Facing the State
Left Analyses
and Perspectives

Facing the State
Left Analyses
and Perspectives

2023

transform!
europe

Edited by
David Broder, Eric Canepa
and Haris Golemis

MERLIN PRESS

transform! Yearbook 2023
Facing the State: Left Analyses and Perspectives

English edition published in the UK in 2023 by
The Merlin Press
Central Books Building
Freshwater Road
London RM8 1RX
www.merlinpress.co.uk

Editors: David Broder, Eric Canepa, Haris Golemis

Managing Editor: Kimon Markatos

Editorial Board: Walter Baier, David Broder, Eric Canepa, Haris Golemis, Javier Moreno, Dagmar Švendová

transform! europe EUPF, Square de Meeûs 25, 1000 Brussels, Belgium
Partially financed through a subsidy from the European Parliament.

Cover Illustration: Stavroula Drakopoulou

ISSN 1865-3480

ISBN 978-0-85036-788-1

Contents

Preface

With this ninth edition of the *transform! yearbook* we turn to a consideration of the social content and character of the contemporary nation-state and left strategies to transform it.

In his 1995 *After Liberalism*, Immanuel Wallerstein, after the collapse of East-West system competition and the seemingly complete triumph of neoliberalism, posed the question of how long such a radically unfettered market regime could last before producing a major crisis. He predicted that in 30 years social democracy would come to the United States, whether through a significant socialist movement or simply the rediscovery by a fraction of the ruling class of the need for public regulation, investment, and adequate welfare measures.

Already in 2008-09 we witnessed the massive intervention of the state when it came to bailing out the banks, but particularly now, with the general recognition of the climate emergency and the need for public health measures to confront pandemics, there is much talk of an indispensable 'return of the state'. The question of what the state actually is, whether its nature is to serve the dominant classes, or possibly the subaltern classes, is a question that historically could not arise before the mode of production and social reproduction, the so-called 'economy', was separated from politics. In a feudal regime, the social relations of the production and expropriation of surplus were transparent and required no social science, no political economy to unveil them. Likewise, there was no need to uncover what social power was being expressed through the state. 'Economics' only appeared with the need to understand how society as a whole, as a mode of life, could economise its limited resources and continue to exist without direct conscious control but merely through impersonal ex post facto market reactions – and when equality – in a system of exchanges based on equivalent 'value' and a political system based on juridical equality – became a condition of existence for the structural inequality in the material mode of life.

The idea that the separation of economy from politics is indispensable to humanity's wellbeing is not just an article of faith of neoliberalism but is rooted in liberalism itself, whose fundamental tenet is that society's direct governing of what and how much to produce, and how to distribute the resulting wealth, is in its essence tyrannical and 'monistic', in that it suffocates the creative, open-ended, and essentially democratic workings of the market, as the realm of freedom. In the twentieth century this view of democracy, in reaction to Soviet-type societies, amounted to the assertion that too much public intervention in the economy, no matter how much democratic participation it involves, leads to the 'gulag'. Thus, neoliberalism's ideal of the 'minimum state' seems the logical development of liberalism's rejection of or antagonism to the state as an instrument of popular sovereignty over the economy.

In reaction to the devastating realities caused by the implementation of neoliberal dogma, several mainstream political scientists in the 1990s, lamenting globalisation's apparent eclipsing of the state, issued calls to 'bring the state back in'. Sam Gindin and Leo Panitch were in the forefront of those who pointed out that, far from being in retreat, the state had taken on a stronger role than ever in facilitating the new level of global marketisation. Being a formal organisation (as distinct from class, which is only a networked force) the capitalist state can in normal circumstances exhibit a relative autonomy. In special cases, particularly when the power of the antagonistic classes are in a temporary equilibrium – with the dominant classes weak or in disarray – it can achieve still more pronounced autonomy from a more direct rule by the dominant class or any of its fractions. Marx called this state of affairs 'Bonapartism' (see Boris Kagarlitsky in this volume). The state, as Göran Therborn emphasises in this issue of the yearbook, is in some ways now more important for capitalism than it was a century ago – for example financial capital is maintained by the state and its banking policies, and the digital revolution in the US was developed out of the military.

Michalis Spourdalakis cites a symbolic document for the process of hollowing out of democracy in the 1990s, which for short can be called the transition from government to 'governance' or 'government through a continuum of actor networks': the 1997 World Bank Report. In it, a consensus-building model is proposed which opts for a specific type of NGO but not labour unions or grassroots associations that would seek to control political outcomes. In rejecting centralised hierarchies, the governance model works through networks, through consultation and more procedural 'participation' within 'civil society' and the market, but not through political antagonism and representation. State administrative control and accountability is ceded to independent administrative agencies and administrative costs to non-governmental institutions and professional associations. The public sphere is redefined as being within the framework of the market.

This post-democratic framework naturally generated apolitical or anti-political sentiment and led to the values of individual 'responsibility' and 'realism' cutting off the wider scope of the political.

Dunja Larise provides a history of Marxist theories of the state and democracy, from Marx and Engels, through Luxemburg and Lenin, crucially restoring the place of the Austro-Marxist theorists' important contributions here – notably those of Otto Bauer, Karl Renner, and Max Adler – but unknown to so many who subsequently developed Marxian state theory – Gramsci, Telò, Althusser, Poulantzas, Bobbio, Altvater, Müller, and Neusüß – whose arguments she also presents.

The nation-state, as Ulrich Brand notes, can no longer be conceived as operating only within its borders. With the end of formal colonial empires, and after the dissolution of the Soviet Union in 1991 and the advent of the US' 'unilateral moment', rather than a retreat of the state, the elites, through the mediation of the nation-state, tended to transfer power to the international scale – to the EU or to supranational agencies or institutions like NAFTA, the WTO and the upgraded World Bank and IMF. Extending Nicos Poulantzas's theorisation of the state as a condensation of social forces, these international state apparatuses can be considered a 'second-order condensation of forces', that is, between nation-states. But already from the 1980s the process of capitalist internationalisation remained very much based in the nation-state, which was reconfigured as a 'competition state' (promoting the international position of businesses in the national territory). However, as Poulantzas also observed, the nation-state was already 'internationalising' by the 1970s as it was permeated by inter-imperialist contradictions, with the contradictions among its ruling fractions already internationalised and partly representing international capital.

The degree to which states are now locked into this international configuration and their limited room for manoeuvre even with significant left presence makes left participation in government hazardous; thus each concrete situation has to be weighed in terms of whether participation can or cannot advance a socialist project. For a left participation that is initially productive can, as the state evolves, typically in the context of neoliberal globalisation, become a liability for the left, as its constituency becomes confused and disillusioned by the identification of the left with government. When the objective parameters do not allow for social gains, particularly with the left in a secondary position, pressure for the mere preservation of the status quo becomes a trap for a left force in government, as the survival

of a coalition often entails giving up crucial and constitutive left goals. This is a dilemma that left-wing governments typically face within the EU's institutional design, a dilemma all the more severe in smaller EU countries, which Portugal's Bloco de Esquerda had to contend with, as its National Coordinator, Mariana Mortágua, relates.

That the state is no longer seen as 'the problem' but the solution to problems like climate change and pandemics and central to a possible future military mobilisation against China and Russia does represents a defeat for neoliberalism. But, as Therborn points out, this does not mean that it is a victory for right-wing nationalism. For major sections of business and finance are advocating a Green New Deal and even radical egalitarian social change, although the Ukraine War has thrown a wrench into this. But by now, with the ramped-up competition between the US and China, it is more accurate to say that we have an extreme centrist and right-wing internationalism – for example 'pan-European Russophobia' and 'all-Western Sinophobia', with the Biden administration dividing the world into allies and partners, on the one hand, and sanction targets, on the other. And now free trade and capital movements are being replaced by national security, with, as Therborn puts it, the 'US elite implementing a strategic retreat to a fortified sub-global circle of friends', which US Secretary of the Treasury Janet Yellen calls 'friend-shoring'.

Despite the increased importance of international institutions, international law scholar Antonios Tzanakopoulos points out that social forces cannot interact directly with international judicial institutions. The irony is that although there is an international legal order it is a de-centralised phenomenon that only exists through the states which enforce the laws. The enforcement of these laws entirely depends on the clout of states, or rather group of states, in pressing legal arguments. Thus, the left needs to be clear that it can only win such battles by building its strength within its own nation-states.

There is, understandably, scepticism as to the possibility of the demos acting in supranational institutions. But according to Walter Baier, president of the European Left, it is erroneous to think of national self-determination and European integration as mutually exclusive, for national feeling and the nation-state are ever present, and that level of struggle for self-determination cannot be elided. On the other hand, if the goal is an eco-socialist transformation with energy transition and European industrial, social, and tax policies this cannot be accomplished in one country but requires a European if not international scale. Moreover, a European frame might be the best level to address the national conflicts within European states.

Regarding the austerity Memoranda imposed by the Troika, Baier points out, the problem is the dominance of international financial institutions rather than the EU. Although the EU carried out the demands of the institutions, the problem does not emanate from the European treaties or institutions themselves. In fact, the only leverage a European country can have in the face of international finance is a democratised European construct that can protect it from such measures.

Transforming Europe into a federal state is not the solution, Baier cautions, as enacting industrial policies, energy transition, etc. first requires a change in people's mindsets, which can only occur through democratic decision-making, which in turn means there is no way around national self-determination. Baier suggests that a commonwealth rather than a federation might be the most appropriate solution. Moreover, in the federal model a European army would, as things are, simply become a pillar of NATO. And one would first have to ask what this army would be for. Military blocs would need to be replaced by common security arrangements.

Post-Marxist theorists, particularly Michel Foucault, reacting to the new reality of the early years of the neoliberal transformation, shifted the locus of power away from the state and the workplace to the more diffuse realm of individual internalised 'micro-power' (sexuality, incarceration). In view of the 'return' of the social question after 2008, especially in the US, and of the consequent felt need for state intervention, this shift of focus certainly seems short-sighted. Nevertheless, Foucault's concept of 'biopolitical' power is fruitful in identifying the progressive expansion of power – and one should add of capital valorisation – to cover ever greater immaterial areas of life itself, most especially the realm of reproduction. Foucault dates its appearance to the eighteenth century when 'population' became the object of modern politics, with biopolitics making population management, the administration of life and the optimisation of the labour force possible, and the nation-state assuming responsibility for basic health. In the neoliberal context we are dealing with a governmental rationality which, in effecting individual internalisation of power and self-responsibilisation through self-interested competitiveness, produces subjects of economic interest rather than of rights and popular authority – to ultimately 'govern less' or at least to govern in less traditionally direct ways. Although Athena Athanasiou endorses Foucault's challenge to the primacy of state-based analysis and politics, one of her aims is to negotiate his thinking into a Poulantzasian theory of the state.

Ankica Čakardić, in her survey of care work under neoliberalism, and its transference of responsibility for social reproduction from the society – as a whole – to the individual, applies the concept of biopolitical power to the privatisation and financialisation of social reproduction in subsuming life itself as a rent-producing sphere. Giulia Russo develops this concept, focusing on how state welfare in post-Yugoslav Serbia has become important to corporations which have invested in tax-financed healthcare and education. The neoliberal plundering of social welfare in the late 1980s, subsequently exacerbated by the 2008 crash, has developed into new forms of capital valorisation in which capital gets a rent on immateriality. With the common now privatised, and this is one of Russo's central points, welfare is no longer just a mode of value distribution but also of value production, with financialised social welfare now having become another basis for accumulation. This privatising and financialising of the commons introduces the logic of private investment into the strategic sector of the 'production of humans for humans', that is, the realm of reproduction that was previously outside the market and capital valorisation.

The centrality of health services to society and the state is evident when we consider that they include not only the pharmaceutical industry and biomedical technologies, demographic and statistical measurements, academic institutions of higher education and professional training, organisms of mutual aid and social programmes, but also the 'invisible' services of cleaning, food supply, and the bodily and psychological 'care' for every individual whether ill or not. Moreover, an interruption in health services could stop society from functioning. And so, in a sense, public health is, as Étienne Balibar points out, a relation to society as a whole – 'a universal relation of society to itself', and one which generates commonality. Neoliberalism, in privatising so much of public services created uncertainty as to which services are public by nature and what the common goods of society or humanity are.

Balibar draws attention to the special conditions in France where, during the pandemic, health-service personnel were able to communicate to the population the systemic nature of the disaster in the public health services and at the same time to identify its cause in accelerated commodification and privatisation. In so doing they were creating a 'community' effect, tantamount to constructing a common without aiming to substitute it for the state. Instead, they tried to obligate the state to serve public service. The vision was that all needed resources ought to be removed from the market and their use planned under democratic control, and in this there was a perception that although public service always needs the state these services do not belong to the state. But for public service to assert its relative autonomy the common has to be politically organised. So, while the public is an object of the conflict between the state and the common it also serves as a mediator. Balibar sees in this development a new political sensibility signalling a 'new modality of change'.

Concentrating on neoliberalism's erosion of the public sphere, Panos Ramantanis casts biopolitics in a more positive light as the exercise of hegemony through the beneficial provision of welfare. Its erosion is the complement of more open forms of repression.

Turning to the issue of transforming the state, Athanasiou keeps open the question of whether the capitalist state – which she calls an 'open force field of relations' – can be transformed and democratised, calling for a 'critical-performative' conception of the state that resists closure, a politics that re-occupies state power to transform it, aware of the risk of being coopted. She also points out that 'injury politics' (Wendy Brown) – the demand of sectors of 'wounded subjects' for protection from the state – is a left politics that, in not trying to build the political antagonism of a majority aimed at transforming the social whole, in a sense depoliticises itself and de-democratises its contestation, a contestation that neoliberalism appropriates. She suggests that critiquing the state paternalism / 'wounded subjects' relation might help the left to win back working-class citizens who have turned to the right.

Hilary Wainwright explores the lessons for state-transformation strategies suggested by the experience of shop floor union activism in Great Britain consciously oriented to production benefiting society as a whole and the environment, as a kind of 'politics of use value' – an experience dating back to the 1970s that re-emerged during the pandemic when workers led the conversion of aircraft to ventilator parts. Wainwright calls this 'transition bargaining' or 'bargaining for the public benefit'.

While this involves an understanding of the political that is broader than an orientation towards simply winning the state, Wainwright points out that social conversion cannot be achieved by a syndicalist strategy that ignores the state, for the conversion plans all showed that state action is necessary to challenge management. However, the state cannot, as it is, be simply captured by left political forces, and so it must necessarily be radically transformed, something that is not possible without a politicised trade-unionism that can represent the interests of society – and break down the compartmentalisation between workplace unionism and parliamentary politics.

To counteract the intimate relation of business, particularly aerospace and weapons, with government ministries, the labour movement would have to build a connection between labour, parties, and social movements that can win the state and establish a labour/state relationship equal to or surpassing that of business and the state. The problem is that the social democrats have accepted liberalism's separation of capitalist markets from the state, resulting in a Parliamentary Labour Party (PLP) that takes care of politics and is distant from the membership party, while the unions take care of industrial relations, in which social change beyond wage issues is not considered a legitimate part of their purview.

While in the 1970s there was a more integral 'in and against' left relation to electoral politics, eventually the ideological and existential changes brought about by neoliberalism, along with the traditional delegation of politics to the PLP, favoured an apolitical tendency in parts of civil-society movements, with the illusion that mass street protests would be enough to break through the constraints of the capitalist state.

Wainwright's conclusion is that something more targeted at breaking capitalist power is required than 'popular mobilisation'. What is needed then is a different relation between organised labour and political parties. Industrial power has to be fused with the wider struggles for social change and over the purpose of production. The move towards a low-carbon economy provides a stimulus to overcome the conservative division between politics and economics.

Göran Therborn reminds us that before both the revolutionary and reform wings of labour movement achieved major results by focusing on the state in most of the twentieth century, the lack of a state orientation we saw in the movements of the 1990s and early twenty-first century also characterised a significant part of labour organisations in the early twentieth century, for instances the anarchists and anarcho-syndicalists but also the IWW and the AFL. A non-state-centred politics of the taming and dismantling of capitalism from within – conceived as paralleling the transition from feudalism to capitalism – had its most cogent theorisation in the work of Erik Olin Wright who, as Therborn points out, ultimately underestimated the violence and power of the state; moreover, the movements inspired by this orientation have by now faded out.

Moreover, as Brand notes, in view of the ecological crisis the left has no alternative but to strategise the state's role. With major fractions of capital, along with other sectors of society, intent on dealing with aspects of the ecological crisis, the left will be confronted with a situation in which, although the state is a major factor in unsustainable economic growth, it will also be central to socio-ecological transformation, which only it can regulate and secure, because, as was clear in the coronavirus pandemic, capital will not protect the public interest, and so the state must. Moreover, only the state can administer the massive, mostly public, investment needed for the transition, and it is inevitable that people will expect the state to take the lead in this.

Aristides Baltas, minister in two Syriza governments (of education in the first, and of culture in the second), asks what can be learned from his party's governmental experience. In the face of the clientelist Greek state, of foreign imposed origin in the nineteenth century and which appeared to be outside and contemptuous of Greek society, never having internally undergone a post-absolutist evolution, it was not known how a progressive left government would affect its functioning. To his surprise many employees in his ministries did indeed want to be good civil servants, and an atmosphere of solidarity was created. But Baltas's broader theoretical concern is with the problems arising from the absence of an 'immanent critique' of capitalism on the part of the 'revolutionary' wing of the left, particularly before the collapse of eastern state socialism, and the faith that both the revolutionary and reformist wings of the left have tended to have in historical 'laws'. In both wings there was an underdeveloped sense of what it means to be 'in and against' the system, to use Wainwright's phrase. In terms of the revolutionary left, the ideal of an actually existing socialism outside of one's own society is no longer possible now that the world is in a sense one capitalist 'nation' with nothing outside of it. The price paid for the illusions of both wings – either that capitalism, through reforms, would gradually and inevitably, arrive at socialism or that capitalism would collapse through a revolutionary act – has been that while the reformism of the social democratic parties was quite easily absorbed by capitalism, the successful revolutions against capital in the end fell back on capitalist relations of production. As an alternative to such historical laws Baltas proposes an orientation to an anthropologically, and possibly biologically, rooted tendency of human beings to move towards a horizon of infinite justice. Arguing against passivity and a static sense of reality leading to the belief that the political is merely the administration of the feasible, Baltas points out that political action can change and enlarge what is feasible. Thus, although thoughtless voluntarism needs to be avoided, at certain moments realities have to be created by deeds.

Alberto Garzón traces the deeply flawed Spanish constitution to the belated and incomplete transition from feudalism to capitalism in the nineteenth century, which preserved the reactionary ideology of the feudal landowners who were transformed overnight into capitalist entrepreneurs, a legacy that still informs Spain's deep state today, and which conditioned the compromise represented by the 1978 constitution, based as it was on the reciprocal weaknesses of each side. This has determined today's power struggles around alternative state projects in the country and the deep state's use of lawfare and various judicial and media-coordinated attrition operations to wear down Unidas Podemos. In 2017, Podemos and other progressive forces tried for the first time to work out a republican and plurinational state project to confront the reactionary project, a development Garzón regards as the first beginnings of a consciousness that there needs to be an alternative, democratic bloc around a new state project.

Boris Kagarlitsky uses Gramsci's concept of 'reactionary Caesarism', whose classic example is the regime of Napoleon III in France, as a prism to make sense of what is happening in today's Russia. With weak social forces unable to achieve predominance, the result is a 'catastrophic equilibrium' in which the state apparatus becomes the decisive force in society. In the case of reactionary Caesarism, however, no matter how radical a policy of restoration it pursues it can never make a complete return to the past, and so reactionary regimes are obliged to make considerable use of the legacy of the progressive period that preceded them, which explains Putinism's ambivalent attitude towards the Soviet past. The other key dynamic of Russia in the 2000s is the over-accumulation of capital. The cash that accumulated with the sale of raw materials and the flooding of the market with liquidity after the crash of 2008-9 but also China's impeding Russia's development by treating it as a mere source of the cheapest possible raw materials – all this resulted in hoarding in the Stabilisation Fund or in the form of villas, yachts, etc. – and it stimulated foreign expansion and the buying up of assets in former Soviet republics, of which Ukraine is a key example. And, fatefully, Caesarism's cultivation of the heroic leader requires periodical military victories to confirm this image.

Gavin Rae, in his survey of Poland's transition from state socialism to a market economy and 'minimum state', points to the paradox that, in the first phase, the brutal primitive accumulation and massive transfer away from the broad working class was only politically possible with the state providing huge amounts of unemployment benefits. Moreover, at a second stage, the right-wing populist Law and Justice Party (Pis), in reaction to the devastations of neoliberal policies, bolstered its popularity by bold state-welfare measures. PiS taxed foreign companies and financial institutions, increased welfare spending, and restored the previous pension age. It enacted a universal child benefit programme which halved child poverty, lowered the retirement age, and raised the minimum wage. Significantly, though, its welfare measures prioritised state services and support to individuals and families while running down public services (health, education), ironically playing up certain state services to cement individual-centred neoliberal policies. Logically, the first wave of protest against PiS's justice and media reforms, and its policies towards women, mobilised better-off sectors, the working class being thankful for state support. But now with the integration of a great number of Ukrainian refugees and increased military expenditures the protectionist arm of the state is weakening and for the first time under the PiS living standards are falling, all of which has broadened the social base of the protests, allowing the left to play a bigger role.

Steven Forti is concerned with the lack of empathy in part of the radical left, a self-referential identitarianism that impedes many from communicating with those who think differently and cuts the left off from large swathes of the working population who are to one degree or another susceptible to right-wing messages. He points out that the modern populist extreme right is too diverse a phenomenon to be reduced to the phalangist militancy of classical fascism, covering as it does a great variety of sensibilities, from economic liberalism to protectionism and welfare chauvinism, from inclusion of ecological concerns and defence of Western values inclusive of LGBTQI+ rights against 'Islamic fundamentalism' to conservative family morality, etc. The causes of its spread among the working population has to do with the abandonment by social democracy of its traditional policies, the cultural dislocations of liberalist globalisation, the difficulty trade unions face in adapting to a fully post-Fordist reality, and the demand for security in the face of AI and job redundancy, etc. He sketches out a number of left policies and an anti-fascism that might fuse feminist, LGBTQI+ and immigrant causes with the concerns of the 99%, as well as strategic alliances with liberals to offset the new attempts by Meloni, Orbán et al. to bring the European People's Party and even the liberals into their camp.

Jukka Pietiläinen surveys the development of Finland's Left Alliance, as it and its electorate – shifting from a working-class to an urban professional base – struggle around the issue of government participation in Finland's parliamentary tradition of power sharing between parties unable to build large majorities.

Since by now almost all parties in Europe have religion-policy spokespeople, including Germany's left party Die LINKE, the question arises of what a left religion policy for the states and the European Union might look like, a question which Franz Segbers tries to address. An immediate obstacle is France's 'nouvelle laïcité' which appropriates left republicanism not to counter a too great influence of religion on the state but to justify anti-Islamic measures, thus shifting the focus from the state's neutrality to the cultural identity of its citizens. But a more diffuse problem within the left everywhere is the image of religions as violent and part of the repressive apparatus and which therefore need to be pushed into the private sphere, a view often based on a non-dialectical reading of Marx's own statements – and additionally problematic considering that the major horrors of the twentieth century had to do with capitalist modernity rather than religion.

Segbers points out the difference between 1905 France when there was a need to resist the Catholic Church's monopoly by a policy of secularism simply to secure democratic values and rights and today's Europe, so altered through individualisation and immigration, where exclusion of religion from public life can only discriminate against minorities. Today the only goal of a republican secular neutrality of the state can be to respect diversity, which is accomplished not by removing religion from public life but by a strict 'non-identification' of the state with any *particular* religion. The idea, in both the 1875 Gotha Programme and Marx's criticism of it, of religion being a private rather than state affair did not at all imply that religious expression could not be public.

Segbers, himself an Old Catholic theologian, maintains that left religion policy needs the critique of religion in Marx's sense of transforming the 'criticism of heaven' into the 'criticism of earth' in order to analyse the forces that hold up the existing order and veil its class antagonisms. He sees religious communities as one of the contested loci in the endeavour to 'overthrow all relations in which man is a debased [...] being'. For Marx religion is always both 'the opium of the people' and a 'protest against real distress'. In Segbers's words, 'it can be liberating or oppressive and set free forces of humanisation, promote visions of a solidary society, or block them'. Thus, the left needs to do still more than promote the non-identification of the state with particular religions. It must discover and tap into the diverse sources of humanity and solidarity and thus advocate alliances with religions and ideological communities which are pursuing the cause of a just, solidary, peaceful, and sustainable society. 'It must bring to bear the emancipatory potential of religions' − but then intervene when practices inside religions violate human rights.

In his moving tribute to Salvador Allende on the 50th anniversary of the Chilean coup and Allende's death, Mario Amorós reviews Allende's development before he came to power and reminds us of the struggles he waged within the government. The Chilean attempt to build socialism with parliamentary democracy and pluralism and the ensuing coup were central points of reference for Europe and the world vis-à-vis the question of the state's relation to class power and how it can be transformed within a socialist perspective. And both it and the Greek dictatorship were central focuses for Poulantzas's analyses.

★ ★ ★

On 11 December 2022, as we were preparing this yearbook, Walter Baier, former coordinator of the transform! europe network, was elected president of the Party of the European Left. The load of his new duties requires him to interrupt his collaboration with our journal, of which he is founder and a longstanding Editorial Board member. We would like to express our sincere gratitude for the crucial role he has played over the years in the planning of our work, as well as for his important contributions through articles and interviews mainly related to European integration and the left in Europe, such as the dialogue published in this issue. Baier's close collaborator in his new tasks is Dagmar Švendová, another member of the Editorial Board for several years, who has also been obliged to leave it after several years of fruitful collaboration, in which we have benefited from her great organisational prowess. We also offer her many thanks for her contribution.

★ ★ ★

The transform! europe network was established in 2001 during the World Social Forum in Porto Alegre by a small group of intellectuals from six different European countries, representing left research institutions or journals, who wanted to coordinate their research and educational work. Today transform! consists of 37 member organisations and observers from 22 countries.

The network is coordinated by a board of eleven members, and its office is located in Vienna. transform! maintains a multilingual website and publishes a continuously growing number of reports, analyses, and discussion papers on issues related to the process of European integration.

We would like to thank all those who have collaborated in producing this volume: our authors, the members of our editorial board, our translators, and especially our publisher, The Merlin Press.

David Broder, Eric Canepa, and Haris Golemis

State Theory

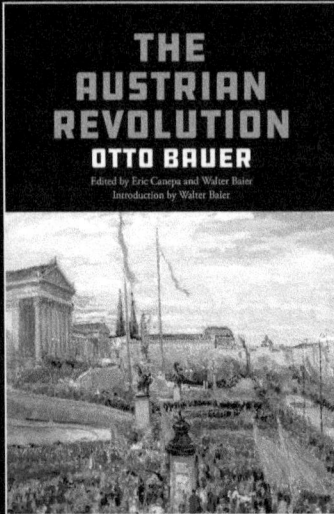

THE
AUSTRIAN
REVOLUTION
OTTO BAUER
Edited by Eric Canepa and Walter Baier
Introduction by Walter Baier

The Austrian Revolution
by Otto Bauer
edited by Walter Baier,
Eric Canepa

Publisher: Haymarket Books
(July 2021)
Language: English
ISBN-10: 1642591629
ISBN-13: 978-1642591620

Otto Bauer's The Austrian Revolution is one of the now largely forgotten gems of the extraordinarily rich literature that Austro-Marxism produced. Thanks to an excellent new translation, this classic work is now available to English-speaking readers in a complete version for the first time. It is one of the classics of Marxist political analysis, only comparable to Marx's The Eighteenth Brumaire of Louis Napoleon or Trotsky's History of the Russian Revolution.

Michael R. Krätke, Lancaster University

State Theory in 'Western Marxism' Revisited

Dunja Larise

Throughout its history, Marxist state theory has pursued different strands of Marx's own analysis of the capitalist state. What elements of Marx's approach were developed depended on his successors' own political strategies. This theoretical diversity was a constant feature of both the First and Second Internationals. The great rift within Marxist theory which split it into two irreconcilable blocs occurred following the 1917 Russian Revolution and the establishment of the new nation-states in Western Europe following the end of the First World War, some of them supported by or under the leadership of the Socialist parties. This was a split between an orthodox and an unorthodox Marxism which coincided with the division of the re-established proletarian International into the Third (Communist) International led and controlled by the USSR, also known as the Comintern, and the International Working Union of Socialist Parties (the so-called 'Second-and-a-Half International') influenced by the Austro-Marxists (renamed after 1923 to Labour and Socialist International).

Alongside the split between orthodox and an unorthodox Marxism there is another division of Marxist theory that is not primarily based on a conceptual chasm and political division, although it is still partially determined by it. This lies in the distinction between so-called Western and Eastern Marxism, introduced during the Cold War and most fully elaborated by Perry Anderson in 1976. Anderson's systematisation is oriented around several markers like the birthplace and birth year of people he counts among Western Marxists. Another yardstick is the point at which they became Marxists. He includes among the Western Marxists all those who came to Marxism 'well after the First World War' (he counts them as a third generation of Marxists regardless of their birth date), or were radicalised by the advance of fascism and the Second World War.[1] So, he does not count Otto Bauer (born 1881), Yevgeni Preobrazhensky (1886) and Nikolai Bukharin (1888) as Western Marxists but as the second generation of

Marxists, whereas Georg Lukács (1885), Karl Korsch (1886) and Antonio Gramsci (1891) are the third generation of Marxists according to Anderson and consequently he counts them among Western Marxism. Another feature of Western Marxists, according to Anderson, is the geography of their origins – all of them (except for Budapest native Lukács) were born west of Vienna. This geographical articulation around a 'West' becomes problematic when attempting to categorise Chinese and other 'Eastern' varieties of Marxism, especially those linked to decolonisation and liberation struggles across the Third World. Some of these problems were signalled by Domenico Losurdo in his 2017 book *Il Marxismo occidentale*. Lastly, this kind of Western-oriented systematisation of unorthodox varieties of Marxism leaves the entire, extremely prolific Central European variety out of the picture. Consequently, it also leaves out Austro-Marxism as an autonomous unorthodox current of Marxism, though according to the German historian Michael Krätke it in fact constitutes the most productive variety of German-speaking Marxism. (2019)

The Russian Revolution was indeed a turning point in the division between orthodox and unorthodox Marxism, although this border did not follow clear geographical lines. The Cold War prolonged the chasm around the old and the new issues of Marxist theory and practice. Most authors have embraced Anderson's systematisation of Western Marxism, which has by now become a kind of self-perpetuating common sense in the historiography of Marxism.

I would tend to accept the division between Western and Eastern Marxism, but only with the qualification that the geographical borders are less clear than the term suggests and that it best applies to the aftermath of the Second World War and the beginning of the Cold War. Otherwise, I prefer the terms orthodox and unorthodox Marxism. The most clear-cut division in the history of Marxism in the twentieth century remains that between Third International dogmatism or Marxist orthodoxy and all the rest, which goes by the name of unorthodox Marxism, which was perpetuated after the Second World War as a division between Western and Eastern Marxism. So, it is important to bear in mind that unorthodox Marxism and Western Marxism are not synonyms and cannot be applied interchangeably.

In what follows, I propose a broader chronology of Marxist state theory. In my view, the first period fell in the years shortly before and after the First World War and the October Revolution and during the 1920s, in which both orthodox and unorthodox Marxist state theories flourished due to the historical challenges that they faced. The second was the revival of the Marxist state-theory debate in France, Germany, and Italy as a consequence of the failed hopes of 1968 and the crisis in the world economy in the 1970s, which opened up the first cracks in the Keynesian welfare states of Western Europe.

My aim is, first, to point out the concepts still relevant for our times. The first part of this article reviews twentieth-century Marxism's theories of the state, which I believe still have relevance for our current problems and struggles. It also shows the cross-fertilisation between different epochs of unorthodox and Western Marxism and sometimes also with orthodox Marxism. The middle and especially the last sections re-open the debates that have direct impact on – and possibly applicability to – the issues of our time. All translations in English of previously untranslated sources in German, French and Italian are my own.

Marx and state theory in Marxism

Karl Marx wrote much on the state, but he did not attempt a coherent systematisation as he did with his economic theory. His early state analysis is to be found in the *Critique of Hegel's Philosophy of Right* (1843). Here he posits the civic (bourgeois) state as an illusion of common interest in a distinct historical form, opposed to civil society. This analysis was deepened in *The Jewish Question* (1843) and the *German Ideology* (1846). The latter contemplated an overthrow of the state and class relations. On the one side, the existing (bourgeois) state was not regarded as instrumental for the workers to radically improve their condition. On the other, the state had to be seized by the workers and eventually overthrown together with class relations. Here the question of the duality of the state, which would be fully developed after the Paris Commune experiment, was approached for the first time. This overthrow would abolish the distinction between the state and society, and the new transitional state, i.e. the commune or community organised through direct democracy, would take its place until there was finally no need for any state. The *German Ideology* is, unlike the two previous texts, a general and abstract theory of the civic (bourgeois) state. In this picture, the civic state is always an apparatus to oppress the workers.

Marx's admiration for the short-lived Paris Commune and its immediate decision-making from below shaped his state theoretical thinking after 1871, although his praise for direct democracy dated back to the *Critique of Hegel's Philosophy of Right*. The two most relevant state-theoretical texts of his post-1871 phase were his writings on the Paris Commune and the *Critique of the Gotha Programme* from 1875 (published posthumously in 1891). There he stated that the *raison d'être* of proletarian state power was to abolish private property, socialise the means of production (to transfer them into common ownership), disband the army etc., and he also spoke of a transitional period of the revolutionary transformation of capitalism into communism which he fatefully termed the 'dictatorship of the proletariat'. In his 1874 notes on Bakunin's book *Statehood and Anarchy*, he again clarified his commitment to direct democracy carried out by all people but not to an electoral democracy of the liberal type.

Both later critics and many of those who believed they were following in Marx's footsteps misunderstood this unfortunately chosen term to mean a despotic dictatorship of (the representatives) of the proletariat over everyone else, while what Marx had in mind was something closer to a combination of direct democracy,[2] socialisation of the means of production, and the abolition of private property by force of arms if not possible otherwise. It is worth remembering that it was not until the late nineteenth century and definitively after the Russian Revolution that the term 'dictatorship' came to have a specifically anti-democratic connotation.[3]

All these ideas were significant parameters in Marx's own state theory, but for Marxist state theory after Marx, another concept was of particular importance. It was his abstraction of the social whole exemplified in another fateful metaphor forged for the preface of *The Contribution to the Critique of Political Economy* from 1859 – the metaphor of the base and the superstructure. It is hardly an exaggeration to say that most of Marxist state theory after Marx revolved around this metaphor or at least referred to it. The relation between the economic system as a system of an entire complex of material and social reproduction, on the one hand, and, on the other hand, the political, ideological, and cultural institutions, including the state, became one of the firmest cornerstones of Marxist state theory but also its most enduring focus of controversy. The dispute about what constituted a superstructure and how it was connected to the base emerged soon after the text was published. Marx gave another clue as to the meaning of the basis and superstructure metaphor in his *Theories of the Surplus Value,* where he claimed that a specific form of material production resulted in a particular structure of society and a particular relationship of people to nature. Both determined their political system and their intellectual outlook.[4] Engels ventured to put an end to this controversy, but his definition ignited it even more. In his 1894 letter to Walther Borgius he explained that: 'Political, juridical, philosophical, religious, literary, artistic, etc., development is based on economic development. But all these react upon one another and also upon the economic base. It is not that the economic position is the *cause and alone active,* while everything else only has a passive effect. There is, rather, interaction on the basis of the economic necessity, which *ultimately* always asserts itself.'[5]

Between two world wars: Antonio Gramsci and Austromarxism

Antonio Gramsci, Otto Bauer, and Karl Renner

If the idea of an east-west divide in Marxist state theory of the 1920s makes sense, it is because of Antonio Gramsci. Not because Gramsci was born west of Vienna or was radicalised 'later' but because his deliberations revolved around the lack of revolution in the West. Contrary to the contemporary picture of him, Gramsci was a Leninist faithful to the Comintern in many respects, but still one deeply aware of the fundamental difference between the structure of the feudal empires in the East and those of the modern nation-states in the West; in the West, he saw complex nation-state democracies and in the East backwards states and colonies. This distinction required not only different revolutionary strategies for each group of states but also a different state theory. It was also Gramsci who saw the state beyond the simplified base-superstructure model characteristic of the economic determinism of orthodox state theory after Marx. The texts of his *Prison Notebooks,* which were, as the name suggests, written in a fascist prison, are neither a unified block of theory nor a structured book. The theory is scattered through the notebooks and thematically incoherent. Some observations are at times inconsistent or even at odds with other observations on the same issue. This is what Perry Anderson dubbed Gramsci's 'antinomies', ascribing them to the precarious conditions in which these texts were written.[6]

Gramsci described the state in the West using a metaphor borrowed from warfare, claiming that the resilience of the modern Western nation-state to crises and revolutions lies in its relationship with civil society, which is in a stable equilibrium. This is the basis of his idea of the 'integral' (i.e. extended) state. As in warfare, the state is the outer ditch behind which there is a complex work of underground trenches and fortresses representing civil society. Crises and the revolutions can wipe away the outer ditches, but they will find the enemy perfectly capable of fighting behind them. This is why the strategy of the Bolsheviks, victorious in Russia, could not be successful in the West.

The power of the Western state is a mixture of its coercive apparatus and activities meant to win the consent of the ruled. Those apparatuses that aim at an ideological hegemony, such as schools, mass media, cultural institutions, etc., create an organic unity between the rulers and the ruled and between civil society and the state. In contrast to the economic determinism peculiar to Marxist orthodoxy, Gramsci emphasises the role of the superstructure in the social whole. Accordingly, the bourgeois state is not to be restricted to its coercive elements; the 'integral state presupposes the taking over of all intellectual and moral means of the leadership of a class over society, the way in which it can realize its "hegemony" [...])'.[7] This is how Gramsci connected the analysis of the state to a study of the power relations which cannot be reduced to the economy, and directed Marxist thinking towards an independent theorisation of the state.

This is also where the concept of hegemony comes into play. Modern democracy in the West was developed as such during the nineteenth century when both state and civil society advanced. The French state before the French Revolution bore more resemblance to a backward state of the East in Gramsci's time than a modern European state at the end of the nineteenth century. In the underdeveloped/backward states, civil society had autonomy from the state because there the state was rudimentary, which is why the French and Russian Revolutions were successful. In modern liberal democracies, the state and civil society became much more fused. In his famous definition, the modern Western 'state is political society + civil society, in other words hegemony armoured with coercion'.[8] In other remarks, he even denied any opposition between civil society and the state, claiming this was a liberal illusion. Accordingly, the appropriate strategy for overturning the state in stable democracies of the twentieth century is, according to Gramsci, oriented to the winning of ideological hegemony – hegemony within a complex civil society.

Otto Bauer approached state theory from empirical perspectives different from those of Gramsci. One of these, and probably the most interesting for our time, was linked to the acute problem of nationalism within the Austrian Empire. Most Marxists regarded nationalism as a lack of working-class consciousness and a bourgeois strategy to mask the class struggle by forging the mythos of shared identity, thus manipulating the working class into wilfully fighting the bourgeoisie's expansionist wars. Hardly anyone felt compelled to analyse nationalism as a constitutional element of the modern nation-state. Most simply embraced Lenin's (and Woodrow Wilson's) doctrine of self-determination without further questions. Otto Bauer was an exception. The problem of nationalities within the Austro-Hungarian Empire impelled him to go far beyond his Marxist contemporaries in inquiring into the nation-state, which he analysed not as a generalised abstraction but as a concrete historical phenomenon which – when one looks at it not as an isolated and abstract unity but as already part of the complex world state system – can follow different evolutionary trajectories. The state's position within this system and its historical evolution are intertwined with its form, function, and structure.

Bauer theorised the distinction between the multinational state as the form most European empires had (although socialist multinational states would later emerge) and the modern nation-state. He was one of the first to foresee the dominant tendency towards a nation-state (as the state of one nation) as a dangerous and potentially murderous principle that could lead to ethnic cleansing and genocide, which indeed manifested itself throughout the twentieth century and continues to account for civil wars and destruction around the world in the twenty-first.

'The fact that the nation-state is seen as the rule, the multinational state as a mere exception, as a remnant of times past, has led to a disturbing confusion in the terminology of political science and politics.'[9] Bauer does not see the nation in the organicist terms typical of the bourgeois national romanticisation of the Belle Époque, nor does he consider it a mere ideology of some illusionary unity created by the bourgeoisie to tranquillise the class conflict; rather he understands it as a historical result of the trajectory towards advanced capitalism. Bauer knew that the nation-state's emergence was not a uniform process. He viewed the evolution of distinct nation-states emerging in early capitalist Italy as entirely different from the nation-states appearing in France and Germany in the nineteenth century. However diverse, all these trajectories were initiated through the development of the capitalist mode of production and distribution. However, the peculiar ways in which each of them evolved into a nation-state were historically conditioned.

Bauer rejected naturalist theories of the connection between state and nation, including the Marxist ones of his time, according to which it was only natural for every nation to want to become a state. He instead asked: Why did it seem 'natural' and reasonable to people that every nation would want the national state, specifically, as the form of its political community? He realised that the principle of nationality included two aspirations: first, the will to national liberation, the rejection of foreign domination, the demand for 'one nation, one state!'; and second, the will to national unity, the rejection of particularism as well as the demand for 'the entire nation in one state!' For Bauer, it was necessary at this point to explain 'how these aspirations could emerge in the nineteenth century and become powerful enough to topple the traditional state system'.[10]

Bauer did not believe in the withering away of the state but in a radical and thorough transformation of the state along the lines of socialism.

From a formal juridical point of view, the modern state constitutes the sovereign territorial corporation. Nothing will change in this respect when the working class takes over power within the state and transfers the instruments of labour to the property of the state and the smaller local associations within the state that are ruled and administered by it. The future polity will also be unable to do without the attribute of sovereignty; in this case, sovereignty will mean that the polity is the highest authority concerning all production and distribution. The proletariat will not initially alter legal norms; rather, it will alter the subjects of the law and the efficacy of legal norms. However, as a result, the state will become a quite new social structure. The modern state first emerged with the monetary economy, which is itself a manifestation of commodity production. The socialist polity, on the other hand, will be based no longer on taxation, but on the fact that it is itself in charge of production and the distribution of the products of labour [...].[11]

For Karl Renner, who approached the theory of the state from the angle of the theory of state and law, the state was the most important means for the emancipation of the proletariat, which was to be channelled through its legal institutions. He posited that the government had to be founded on the majoritarian principle, but control must be in the hands of a minority. In these terms, he demonstrated an awareness of the antinomies of the individual and particular will, formalised as individual freedom and collective will and public needs. For him, this problem would always remain the basis of every sociology, as its fundamental predicament.[12] In this, he proceeded in the same direction as Hans Kelsen. At this point, he opened a debate about equality which could not be guaranteed in the state of nature, as liberals and anarchists claimed, but only within the state as a society regulated by law.

For Renner, democracy was of paramount importance for state legitimacy, but democracy was not only a political democracy as liberal democratic theory suggested; rather, it also included economic democracy. The structure and the scaffolding of an economic democracy were unions, associations, and workers' parties within the state's architecture. The socialisation of the key industries was the first step towards an economic democracy but not tantamount to economic democracy itself. Thus he opposed a bureaucratic state imposing economic democracy from above and instead advocated free cooperative work between different participants in the free society.

In the context of the socialisation of the key industries, Renner differentiated between active capital and passive capital and between small entrepreneur and big capital. He was vehemently opposed to general expropriation and general socialisation of property and was one of the rare Marxists to see the danger in expropriating all capitalists by simply redirecting their property to management by a state bureaucracy since, in his view, this would not change the nature of the existing exploitation and even less likely result in socialism, but would instead make the state into the only capitalist and all citizens into proletarians under the yoke of an omnipotent bureaucracy like that of the Soviet Union. He thus anticipated what Poulantzas concluded in the 1970s regarding eastern state socialism with the remark that 'what has taken place there was a statisation and not a genuine socialisation of production'.[13] Renner advocated for a partial socialisation limited to the financial sector and big industries.

Even a cursory glance at Renner's writings makes it clear that he was no advocate of the thesis that the state was necessarily a tool for the oppression of workers. On the contrary, he held that only the state and its legal system could guarantee the permanency of the hard-fought victories the working class had already won against capital. Without the state, every victory remained precarious and ephemeral. 'The classic Marxists fail to recognise this; they are natural law worshipers who rely on storms and floods and consider it outrageous to want to achieve something by the law and with human hands. They forget the specific task set for the Marxian school today, to analyse the fabric of society and raise it to a system – but this technique is called state and law; there is no alternative. And it does not abolish Karl Marx, but fulfils him.'[14] Further: 'The economic institutions of the working class are the backbone of its economic power. Through them, the class struggle is declared permanent; without them, the declaration of permanence is a phrase.'[15] In this light, we can understand Renner's famous claim that the country's labour laws are the legal index of class economic power.

In his book *Staatswirtschaft, Weltwirscthaft und Sozialismus* (State Economy, World Economy, and Socialism), Renner reiterated that the idea of the state as a tool of oppression arose from early liberalism in a particular historical situation when it served as the ideology of the liberation of the bourgeois classes, set against the aristocracy. Already Lassalle criticised this aspect of liberal state theory. Eventually, it was uncritically integrated into Marx's state theory. Liberal theory had already established that the state as a tool of oppression accounts for the difference in property, which enables the wealthy to abuse the state to preserve their wealth. Against this background, Renner represents the so-called instrumentalist view of the state, in which it can be both a tool for repression and the emancipation of the working class, the outcome depending on the strength of organised labour.

The state debate in the 1970s

Louis Althusser

In *Reading Capital*, Althusser accused Gramsci of following Croce's teleological Hegelianism in political theory.[16] However, in his 1970 essay on state theory, *Ideology and Ideological State Apparatuses*,[17] Althusser felt a connection to Gramsci. In a footnote to this work he credited Gramsci: 'To my knowledge, Gramsci is the only one who went any distance on the road I am taking. He had the "remarkable" idea that the State could not be reduced to the (Repressive) State Apparatuses but included a certain number of institutions from "civil society": The Church, the Schools, the trade unions, etc. Unfortunately, Gramsci did not systematize these intuitions, which remained in the state of acute but fragmentary notes.'[18]

Along with Gramsci and many others, Althusser's contribution to the Marxist understanding of the state presupposed his own interpretation of the 'base-superstructure' concept. To his understanding, the so-called superstructures including ideology and the state were not secondary 'epiphenomena'. Rather, from the point of view of reproduction, the 'superstructures' were constitutive of the existence of the social whole.[19] The social whole that Althusser understood as a complex structure with a dominant element could not be reduced to an essential feature such as 'the economy'. This dominance of the economic authority that applies exclusively to capitalism could only be grasped by referring to the ideological and political authorities which established the framework for the operation of the economy.

In the classical Marxist but also the orthodox Leninist theory of the state, Althusser distinguished two central points of reference: first that the state was apparatus and, second, that it was a repressive apparatus. Such a state apparatus had no other purpose than power. Nevertheless, the state apparatus may survive political events that affect who is in possession of state power.[20] The distinction between state power and state apparatus is part and parcel of the orthodox theory of the state. The state apparatus of orthodox Marxist state theory consists, according to Althusser, of government, administration, army, courts, prisons, etc. For him, these institutions are not the state apparatus per se but only a part of it – the Repressive State Apparatus (RSA). The other component is the Ideological State Apparatus (ISA). 'I shall call Ideological State Apparatuses a certain number of realities which present themselves to the immediate observer in the form of distinct and specialized institutions.'[21]

Althusser left the list of the ISA provisional and subject to change. He counted as components of the ISA religious, educational, family, legal, and political institutions, trade-unions, communication media, and cultural fields. A reader used to liberal state theory may ask why Althusser counts private institutions as part of a state in the first place. He explained this as follows: 'As a conscious Marxist, Gramsci already forestalled this objection in one sentence: The distinction between the public and the private is internal to bourgeois law and valid in the (subordinate) domains in which bourgeois law exercises its "authority". The domain of the state escapes it because the latter is "above the law".[22] For Althusser, the state, which is the state of the ruling class, is neither public nor private; it is the precondition for any distinction between public and private. So, to count institutions as a State Apparatus of some kind, the decisive criterion is not whether they are public or private under the liberal law, but rather the function they perform.

Within capitalism, the components of the ISA are multiple and struggle for domination. In feudalism, the ISA had only one component – the church. It took the bourgeoisie one century to establish its hegemony in a space occupied by the church. In doing so it relied on the new political, parliamentary-democratic, ideological state apparatus, combining universal suffrage with party competition and the educational apparatus.

The Italian, French, and German Debate on Althusser's 'Crisis of Marxism'

When Althusser proclaimed, 'Enfin la crise du marxisme s'est éclatée' from the stage of the *Il Manifesto* conference in Venice in November 1977, it struck like a bomb. He ignited a debate in which the crème de la crème of the younger Western Marxist generation took part. *Il Manifesto* published their interventions in a series of articles between April and September 1978. In Italy, the debate over a Marxist theory of the state had been reignited just a year previously with the theses of Norberto Bobbio. Soon the discussion reached Germany, where the state theory debate had just underwent a lively revival under the auspices of state derivation theorists.

Althusser's speech deeply polarised Marxist workers in Italy. Some saw in his diagnosis of the current crisis of Marxism an opportunity for renewal (as did Althusser himself), but others took it as an insult to all organised workers' parties and, above all, to the Italian Communist Party (PCI).[23] But what did Althusser's provocation mean in the first place?

Althusser's central claim was that there was no state theory in Marxism and that this was not only a problem for Marxist political theory but was also responsible for the grave mistakes Marxist political parties made and still make in their practice. The insult was Althusser's claim that the crisis of Marxism was not a mere crisis of theory. He pointed out that the large workers' parties, not least the Italian Communist Party, had fallen into an identity crisis that affected the membership, the voters, the political self-image of their intellectuals, and their active leadership groups. He criticised not only the official line of the Communist Parties in France and Italy but also questioned the form of the political party itself as the agent of social change. It was obvious that his criticism was directed at the PCI's decision to take part in a ruling coalition by supporting the Christian Democrat-led government and taking key positions in the state apparatus in 1976. His criticism had a completely different weight in Italy than in a German debate where Marxist parties were atomised political presences and Marxists were almost exclusively intellectuals with scant political influence. To add insult to injury, Althusser further claimed that the current crisis of Marxism not only sidelined the traditional bearers of the interests of the working class, like parties and unions, but also gave birth to different 'movements' which questioned the very organisational form of traditional Marxist workers' politics.

There was a danger, according to Althusser, that when mass communist parties (like the Italian and French parties) became a part of the government, a part of the state apparatus, this would not have the effect of bringing the working masses into the state to make it their own state, but, on the contrary, the party would lose the unity with the working masses and their organisations. Mario Telò, who took part in this debate, agreed and added that the split occurred between the traditional labour movement and its organisations, in the course of which the workers' parties, in this case the PCI, found themselves in the state's sphere of domination (as had long since happened with social democracy), while the movements surging to fill its place within civil society from below were divided into a large number of those incapable of action and those only capable of representing corporatist interests.[24] Even more worrisome was the concern raised by Rossana Rossanda[25] that being part of the ruling bloc would make the PCI co-responsible for the economic deprivation of the masses in times of crisis and for other unpopular social policies they were too weak to prevent. This concern is reminiscent of the unease the Austro-Marxist Helene Bauer[26] expressed concerning socialists being in government in Britain and Germany during the 1929 financial crash. In general, the same question of whether Marxist workers' parties should participate in a ruling coalition with a bourgeois party, around which the debate initiated in Italy by Althusser's address in Venice turned, was one of the central issues of the political debates Austro-Marxists had conducted in the 1920s. As we know now, history proved most of these concerns valid.

The debate Bobbio initiated in Italy revolved around liberty, democracy, state, and socialism. One of the most striking remarks in Bobbio's text 'Quale democrazia?' from the volume *Quale socialismo?* aimed at what he regarded as the complete absence of a Marxist theory of democracy that could serve as a counterweight to the bourgeois concept of liberal democracy. Apart from Lenin's 1917 *State and Revolution*, which harks back to Marx's analysis of the Paris Commune and which Bobbio deemed useless for the understanding of the modern socialist states,[27] he saw no theory of democracy in Marxism. However, what this actually shows is that the Marxist theory of the state in 1970s Italy was apparently clueless about the Austro-Marxist contribution to the theorisation of the state and democracy, which in reality represented the most highly developed work in these fields ever written under the banner of Marxism. The exceptions were Giacomo Marramao, Giovanni Battista Gardoncini, and Lucio Lombardo Radice, who did write on Austro-Marxism, but to my knowledge were not involved in this debate itself. Bobbio noted that in the 1970s there was not a single Marxist analysis of the real existing socialist states of his time and that all studies, among which those of Poulantzas and Miliband stand out for their quality, revolved around the Western capitalist states of their time.[28] Knowing only Gramsci and Lenin as Marxist state theorists but not the Austro-Marxists, Bobbio concluded that Marxist state theory made more contributions to the theory of political parties than to the theory of the state.

For Bobbio, the central problem of state theory was the relationship between socialism and democracy. The system of liberal parliamentary democracy does not allow for system change – the overthrow of the capitalist system by democratic means. The consequence is that the only major change that can be achieved within the system of liberal democracy is the construction of a welfare state, which, as we now know, can be easily dismantled.

In the 1970s, the position of Marxist intellectuals in Germany was predominantly academic. Marxist positions were articulated only on the fringes of parliamentary democracy, forming a 'culture of the opposition'.[29] The debate, which was launched by Wolfgang Müller and Christel Neusüß in a 1970 article that charged the 'reform coalition' (Social Democrats and liberal Free Democrats), and the accompanying euphoria for Keynesian planning, with 'welfare state illusionism', tried above all to show that the state was not a 'neutral instrument' but fundamentally intertwined with the imperatives of capitalist accumulation and that therefore all expectations that the state could tame capitalism were, in the long run, illusory.[30] Taking their cue from Marx's *Capital*, the authors saw the concrete state as derived from the tangible form of socio-economic reproduction, endowing the base-superstructure metaphor with new content. By contrast with the vulgar economism epitomised by Lenin, they also argued against the idea of a state independent of socio-economic reproduction and autonomous in relation to it. The state can produce legislation in favour of or against the working majority, depending on the conjuncture of the class struggle. In this sense, the state has a Janus face, representing the antagonism between the working class and the bourgeoisie. The state is part and parcel of society and its economic reproduction, so it can hardly be expected to regulate both independently. The regulation and redistribution policies the state introduces in certain epochs depend on political relations of power and concrete socio-economic relations, reducing the state's ability to transform the economic system radically. This was directed against the view widely accepted among the German social democrats in the years of the economic miracle, who regarded state intervention as the promise of a crisis-free economy and welfare.[31] Similar criticism of the idea of the state's externality as an agent of intervention was also made by Elmar Altvater in 1972.

The state-derivation theory argued by Müller, Neusüß, and Altvater – merged with state theory as inspired by Nicos Poulantzas – is the most active branch of state theory among Marxists and neo-Marxists. It has inspired today's Marxist state theories, particularly in providing an explanatory model for the economic governance of the European Union as an authoritarian statism.[32]

Nicos Poulantzas

Nicos Poulantzas was among the thinkers who most profoundly developed the Marxist theory of the state in the French context of the 1970s. During the 1960s he was influenced by the circle around Althusser. *Political Power and Social Classes* still used Althusserian vocabulary in which a mode of production involves different levels or instances (the economic, political, ideological, and theoretical), the peculiarity of the capitalist mode of production lying in the fact that economic authority dominates within the complex structured whole.[33]

In the 1970s, he developed a theory closely associated with his name of the state as a balance of power or as a material condensation of these relations. It is in his last major work from 1977, *State, Power, Socialism*, that he develops his 'relational' concept of the state. In contrast to the 'class-functional' argument outlined in *Political Power and Social Classes,* he no longer argues that the state represents a specific structural level with the primary function of cohesion in the class-divided capitalist society. Poulantzas had already self-critically argued that Althusser's position was too formalistic. The conception of the structural levels suggests that the economy represents a self-reproducing and self-regulating entity and that the state, expanded to include the ideological and repressive state apparatus, only serves 'to fix the negative rules of the economic "game"'.[34] Such ideas ultimately entail an instrumental and neutral understanding of the state.

The ideological and political relationships play an essential role in reproducing the relations of production in which the state is the concentration and condensation of the political-ideological relationships in the relations of production and their reproduction.

Such an understanding, however, still does not entirely answer the question, already posed by Bauer in 1907, as to why the bourgeoisie generally falls back on the nation-state, a specific kind of modern representative state with its particular institutions, and not on another kind of state. 'Why, in general, does the bourgeoisie seek to maintain its domination by having recourse precisely to the national-popular state – to the modern representative state with all its characteristic institutions?'[35]

Poulantzas follows both Marx and Althusser in holding that the separation of politics and economy forms the basis of the peculiar institutional structure of the capitalist state. This conclusion conveys that this separation must not be grasped in the sense of a real externality of the economy in relation to the state, expressed in a belief in the miracle of state intervention in the economy from outside it. On the contrary, the separation of state and economy in capitalism is part of the hard core of the capitalist mode of production; it is a structural feature that characterises capitalism. The crucial point is that, according to Poulantzas, this separation is facilitated by the law. The separation is juridical – and this fact brings us back to Renner. Both Poulantzas and Renner agree that the main feature the state brings to the reproduction of the relations of production, meaning economy, is first: the 'economic property relationship', which means property in the legal sense, and, second, the factual, immediate 'ownership relationships' and the fact that the law sets limits to the exercise of power, but only when the relation of class forces stands in favour of the working class.[36] The function of the law as a barrier against the power of money depends directly on the power of the working class.

Here, finally, the conviction Poulantzas shares with Renner emerges with exceptional clarity: the need to rethink the juridical element and its potential to alter the balance of power in the state. It is especially relevant for rethinking the political strategies within the global neoliberal order and the specific state structures emerging from it. Following both Poulantzas and Renner, it becomes clear that juridication of the class struggle is the pivotal moment in the materialisation of the class struggle and its achievements. But the direction in which this materialisation will turn, on the side of capital or the working population, depends directly on the power of the working class to impose the juridical regulation in its favour. This, however, following Renner, depends directly on the level, structure, and power of the organisations representing wage workers. The concrete way in which these organisations were structured during most of the twentieth century is no longer viable and must be subjected to radical re-evaluation. Nevertheless, the class struggle and its different forms of organisation are still, as ever, the fundamental issue in any state theory that takes into account the dependency of the juridical structure of the state on the inequality within society. So, let us take a closer look at Marxist theories of class struggle and of the state.

The paths to the future

State and class struggle: Poulantzas, Althusser, and Renner

The relationship between the state and class struggle was one of the crucial points of Marxist state and political theory in general. From this angle, Poulantzas moves beyond Althusser's concept of the state and broadens it with the 'economic state apparatus'. Since Poulantzas argues that the state is no homogenous entity but a relationship of forces, political practice is political only insofar as it aims to transform these relationships as well as the form of the state apparatuses, which are the condensation of the relationship of forces between classes.

The affirmation of the state as a political field of class struggle is also decisive for the instrumental role Karl Renner ascribes to the state. For Poulantzas, too, the state is a field of politics, and all political parties are always already within the state, so every exteriority of the struggle is a myth. Against this background, Poulantzas accuses both Gramsci and Althusser of taking the dual strategy concept of the state over from the orthodox Marxists. 'Either the popular masses are included, "integrated" in it, and thus contaminated by the bourgeois plague that infects the fortress, or they remain pure in their search for their "for itself"/class consciousness (party), and are thus situated radically outside.'[37]

Against this background, Poulantzas attacked Althusser's idea that workers' parties should function outside the state.[38] For Althusser, class struggle is separate from the state, but this does not mean that for him there is no intrinsic relation between the two spheres. On the contrary, the tension between the forces of the dominant classes and that of the dominated classes gives structure to the state. This is what Althusser called the 'pseudo-circle' or 'great mystification' of the state: its formal separation from the class struggle. While the state is indeed the condensation of class struggle, as Poulantzas sees it, according to Althusser it is traversed only by the dominant form of struggle. It does not allow itself to be traversed by other forms of struggle. This is why Althusser argues that whoever believes that 'the state is by definition traversed by class struggle' is engaging in wishful thinking.[39]

For Renner, the class struggle was central to the nature of the state. If the workers' organisations are strong within the state, it serves the purposes of the proletariat; if they are weak, the state becomes an apparatus of oppression. Renner was well aware, however, that the classes are not static entities and that their structure changes together with the changing fate of the state. He was one of the first to see the new bureaucratic class arising from the state administration and forever changing the dual concept of the social class established by Marx. Where for Poulantzas the state is the densification of the class relations, for Renner the law is the stabilisation of the achievements of the class struggle. The institutionalisation of the class struggle and its transfer to the juridical plane is the most fundamental issue for his state theory. In this way he avoids the pitfalls of a base-superstructure metaphor in a unique way by affirming the role of the economic institutions of the working class firmly set within the state's law. 'The working class's economic institutions are the background of economic power.'[40] In this way he affirms the pre-eminence of the economy, together with the power it has, and brings it into direct connection with the state and its law in a circular form of mutual interdependence without having to subject either to vulgar economic determinism or to reiterate the liberal dogma of the division between the spheres of the economic and the political.

The question of democracy: Max Adler, Nicos Poulantzas, and Norberto Bobbio

As Bobbio noted in the 1970s, democracy was one of the elements barely discussed within the Marxist theory of the state in the twentieth century. This observation gains particular weight in the global neoliberal systemic constellation since democracy evolved as a pivotal legitimation ideology of neoliberalism. It not only serves as an omnipresent legitimation for almost every military intervention of the West around the globe but also as an indispensable condition for economic and political inclusion in the global 'rules-based system'. These rules, however, enforce a particular form of liberal democracy, which is thoroughly cleansed of any idea of democratic decision-making within the realm of the economy. This is also the main reason for the dissatisfaction of democratic movements around the world with liberal democracy, why democratic revolutions in the Middle East failed to deliver on the people's hope for democracy, and why authoritarian alternatives often hijacked them. It is not that the people are generally dissatisfied with democracy; rather, they expect more from democracy, above all, a concomitant improvement in their living and working conditions, which liberal democracy is unwilling and unable to deliver.

The Austrian Marxist Max Adler was concerned with the questions of democracy in liberal and socialist states. He followed Saint-Simon, who was one of the first to recognise that wealth was the true and only basis of all political influence and value. Consequently, he concluded that 'The law that determines the competences and form of government is not so important and does not have as much influence on the wellbeing of peoples *as the law that determines property rights and regulates their exercise*'. And in fact: under the bourgeois property order, under the capitalist mode of economy, which quite necessarily creates and maintains the difference between rich and poor, between entrepreneur and worker, between master and servant, all ideas of democracy must always be presented as mere pressure, as a tragic self-deception of a striving that wants good but always creates evil.[41]

The idea of democracy, according to Max Adler, can only acquire real social content if democracy is built on a system of economic equality, that is if all economic enslavement and dependency have been radically eliminated. This is possible only by overcoming the order from which economic inequality originates, i.e. the capitalist order. The realisation of democracy thus demands the decisive step beyond the world of the civic state and beyond the world of capitalism to a new socialist order, in which private ownership of the means of production no longer divides the people into a small class of masters and an overwhelming mass of pariahs in society and in which profit is no longer the actual motor and organiser of social and cultural life, but in which all available goods and forces of society are deployed for the benefit of each and all. This, for Adler, is the actual content of the call for freedom, equality, and fraternity formulated already within the French Revolution. From this perspective, anyone who earnestly strives for democracy but who also has learned from history and recognised why democracy acquired so little content in a hundred years cannot stop halfway with liberal democracy but must go forward to socialist democracy, which can only be achieved in a socialist state.

The socialist state that Adler advocated has never been created in Western Europe, and the socialist republics of the Eastern Bloc never became democracies. This contributed to the somewhat disillusioned view of the Western Marxists of the 1970s regarding the prospects for socialism and democracy. It was a pessimism expressed both by Poulantzas and Bobbio concerning a feasible democratic theory of socialism.

Being disillusioned by the social democratic struggle through the institutions of the state, Poulantzas rejected such a strategy and experimented instead with the direct democracy he found in Marx's writings on the Paris Commune. He was equally disappointed, however, with the attempts to emulate it in the universities during the 1968 protests. In an interview with

Henri Weber, he elaborated on some of his thoughts about direct democracy. For him, direct democracy, as Marx understood it, referring to the Paris Commune as a *mandat impératif* (formal instructions), revocable at the will of delegates', is not viable. 'If we want to preserve political freedoms and formal freedoms, this implies, I believe, the maintenance of certain institutions that embody them, and also representativeness, that is to say, centres of power, assemblies that are not directly modelled on direct democracy.'[42] This is precisely the point (which Poulantzas reiterates) on which Rosa Luxemburg reproached Lenin. All attempts at direct democracy from the base, without a clear idea of how it could work without preserving the institutions of representative democracy for a specific time of 'transition' until they 'are no longer needed', failed.[43] 'Believing that we will have a direct democracy, in the absence of the specific institutions of representative democracy, with political freedoms in addition (pluralism of parties, between others), well, what I know is that it never worked. Direct democracy, as a direct democracy in the Soviet sense, has always and everywhere been accompanied by the suppression of party pluralism and, afterwards, the suppression of political freedoms or formal freedoms.'[44] For Poulantzas, it is naïve to believe that civil liberties will continue to exist just by inertia if there are no institutions which guarantee them.

To elaborate a new concept of socialist democracy for the twenty-first century remains one of the most urgent tasks for any contemporary Marxist or Marxist-inspired state theory.

NOTES

1   'By contrast the second generational "set" within the tradition of Western Marxism was comprised of men who came to maturity well after the First World War, and who were politically formed by the advance of fascism and the Second World War.' Perry Anderson, *Considerations on Western Marxism*, London: Verso, 1976, p. 68.

2   The Marxist concept of direct democracy should not be confounded with the current liberal notion of direct democracy, which indicates plebiscitary democracy.

3   In the words of Nicos Poulantzas 'In Marx's statement the term "dictatorship" refers to the precise fact that every state is organised as a single functional order of legality and illegality, of legality shot through with illegality.' Nicos Poulantzas, *State, Power, Socialism,* London, Verso, 2014, p. 202.

4   Karl Marx, *Theories of Surplus Value*, Karl Marx and Frederick Engels, *Collected Works*, vol. 31, New York: International, 1989, p. 182.

5   Friedrich Engels, Letter to Walther Borgius, 25 January 1894.

6   Perry Anderson, 'The Antinomies of Antonio Gramsci', *New Left Review* I/100 (November/December 1976).

7   Christine Buci-Glucksmann, *Gramsci and the State,* London: Lawrence & Wishart Ltd, 1980, p. 88.

8   Antonio Gramsci, [Notebook 8, §185], *Selection from the Prison Notebooks*, translated
       and edited by Quintin Hoare and Geoffrey Nowell-Smith, New York: International
       Publishers, 1971, p. 263.

9   Otto Bauer, *The Question of Nationalities and Social Democracy*, Minneapolis, University
       of Minnesota Press, 2000, p. 144.

10   Bauer, *The Question of Nationalities*, p. 145.

11   Bauer, *The Question of Nationalities*, p. 405.

12   Karl Renner, *Mensch und Gesellschaft – Grundriß einer Soziologie*, Vienna: Verlag der
       Wiener Volksbuchhandlung, 1952, p. 148.

13   Poulantzas, *State, Power, Socialism*, p. 127.

14   Karl Renner, *Marxismus, Krieg und Internationale. Kritische Studien über offene Probleme
       des wissenschaftlichen und des praktischen Sozialismus in und nach dem Weltkrieg*, Stuttgart:
       J.H.W. Dietz, 1917, p. 59.

15   Karl Renner, *Was ist Klassenkampf?*, Berlin: Singer, 1919, p. 18.

16   Louis Althusser et al., *Reading Capital: The Complete Edition*, London: Verso Books,
       2015 (first published 1965)

17   Louis Althusser, *Essays on Ideology*, London: Verso Books, 1984.

18   Althusser, *Essays on Ideology*, p. 16.

19   Althusser, *Essays on Ideology*, p. 10.

20   Althusser, *Essays on Ideology*, p. 14.

21   Althusser, *Essays on Ideology*, p. 17.

22   Althusser, *Essays on Ideology*, p. 18.

23   One can get a sense of the polarising effect Althusser's address had on Italian Marxists
       from a letter to the editors of *Il Manifesto* signed 'Benni', shortly after Althusser's talk.
       The writer suggests *Il Manifesto* should offer a platform around which Althusser's
       theses could be productively discussed. Here is an excerpt: 'Dear comrades, I'm pretty
       worried. Last night, while we were standing around outside the bar, engaged in a
       discussion with Althusser over the Italy-Brazil soccer match, we heard a huge crash.
       On the third floor of the house across the street, a woman smashed dishes on her
       husband's head because he hadn't gotten home until five o'clock that night from a
       long discussion with Althusser. Of course, we immediately called the police just to
       find out that all the patrols had already been dispatched to the Piazza Maggiore, where
       a discussion with Althusser had turned into a huge fist fight'.

24   Mario Telò, 'Formen und Widersprüche des erweiterten Staates', in Elmar Altvater
       and Otto Kallscheuer (eds), *Den Staat diskutieren*, Berlin: Verlag für Äasthetik und
       Kommunikation, 1979.

25   Rossana Rossanda, 'Kritik der Politik und ungleiches Recht', in Altvater and
       Kallscheuer, eds., *Den Staat diskutieren*.

26   'But the mere fact that when the acute crisis broke out in both countries [England and
       Germany) the governments wore a socialist label was enough to make the two workers'
       parties appear co-responsible in the eyes of the masses for everything they were too
       weak to prevent' (Helene Bauer, 'Im vierten Krisenjahr', *Der Kampf* 25,12 (1932): 493-
       9.

27   Norberto Bobbio, *Quale socialismo – Discussione di un'alternativa*, Turin: Einaudi, 1976,
       p. 4.

28   Nicos Poulantzas, *Pouvoir politique et classes sociales*, Paris: Découverte, 1968; Ralph
      Miliband, *The State in Capitalist Society – An Analysis of the Western System of Power*,
      New York: Basic Books, 1969.

29   Elmar Altvater and Otto Kallscheuer, 'Reaktionen auf eine Provokation – wie die
      Linke in Italien die Krise des Marxismus diskutiert', in Altvater and Otto Kallscheuer,
      Den Staat diskutieren.

30   John Kannankulam 'Materialistische Staatstheorie' in Rüdiger Voigt (ed.), *Handbuch
      Staat,*Wiesbaden: Springer, 2018.

31   Wolfgang Müller and Christel Neusüß, 'Die Sozialstaatsillusion und der Widerspruch
      von Lohnarbeit und Kapital', *Probleme des Klassenkamps [PROKLA]* Sonderheft 1
      (1972): 4–67, here 52.

32   Martin Konecny, 'Die Herausbildung einer neuen Economic Governance als
      Strategiezurautoritären Krisenbearbeitung in Europa – gesellschaftliche Akteure und
      ihre Strategien', *Prokla*, Verlag Westfälisches Dampfboot, 168 (2012): 377-94.
      Jens Wissel, *Staatsprojekt Europa: Grundzüge einer materialistischen Theorie der europäischen
      Union*, Münster: Westfälisches Dampfboot, 2015;

33   Poulantzas, *Pouvoir politique et classes sociales*, p. 12.

34   Poulantzas, *State, Power, Socialism*, p. 85.

35   Poulantzas, *State, Power, Socialism*, p. 44.

36   Poulantzas, *State, Power, Socialism*, p. 216.

37   Nicos Poulantzas, *Repères: Hier et aujourd'hui*, Paris: Découverte, 1980, pp. 172-3.

38   Louis Althusser, 'Marxism as a Finite Theory' [1978], *Viewpoint Magazine*, December
      14, 2017.

39   Louis Althusser, 'Marx in his Limits', in *Philosophy of the Encounter: Later Writings,
      1978-87*, London: Verso, 2006, p. 80.

40   Renner, *Was ist Klassenkampf?*, p. 18.

41   Max Adler, *Politische oder soziale Demokratie – ein Beitrag zur sozialistischer Erziehung*,
      Vienna: "Tribüne" 1982, p. 42.

42   Nicos Poulantzas, 'L'État et la transition au socialisme – interview de Nicos Poulantzas
      par Henri Weber', *Critique communiste* (May 1977): 15-40, here 25.

43   Poulantzas, 'L'État et la transition au socialisme'.

44   Poulantzas, 'L'État et la transition au socialisme'.

Decentring the State

Athena Athanasiou

The state is an embattled terrain of epistemic and political signification. It conjures different sites, geographies, and temporalities of violence and injustice that underwrite the global present. Tangled in the historically sedimented, interlocking contours of racialised, gendered, ableist, and classed power relations, the state refers to multiform, heterogeneous, and trans-local coordinates that remain challenging sites for left critique and engagement.

To what extent can 'the state' be a useful concept, then, for a left critical imaginary and reconfiguration of our present? Is a critical concept of the state possible in these times of global neoliberal governmentality, militarised securitisation, and far-right and neofascist authoritarianism? How can we think about the state in the register of radical democratic, emancipatory, and revolutionary struggles and movements in the 'here and now'?

In asking such questions, I would like to argue that this critical work requires attending to theorisations that problematise the primacy of state-based politics, dislodge the premises of state sovereignty through a transnational frame, and revisit the theories of the state through a de-substantialised perspective on power. Such theorisations resonate with Michel Foucault's famous programmatic statement from *The Will to Knowledge*: 'In political thought and analysis, we still have not cut off the head of the king.'[1]

In this text, I propose to explore how the analytics of the state persists or returns in the left's political imaginary at this critical time of neoliberal capitalism and the rise of neofascist formations and regimes. I am interested in revisiting the state through questioning the paradigm of sovereign authority, inaugurated by Hobbes' *Leviathan*, and its attendant essentialised reduction of power to state-centred, juridical frames. At the same time, I seek to attend to the political figuration of the social state – in all its contradictory complexity and differentiated plurality – as a performative resource for the possibility of a radical democratic engagement and contestation for the present, in the face of the neoliberal dissolution of welfare policies and public infrastructures.

Thus, in view of the neoliberal turn of capitalism, a left engagement with the state requires a double gesture of resistance and transformation; it calls for a simultaneous critique and reconfiguration of the established notions of citizenship, welfare, and democracy. Drawing on feminist scholarship on the state, such engagement might complicate the received logic of the state as either a protective or a merely coercive force. Instead of uncritically dismissing or uncritically endorsing state-oriented politics, at stake in left theory and praxis is a decentred, agonistic democratic, and redistributive reappropriation of the state. This venture would entail enacting collective democracy to counter institutionalised injustice, and embracing the task of instituting it in fundamentally different, more just and equal, ways.

Seen from this perspective, the task of the left in response to the present exigencies involves rethinking and re-enacting a politics of civic engagement and dissent in the face of oppressive state violence, and devising strategies of resistance to this violence and its attendant technologies and mechanisms of regulation, in step with radical democratic and emancipatory social movements and collectivities. This struggle does not occur, however, only within the realm of the state. It keeps the question of whether the capitalist state can be transformed and democraticised open to the contingencies of collective agency. This multilayered task involves crafting and reinhabiting places and times from which to engage in collective practices of making life more bearable in the present, in light of forced social suffering and exhaustion.

In this respect, I would like to call for a critical-performative conception of the state as a modality of political agonism that resists closure and finality, and opens ways of transfiguring the power/knowledge matrices that regulate the present.

States of crisis

As the colonial history of the modern European state shows, state power as a universal form of order-making bestowed with a monopoly over regulatory rationality and the use of violence has been historically established through the power/knowledge constructions of 'Western civilisation' and its racialised and gendered 'others'. As Veena Das and Deborah Poole have explained, the margins of what is recognised as the terrain of unquestioned legitimacy are imagined as sites of the 'state of nature' (construed as savage and lawless but also idealised as primordial by early theorists of the state, such as Hobbes, Locke, and Rousseau) where the state refounds its modes of order.[2] Colonial power introduced a new matrix of epistemic, affective, and political protocols, akin to what David Scott refers to as the 'governing effects on colonial conduct'.[3] The modern state, in its historically contingent ways of drawing on and diverging from the history of the empire, is an epistemic object that is put to work in a genealogy of spatio-temporally contextual governing practices and knowledges that underwrite today's world.

Such explorations of the modern state's colonial history have drawn attention to the state not as a monolithic entity but rather as a lived history and an open-ended force field of relations.[4] What constitutes a state at specific times, what truth-claims, narratives, fantasies, tropes, and matrices of intelligibility it is premised upon, and what technologies of demarcation and (un-)belonging it registers are at the heart of what makes up authorised accounts of state politics in colonial capitalism.

In order to address and engage with the crucial question of the historically produced epistemic space of the state in our political present, it seems important to account for the ways in which current and ongoing crisis-oriented post-democratic and anti-democratic formations provide the ground for today's rearticulation of the state and its techniques of governmentality. This is a pursuit that calls for critical epistemologies and imaginaries capable of countering the biopolitical timescapes of a present structured through what Lauren Berlant has called 'crisis ordinariness'.[5]

The current regimes of crisis, governmentality, and precaritisation, as well as their meshes of subjectivation and power/knowledge, call for a critical re-engagement with, and re-imagining of, the political performativity of the state. This, however, makes sense within the framework of a wider and sustained questioning about how radical social transformation can be enabled and how the political is agonistically rearticulated. It connects with understanding the complex ways in which the state (re)produces, maintains, and perpetuates social inequalities and oppressions, such as those of class, gender, and nationality. At the same time, it connects with practices of defending and rearticulating the unconditionality of non-corporate, non-commodified public spaces, in the face of the anti-democratic governing reason of neoliberalism that dismantles the social state, dispossesses public goods and infrastructures, and undoes the constituent terms of democracy – freedom, equality, and popular sovereignty.[6]

Neoliberalism is not only anti-statist, however, despite the 'mistaken notion that, in going global, capitalist markets were escaping, by-passing, or diminishing the state'.[7] There has been a diverse literature on the ways in which markets and states are intimately connected and work in tandem with one another in modern global capitalism. Indeed, despite the normative discourses about a 'lean state', state power is a core force that sustains the encroachment of the market in all social and economic fields. As David

Harvey has put it: 'Neoliberalism does not make the state or particular institutions of the state (such as the courts and police functions) irrelevant, as some commentators on both the Right and the Left have argued. There has, however, been a radical reconfiguration of state institutions and practices (particularly with respect to the balance between coercion and consent, between the powers of capital and of popular movements, and between executive and judicial power, on the one hand, and powers of representative democracy on the other)'.[8]

As a mode of governing reason, neoliberalism remakes the state into an authoritarian, anti-democratic mechanism that legitimises, facilitates, and superintends the privatising entrepreneurial economic order. This process of state neoliberalisation is reflected in the policies of 'austerity' and public spending cuts as well as the business-based model of governance. The state retreats from its responsibility for providing the common goods and services – healthcare, education, welfare and pensions – that were previously the domain of the public sector while taking on responsibility for economic activities of private business entities to ensure their profitability and competitiveness. As Wendy Brown has incisively demonstrated, the neoliberal state is a de-democratised state, operating as a manager of the 'free market' and its crises. As she suggests in her book *In the Ruins of Neoliberalism*,[9] the rise of far-right formations, associated with figures like Donald Trump, Recep Tayyip Erdoğan, Viktor Orbán, and Jair Bolsonaro, and premised on racism, ethno-nationalism, and anti-feminism, is not to be understood as a reaction to neoliberalism. The anti-democratic, authoritarian, and self-investing individualistic politics of the contemporary right are conditioned by, albeit not reducible to, the deregulating force of neoliberal rationality. The neoliberal right and far right converge in an antidemocratic, possessive-individualistic logic; they disdain and denounce the social state while promoting strategies of market-based technocratic and repressive statism that Nicos Poulantzas encapsulated with the term 'authoritarian statism'.[10]

Poulantzas introduced the term 'authoritarian statism' to describe the form of capitalist state and governance that had been consolidated and intensified by the political crises of the 1970s and in response to the rise of left-wing movements. This form of capitalist governance included a centralised and all-powerful administrative and executive control of the state over all registers of political and socio-economic life, along with an abolition of some of its former economic functions, a weakening of the institutions of political democracy, a decline of the rule of law, an accentuation of repression, and a curtailment of formal rights and liberties – all characteristic of exceptional regimes.[11] In theorising 'authoritarian statism' at a time of rising left-wing movements and their brutal defeat by military dictatorships (i.e., Greece and Chile), Poulantzas highlighted the constitutive role of 'exceptional' turns in capitalist management in ways that also accounted for the beginnings of neoliberalism. Advancing a critique of Marxist theories of the state, but also thinking through Michel Foucault's theory of power, Poulantzas articulated the workings of authoritarian statism as a way to capture how the capitalist state, in condensing class relations, deploys disciplinary technologies of power that defy the distinction between 'normal' and 'exceptional'.[12] The compelling aspect of Poulantzas' nuanced neo-Marxist framework of authoritarian statism is that it takes us beyond the problematic accounts of the state as being either strengthened or weakened in response to contexts of capitalist crisis. This perspective offers conceptual means with which to analyse the intensification of 'exceptional' features and the integration of 'extraordinary' executive regulations into formal liberal democracies under neoliberal governmentality.

In this sense, the state of crisis as a mode of authoritarian neoliberal statism raises questions about the complex intersections of crisis, capitalist state, and democracy. The managerial and anti-democratic aspects of neoliberalism eviscerate, in Wendy Brown's terms, the very space of the *demos*: the democratic space in which people assemble to articulate and bring forth common claims of freedom, equality, and justice. As capitalist democracy becomes increasingly dispossessed of the demos, it is reduced to its function of *-cracy*: the state is being relegated to an authoritative medium and guarantor through which 'human capital' is administered by the market and the interests of the ruling classes are served. Rather than a differentiated, open-ended, and plural body politic that creates the ongoing conditions for multiple and transversal forms of belonging, the body politic amounts to the territorial and administrative coordinates of the nation-state, free-market economics, and self-interested possessive individualism. Rancière has aptly addressed post-democracy as an inflection of liberal democracy that neutralises the central element of political antagonism: 'Postdemocracy is the government practice and conceptual legitimation of a democracy after the demos, a democracy that has eliminated the appearance, miscount, and dispute of the people and is thereby reducible to the sole interplay of state mechanisms and combinations of social energies and interests'.[13]

Various scholars have addressed the interplay between sovereign power and neoliberal rationality.[14] Indeed, the regulatory demarcation and management of the *demos* is a defining aspect of neoliberal statism and its functions in citizenship and the economisation of political life. The elimination of what Étienne Balibar defines 'equaliberty', as 'nothing other than the demand for a popular sovereignty and autonomy *without exclusion*',[15] is a condition on which neoliberal governmentality is founded. Neoliberalism undermines the (always already antinomical) principles of democratic citizenship and representation as such. Achieving equaliberty requires, in Balibar's terms, a democratisation of democracy in the existing state and its institutions.[16] This pertains also to the democratic reflexivity of political movements: 'a force or a political movement can only democratise society if it itself is fundamentally more democratic than the system it opposes, both with respect to its objectives and to its internal operation.'[17]

In line with this scholarship on radical democracy, we might trace possible ways in which the *demos* could be reclaimed as a plural and open-ended vantage point for a transformative and potentially revolutionary critique of the states of emergency that structure our present condition of neoliberal and authoritarian governmentalisation.

Revisiting the state through a governmentality perspective

In the fourth lecture of *The Birth of Biopolitics*, Foucault states: 'I must do without a theory of the state, as one can and must forgo an indigestible meal.'[18] I would like to argue that the left cannot do without a theory of the state; however, it must account for and engage Foucault's and others' critique of theories that tend to assume the state as a fixed, unitary, universal, and essential(isable) empirical given. And so the challenge for the left is to resist this reification and instead theorise the state within social relations, institutional forms, everyday embodied affiliations, and power configurations through which it comes to depict itself and to be experienced or imagined by the body politic as singular and coherent.[19]

As Foucault's analytics of power has shown, a theory of governmentality necessarily includes a notion of the state. Foucault was concerned with the power effects of the state: 'The problem of bringing under state control, of "statification" [*étatisation*], was the heart of the questions I have tried to address.'[20] The process and practice of 'statification' is an aspect of governmentality: 'The state is nothing else but the mobile effect of a regime of multiple governmentalities.'[21] In deconstructing perspectives that take for granted the institution of the state as a central site or unilateral source of power, however, he calls for theorising power outside the dominant 'discursive-juridical model' (i.e., the model of Leviathan), which is focused on the logic of sovereignty and law. In this sense, Foucault departs also from Max Weber's location of power in the terrain of the state. The Foucauldian analysis has enabled the comprehension of power in its de-centralising modalities and 'capillary ends'. Hence his notions of biopolitics and disciplinary power, through which he deals with the microphysics of power (i.e., incarceration, sexuality) but also macro-power (i.e., governmentality). It is by accounting for the interrelation between 'micro' and 'macro'-powers that the workings of subjectivation through and inside the subjugating modes of power/knowledge can be mapped out.

In Foucault's analysis of state formation, 'population' became the object of modern politics and episteme during the eighteenth century. Embedded in disciplinary techniques, and contextualised in the expansion of capitalism, biopolitics makes population management, administration of life, and optimisation of the labour force possible. Populations are managed, policed, optimised, and normalised through technologies of power that are more diffuse, complex, transversal, and intense than those operating by the single and centralised authority of the state. This does not mean, however, that the nation-state is deprived of its powers of oppression. In Foucault's thought, neoliberalism, as a new mode of governmentality, defines a diffuse regime of truth and subjectivation that focuses on the ways, or mentalities, in which people are governed and govern themselves by means of self-responsibilisation and self-interested competitiveness. The mode of subjectivation akin to neoliberal governmentality is enacted by producing and regulating subjects of economic interest rather than subjects of rights and popular authority: 'Homo economicus is an entrepreneur, an entrepreneur of himself.'[22]

In light of the interrelation of sovereignty, discipline, and biopolitics, 'life' is administered, enhanced, and secured through mechanisms that expose lives to lethal power effects, including those that seek to fabricate useful, docile, and governable bodies. In *Security, Territory, Population*, Foucault addresses the 'pre-eminence over all other types of power – sovereignty, discipline, and so on – of the type of power that we can call "government"'.[23] And in *The Birth of Biopolitics*, pursuing the theme of a governmental rationality which seeks maximum effectiveness and intensity (in mastering and saturating the field of life) by governing less, he focuses on a detailed analysis of the forms of this liberal governmentality, including the role of neoliberalism in twentieth-century politics.

In this respect, neoliberal rationalities and techniques of power involve a multifaceted articulation between 'productive' and 'destructive', economic and uneconomic, repressive and 'free market'-based aspects of subjectivation. Tracing the idea of natural order that underlies the free-market economic thought, Bernard Harcourt has emphasised how market naturalism and government-run penal autarchy have come to work in tandem in the framework of the neoliberal state.[24]

The current crises of late capitalism, made possible by neoliberal governmentality and by its having become the norm, threw into crisis the bipolar conceptualisation of the relation between the liberal–capitalist logic of welfare and the authoritative production of dispensable and disposable populations through austerity and the precaritisation of the labour force.

Thus, as manifested in the Greek context of neoliberal austerity as well as in other contexts of the Global South, steep economic disparities, public-sector degradation and divestment, deprivation or loss of healthcare access, and the widespread condition of precarity are combined with, and supplemented by, various repressive and coercive mechanisms, such as the forced compliance with debt service, tightened migration policies and 'detention centres', police brutality, state practices of quelling public protest, institutional power abuses, and the curtailment of rights.

Neoliberalism is more than just a mode of post-Fordist capitalist financialisation. Rather, it is a more encompassing regime of governmentality, which regulates the terms of citizenship and livability by unevenly distributing resources among differently economised, racialised, and gendered subjects. It includes particular modalities of power and subjectivation, which assume the interwoven forms of biopolitical (self-)management, market economisation, competitive individualisation, securitisation, responsibilisation, and a reconfigured relation between public and private.

Equal before the law? A feminist critique of the state

In her classic book *States of Injury*,[25] Wendy Brown argues that the state is legitimised by portrayals of wounded subjects as helpless victims in need of institutional protection in liberal capitalist societies. Working on an integrated Foucauldian and Marxist frame of analysis, she addresses the disciplinary role that institutionalisation and the law play in this process of attributing to the state the power of acting as arbiter of injury: 'the heavy price of institutionalized protection is always a measure of dependence and agreement to abide by the protector's rules.'[26] This process works to obscure and sustain the structural force of late modern state power in producing and multiplying conditions of injury. Brown deconstructs the depoliticising and de-democraticising effects of this regulatory discursive formation of injury politics. Seen through this perspective, we might acknowledge how certain state-focused left political projects inadvertently enhance the very power configurations they seek to disrupt.

The social contract theory of state formulated by Rousseau, Hobbes, and Locke has been severely criticised by feminist theory, pointing to the androcentric nature of the state and the social-sexual contract.[27] Feminist critiques of the state have addressed the paradoxes that underlie certain appeals for gender justice addressed to the state. Such feminist scholarship has tracked and denounced the disciplinary frames of welfare-state policies. If the state is a tool of biopolitical management, premised upon, and saturated with, unequal and unjust power relations in terms of gender, class, ethnicity, race, and (dis)ability, could it eventually function to achieve gender equality (as liberal feminism uncritically assumes)? Although critical of the liberal state, legalist discourses of rights, and welfare policies, feminists – especially those who draw on socialist and poststructuralist currents of scholarship – make agonistic demands on the state in the key areas of feminist concern, like violence against women, queer and trans people, reproductive justice, and also, more widely, in terms of uneven allocation of resources. The domain of governance is critically rethought and problematised as a form of cooptation by the status quo but also as a performative site of resisting and opposing structures of power as well as inciting social change. Feminist critique pays attention to, and politically mobilises, the performative contradictions inherent in a politics that seeks to transform the diverse mechanisms of the state. Most significantly, poststructuralist, queer, and intersectional feminist scholars promote a feminist critique of power (rather than of the state); for (this) feminist theory, power is the decisive concept and unit of critical analysis.[28]

In this respect, the feminist/queer critique exposes the appropriation and depoliticising instrumentalisation of feminist claims and gay rights by neoliberal governmentality. It seeks to problematise and counter the violence and injustice built into the state and legal apparatuses, by asking 'who' the subject of the law might be and how it is formed as a gendered subject through the law, whose claims and rights are recognisable, and what requirements of gender, race, and class determine access to the law.[29] The conceptual implication of 'law' is analytically expanded to include juridical, discursive, disciplinary, and regulatory power formations that are performatively involved in reiterative processes of social identification and subjectivation. Differently situated subjects become identifiable and intelligible by reiterating the social norms through which they have been interpellated. At the same time, problematising the hegemonic domains and apparatuses of legal standing is an open-ended, historically contingent possibility. Judith Butler's feminist account of norms in their relationship to legal violence has been key to our understanding of critique and social transformation in the midst of diverse and intersecting forms of power. As she has put it: 'We need this kind of analysis so that we do not assume that everyone is equal before the law. Not yet. That struggle for legal standing only arrives as the effect of a broader struggle for political equality, or so it seems to me. In the end, the power to wage a revolution is more important than the fight to file a lawsuit – but sometimes they are connected.'[30]

Elucidating the complex intersections of normative frameworks, discursive and legal violence, citizenship, resistance, and change, this line of analysis is needed to understand and overcome the systemic violence that is waged with impunity by structures of power against those subjectified by the intersecting forces of gender, race, class, and ableism. It is essential in producing a new understanding of how gendered subjects are made to be dispossessed and precarious by patriarchal and heteronormative domination intersectionally combined with racialised violence, neoliberal exploitation, or neofascist actions, but also how such discourses of subjection can become performative occasions for radical expropriation, reoccupation, and transformation of hegemonic intelligibility. In this sense, legal battles make sense as steps and aspects of broader and multi-sited processes of political critique, resistance, and mobilisation.

Drawing on a genealogy of Black feminist and feminism-of-colour critiques of institutions and the state, Sara Ahmed has offered a consideration of how institutional structures promote racism and heteropatriarchy and, at the same time, how institutional change becomes possible. Drawing attention to testimonials of students and employees who have complained to university authorities about harassment and inequality, she highlights the persistence and resistance of those who fight for justice within institutions against institutional injustice.[31]

This feminist politics seeks to extend across the boundaries of the nation-state and build transnational alliances and solidarities. Moreover, with the catalytic role of a vibrant women-of-colour feminist movement, it provides a critique of white liberal feminism and promotes the mobilisation against police brutality and systemic violence against black people. The mobilising power of feminism across Latin America, but also in Europe as well as throughout the world, has become a crucial component of today's emancipatory and radical democratic politics. It can no longer be disregarded by the left.

Agonistic democracy and the public

The antidote to the present and ongoing political and economic crises and authoritarian shifts effected by state neoliberalisation cannot be a 'stronger state'. To be sure, in view of authoritarian alt-right statism and neoliberal post-democratic statism, a critically situated epistemology and politics of a progressive social state is something the radical left cannot do without. 'Not doing without it' requires an interminably complicated critical labour of collective thinking and acting in ways that challenge and do not re-entrench the existing unjust power relations.

The world-changing Covid-19 pandemic has brought to the fore the neoliberal debris that austerity policies and the bailout of the banks had left behind. The apparatus of the pandemic disaster intensified the pre-existing and longstanding crises within the crisis: poverty and precarity, the decimation of healthcare systems, structural oppression, the exploitation of migrant labour, racism, able-bodiedness, sexism, and homophobia/transphobia. Power/knowledge configurations of the pandemic, in all their lived embeddedness, implicated the neoconservative biopolitics and bioeconomics of crisis management. The coronavirus outbreak in Southern Europe took place in the aftermath of the 2008 financial disaster and on the basis of the social radical inequalities in terms of the intersecting powers of class, race, gender, sexuality, care, and access to public healthcare.

Under these circumstances, and in light of the neoliberal governments' retreat from the state's obligations to provide social care, a public awareness emerged regarding the induced conditions of unlivability in which bodies are differentially treated by the market-driven governmentality of profit, debt, and precarity. A dissident public awareness emerged regarding the need for a social state. This has been manifested in public enactments of collective agency that seek to turn the inscriptional space of 'the state' into a domain of agonistic contestation.

The politics of bringing an agonistic account of the state to bear on a left theory of the political involves – but is not reduced to – claiming and taking state power. The left turns to legislative powers and the state in order to radically reoccupy and transform them, sustaining a critical and (self-) reflexive relation to them, and thus running the risk of becoming co-opted by them, but hopefully without succumbing to this risk.

However, recognising that notions of protection and sovereignty are already embedded in the neoliberal doctrine of managing crises, the left should not acquiesce in a defence of the status quo but should rather combat the regimes of uneven distribution of social vulnerability and push for radical changes of social intelligibility, through egalitarian demands for social and economic justice, collective freedom, and democratic institutions.

This struggle entails defending and enhancing the democratic gains that had been previously achieved by subaltern classes and oppressed groups; defending these collective achievements against the neoliberal and the new right's assault on welfare services, public institutions, and social rights. Our critical task is to foster a reinvigorated vision of democratic socialism with antiracist and feminist/queer politics at its centre against the neoliberal doctrine that 'there is no alternative'. Such a vision beyond the pragmatic management of the status quo and conventional modes of state administration might help to reclaim for the left disenfranchised and working-class citizens who have turned to the right, and to create a new popular base for democratic socialist mobilisation.[32]

This counter-hegemonic pursuit requires collective mobilisation demanding equal and just allocation of resources, efficient and inclusive public services, and institutional justice. Thanks to protest movements of the 2010s, such as the Indignados in southern Europe, Occupy Wall Street in the US, and Occupy movements in Turkey, Brazil, and elsewhere, which, drawing on the 1999 anti-capitalist Seattle protests, denounced the displacement of democracy by neoliberal injustice, we now have the capacity to conceptualise left political commitment in social mobilisation beyond conventional binaries such as horizontal versus vertical organisation or spontaneity versus vanguardism.[33]

From the Movement for Black Lives in the US, the Ni Una Menos in Latin America, and collective practices opposing gendered and racial injustice, to the struggles for self-determination by occupied and Indigenous people, the 'march of hope' from Budapest to the Austrian border in 2015, in which thousands of refugees were involved, and the rise of left social movements opposing neoliberal privatisation and austerity, authoritarianism, and de-democraticisation around the world – these collective modes of the political have offered empowering glimpses of hope in these times of despair. Challenging and rearticulating established notions and demarcations of who counts as 'citizen', such movements disrupt the nationalist and statist frames of bounded nation-states. They signal that the nation-state is no longer the exclusive and unquestioned domain of emancipatory and democratic struggles. Taking place within contested public spaces, or within contested realms of embodying public space, those movements and alliances practice democracy through agonistic ways of attending to, and transforming, the harrowing conditions and contingencies of the present.

As I have attempted to show in this text, not essentialising the state does not mean epistemologically and politically disregarding the insurgent and constituent agency related to it. The left critique of the state entails combining struggle from within the capitalist state with enacting radical democracy outside it, while also transgressing and reappropriating that contestable dichotomy. This challenge requires embracing the task of tracking and mobilising the cracks within institutional power. It also entails acknowledging the revolutionary potential of such performative contradictions.

NOTES

1   Michel Foucault, *The Will to Knowledge: The History of Sexuality*, vol. 1, London: Penguin Books, 1998, pp. 88-89.

2   Veena Das and Deborah Poole (eds), *Anthropology in the Margins of the State*, Santa Fe: School of American Research Press, 2004, p.8.

3   David Scott, 'Colonial Govermentality', *Social Text* 43 (August 1995): 191-220, 204.

4   Nicos Poulantzas, *State, Power, Socialism*. London: Verso, 2014 (first publication: 1978, New Left Books); Bob Jessop, 'Poulantzas "*State, Power, Socialism*" as a modern classic', in Alexander Gallas et al. (eds), *Reading Poulantzas*, Pontypool: Merlin Press, 2011.

5   Lauren Berlant, *Cruel Optimism*, Durham: Duke University Press, 2011.

6   Wendy Brown, *Undoing the Demos: Neoliberalism's Stealth Revolution*, Cambridge, MA: Zone Books, 2015.

7   Leo Panitch and Sam Gindin, *The Making of Global Capitalism: The Political Economy of American Empire*, London: Verso, 2012, p. 1.

8   David Harvey, *A Brief History of Neoliberalism*, Oxford: Oxford University Press, 2005, p. 78.

9   Wendy Brown, *In the Ruins of Neoliberalism: The Rise of Antidemocratic Politics in the West*, New York: Columbia University Press, 2019.

10   Poulantzas, *State, Power, Socialism*; Jessop, 'Poulantzas' "State, Power, Socialism"'. As Bob Jessop has put it: 'A stronger emphasis on issues of national security and pre-emptive policing associated with the so-called war on terror at home and abroad has reinforced the attack on human rights and civil liberties' (*The State: Past, Present, Future*, Cambridge, UK: Polity Press, 2016).

11   Poulantzas, *State, Power, Socialism*.

12   Foucault's reflection on the state is also an engagement with Marxist discussions on the state at the time, including, most notably Poulantzas's non-reductionist conceptualisation of the capitalist state (in *State, Power, Socialism*).

13   Jacques Rancière, *Disagreement*, Minneapolis: University of Minnesota Press, 1998.

14   Brown, *Undoing the Demos*; Bernard Harcourt, *The Illusion of Free Markets: Punishment and the Myth of Natural Order*, Cambridge MA: Harvard University Press, 2011.

15   Étienne Balibar, 'Is a Philosophy of Human Civic Rights Possible? New Reflections on Equaliberty', *South Atlantic Quarterly* 103,2-3 (July 2004): 311–322, 319.

16   Étienne Balibar, *Citizenship*, Cambridge UK: Polity Press, 2015, p. 124.

17   Balibar, *Citizenship*, p. 128.

18   Michel Foucault, *The Birth of Biopolitics: Lectures at the Collège de France, 1978–79*, Basingstoke: Palgrave Macmillan, 2010, pp. 76-7.

19   Aradhana Sharma and Akhil Gupta (eds), *The Anthropology of the State: A Reader*, Malden, MA: Blackwell Publishing, 2006.

20   Foucault, *The Birth of Biopolitics*, p. 77.

21   Foucault, *The Birth of Biopolitics*, p. 77. And see Mathias Hein Jessen and Nicolai von Eggers, 'Governmentality and Statification: Towards a Foucauldian Theory of the State', *Theory, Culture & Society* 37,1 (2020): 53-72.

22   Foucault, *The Birth of Biopolitics*, p. 226.

23   Foucault, *Security, Territory, Population: Lectures at the College de France 1977-78*, Basingstoke: Palgrave Macmillan, 2007, p. 108.

24   Harcourt, *The Illusion of Free Markets*.

25   Wendy Brown, *States of Injury: Power and Freedom in Late Modernity*, Princeton NJ: Princeton University Press, 1995.

26   Brown, *States of Injury*, p. 169.

27   Carole Pateman, *The Sexual Contract*, Cambridge UK: Polity Press, 1988.

28   Amy Allen, *The Power of Feminist Theory: Domination, Resistance, Solidarity*, New York: Routledge, 2018 (first published 1999).

29   Judith Butler, *Gender Trouble: Feminism and the Subversion of Identity*, New York: Routledge, 1990.

30   Judith Butler, 'Sexist violence and forced migrations demand a transnational mobilization', interview, LATFEM, 20 April 2019, <https://latfem.org/judith-butler-sexist-violence-and-forced-migrations-demand-a-transnational-mobilization/>.

31   Sara Ahmed, *Complaint!*, Durham: Duke University Press, 2021.

32   Panitch and Gindin, *The Making of Global Capitalism*.

33   Rodrigo Nunes, *Neither Vertical nor Horizontal: A Theory of Political Organization*. London: Verso, 2021.

State Transformations: From the 'Powerless' to the 'Entrepreneurial State'

Michalis Spourdalakis

The state has gone through several transformations over the last four decades, both conceptually and in its actual operation. At the heart of these transformations are: capitalist integration at a global scale; so-called 'globalisation'; the unprecedented developments and challenges of the triple transition in the countries that comprised so-called actually existing socialism; the rise and the fall of social democracy in the 'West' and particularly in Southern Europe of the 1980s and 1990s; the limited impact of the so-called anti-globalisation movements; the historical experience of pink-tide governments in Latin America; and finally, the rise and the retreat of the various radical-left attempts in government.

However, to date, the analysis of all these distinct changes and debates over the conundrum of state power has been rather descriptive, with little room for a more comprehensive understanding of these changes, an understanding that could have updated and enriched the theories of the state developed in the late 1970s and early 1980s. This failure to capitalise theoretically on the rich historical experience of the last thirty plus years is due to what has been insightfully called the 'impoverishment of state theory'.[1] However, this ought to be no surprise, given that 'the retreat from class' has been a dominant trend not just among mainstream intelligentsia but even among those inspired by the Marxist tradition.[2]

The purpose of this essay is not, of course, to fill the gap left by the state theory so impoverished over the last few decades. Rather, it is to note the weak, descriptive perceptions of transformations of the state, unable to facilitate critical understanding and therefore be strategically operational for those parts of the left who still aspire to the social transformation of capitalism. However, even this modest goal cannot be fully realised. The size of the related literature and, at times, the complexities of its arguments can only be presented in an eclectic fashion. Thus, I will touch on the way in which state theory was impoverished and the efforts to make up for this through the call to 'bring the state back in', and then turn to the idea of the 'powerless state', such as it developed out of the dynamics of globalisation. I will examine the idea of the need for a new type of state, as a response to the aggressive neoliberal reconstruction of the state and the state policies promoted by the highly influential 1997 World Bank Report; the transition to 'new governance' and finally the recent post-COVID call for an 'entrepreneurial state'.

The above developments in state theory correspond to the key moments in the actual transformation of the functions and/or structures of state power. However, my main thesis is that in effect – regardless of their analytical capacity and methodology – all of them function as a cover for (and legitimating justification of) unequal social and political power and the capacities of the capitalist social formation. Thus, the challenge for the radical left is not just to acquire a critical understanding of all these 'new' pseudo-theories but also to reflect on their various shortcomings, in a way that allows for a new revival of state theory. This means a state theory that will not only point to an understanding of the characteristic features of state power in the current moment but also serve as the background for a strategy for not simply 'entering' the state but transforming and democratising it.

There is little doubt that evaluations of the radicalism of the 1960s and the miraculous year 1968 provided a serious qualitative boost to state theory. The reconsolidation of Gaullism, after it had been seriously challenged by powerful radical and militant movements, and soon afterward the coup d'état in Chile, a country with the longest and most stable democracy in South America, spurred political scientists and sociologists to analyse the grounds upon which the state's reproductive capacity of capitalism is based.

Until then, social scientists with a critical background criticised pluralism – something that E.E. Schattschneider had done in his own unique way since the 1940s.[3] At the same time, they followed the debates on the research on political power as it was approached by authors such as C. Wright Mills, John Kenneth Galbraith, and others. Thus, state theory really took off in the late 1960s and 1970s, when relatively young Marxists decided to go beyond critical comments and develop an alternative theoretical approach to the state, capitalising on both the Marxian and Marxist analyses as well as on insights from mainstream traditions. In the first and founding theoretical contributions to the field, it became clear that these new Marxists' theoretical contributions were far from the mainstream of the instrumentalist and simplistic ideological approach of most communist parties. These social scientists did not disregard the advances of the Marxist tradition; it is no exaggeration to say that their perception of state power was very much along the lines of a Gramscian understanding of the state: '[As the state is an] entire complex of practical activities with which the ruling class not only justifies and maintains its dominance, but manages to win the active consent of those over whom it rules, then it is obvious that all the essential questions of sociology are nothing other than the questions of political science.'[4] This definition of Gramsci's vividly describes the sophistication of state theory that was then being initiated.

What followed over the next decade or so, is well known. The work of Ralph Miliband and Nicos Poulantzas, the debates between them as well as those of a good number of students from almost all the fields of social sciences, took on both the theoretical complexities of state power and the political challenges imposed by the conjuncture of the time. Thus, the key traits of this problematic produced analyses that tried to sharpen the tools of the understanding of class as a determining factor of the capitalist state's structure and function.

Based on the European experience, Miliband's effort was focused on identifying the site where fractions who hold political power meet and link up with the dominant classes. Thus, his major contribution was to concretely display the elements through which and the ways in which the unity of dominant classes and political power is sealed. On the other hand, Poulantzas' effort was to theoretically determine the distinct character of the political within the capitalist mode of production. Consequently, his emphasis was on identifying the sites and the elements of detachment between the dominant classes and those who hold political power. This difference in their analytical emphasis governed the often-controversial debate over the 'relative autotomy of the state'. Thus, while Poulantzas saw the relative autonomy of the state as subject to a framework of determinations and called for its study in this context, Miliband's concept of state autonomy understood it in terms of its relative freedom of action.

Despite the great impact that these analyses had on state theory – as exhibited by the prolific theoretical production at the time – in the 1980s, as Panitch aptly later argued, 'the advances made in Marxist state theory set in and soon became quite unfashionable ... [since they were] swept away as part of the general post-Marxist, post-structuralist, post-modernist trend' in the academic world.[5] This led to a change of 'focus of attention for the state and class struggle to the micro-physics of power and the problems of identity formation'.[6]

This latter development, in combination with the superficial adoption of the idea of 'the relative autonomy of the state', further impoverished the advances of Marxist state theory, which was objectively very critical of the naïve social democratic understanding of the state. It also contributed to an approach to the state and the market as an ahistorical or at least a vague concept. In turn, this led social democracy and several other left-wing and radical political forces to adopt policies which implied that they could withstand and manage the perils of capitalist crisis. These policies were based on the argument – as against the neoliberal right – that state intervention in the economy is neither anti-business nor irrational and inflationary. Through this development both in theory and in concrete politics, the sophistication and advancements of state theory that emerged from the political rejuvenation of Marxism in the 1960s and 1970s has been reduced to a mere challenge to pluralism and not seen as a contribution to the challenge to capitalism.

Nevertheless, the impoverishment of Marxist state theory does not mean that the mainstream or even anti-Marxist scholars of this field were indifferent to it. In the mid-1980s, a number of serious social scientists noted – contrary to their counterparts of the so-called critical or 'unorthodox' tradition – that they did not approach the state as a set of organisational structures with an autonomous capacity as an actor. This indirect recognition of the rigorous advancements of Marxist state theory led to a ground-breaking study in the field of comparative social science, funded by the Social Science Research Council in the United States, which issued a call to 'Bring the State Back In'. This development briefly brought some relief to radical students in the field. The aim was to reconsider and reconceptualise the state as a key factor in social structures, and its operations as a proper subject of research. However, this effort, despite its impact on academia, had much more modest aims than initially believed. The concluding paragraph of the chapter which introduces the founding volume of this methodological proposal itself points to its infection by Marxist theorisations.

As we bring the state back in to its proper central place in explanations of social change and politics, we shall be forced to respect the inherent historicity of sociopolitical structures, and we shall necessarily attend to the inescapable intertwining of national-level developments with changing world historical contexts. We do not need a new refurbished grand theory of 'The State'. Rather, we need a solidly grounded and analytically sharp understanding of the causal regularities that underlie the histories of states, social structures, and transnational relations in the modern world.[7]

Post-structuralist and post-modern theories and identity politics, in combination with the political naïveté of modernisers (both new social democrats and other ex-radical leftists alike) and segments of academia who sought to 'bring the state back in', were instrumental in freezing and in effect undermining the advances of Marxist state theory. However, it was globalisation that changed the debate on the question of state theory.[8] Since globalisation is a process that leads to capitalist integration at the global level, it contains a number of different functions and develops certain institutions that used to come under the authority of nation-states – an authority which determines political, institutional, and social dynamics within a certain territory. However, there are no common criteria for measuring globalisation, and this has provided an opportunity for some analyses to dispute its dynamic as a novel face of international economic, political, and cultural relations.[9]

This scepticism was expressed in the late 1990s and has resurfaced again in the last few years. Yet there is virtually no doubt that globalisation has produced very important and extensive changes both at the structural and functional levels, with the following key traits: 1) The necessary goods and services for the material needs of every society are no longer produced predominately by those who live in the territory of a given state. Rather, they are produced in several states, primarily for the world market and much less for the local, state defined, market. 2) Financial structures, i.e. the system created to finance production and trade, are no longer confined within the nation-states and are now electronically linked, having developed on a world scale. The local, state-confined, banks are no longer independent as they have become part of a global financial system which is coordinated by powerful institutions. 3) The most perplexing dimension of globalisation is a clear tendency towards global homogenisation. Although there is no doubt that regions' and small territories' cultural characteristics persist, there has developed a clear trend toward the convergence of tastes, perceptions, beliefs, and ideas at the global level.

These developments have opened up an extensive academic debate regarding the role of the nation-state. These analyses' main concept holds that the role and the capacity of the state have been 'eroded' and its political power has become more diffuse because of the heavy impact of the dynamics of the world economy.[10] There have been many variations on this analysis, seeing as in everyday politics it seemed that governments and states were overpowered and undermined by the processes of globalisation or outflanked by the rise of ever more powerful international institutions. Part of this approach is the much-celebrated work of Hard and Negri,[11] who in their defence of globalisation argued that it abolished both the form of the state apparatus, and the national bourgeoisies. Others, however, opposed this 'retreat of the state' and argued that this apparently 'powerless state' is simply a 'myth', given that the state maintains its capacity to adjust to the challenges of the global economy.[12] This argument was usually put forward by those who continued the tradition of Marxist state theory. Thus, since the state, in a given territorial jurisdiction, is key in maintaining order and the discipline needed for capital accumulation and securing the necessary consensus, it has become an agent of globalisation and even its real 'author'. The argument here is that globalisation is misunderstood if we do not recognise that this apparent internationalisation is very much composed of states which, within the given democratic structures, are still embedded in economic and political power at the national and even subnational levels.[13] To these authors, the 2007-8 crisis was a 'vivid' verification of 'Marx's insight in the *Communist Manifesto* (that) while capitalism is international in substance, its reproduction remains national in form'.[14]

It seems to me that this view of state power and governmental capacities fits more with our European (or rather, EU) experience. I do not think that there are many people who could convincingly argue that, for example, in the Maastricht or the Lisbon treaties, the nation-states through their respective governments were absent. The argument that the power and the role of the nation-state has evaporated is quite superficial. Even the key thinkers who maintain that the nation-state does not have the capacity to intervene in economic production and distribution, recognise that its role has not been nullified; it may have been reduced, but we should take seriously its capacity to administer and police social dynamics in order to guarantee a positive climate for economic investment.[15]

As the dominant neoliberal globalisation evolved − and through the extensive reforms that promoted, caused, or contributed to the capitalist integration of our planet − its contradictions have become increasingly vivid. The spirit of deregulation inspired by the Thatcherite dictum against the 'nanny state' has brought several contradictions to the fore, especially regarding its management and apparent lack of democratic legitimisation. It was in this context that in 1997 the World Bank issued an extensive and widely hailed report under the title *The State in a Changing World*.[16] The impressive background of the researchers involved, and particularly the all-out warfare it wages against the state's responsibility to secure social cohesion, briefly led some radical academics to welcome the report as a landmark which could change the political orientation and the role of the state.

However, shortly afterward it became clear that the report did not aim at changing the political orientation of the state, but rather at renewing its practice so that the state could be more 'effective' in opening 'windows of opportunity' through the "compensation of potential losers [...] and building consensus'.[17] Thus 'The Agenda of Change',[18] aimed at making the state more effective, requires a better mix between coercion and consent. This did not mean, as some thought at the time, the idea of 'bringing the state back in' but a plan for how political elites could secure their hegemonic rule. All the rhetoric of the Report about 'participation', 'involvement' and 'consultation' is meant to secure the acquiescence of those social classes and strata which are more likely to oppose the dominant policies. A typical example of this is the choice of a particular type of NGO and the exclusion of the unions and associations of subordinate strata (workers, farmers, etc.). Here, NGOs seem to act as institutions to oversee Total Quality Management, and not as promoters of grassroots control of political outcomes.

Besides the debates around the development and the understanding of state power, there is little doubt that a major change in recent history is a dramatic 'hollowing out of the state'. It is a transformation that can be described as a transition from government to governance.[19] A transformation that seems to have changed the logic, the functions, the structures, and the apparatus of the state.

In the nineteenth century, the governments of the liberal state had to coordinate several, often contradictory or at least competing functions in order to maintain the conditions of accumulation with social peace and harmony. These tasks were not so simple, as the governmental power had to recognise, strengthen, and regulate a number of institutions (e.g. schools, organised interests, prisons, etc.) which could improve its political efficiency. At the same time, governments reached out and integrated several initiatives and practices into their logic, such as attempts at self-government that evolved into institutions of the local and regional state, and urban civil rights movements.

In the twentieth century and especially after World War I, state power became embedded within the framework of government. This governmentalisation of the state addressed the key areas that required governmental management, regulation, and control: urban planning, social security, economic life, as well as the society's ethical values. It was in this context that government grew enormously and became 'big government'. This was a fair description in the literature and had both qualitative and quantitative dimensions. It was this development that sparked criticism from both the left (Habermas's 'colonisation of the lifeworld' and 'legitimation crisis') and the right (in opposition to statism that controls socio-economic dynamics and represses personal life, leading – according to Hayek and Friedman – to inefficiency, to 'serfdom' and to injustice).

As 'big government' became the centre of neoliberal polemics, the government had to be redefined. This process of redefining government started in the late 1980s and was centred upon the dominant assumption that 'good government' means 'less government', itself based on the principles of 'New Public Management'. With strong 'suggestions' from international Institutions – the Washington Consensus, the World Bank, the IMF, the White Paper on European Governance – government now had to respect the principles of governance. These latter are expressed, on the one hand, by applying the whole neoliberal menu (privatisation, promoting and supporting private entrepreneurship, shrinking the state apparatus and state functions, and the fractionalisation of administrative functions now assigned to non-state institutions, etc.). On the other hand, at the institutional and administrative levels, serious reforms had to be introduced to the whole structure of the political management, to transform government into governance. Thus, politics would now simply mean the exchanges and relations between public, private, and voluntary organisation. Governance is simply a continuum of 'actor networks', 'self-regulatory mechanisms', 'trusts' and 'informal obligations'. In other words, governance takes place not through centralised hierarchies or through societal antagonisms, but through networks.

As governance has replaced government both institutionally and functionally, it has become more and more established within the context of post-democratic politics. It has been further strengthened in the recent conditions of crisis, and it displays clear signs of the diffusion of state power. More concretely, the move from government to governance means that the state authority and its responsibilities have gradually been transferred in three directions: a) outside the national territory and to supranational institutions in which the state participates (e.g. the EU, AFTA, etc, b) to lower authorities e.g. local and peripheral institutions, and c) to civil society and the market. This trend has redefined the jurisdictional boundaries between the state, the market, and civil society. This in turn has led to the redistribution of state administrative control and accountability to independent administrative agencies and the transferring of the respective administrative cost to non-governmental institutions such as NGOs and various professional bodies. The old governmental / state institutions are denounced as dated or incapable of securing popular consent and legitimation. They are now ever more dependent on NGOs, on various ephemeral agencies, and on strong media and communication systems.

This is not to say that these developments are without antinomies and contradictions, which themselves seem to have very negative effects on democratic politics. In this sense, an analysis of the structures and functions of contemporary democracies requires separate attention. However, a brief reference to this here could provide a better understanding of state transitions and contribute to a further research agenda.

Even a superficial understanding of the logic of governance makes clear that we are faced with new types of representation. Although this representation promotes the institutional participation of the society, its political power is diminishing. Indeed, the prolific rhetoric about the role assigned to civil society in restructuring the institutional and procedural functions of democracy which was expected to revitalise political participation did not bring any results. On the contrary, increased societal participation through the processes of 'social dialogue' among 'social partners', instead of leading to effective political participation further contributed to define the public sphere within the strict framework of the economic market. This 'market first' logic led to a distortion of the liberal and democratic understanding established in most advanced capitalist democracies. Furthermore, it led to a change in the basis of legitimation. In the past, this was secured by social negotiations, deliberations, and dynamics. Now the values of these processes are becoming marginal, in conditions in which post-democratic structures are gaining strength.

As the move from government to governance further reduces democracy to its procedural dimension, it has become clear that citizens' political impact and power was depleted as society's formal and institutional participation increased. This development has drastically changed political attitudes which now question the positive dynamics of democracy. These attitudes can be described heuristically as: a) a sub-political societal feeling, which leads to the belief that citizens can only have an effect on very marginal issues; b) an antipolitical sentiment that leads to – and largely explains – rising political apathy and falling voter turnouts worldwide; and c) a selective realism and tamed by a narrow sense of individual responsibility, which restricts most initiatives that might widen the scope of the political.

The enduring crisis that began in 2007-8 expanded the 'crisis of legitimation' which had taken root already at the end of the twentieth century. This was concretised as a multifaced crisis of representation and, in not a few cases, as a crisis of democracy. The rise of undemocratic political parties is a case in point. The neoliberal deregulation policies that undermined the state's capacity to secure the reproductive patterns of capitalist societies has given actual content to Habermas' 1970s concept.[20] However, it was the pandemic crisis of the last few years that exposed in the most dramatic fashion the shortcomings of neoliberal politics. Governments' huge spending to deal with the intense public-health issues and to support the economy in order to reduce recessionary tendencies, momentarily gave the impression that states were breaking out of the neoliberal straitjacket.

These Keynesian initiatives were short-lived. However, this experience has reopened the debates on alternative polices for the governments of our time. In this context, some innovative social-democratic proposals along the lines of the 'entrepreneurial state', voiced already a few years before the last crisis, once again entered the debates on the transformation of the state. These proposals were prompted by Mariana Mazzucato's much-celebrated book *The Entrepreneurial State: Debunking Public vs Private Myths in Risk and Innovation*[21] in which the author refers to a number of case studies of economic successes and failures, but her primary focus is US economic development, which is considered, overall, as a successful example. At the heart of Mazzucato's argument is the claim that this should be attributed to the strong US government investments in innovation and technology. In this way, she dismisses the dominant neoliberal belief that only the small state and market-driven investment can bring about economic prosperity or be an answer to austerity. Her analysis is clearly inspired by a heterodox political economy and she indirectly challenges the dominant economic dogma, as for her it is not up to the taxpayer but the state to protect the private sector from risks. However, left-wing critics pointed to serious omissions in her analysis such as the socially defined preference in the production of goods and services. On the other hand, conservative critics, even those who recognise that the idea of the 'entrepreneurial state' is worth discussing, have remarked that Mazzucato omits mention of numerous endeavours in state investment. In sum, even though the idea of the entrepreneurial state is a relatively vague theoretical analysis and cannot be translated into concrete policies, nor in any concrete way contributes to state theory, it is well worth discussing. That is, not as a new dogma, but as an idea which, even in its reasoned rejection, can help us to revisit and rejuvenate the Marxist theory of the state.

The longstanding deregulation of the law, at least within the legal order of the EU's nation-states, has alarmed the critical-academic community. Specifically, the argument here is that the tendency towards the Europeanisation of the nation-state's legal system, in the context of frequent crises, has led to a separation of sovereignty, to the dispersal of public institutions, to a multiplying system of conflict between institutional authorities, and to a rising tendency of privatising legislation whereby the law is instrumentalised and constitutional authority is challenged by the uncontrolled powers of the big centres of private capital. This is a critical description of state transformation, which has been described by public law scholars as 'neo-feudal constitutionalism'.[22]

The various expressions of state transformation over recent years are so intense and varied that they are bound to rekindle interest in state theory. There is no doubt that left-wing parties' failures in real-world politics over the last decade (Greece, Portugal, UK, US, and elsewhere) will force us in this direction, just as in the late 1960s, the rich historical developments at the time led to an unprecedented rekindling of Marxist state theory. However, very little effort has been made to develop a plan for a political strategy which could take advantage of the transformations of the state and advance a socialist project. Of course, in addition to the theoretical understanding of changes in state power, this presupposes a good analysis of the recent failures of the left – something which is long overdue. Activist academic thinkers have tried to draw some conclusions as a point of departure for such a debate. The authors of *In and Out of Crisis* have made some very useful points to contribute to this discussion:[23] a) there is no use in planning to return to the pre-neoliberal framework, since there is no similarity between the conditions then and now, seeing as the 'working classes have been integrated into the financial markets'; b) the primary goal of social(ist) transformation is to strengthen the capacities of the subordinate/popular classes in a way that undermines the capitalist logic, but this priority should be pursued in a way that includes an efficient response to their immediate material needs; c) democracy should not be limited to the way it is understood in the mainstream, simply as the process of forming a government, but should be a hallmark of society and the basis upon which to eventually democratise the economy; d) as the crisis has exposed, 'states are enveloped in capitalism's irrationalities', and building new political parties and movements is a must if we want to transcend capitalist markets and states.

On numerous other occasions, intellectuals of this tradition have underlined the fact that even worse than the left's inability to confront the crisis is its lack of ambition to do something innovative and effective. To this end, they have suggested some basic reforms such as placing the banks under social control and turning them gradually into public utility institutions, free health care, free education, and free city transport, which will bypass capital's tendency to turn public needs into commodities for profit making. It is clear that all these proposals cannot be achieved by an ad hoc academic or theoretical debate within the context of the left-wing intelligentsia. This is a job for the movements initiated by the subordinate classes and for political parties which will have the courage and will to supersede the shortcomings of both social democracy and the various Leninist advances of the past.

NOTES

1   Leo Panitch, 'The Impoverishment of the State Theory', Stanley Aronoviwitz and Peter Bratsis (eds), *Paradigm Lost: State Theory Reconsidered*, Minneapolis: The University of Minnesota Press, 2002, pp. 89-104.

2   Ellen Meiksins Wood, *The Retreat from Class: A New 'True' Socialism*, London: Verso, 1986/1998.

3   E.Eric Schattschneider, *Party Government*, New York: Farrar & Rinehart, Inc., 1942; Schattschneider, *The Struggle for Party Government*, College Park, MD: University of Maryland - College Park, 1948; and later his classic *The Semi-Sovereign People: A Realist's View*, New York: Holt, Rinehart and Winston, 1961.

4   Antonio Gramsci, *Selections from the Prison Notebooks*, Quinton Hoare & Geoffrey Nowell Smith (eds), London: Lawrence and Wishart, 1971 p. 244.G

5   Panitch, 'The Impoverishment of the State Theory', p. 92.

6   Bob Jessop, 'On the Originality, Legacy, and Actuality of Nicos Poulantzas', *Studies in Political Economy*, 24 (1991): 92.

7   Peter B. Evans, Dietrich Rueschemeyer and Theda Skocpol (eds), *Bringing the State Back In*, Cambridge: Cambridge University Press, 1985, p. 28.

8   For a useful history of globalisation, see Robbie Robertson, *The Three Waves of Globalization*, London: Zed Books, 2003.

9   Paul Hirst and GrahameThompson, *Globalization in Question: The International Economy and the Possibilities of Governance*, Cambridge: Polity, 1996.

10 For example: Susan Strange, 'The Erosion of the State', *Current History*, 96,613 (November 1997): 365-370; Strange, *The Retreat of the State. The Diffusion of Power in the World Economy*, Cambridge: Cambridge University Press, 1996.

11 Michael Hardt and Antonio Negri, *Empire*, Cambridge, MA.: Harvard University Press, 2000; Hardt and Negri, *Multitude. War and Democracy in the Age of Empire*, New York: Penguin, 2004.

12 Linda Weiss, *The Myth of the Powerless State*, Ithaca, NY: Cornell University Press, 1998.

13 Leo Panitch, 'Globalisation and the State', *Socialist Register 1994*, London: Merlin Press, 1994, pp.60-93; Panitch, 'Rethinking the Role of the State', J. H. Wittelman (ed.) *Globalization: Critical Reflections*, Boulder: Lynne Rienner, 1996, pp. 83-113.

14 Greg Albo, Sam Gindin and Leo Panitch, *In and Out of Crisis: The Global Financial Meltdown and Left Alternatives*, Oakland: PM Press, 2010, p.126.

15 Zygmunt Bauman, *Globalization. The Human Consequences*, New York: Columbia University Press, 1998, esp. pp. 55-77.

16 The World Development Report 1997, *The State in a Changing World*, Oxford: Oxford University Press, 1997.

17 The World Development Report, p. 156.

18   The World Development Report, pp. 157-167.

19   See for example: R.A.W. Rhodes, 'The New Governance: Governing without Government', *Political Science* XLIV (1996): 652-667.

20   Jürgen Habermas, *Legitimation Crisis*, Boston: Beacon Press, 1975.

21   Mariana Mazzucato, *The Entrepreneurial State: Debunking Public vs Private Myths in Risk and Innovation*, London: Anthem Press, 2013.

22   For an excellent exposé of the legal transformation of the state see: K.T. Giannakopoulos, *Neo-Feudal Constitutionalism*, Athens: Sakkoulas Ed, 2022.

23   Albo et al., *In and Out of Crisis*, pp. 126-129.

State Transformation and Its Effects

Download our e-publications at the website
www.transform-network.net/publications

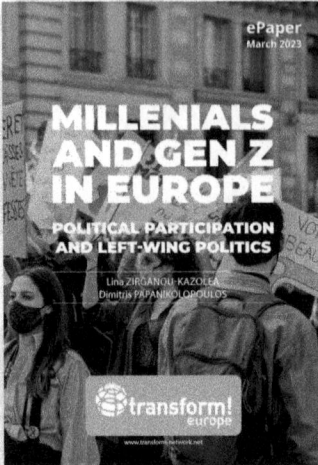

Youth expresses the most militant and promising part of the political left, playing a central role in social mobilisations and political uprisings. But are left-wing parties in Europe credible to Millennials and Gen Z? Why do even the radical parts of the politicised youth not see the left parties as spaces of participation and collective struggle?

Selected contributions from last year's annual Strategy Seminar organised by transform! europe and the Rosa-Luxemburg-Foundation, which took place in Paris in November 2022 and focused on the sociology of the left vote and various conglomerates of the radical left.

Subscribe to *transform! europe's* monthly newsletter to stay informed about the transform! network's activities and current events.

www.transform-network.net

f /transformeurope　　**𝕏** @transform_ntwrk　　**▶** @transformeurope

On the State, the Public, and the Common: Thoughts from the Pandemic[1]

Étienne Balibar

In this essay, I will assemble some hypotheses about the three notions – the state, the public, and the common – which subtend the discussions about power relations, collective practices and political responsibilities emerging from the experience of the Covid-19 pandemic between 2020 and 2022. They mainly apply to Europe, though some surely have a more universal significance.

Learning from and within the crisis

The following reflections are closely linked to what I believe that I – in conversation with many others – have learned during the recent pandemic.[2] These reflections are as fragile as the conjuncture itself is ever-shifting, both in terms of the developments in the public-health situation and in the political and economic consequences that they produce over time. We have behind us suffering, destruction, lockdowns, but also protests, social movements, and political initiatives – and other developments still to come. They affect the very meaning of the categories we use; this makes the interpretation of tendencies more hazardous, but we must take the risk of identifying and naming what we can see already.

Such a strange situation may in fact prove useful. Indeterminacy makes it possible to grasp the *historic dimension* of the crisis in which we find ourselves: it is not just a temporary interruption in the life of society, or an occasion for a shift in the exercise of power, but a *change in the modality of change* itself, which forces us to anticipate unknown mutations. When we gather our experiences and theories in order to imagine what could happen, we are looking for the 'signs of the times' that suggest *questions* rather than answers based on yesterday's forecasts. In this respect, I am betting on the *irreversible character* of the break provoked by the pandemic and what follows from it. Many institutions will continue and defend their legitimacy, but a simple return to the standards of the past will ultimately prove impossible. This is not a prophecy; it is, rather, a description of the existing state of affairs. What the crisis reveals are conditions incompatible with a 'reproduction' of the former regime, including its acceptance by the 'governed'. As Lenin famously wrote: 'the lower classes do not want to live in the old way, and the upper classes are unable to live in the old way.' In the crisis situation, social relations are stretched to the extreme, in terms of the working of administrations, models of economic growth, debt sustainability, the acceptance of inequalities and discriminations, and obedience to the decisions of authorities. This is tantamount to saying that we have already entered a *transition process*, but one whose orientations and goals remain indeterminate. We can only assert that it will create other institutions, other modalities for labour and life in common, other creeds and collective values. The question that haunts our speculations is quite simply: *how do civilisations change* in history? By means of what violences, inventions or conversions do they change? Other generations in the past had to confront this question, and they never gave unanimous answers.

These are, surely, big words. We ought now to qualify them. First, as I indicated, powerful organised forces are convinced that *everything can continue as before*. They even believe that they can use what (in Naomi Klein's words) we may call the 'shock therapy' of the crisis in order to intensify the changes that they had already planned in the previous period, which we can summarise under the term *neoliberal programme of social change*. When calls for a 'reboot of the economy' are made, we may identify a 'global' project for the *acceleration* of neoliberal tendencies: a greater hegemony of financial capital, generalised indebtedness of individuals and nations, a digital revolution in the division of labour, the commodification of services and the environment, etc., with devastating effects on everyday lives and solidarities. But all this is going to collide with equally powerful obstacles. The dominant forces of capitalism must *invent a new strategy* of domination and a new ideological project for themselves and for others. This is a risky 'interregnum' (in Gramsci's words), ripe with conflicts of hegemony. The result cannot be the 'enlarged reproduction' of the neoliberal economy, but – as my late friend Immanuel Wallerstein never tired of explaining to his socialist comrades – it can also be *worse*.[3]

At this point, a second clarification is in order. In its current form, *globalisation* has produced a degree of interdependency among economies and societies which is unprecedented in history, but it has absolutely not uniformised political regimes, it has not levelled inequalities of wealth or brought together cultural traditions in the 'world-system'. The polarities between North and South or East and West are stronger than ever: they might lead to confrontations or wars on different borders and 'fault lines'.[4] Every analysis of a local situation involves a definition of the *place* that it occupies in a field of unstable geopolitical relations. Which adds to our conviction that we live in a time of great uncertainties, for which we must seek new categories of both thought and action.

A strategic component: the crisis of public services

From these general comments, I draw the conclusion that it would be useful to identify the *strategic link,* in which current problems are crystallised at the same time as long-term contradictions are taking shape. My aim is not to project a political agenda onto the embarrassments of the pandemic, which would be completely artificial, but to tentatively unravel the latent 'politicality' within the institutions which have been tested by the pandemic. In my country (France) but also in others, this strategic link was represented by *public service*. The crisis essentially affected how it works, which functions it performs, which conflicts emerge in its core and how they develop.

The most striking thing, indeed, is the fact that across a long period the whole life of a country – from its economic activity to the private lives of its citizens – was conditioned by the quality, the resources, and the defects of its public health system. As everyone agrees, medical care then becomes central to the political; it does so not just as an institution fulfilling one necessary social function among others, but as *the primary 'service'*, whose interruption or malfunctioning can stop everything working: this is the reason why it needs preserving 'whatever it takes'.[5] This validates the idea, proposed by Michel Foucault, of rethinking the whole conditions of possibility of politics in terms of a *biopolitical imperative*, whereby 'making live and letting die' does not concern only a *particular domain*, but the primary object of government and the foundation of power relations. However, Foucault does not really discuss the function of medical and healthcare institutions as *public services* with their contradictions, due in particular to his ambivalent attitude with respect to the juridical dimensions of politics, and more generally his reluctance to envisage a *theory of the state* that makes it the dominant power within society. But precisely what the current health 'state of exception' has put into question is the exact nature of the relations between state policies (whether liberal, socialist, or neoliberal), the historical forms of the capitalist state itself, and public services' role in sustaining society. Now, the heavy constraints imposed on the staff of doctors and nurses who keep the health service going, plus their increasingly conflictual relationship with administrations, have struck at the core of an institution (the public hospital) which (in France in particular) was already in revolt against the government. This creates a *problem* which may strategically command their relations of forces in the coming period. The categories of *public service, public authority, public order,* and *public budgets* gravitate around the protection and the destination of health. They call for a reflection which articulates immediate, urgent issues with long-term perspectives. This itself requires some preliminary definitions and clarifications.

To begin with, *health* is a very complex kind of 'service', which cannot be reduced to the workings of hospitals and professional medicine. It must be articulated with many other practices and institutions, which cover practically the whole of society. These range from scientific research to the pharmaceutical industry and biomedical technologies, demographic and statistical measurements, but also academic institutions for higher education and professional training, mutual aid bodies and social programmes. As the crisis has made clear, we should also include the hitherto 'invisible' services of cleaning, food supply, and bodily and psychological 'care' for every individual, considered ill or otherwise. It appears that public health is not a *specialised* service, but a relationship to society as a whole, in fact a *universal relationship of society to itself,* that generates commonality. Only education, perhaps, has the same extension and degree of multiplicity.

There is permanent controversy, however, about the definition of 'public services', regarding their social function, the legal status of facilities providing them, the financing on which they depend, and whether or not they are incorporated into a state institution. Such debates considerably vary from one country to another and across different periods. After the 'golden era' for public services in the 20th century, when a reformist capitalism established 'social citizenship' (T.H. Marshall) in the framework of a both 'national' and 'social' state – hence placing it at the core of the material constitution of the country – neoliberal policies reversed this course. They aimed at 'rationalising' the management of 'public services' and 'privatising' as much of their facilities as possible. This was a 'revolution from above', affecting the living and working conditions of the population and generating a considerable uncertainty as to *which services are public by nature,* in other words not to be entrusted to private entrepreneurs. This is similar to the question of what the *common goods* of society or even humanity are. Contemporary 'neo-communists' tend to develop a category of the 'common' that is not the same as the 'public', or even contradicts it.[6] Rather than engage in a complete discussion on this score, let's note an important point: there exists a *plurality* of services, which remain widely heterogeneous, with different, even antinomic connections to social citizenship, hence their completely different management by the state. This can be illustrated by the extreme examples of (1) the *school system*, 'serving' education and individual professional training, but also (in democratic countries) instituting the 'equal opportunity' which is supposed to reduce social inequalities, and (2) the *police*, 'serving' safety and public order, hence officially 'protecting' citizens against the consequences of their own unruly behaviour (as illustrated these days by the enforcement of rules of confinement and 'social distancing' – with China constituting the most extreme case). These examples already indicate that the problems raised by the articulation of public services with the state and the society in general are very diverse. However, they remain *political* in every case, i.e. never reducible to 'technical' or 'administrative' issues. The neoliberal phase with the (sometimes massive) resistances it produces, gives a clear illustration of the way the political situation impacts the notion of a public service. But we are above all interested in the *feedback effect* of the debates on public services upon politics itself.

Actually existing public services, constructed in history, harbour an acute conflict between the principles of *universality* and *equality*, which can take different forms. They do not always reach extremes, but they always *destabilise* the services, and they are now crossing a line in the public healthcare crisis, which produces consequences which are hard to sustain. Citizens who are supposed to enjoy 'equal rights' prove widely *unequal* when confronted with the pandemic and its means of containment. While governments invoke patriotism and national unity in a 'war against the virus', considerable differences in rates of contamination and mortality are observed, which are correlated to massive class determinations (as already manifested in different life expectancies depending on professions and social environment). This is compounded by the unequal distribution of medical resources among urban and regional areas. The inequality is even more striking when it comes to the rules of the 'health state of exception', since a massive proportion of the workers who *must* continue to work in the outside world, with little or no protection against contamination, are manual workers (often migrants, sometimes undocumented). They are largely the same people for whom remaining confined in small housing units, deprived of comfort, proves impossible or unbearable. To which we may add the consequences of the lockdowns and shifting to 'remote working'. A both symbolic and material social contradiction becomes extremely visible in the same institutions that I gave as examples of antithetical figures of public service: the school and the police. When teaching 'in person' is interrupted, children from the lower classes who are deprived of private cultural and financial resources are 'left behind' irreversibly. Similarly, an intensification of police controls on citizens' movements leads to increased racist violence in poor neighbourhoods. But in the one case, the discrimination is officially discussed, whereas in the other it is completely denied. This can be summarised through the inversion of the previous formula: public service *does not create a commonality*, it destroys it, hence contradicting the universality which a republican regime proclaims as its *raison d'être* and instils in its own 'servants' as a moral standard. This contradiction always existed, but it becomes acute in the public health crisis. We must now tentatively propose an interpretation that both clarifies the historical function of public service in a capitalist society, at a general level, and helps understand the *political dynamic* generated by this specific crisis.

The state and public service

Suddenly, the 'return of the state' (in society, in the economy), but also the question of its formal and material constitution, has become a politically pressing issue. The discussion is dominated by the alternative inherited from 20th century ideological conflicts, which tells us that *state interventionism* and *business activities* are polar opposites. French president Emmanuel Macron made statements at the beginning of the crisis which directly proceeded from this paradigm, when he declared that vaccines ought to be considered 'public goods' which, as such, do not come under the 'laws of the market'. Given his personal background, these statements were met with some surprise, but they also involved a huge ambiguity. After all, the 'non-market' embodied in the initiatives taken by the state can fluctuate widely: between, on the one hand, public investment, the nationalisation of industries, or planning, and on the other, the establishment of free services which correspond to 'fundamental human rights'. In other words, the alternative refers either to a *limitation* of the range of competition and the imperative of profitability, which does not affect the commodity-form as such, or lead to a substitution by new 'common' values which negate the commodity-form itself. The general question then becomes: what does it mean to create *an exception to the market* and its 'laws' in a society where they have become *generalised*? Which political instruments could conceivably make this possible?

Equally fundamental ambiguities emerge in all the current questioning on the modern 'Leviathan': is there something invariant in its structure, that has been there since the 'origins'? Alternatively, what would have been transformed after the contemporary revolutions, which began with a consolidation of the 'social policies' within a capitalist economy and continued with an attempt at dismantling them, thus first reinforcing the national state, then transferring some of its functions to supranational institutions? And there is no less ambiguity in the relationship among the people, between the 'governing' and the 'governed', which can be seen as the *elementary structure* which the political instituted in the 'state-form', that oscillates between authoritarianism and democratisation, centralism and federalism (or the autonomy of territorial communities). I make no pretence to summarise all these discussions. But I would suggest that the current crisis is pushing them in directions which confer a strategic function upon the organisation of public services. On one side, we have the new configuration of what Jacques Rancière called 'the police' in a general sense, namely the combination of administrative constraints which are necessary in order to provide universal services, and practices of normalisation and control of the population, imposed on those who 'benefit' from these same services. On the other side, we have the renewed question over *the 'public' and the 'common'*: do these terms name a single dimension of social life, or should we find a more complex (less binary, less stable) articulation of these categories : the state (and the state-owned), the public, and the common? The two issues are not independent.

Let us begin with 'police'. Some prestigious minds have offered descriptions of the lockdown and its possible replacement by electronic tracking of individual movements, encounters, etc., which seem to me sometimes to border on paranoia. This is said to be the totalitarian regime that capitalism always dreamed of installing in order to crush resistance to its economic order, finally made possible through the 'miraculous' encounter of a technological revolution (big data, facial recognition and individual smartphones) and an anthropological catastrophe (the pandemic).[7] Without endorsing this 'conspiracy' scenario, we may agree that the declaration of a global health threat to the lives and activities of people has opened a possibility of accelerating the evolution towards what Deleuze called a 'society of control', which goes beyond the simple forms of discipline and morality arising from the combination of rights and protections in the 'social-national state'. This acceleration is really taking place under our eyes, with variations from one country and one political regime to another. Hence, the *state-formation,* in the broad sense – a formation that does not exist in isolation, 'above' or 'outside' the civil society, but *penetrates* its fabric – is now changing with it. The function of the state is no longer (if it ever was) just to 'dominate' the society, but to *organise* it, trying to find a balance between upholding certain interests of class, race, gender, culture, and the official establishment of a 'right to have rights' for all citizens. Gramsci called this kind of balance a 'hegemonic' system. It is currently changing meaning and shape: if the whole society must be controlled as much as protected, if government agencies and public services in the realms of education, care, information, assistance, employment, census, and surveillance, insert the state into every 'social relation', then the range of public service becomes infinite; it amounts to a universal machine of subjection of individuals to the state. What philosophers like Habermas call the 'normative' aspect of the state (or its articulation with citizenship) is perverted and ultimately erased. However, this is a problem that we cannot resolve just by 'returning to the principles' of the democratic state, since it is rooted in the principles themselves. For this reason, we must consider more radical alternatives to the infinite 'socialisation' of the state: and this is what current debates about the idea of the 'common' seem to propose.

The 'common' and the effect of political community

I will consider a summary version of these debates in order to highlight the necessary choice between *binary* approaches, in which 'public service' must *decide* between forming an agency of the state and an expression of the common, and a more complex problematic in which it acquires the status of a *third term* in its own right, with at least a relative autonomy.[8] The binary argument essentially relies on the idea that there exist 'basic' needs of society, which are historically constituted. It is the recognition of these needs that institutes fundamental rights. On this basis, a conflict arises between antithetical ideologies: if for liberalism the sphere of needs and rights regulated by the state must be as limited as possible, for socialism (or 'solidarism', the preferred name in the French tradition), this is an expansive realm. Yet this is a rather static alternative ... In the current debates, we are concerned rather with a choice between the idea that the state by nature *represents society* and incarnates the 'common good', and the idea that the state forms (in Deleuzian terms) a 'capturing machine' that *seizes for itself* certain functions that citizens ought to be able to exercise in their own interest, while acquiring the capacities and inventing the modes of governance suited to this mission. In this perspective, the 'public' agency cannot be really autonomous: either it is just a name for the *social function of the state*,[9] or it is another name for the *society itself inasmuch as it also become a community*, a self-governing political body. In a way, we are returning to the old antithesis between the categories of sovereignty, representation, political mediation among the interests of social groups, without which they are not able to overcome their conflicts (as argued by Hobbes, Hegel, even Rousseau in a more contradictory manner), and the categories of autonomy, immanence, the equal capacity of citizens to govern and organise their own lives (as argued by Proudhon and Marx, who do not disagree on this point). Of course, this traditional opposition can be resolved in one sense or the other, but it is also quite naturally associated with the theory that society is dominated by relations of exploitation and mechanisms of expropriation which are essentially enforced by the state or controlled by it (a theory that I find hardly disputable).

However, we find ourselves now experimenting historical developments which suggest overcoming this simple binarism. *The notion of public service is becoming more autonomous*, both in relation to the state and to the Common, it emerges with a type of conflictuality that calls at the same time for theoretical analysis and political initiative. This is not so much a question of defining a special 'sphere' of the public in juridical-political terms, as of finding a concept for *the competition between the two logics* to which it is subjected, and the two kinds of 'powers' which generate conflicts in its operation, from the local plane of everyday life to the global, indeed virtually planetary space. The current experiment is constrained by urgency, but also nourished by the lessons and memories of previous episodes. What I find especially significant is the following: 'caretakers' (doctors, nurses, etc.) succeeded during the pandemic in communicating to the population at large the 'systemic' nature of the misery in public health services, made of insufficient planning and resources, authoritarian management, injustices and discriminations bordering on cruelty towards 'weak' people (e.g. the elderly poor), identifying their roots in accelerated commodification and privatisation. As a consequence they generated a 'community-effect' which was not only moral (and certainly was not free of contradictions, since it did not cancel every hierarchy or inequality), but was profoundly political. It was conscious of its own demands, the forces that supported it, the values it expressed. They build a 'common' in actual practice. But they did not aim at substituting the common for the state. Rather, they tried to impose an obligation to *serve public service* upon a state which, in the last period, has been essentially acting in the service of the dominant classes (or even the wealthiest part of the dominant classes). In particular this proceeds by taking all the necessary resources away from the market, and planning their use under a democratic control. The common sense (which is quite correct in this case) is that public service always *needs the state*, from its top executives to the bottom, the civil servants or even the ordinary citizens who take part in administrative functions or try to control them from the inside.[10] However the same common sense *sharply distinguishes public service from the state*, as it does not accept that public services *belong to the state*, are 'owned' by it, and form a mere detachment of its organisation. The boundaries between the two are surely imprecise, and they are bound to be permanently disputed. This explains why public service cannot assert its relative autonomy if the common, for its part, is not politically organised, raising its voice, and confronting the government with adequate demands and critiques. This makes the public at the same time *a mediator and an object* of the conflicts between the state and the common. This is a permanent dialectic, for which the pandemic (and probably also the environmental crisis) is creating new conditions and locations.

★

I hope it is clear that here, I was not proposing a programme for a movement. I was trying to find the best formulation for a question which touches on both issues of *citizenship* (emphasising the control of the governed upon the governing agencies) and issues of *civility* (the modalities of conflicts which permeate society, without engulfing it in civil war). It remains to be seen if these formulations shed light on the questions posed by the recent experience imposed by the pandemic. Other questions arise from this, of course: particularly in terms of the regulation of the market, which has in neoliberalism acquired a seemingly unlimited capacity to shape our lives and our environment after its individualistic models of 'adaptation' to competition.[11] In practice, the two questions are inseparable. But it is important not to erase *the specificity of the 'biopolitical' crisis* which becomes concentrated around the functions of public service, for the sake of a general critique of the fetishism of commodities and the domination of capitalism. This critique makes sense only if it is articulated with concrete problems of governmentality and agency in the field of health and care.

NOTES

1   This contribution to the 2023 transform! yearbook is adapted from my previous essay: 'l'Etat, le Public, le Commun. Trois notions à l'épreuve de la crise sanitaire', published in *Dessine-moi un pangolin*, edited by Pierre Jacquemain, Vauvert: Éditions Au Diable Vauvert, 2020.

2   Which, lest we forget, is still going on, although in different forms influenced by the mutations of the Covid-19 virus (with the emergence of new 'variants') and the policies which have been implemented locally and globally to control it.

3   See Immanuel Wallerstein, *The Global Left. Yesterday, Today, Tomorrow*, London: Routledge, 2021.

4   This was written before the outbreak of the war unleashed by the Russian invasion of Ukraine.

5   The phrase from Mario Draghi, President of the European Central Bank, during the 'Eurobonds crisis', that was mimicked by French president Emmanuel Macron with respect to the pandemic in 2020.

6   Despite their divergences, both Hardt-Negri and Dardot-Laval agree on this point: see Michael Hardt and Antonio Negri, *Commonwealth,* Cambridge, MA: Harvard University Press 2011; Pierre Dardot and Christian Laval, *Commun. Essai sur la révolution au XXIe siècle*, Paris: La Découverte, 2014.

7   I am thinking of course of Giorgio Agamben's critique of the 'state of exception'
     embodied by lockdowns, mandatory vaccination and travel restrictions or domestic
     health passports: see Giorgio Agamben, *Where Are We Now? The Epidemic as Politics*,
     London: Rowman & Littlefield, 2021.

8   Regarding the opposition between the two logics of the State and the Common, I
     am inspired by the lucid presentation in Pierre Dardot and Christian Laval, *Commun.
     Essai sur la révolution au XXIe siècle*, Paris: La Découverte, p. 514, etc: 'Les services
     publics doivent devenir des institutions du commun' ['Public services must become
     institutions of the common'].

9   Which is just what the great French legal theorist, a founding figure of 'solidarisme',
     called the 'material content' of the state, directly opposed to 'social disorder': see
     Les transformations du droit public (1925), cited by Thomas Boccon-Gibod, *Autorité et
     démocratie. L'exercice du pouvoir dans les sociétés modernes*, Paris: L.G.G.J, 2014.

10   A young French philosopher (Marc Pavlopoulos) has written in this respect, during
     the pandemic : 'l'Etat c'est nous!' (We are the State).

11   See the excellent book by Barbara Stiegler, *« Il faut s'adapter » : Sur un nouvel impératif
     politique*, Paris: Gallimard, 2019. Stiegler has produced an analysis of the political
     effects of the pandemic with which I have some disagreements, but which is well
     worth reading: *Santé publique année zéro*, Paris: Gallimard, 2022.

Transforming Production to Save the Planet: What Does This Mean for the Left and the State?[*]

Hilary Wainwright[1]

'The real differences between social democrats and communists (or radical leftists) remain', says Luciana Castellina in her dialogue with Donald Sassoon in the 2022 volume of the transform yearbook.[2] 'But [they] have no longer mainly to do with questions of income distribution, welfare and so on, as in the post-Second World War years. Instead, the dimension now involved is that of a complete change in the way we consume and produce, which needs to be more related to use-value than to exchange-value, as it is today.'

The determining importance of production

Castellina implies that fundamentally transforming production is a necessary condition for reducing carbon emissions and slowing down and ideally reversing climate breakdown. Social democracy, by contrast, leaves production to the play of the market, relying on Keynes's macroeconomic tools to create full employment through regulating demand and interest rates and, through taxation, to redistribute wealth from private production to the welfare state and public infrastructure.

Not only has the efficacy of these tools of macroeconomic management by national governments been undermined by the corporate (mainly US)-driven global market. They are also unable to address the industrial structures, purposes, and power relations of production that lie behind high levels of carbon emissions. By contrast, a move towards a low-carbon economy requires a radical transformation of production in purposes and products, and methods, speeds, and levels of production. In other words, such a move requires a political strategy that challenges contemporary capitalism's fossil fuel-driven overproduction and overconsumption.[3]

[*]   In memory of the inspiring eco-communist Javier Nvascués (1957-2018).

In Marx's (and Castellina's) terms, Keynesian macroeconomic tools shaped to intervene in the sphere of circulation are incapable of changing the use-value of what is produced – for example, in the aerospace industry, shifting from petrol-consuming, carbon-emitting aero engines to wind turbines or other low-carbon products; or, in the fashion industry, moving away from the 'buy, wear, and chuck' levels of consumption and waste of today's mass fashion industry, and towards sustainable textiles and long-lasting clothes.

This focus on production, therefore, is not about belatedly adding microeconomic tools to Keynes's macroeconomic toolbox. On the contrary, Castellina's central insight, drawn from Marx, starts from the determining importance of production, and the labour process on which it is based, over the spheres of distribution and circulation.

Context

In this essay, I describe how a minority of trade unionists are attempting to extend collective bargaining to include the purpose and character of their work. Such moves beyond trade unions' traditional focus on wages and conditions are unusual and historically have always been resisted as a threat to managerial prerogatives.

The context – the wider social and political circumstances that influence trade unionists as citizens as well as workers – is important. The current context, with a growing awareness that climate breakdown is the result of high-carbon production coinciding with a crisis in public service provision, has the potential to stimulate a broadening of trade-union concerns. In these conditions, could traditional trade-union concerns with decent wages, dignified working conditions, and secure jobs flow into questions of how services are funded and organised and, in the private sector, what socially useful alternatives to current production 'redundancy' workers have the skills to produce?

To get a historical bearing on this possibility, I summarise the late 1970s' experience of the Lucas Aerospace workers' 'alternative corporate plan for socially useful production',[4] to which today's trade unionists in engineering industries often refer as they resist redundancies and factory closures with proposals for 'green' alternatives. In the 1980s, this industrial experience influenced a municipal political experiment by the former Greater London Council,[5] which developed an industrial strategy that sought to nurture the capacity of organised workers, directly and in alliances with communities, to transform production more radically than is possible by state intervention alone.

I go on to summarise two recent trade-union-led experiences. One occurred at the height of the Covid pandemic when shop-floor trade unionists led the conversion of aircraft manufacturing capacity to the production of ventilator parts. The other was a collaboration between shop stewards at Rolls Royce faced with the threat of job losses and the Coventry Green New Deal campaign. Together they developed a green alternative, with which they challenged management's attempt to declare workers 'redundant'.

I then explore theoretical tools for understanding how far and under what conditions these transformative initiatives can be generalised. I develop these tools from Andreas Malm's theory of 'fossil capital', from Marx's theory of labour power (especially his distinction between exchange-value and use-value) and from Nancy Fraser's theory of 'cannibal capitalism'[6] to try to draw insights for developing strategies of transition towards a low-carbon economy. Malm's historical explanation of the choice of coal as the source of energy driving capitalist industrialisation and Marx's study of capital's relentless drive to accumulate enable us to identify the potential for organised labour to play a vital role in reversing the high carbon emissions of this promethean economic system to move towards a low-carbon economy.

What does this argument about the importance of transformative power from within production suggest for the role of the state in broader strategies for socialist change? My emphasis on production does not imply a syndicalist optimism about the possibility of trade unions being able to transform the economy and society without engaging with the state. Nor, however, can 'the state' simply be captured by a left party as a neutral superstructure to be deployed against capital.

I argue that the nation-state provided essential conditions for capitalist development – a legal framework for markets, the protection of private property and more[7] – and, in the era of financialised capitalism, remains integral to its reproduction on a global scale, mainly through the empire state of the USA. Action by a democratically elected government deploying the rule of law against private capital, especially financial capital, which is destructive of the public good, is essential for the protection of the planet, the basis of human survival.

Here, however, we come up against the reality that nation-states are themselves the products and the agents of capitalist development. We face the problem, therefore, of how they can be radically transformed to act against their own historical partner. I argue that such a necessarily radical transformation is only possible through the agency of organised labour as a productive power with autonomy from the state. How such a productive power is created is a matter not only of traditional trade unionism but requires a new kind of politically minded trade unionism, concerned with the wider interests of society including the planet on whose thriving it depends. This involves a strategic thinking that overcomes the deeply ingrained division of roles between active workplace trade unionism and electoral, or parliamentary, politics.

I conclude by showing how this logic points to the need for a radical shift in the left's traditional ways of organising towards an active political engagement with grassroots trade unionism. This breaks with the tendency to take for granted the trade unions and their membership as simply a mass base for political representation or party membership.

The politics of use-value: collective bargaining and municipal intervention

The Lucas Aerospace workers' 'alternative plan for socially useful production'
A notably coherent political experience based in production in the late 1970s, the Lucas Aerospace workers' 'alternative plan for socially useful production', provides a laboratory through which to explore what is involved in transforming production and to raise questions about the support a left government could give to strengthen trade-union power rooted in workers' organisations and inside knowledge of production.

The 1970s was a period when, faced with an increasingly competitive market, British-based engineering corporations – Lucas Aerospace, Vickers, British Leyland, Chrysler – were attempting to rationalise their sprawling assets with factory closures and 'redundancies'. Self-confident shop stewards' committees, increasingly organised on a company-wide basis and with considerable bargaining power developed under the post-war boom, refused to accept that they and their members, mainly skilled engineers and creative designers, were 'redundant'. To resist management plans, they not only took industrial action but also proposed 'alternative plans', insisting that management consider alternative ways to deploy their skills for public benefit. The most developed of these came from the shop stewards' combine committee at Lucas Aerospace.[8]

The Lucas Aerospace shop stewards had been asked by the radical minister for industry in the 1974 Labour government, Tony Benn, what they thought about bringing the aerospace industry into public ownership. At first, the combine committee members were doubtful. Their experience of previously nationalised industries made them question whether public ownership would necessarily lead to secure employment. They responded by drawing up their own plan – in effect, their autonomous terms on which any form of state intervention in the company should take place. They called it an 'alternative corporate plan for socially useful production'. Based on the ideas of union members across the design offices and shopfloors of the company, it included around 150 products of medical, environmental, and transport use that they could design and manufacture to save jobs – and as an alternative to the military components that were the core business of Lucas Aerospace.

The shop stewards intended that these proposals should be part of their collective bargaining with management. They hoped, on the basis of their discussions with Tony Benn, that the government would support their plan and shift contracts for military aerospace to medical and environmental equipment. They were, in other words, demanding that collective bargaining go beyond exchange-value (wages) to address issues of use-value (the purpose and products of their labour).

Management refused to negotiate over the alternative plan. The Lucas Aerospace CEO James Blyth, speaking to MPs impressed by the plan, put it bluntly: 'We do not need the combine committee to tell us to diversify.' The stewards had had the temerity to challenge managerial prerogative. The Labour government finally sided with management, though the trade-union campaign did succeed in winning a minor reduction in the number of redundancies.

In retrospect, this could be said to be an early precedent for what is now termed 'transition bargaining' or 'bargaining for public benefit'.

Socially useful production versus militarised market production – a municipal political experiment

In the early 1980s, Ken Livingstone's radically socialist Greater London Council, across the Thames from Margaret Thatcher's determinedly neoliberal government, pioneered an unusual industrial strategy to address the high levels of unemployment in London. The experiences of the Lucas Aerospace workers were an important influence.

The Labour Party activists and would-be councillors responsible for the party's GLC manifesto made a commitment to give full support to trade-union alternative plans that shared the objectives of their electoral mandate. The result was the Council's London Industrial Strategy, which saw a local state administration working directly with workplace trade unionists to guide public investment to maximise public (including planetary) benefit rather than private profit.

This work was led by the late Robin Murray, who, like Luciana Castellina, insisted on the importance of production.[9] Murray started from the view of contemporary capitalism as a political economy in which 'the overriding priority is given to private market production and to the military sector, to increased intensity of work within the factory and the technological replacement of awkward labour'.

'We can call this *militarised market production*', Murray wrote in the introduction to the London Industrial Strategy. 'It represents the economics of capital.' He went on to argue that 'there is an alternative, which we shall call *socially useful production*'. This, he said, 'takes as its starting point not the priorities of the balance sheet, but the provision of work for all who wish it, in jobs that are geared to meeting social need.' William Morris, he added, 'referred to it as useful work rather than useless toil. It represents the economics of labour.'

This perspective has profound implications for transforming production for socially useful purposes – in particular, a radical reduction of carbon emissions – and how to transform the state to assist this labour-driven process of decarbonising production. There are important limits to what can be generalised from a municipal experience, but we can gain some insights as to how state institutions could be transformed to actively support the initiatives of labour for the public good.

Aircraft parts into ventilator components

Whereas the Lucas Aerospace workers showed what *could* have been done to transform production, 40 years later in 2020, with the UK coronavirus crisis at its height, the Unite union branch at the Broughton Airbus factory in north Wales achieved an example of successful bargaining for public benefit. These trade unionists led the conversion of the factory's research and development facility in a matter of weeks to become an assembly line producing components for up to 15,000 ventilators for the NHS. More than 500 Airbus workers, previously employed on the production of aircraft wings, rather than losing their jobs due to the collapse of the aircraft market as a result of the pandemic, turned their skills to working round the clock as part of a consortium to produce 1,500 Penlon Prima ESO2 ventilators each week.

The organisation of the conversion process, the speed at which it was achieved, and the flexibility of the workforce in adapting to the challenge was impressive. This was due in no small part to the role of the trade-union branch that organised the aircraft-turned-ventilator workers. Moreover, in the context of a crisis in the supply of ventilators to meet the needs of Covid patients, management could hardly stand on its prerogative and resist the union's efforts to find a solution.

As well as helping to meet immediate needs in a public health emergency, this worker-led conversion also offers a hopeful example of the possibilities of moving from a high-carbon to low-carbon economy without loss of jobs. Not least among its various lessons, the experience points to the importance of a well-unionised workplace for the efficiency of such a transition.

Rolls Royce shop stewards making aerospace engines, now pressing to develop low-carbon alternatives

The decline in aerospace markets during and after the pandemic was also a stimulus in leading the shop stewards in two West Midlands factories to contact the local Green New Deal campaign group associated with Coventry Trades Council. Faced with the threat of redundancies and yet confident in the usefulness of their skills, they specifically wanted to learn from the Lucas alternative plan to resist job losses with proposals for alternative products. As in the case of Lucas Aerospace, the Rolls Royce shop stewards insisted that 'there is an alternative' to redundancies based on the usefulness of their skills to wider society.

As with Lucas Aerospace, management at Rolls Royce has been resistant to a challenge to what they consider to be their prerogative to decide on products and investment. But there is a contrast with the Lucas Aerospace experience: the movement for action in the face of the climate crisis, especially among the young, has reached the point where Rolls Royce management has sensed that the reputation of their brand is endangered if they are not at least *seen* to be reducing carbon emissions. This vulnerability has given the shop stewards an additional source of strength to challenge management. Increasing concern about climate breakdown has also had an impact on workers' own awareness of their moral and political duty, and potential power, to question their complicity in high-carbon production.

Initiatives such as those at Rolls Royce have emerged alongside other environment-driven developments within trade unions. These include Unite's new environment taskforce, the Green Jobs Alliance, and the convergence of Friends of the Earth and the Scottish TUC to campaign around the COP26 UN climate conference in Glasgow in 2021. The Yorkshire and Humberside TUC and the TUC nationally have made specific appointments to support trade-union conversion plans, further underlining trade unions' increasing interest in strategies for conversion to low-carbon production. There is amongst a growing minority an intensifying sense of urgency and with it a sense of workers' role as citizens needing to respond to social movements sounding the alarm on climate breakdown.

The power of shared practical knowledge, the limits of individual examples

These examples – and there are more in the making[10] – of innovative and potentially transformative trade-union initiatives illustrate the potential power that workers have through their practical knowledge of production, potentially sharable across the whole labour process by their workplace organisation. This knowledge lies in workers' skills. It is tacit rather than the codified knowledge that is conventionally the basis of public policy.[11] This points to the need for ways of trade-union organising that facilitate the sharing of this tacit social knowledge, producing a comprehensive 'underview' of the production process.

The initiatives in these examples are at the company level, but the systemic transformation of production necessary to overcome the climate crisis is unlikely to come factory by factory or company by company, especially in today's global market and financialised capitalism. Moreover, the climate crisis now converges with a cost-of-living crisis to a point where workplace union organisations are overwhelmed by struggles to defend their livelihoods. In such conditions of general austerity, management has the upper hand – which is very different from the years of the post-war boom during which the trade unions in Lucas Aerospace developed their strength.

However, in the cases of the ventilator conversion and the tentative extension of collective bargaining at Rolls Royce, public opinion and corporate concern about the 'greenness' of their brand image weakened management's ability to ensure that collective bargaining remained restricted to wages and conditions. (Rolls Royce has done its best to promote a green image through a variety of claims for its own supposedly 'green' forms of diversification to nuclear power and hydrogen as sources of 'green' aircraft fuel.[12])

We can learn much from these trade union initiatives to change the high-carbon direction of production, but they do not, on their own, provide a strategy. To develop such a strategy, we need the theoretical impetus to make an imaginative leap.

Beyond telling individual stories: the tools to theorise and generalise

To understand the conditions under which the potential for transforming production can be realised we need to draw on three sets of theoretical tools, referred to earlier.

Andreas Malm on the choice of coal-driven energy

Andreas Malm explains how coal became the basis of capitalist industrialisation in the home of the first capitalist industrial revolution at the expense of other sources of energy, most notably water.

Britain's embrace of coal came relatively late. Waterpower remained dominant for decades after James Watt's invention of the steam engine. Fossil capitalism arose from a desire to concentrate industry in cities, thereby avoiding the complex engineering needed to sustain water-powered production, which would have necessitated co-operation between mill-owners – an option inimical to these early capitalists at a time of intense competition. It also allowed for a greater concentration of labour, more easily disciplined and exploited. Malm argues that it is possible to imagine an alternative industrialisation, based on wind and water (and recently including solar power) but it would not have produced such high rates of profit as coal.

Malm's explanation and detailed historical analysis of the fossil-driven nature of capitalist industrialisation is important and points to the powerful vested interests that protect the fossil-driven energy underpinning the past two centuries of capitalist political economy, with all its cumulative damage to the atmosphere. But to understand the role of labour in the reproduction and hence relentless growth of high carbon emissions we need to understand the inner social relations between capital and labour in the process of exploitation, profits, and accumulation. Most central here is Marx's theory of labour power.

From Marx: the importance of workers' collective struggle over use-value

In Marx's words, 'labour power', or the capacity for labour, is to be understood as 'the aggregate of those mental and physical capabilities existing in a human being', exercised whenever one produces 'a use value of any description'.[13] Marx highlights the fact that under capitalism, workers 'alienate' (or sell) their capacity to work in exchange for a wage or salary. Workers therefore lose control over their labour power. How their capacity for labour is deployed – to what uses and for what purposes – is the prerogative of capital. Trade unions have historically won the right to organise over the terms on which workers sell their capacity to work. They rarely challenge capital's *control over a worker's capacity to work*.

If we apply Marx's crucial distinction regarding the value of the product of labour, between its *exchange-value* and its *use-value*, we can understand conventional trade unionism as being essentially about bargaining over the exchange-value of the sale of their members' labour power.

This understanding of conventional trade unionism, and its limits, immediately raises the question of what would be involved for trade unions to bargain over the use-value of labour's product. This, surely, is what workers extending their control over the purpose of their work would amount to.

It is what the workers in Lucas Aerospace, Airbus, and Rolls Royce were attempting to achieve in their efforts to extend collective bargaining. We can also find such experiences in the public sector, most notably in initiatives to improve the public-benefit efficiency of public services as an alternative to redundancies or privatisation.[14]

The struggle over use-value, if not delegated to the state

Two points arise about struggles around use-values. First, there is no seamless flow from struggles over exchange-value to struggles over use-value. In the examples just given, the trade-union initiatives arise from a crisis of some kind leading to a breakdown or by-passing of conventional collective bargaining. In the cases of Lucas Aerospace and Rolls Royce, it was the threat of factory closures and redundancies. In the case of Airbus, it was the collapse of aircraft markets due to the pandemic.

These disruptions of the day-to-day routines of conventional trade unionism opened space for those with a definite idea for how a change in the purpose of production – a change in use-value – could provide a solution. Sometimes this involved an external organisation, as with the Coventry Green New Deal and the Rolls Royce shop stewards. In the case of Lucas Aerospace, the initial encouragement came from a minority in the Labour government[15] and two political but non-party organisations – the Institute of Workers Control and the British Society for Social Responsibility in Science.

Could this role of an external force rooted in non-economic life – whether concerning the planet, care systems, or other non-economic conditions of capitalism – be generalised to a new kind of political movement, which instead of being oriented to elections is oriented towards allying with workers to achieve a systemic change in the profit maximising, accumulation-driven purposes of production?[16]

The second key point is that struggles over use-value tend to be unrecognised and their potential unvalued. At present, they fit into no one's political framework. On the one hand they tend to be seen as too political by moderate trade-union leaders, while on the other hand they are seen as insufficiently political by the traditional state-focused left. We need the tools to theorise a wider understanding of 'political' that refers to the totality of social and environmental conditions of capitalist reproduction rather than simply the state.

Nancy Fraser on the importance of the non-economic conditions for the support of capitalism

The invisibility of struggles over use-value stems in part from a tendency on the left to adopt an economistic understanding of capitalism as simply an economic system of exploitation, with everything else being superstructural. Here, Nancy Fraser's theory of 'cannibal capitalism' is useful, based as it is on analysing the non-economic conditions for the existence of capitalism as an economic system of exploitation.[17]

Fraser points to the material importance of non-market systems of care for the reproduction of labour (the welfare state as well as the family); of the non-human resources of the planet, and the thriving of nature on which capital depends and feeds; of the availability of the resources of raw materials and unfree labour outside the market from which capital extracts; and of state institutions, especially (in the history of capitalism) the institutions of the nation-state, with the legitimacy to maintain law and order – which includes protecting private property, disciplining labour, and facilitating ever-extending commodification and new markets. Most originally and importantly, she goes on to show how the drive to accumulate leads capital to devour those non-economic spheres on which it also depends.

Two insights are inspired by bringing together Marx's theory of labour power and Fraser's theory of the non-economic conditions of capitalist development. First, by combining Marx's theory of capitalist exploitation with Fraser's exploration of the conditions for the reproduction of capitalism, it becomes clear that struggles over use-value (for example, to convert to low-carbon production or to extend the quality of healthcare, or to overcome the gendered division of labour) are in effect also struggles to protect – and sometimes to gain popular control over – these non-market forms of material life.

Second, Fraser's analyses of state institutions point to why struggles over the state are ambiguous. As she argues, the nation-state is 'a condition of existence of capitalism', but it is also more. It has been and continues to be an active facilitator of capitalist development. So, the struggle over the state is on the one hand a response to the 'cannibalisation', or commodification, of aspects of the nation-state's support for capital – most notably, the public provision of the care and infrastructure of the welfare state. On the other hand, this resistance to marketisation, while able to win one-off victories, tends to be too weak to stop a steady, and more-or-less stealthy, process of cannibalisation as capitalist financialisaton hollows out democracy through privatisation and the corruption of elected politicians.

Here we must face up to the nature of the 'actually existing' state, its role in facilitating capitalist accumulation, and why struggles over the use-values of production are central to a strategy for effective socialist transformation.

The necessity of state action, and of transforming the state

I have highlighted trade-union initiatives that go beyond the normal limits of trade-union bargaining and address issues conventionally considered political – such as a shift from military or high-carbon production to socially useful low-carbon products. These initiatives all indicate the necessity for state action to challenge the prerogatives of management, accountable only to corporate shareholders, and to facilitate these alternative plans developed in the process of resistance to job loss, becoming the basis of a socialised economy. However, these experiences – especially that of the Lucas Aerospace workers and the minority of Labour ministers who supported them – also reveal how closely the state apparatus works with the corporations whose purposes the local trade unionists are trying to change – and how rare it is for elected politicians (for example, in the case of Tony Benn) to challenge this.

The government funded and gave contracts to Lucas Aerospace to such an extent that the company and many like it were almost annexes of the ministries of defence and industry, separated only by 'revolving doors'.[18] This closeness between corporate management and the state explains why the Labour government ended up on the side of Lucas Aerospace management opposing the shop stewards' combine committee – and why, when Tony Benn as industry minister opened his doors to shop stewards rather than management and attacked 'industrial policies discussed in the comfortable atmosphere of Westminster, Whitehall, and Fleet Street', the establishment saw him as such a danger.[19] It was not long before he was sacked as minister.

But a lesson was learnt that the 'fundamental and irreversible shift in the balance of wealth and power' such as was promised in Labour's 1974 election manifesto cannot be achieved through the existing parliamentary states of today, which effectively protect the wealthy and the powerful.

To understand the importance of radical socialist parties, in preparation for, and as a condition of, a radical socialist government, having an active alliance with organised labour at the point of production, and what that implies, we need a historical perspective on the nature of the state's relation to capitalism. This will enable us to understand how the kind of alliance that is needed is very different from today's institutional links with national trade-union apparatuses.

A historical perspective on nation-states' facilitation of capitalist development

My focus is on the British state, which is a distinctive (old) empire-state, but as the first capitalist industrial nation it is of some interest for a more general consideration of questions of left strategy towards the state. The experience of capitalist industrialisation in Britain points to the role of the nation-state as a facilitator of capitalist development, indeed a condition of capitalism's development.

The corollary of this is that the administrative and legislative institutions of the British state, with all the trappings of the United Kingdom and the legacies of the British empire, have been shaped in response to the needs and activities of capital. Other than at times of war, the role of the state was to provide the framework of a market economy, including the legal protection of private property, and to act as the guarantor of last resort to ensure a relatively stable system of banking and finance, including public subsidies to ensure continued production and maintain Britain's competitive position.

The military-industrial complex: the state's integration with capitalism

By the 1970s, meetings with corporate managers would be a routine part of government processes in the departments of industry and defence.[20] C. Wright Mills's 'military-industrial complex'[21] is a description far closer to the reality than the metaphor of government as a wheel to be steered according to the objectives of whichever party is elected to govern. The result was that when a left(ish) government intervened in industry and therefore depended on a partner with inside know-how of production, the partner already built into the social relations of the state was business – and that meant management and at best national union officials, not the unions at the point of production.[22]

Aneurin Bevan, best known as the former Welsh mineworkers' leader who as a Labour minister founded the National Health Service, anticipated the consequences of the post-war Labour government's intervention in industry, even before seeing them first-hand as a cabinet minister. He put it this way at the 1944 Labour Party conference: 'In practice it is impossible for the modern state to maintain an independent control over the decisions of big business. When the state extends its control over big business, big business moves in to control the state. The political decisions of the state become so important a part of the business transactions of the corporations that it is a law of their survival that most decisions should suit the needs of profit making.'[23]

The decisions Bevan was referring to are multiple and the relations between government and business have been deepened by successive Conservative administrations and under Tony Blair's premiership from 1997.[24] These entrenched vested interests would be resistant to the will and electoral mandate of any new government coming in from the left. Unless such a government had the backing of organised labour at the point of production to create a combined bargaining power of an organised and knowledgeable workforce and a strong administration with a public mandate, any radical industrial and environmental policies would be ruthlessly undermined.

In sum, then, the implication of the integral relation between capitalism and the nation-state – and with globalised capitalism between the US state (as the dominant capitalist nation-state) and US multinational corporations – is that an adequate counter strategy requires building the power and capacity of labour, ultimately on a transnational level, as an essential ally for a left government intent on implementing industrial polices for public and planetary benefit.

Such power cannot be turned on overnight with the election of a left government. So how can it be built in the here and now as part of a shift in the balance of power between capital and labour that is a condition for the very possibility of a radical left government?

Reversing the state's reliance on capital: a transformative alliance with labour

The answer lies, surely, in developing a trade unionism that can answer the integral relations between business and the state with equally close and productive relations between the trade unions and the political movements and organisations of the left. By 'integral relations' I mean rooted in struggles to extend collective bargaining and local-authority power to maximise public benefit rather than private profit. Only with this *material*, productive alliance could a left government challenge the otherwise ineluctable tendency, as observed by Nye Bevan, for private business to control government.

This presents a major challenge, especially to labour movements dominated by social democracy. Social democracy tends to carry over from liberalism the principle of liberal political economy that the economy (that is, capitalist markets) is separate from politics. Given the reality of the integration of capitalism and the state, to a point where the state has been a driver of capitalism and is now essential to its reproduction, the liberal and social democratic insistence on the separation of politics from economics, the state from the market, seems to function more as an ideology than as an analysis of reality.

This is especially the case when one observes how the impact of the translation of this principle into the separation of politics and industrial relations has worked in the UK. The separation of the Parliamentary Labour Party (politics) and the trade unions and collective bargaining (industrial relations) has served to protect the prerogative of private business over any decisions that concern the social and environmental impact of their companies.

Overcoming the institutional divide between economics and politics

The conventional understanding of trade unionism as limited to bargaining over exchange-value has meant that trade unions aspiring to be agents of wider social change effectively delegate responsibility for such change to the historic political representatives of labour with which they have an institutional tie (as with the British Labour Party) or a close informal relationship (in Germany, Scandinavia, and, in the years of Pasok, in Greece). Social change beyond the wage bargain is not understood as a legitimate cause for industrial action or collective bargaining. Instead, it is to be pursued through conference resolutions about what a government or party should do, by making policy statements and, sometimes, joining campaigns through demonstrations and other such expressions of pressure on government. In the extreme case of the UK, where the Labour Party has until recently had a monopoly of working-class political representation,[25] this has historically taken the form of affiliation to the party as the parliamentary representation of workers' interests – from protection of employment rights to welfare provision.

These institutions tend to shape the terrain facing the radical left today.[26] In the case of Britain, the often rigid role division between the industrial and the political (understood as parliamentary) is reinforced by a disproportional electoral system (and therefore assumed allegiance to the Labour Party). This division is notably stultifying for the development of a deeper transformational politics, favouring an apolitical tendency in parts of civil-society organisations.

Stirrings, past and present, beneath the institutions

In moments of crisis, however, a more political consciousness sometimes breaks through the institutions. This was especially notable in the years between 1968 and the rise of neoliberal politics marked by the Conservative election victory under Margaret Thatcher in 1979. That decade witnessed the emergence – and glimpse of the possibility – of what this transformative politics could be.

This is not the place for a long digression on the character of the transformative movements of that time including radical trade unions organisations (like the shop stewards at Lucas Aerospace and elsewhere). Suffice it to say that they were deeply political in the sense of desiring and attempting to prefigure radically transformative change, with a very different kind of vision from the left traditions of the past. The notion of 'prefigurative' can best sum up their independent approach to change, conscious of themselves as the agents of change, rather than delegating agency upwards to the political class and simply 'making demands'.

Creating alternatives in the present to prefigure and prepare for the future

Prefigurative politics involves the commitment to creating experiences of a new society within, and in conflict with the shell of, the old. Or, to put it another way, it involves organising now to illustrate in practice the values of the society we envision for the future.

The emergence of prefigurative politics with the social movements of the 1970s, especially the women's liberation movement, was in part a desire to move beyond the instrumental politics of both Leninism and social democracy in which the end – state power through insurrection or elections respectively – justified the means.[27] For would-be feminist activists at the time, the creation of solutions to the day-to-day consequences of their subordination was essential if they were to be active and autonomous in the way they desired.

The creation of community childcare for example, was very important. Consequently, the early days of the women's movement saw numerous experiments in community childcare in which the parents and local community were in control. Some of these went on to be funded by local councils and became models for public childcare policies. In this way, a prefigurative culture and social movement can play a part in enriching public policy.

The impact of neoliberalism on a new left politics

Prefigurative politics also provides a good description of the work of radical trade-union organisations like the Lucas Aerospace shop stewards or, to give another example relatively common at the time, community organisations resisting property developers and developing their own alternative 'people's plans' for their neighbourhoods. These were often later supported by the more radical Labour municipalities.[28]

How this emergent politics could have changed the left's relation to the state was never fully realised. Certainly, it involved a break from both the social democratic and the command-economy models of socialism. The implicit positive model remained fuzzy, to be developed in practice as much as in theory. But political time waits for no one, and time was called by the victory of Thatcher and Reagan and the new neoliberal era they inaugurated.

The neoliberal offensives of the early 1980s hit the emerging radical left politics hard. Between them, Thatcher, Reagan, and an increasingly neoliberal European Economic Community (later the European Union) destroyed the institutional supports that this social-movement-based alternative had begun to build in the local state and at the base of the trade unions.

Nevertheless, the glimpses of a radical socialist politics witnessed in the 1970s has remained in the imaginary of a whole generation and shaped their ambiguous 'in and against' relationship to electoral politics. The memory has been periodically enlivened by moments of radical creativity: the transnational, anti-hierarchical networks of the 'alter-globalisation' movement at the turn of the century; the direct action of the Occupy movement creating new spaces for alternatives; the anti-racist and pro-LGBT rights movements; and all the new forms of community organising stretching across these years.

Then came the inspiration of the 'Arab Spring' and the mobilisations in the squares of southern Europe. These created movements eager for a platform and opportunities for political change. New leaders emerged in and (to differing degrees) against the political system. The energy of the movements lifting them into office created the seductive illusion that mass street mobilisation would be somehow sufficient to dissolve the constraints of the capitalist state. The defeat of these experiences, especially in Europe, particularly in Greece and in different ways elsewhere, was demoralising and led to dispersal and fragmentation.

Yet despite defeat and demoralisation there is – not surprisingly, given the existing extremities of injustice, corruption, inequality, and greed alongside climate breakdown and war – an energy and a hunger for change. This is often focused on specific issues but with a consciousness of system breakdown and an urgent sense, albeit vague, of the need to be grasping every opportunity for alternatives.

Lessons from the latest attempts to gain office but not power

The belief in the power of winning an election and then steering a neutral state runs deep in the institutions of the Labour Party and the mentalities that they shape. Even the leadership team around Jeremy Corbyn, one of the most radical leaders the party has ever had, with a long record of extra-parliamentary campaigning, tended, in the words of James Schneider, a leading spokesman for Corbyn, 'to treat the party programme as something that could be implemented through existing state machinery, without mass mobilisations and with little establishment backlash'.[29] The problem, as Schneider sees it, is how to combine mobilising to win public support for electoral success with sustaining for the long term the popular mobilisation to carry out the radical programme against establishment backlash.

Schneider makes useful suggestions concerning political education – through practice as much as through study – and using the public economic powers of local councils to the maximum to prefigure elements of a socialised economy. My arguments concerning the importance of production point to a further step in this dimension of popular mobilisation behind a radical programme.

Schneider is right to emphasise the power of 'the establishment' to derail a radical programme. But a strategy to win needs to take account of not only 'establishment backlash' but the very nature of the state. I have sketched above the nature of the state that underlies the 'state machinery' to which Schneider refers, its extensive integration with corporate decision-making and, vice-versa, corporate integration with state decision-making. In the face of this mutual corporate state integration, something more specifically aimed at breaking capitalist power over the state than 'popular mobilisation' is required. And this in turn requires a very different relationship between organised labour and the political parties that have claimed to govern in its interests.

Fusing industrial power with the wider struggles for social change

An alternative approach, fusing industrial power with the wider struggles for social change, would be to use industrial power to resist the alienation process – the selling of workers' capacity to work – and to struggle for control over the purpose of production itself. The growing sense of urgency around the need to move towards a low-carbon economy provides a necessary and feasible stimulus to overcome the conservative division between politics and economics, between narrowly trade-union functions and wider issues of social change.

This takes us back to Luciana Castellina's insistence that instead of a politics of distribution, the radical left needs to work for 'a complete change in the way we consume and produce, which needs to be more related to use-value than to exchange-value'. By leaving production to the market, social democracy is in effect complicit in the high carbon emissions that contribute to climate breakdown. Moreover, this complicity is not just a matter of what a social democratic party does in government. The current separation of politics from trade unionism inhibits trade unions from making use-value, and in particular a transition to a low-carbon economy, part of their bargaining strategies. A reversal of that separation would not only encourage trade unions to push forward immediate steps towards a just decarbonising transition; it could also create the conditions for dismantling the state's integration with business and build instead a powerful ally in production for a government intent on achieving the increasingly popular goal of a low-carbon economy.

ADDITIONAL LITERATURE

Huw Beynon and Hilary Wainwright, *The workers' report on Vickers : the Vickers Shop Stewards Combine Committee report on work, wages, rationalisation, closure and rank-and-file*, London: Pluto Press, 1979.

Michael Cooley, *Architect or Bee: The Human/Technology Relationship*, Boston: South End Press, 1999.

David Harvey, *Seventeen Contradictions and the End of Capitalism*, Oxford: Oxford University Press, 2014.

Matthew T. Huber, *Climate Change as Class War: Building Socialism on a Warming Planet*, London: Verso, 2022.

Leo Panitch and Colin Leys, *The End of Parliamentary Socialism: From New Left to New Labour*, London: Verso, 2001 (second edition).

NOTES

1   With many thanks to the Rosa Luxemburg Foundation (especially Nessim Achouche), the Transnational Institute, and the Trade Union Congress (especially Policy Officers for Industry and Climate, Mika Minio-Paluello and Anna Markova) for their financial support and intellectual/political stimulus and encouragement. Also thanks to Haris Golemis, David Ridley, and David Whyte for their comments on earlier drafts. This essay is adapted from a presentation to the Centre of Social Movements Study (COMPAS), Scuola Normale Superiore, Florence; thanks to COMPAS for their encouragement and collaboration, especially Donatella Dalla Porta, Guglielmo Meardi, Mario Pianto, Riccardo Emilio Chesta, and Francesco Bagnardo.

2   <https://www.transform-network.net/en/publications/yearbook/overview/article//transform-yearbook-2022-1/>.

3   See Andreas Malm, *Fossil Capital: The Rise of Steam Power and the Roots of Global Warming*, London: Verso, 2016.

4   For a detailed analysis of this initiative and its wider significance (written in collaboration with the Lucas Aerospace Shop Stewards Combine Committee) see Hilary Wainwright and Dave Elliott, *The Lucas Plan: A New Trade Unionism in the Making*, London: Allison and Busby, 1979.

5   It was abolished by Margaret Thatcher in 1986.

6   Nancy Fraser, *Cannibal Capitalism*, London: Verso, 2022.

7   See Tom Nairn, *Faces of Nationalism: Janus Revisited*, London: Verso, 1998.

8   For a comprehensive overview of these initiatives and the responses of the 1974-79 Labour government, see Coventry, Liverpool, Newcastle, and North Tyneside Trades Councils, *State Intervention in Industry: A Workers' Inquiry*, Spokesman Books, 1981.

9   Interestingly, both of these creative Marxist public and actively engaged intellectuals were very influenced by the rebellions of 1968, which marked a critical rethinking of the role of the state and political party as having a monopoly on political change and also a valuing of the transformative role of grassroots social and labour movements. On Robin Murray see Michael Rustin (ed.), *Robin Murray – Selected Writings*, London: Lawrence & Wishart, 2020.

10 The TUC and Unite's environment taskforce are supporting efforts to survey their members to identify such emergent alternatives.

11 See Michael Polanyi, *The Tacit Dimension*, Garden City: Doubleday 1966.

12 Negative cases where management has adamantly and persistently refused to consider diversification, even in the face of public pressure – for example, BAE systems, the manufacturers of the Trident nuclear missile in Barrow in Furness – also prove the point, in that Saudi Arabia, Qatar, and India, which are among the markets for BAE systems, are not, at present, influenced by the peace movement. BAE appeals to concepts like 'national security' to legitimate its activities, insofar as it has to, to a wider public.

13 Karl Marx, *Capital*, vol. 1, Karl Marx and Frederick Engels, *Collected Works*, vol. 35, New York: International, 1996, p. 177.

14 See Hilary Wainwright, with Matthew Little, *Public Service Reform – But Not As We Know It: A Story of How Democracy Can Make Public Services Genuinely Efficient*, Hove: Picnic Publishers, 2009 (e-book).

15 See Wainwright and Elliott, *The Lucas Plan*, pp. 7-15 (1979 edition) for a report on the combine committees' discussion of Tony Benn's question concerning nationalisation of the aerospace components sector.

16 Do we need organisations like the Institute for Workers' Control and the British Society for Responsibility in Science adapted today's conditions – as non-party organisations that are nevertheless working to change society? See Joe Guinan, 'Bring back the Institute for Workers Control', *Renewal* 23,4 (2015).

17 See Fraser, *Cannibal Capitalism*.

18 Readers will be familiar with the well documented phenomenon of the 'revolving door'. See David Miller and William Dinan, *Revolving Doors, Accountability and Transparency: Emerging Regulatory Concerns and Policy Solutions in the Financial Crisis*, Paris: OECD, 2009.

19 The Permanent Secretary of the Ministry of Industry Anthony Part came – like a message boy of the establishment – into Benn's office, effectively reprimanding his elected boss. 'You're inflaming people,' said Part. 'You're raising temperatures.' Benn read him a sentence from the Labour Party's manifesto – the basis of government's popular mandate, as Benn believed: 'The first objective of the manifesto is about a fundamental and irreversible shift in the balance of wealth and power in favour of working people and their families.' Benn reports the moment in his diary. He also reports Part's response: 'Well, I have never known a minister in the whole course of my life in any party who has been like you.' A minister in other words who believed his job was to implement the party manifesto. Not long after, Benn was sacked as industry minister.

20   This originated in the years following the war and even more so after the fall of the
      post-war Labour government when business was *in* government, part of ministerial
      decision-making, and administrative implementation. Initially, after the war and
      following Labour's election victory over Churchill, these relations tended to be
      corporatist, with the trade unions also being consulted over the infamous 'beer and
      sandwiches'. Once Tory hegemony had been established under Macmillan, labour
      reps were pushed to outer-circle quangos (quasi-autonomous non-governmental
      organisations) at best. The National Economic Development Council (NEDC) and
      its sectoral NEDs (or 'neddies' as they were called) were attended by trade-union reps
      but they had no practical influence over them.

21   See C. Wright Mills, *The Power Elite*, Oxford: Oxford University Press, 1956.

22   Senior civil servants would know how to contact national trade union officials, but
      this would not be normal and a direct relationship with workplace representatives
      would be out of the question.

23   Quoted in Michael Foot, *Aneurin Bevan: A Biography – Volume One: 1897-1945*,
      London: Macgibbon & Kee, 1962.

24   The Labour government of 1997 created committees in every government
      department to which a corporate CEO was appointed.

25   Broken recently by the rise of leftish national independence parties in Scotland and
      Wales

26   Though a number of factors are destabilising these deeply conservative institutions in
      ways that can be contradictory. These include the fragmentation and casualisation of
      the labour force (which has also led to the creation of new militant organisations of
      these workers, which are now gaining some support from major unions and winning
      victories against the worst employers, such as McDonald's and Wetherspoon's); and
      the increasingly aggressive strategies of employers making the most of the Tory attacks
      on labour rights (which favoured the election of a new leader of the UK's largest
      union, Unite, who places more emphasis on winning at the workplace and shifting
      the balance of power there, deploying more resources to do so, than on spending
      energy and funds on the Labour Party).

27   See especially Sheila Rowbotham in Sheila Rowbotham, Lynne Segal, and Hilary
      Wainwright (eds), *Beyond the Fragments: Feminism and the Making of Socialism*, London:
      Merlin Press,1972, second edition 1980, third edition 2013.

28   See Maureen MacIntosh and Hilary Wainwright, *A Taste of Power: The Politics of Local
      Economics*, London: Verso, 1987, for the example of the People's Plan for the Royal
      Docks and also the role of a community plan in the struggle over the future of Coin
      Street, Waterloo.

29   For Schneider's full analysis, see James Schneider, *Our Bloc: How We Win*, London:
      Verso, 2022.

The Role of the State in Social-Ecological Transformations: Some Theoretical Considerations and Current Observations

Ulrich Brand

One of the most striking features of the current debate on emancipatory alternatives is that it implicitly or explicitly refers to the local or national scale, and only rarely to the international one. This may have to do, firstly, with the fact that it is when we look beyond the local and national levels that things really become complicated. How is it possible to reorganise global commodity chains which are becoming increasingly complex? How is an alternative thinkable and practicable, beyond the political games of the powerful states?

Secondly, the absence – or at least weakness – of truly global political alternatives may stem from the fact that common experiences of social protests, struggles, and alternatives are often had at the local, regional, or national levels and rarely at the international one. Of course, things are different when we think about Latin America, where people can more easily be informed about what is happening in neighbouring countries than between African or Asian countries. Or indeed in the case of the European Union, where many political initiatives from above are formulated at the European level. But here, too, when it comes to alternatives, the respective debates and practices largely ocur at the national level.

I would contend that the aforementioned absence of global alternatives thirdly has to do with a strong historical experience of alternative thinking and practice, in which the national state is the main framework for ensuring a certain durability of emancipatory achievements. This is quite obvious when it comes to anti-colonial struggles (historically framed as 'national liberation') or the welfare state in the global North and some countries of the global South. The state is also the main addressee of political demands from various actors and interest groups.

Moreover, the very mechanism of the political – public debates, information in mass media, the imaginary of a 'national culture,' and also the economy – is oriented to the national scale. We may think, for instance, of the perception of production units, growth or employment rates, economic policies, and state interventions in times of crisis. When I travel between Austria and Germany (the two countries where I live) it is always interesting to see how country-centred the mass media are.

The question of the state

The initial argument of this chapter is that the national state plays a crucial role in the reproduction of social structures and processes, and is itself such a structure and process. Put differently, the state is a social relation. Its enormous material resources; its legal, bureaucratic, and coercive functions; its power to set norms and to sanction (even powerful economic actors); and the fact that, despite all its dysfunctions or its repressive character, it is usually accepted by large parts of the people as the state – these are the bases of its outstanding role in our societies. The state has discursive power (e.g. constantly framing its decisions in terms of 'progress', 'growth', 'the migrant problem') and it also creates knowledge about society and the economy in order to steer and control it more adequately, i.e. through population-related, economic or environmental data, through studies and expert commissions, etc. Moreover, the state is active within the economy and the provision of services, or the creation and maintenance of physical and social infrastructures, through state-owned or public enterprises; it may also receive rents resulting from the extraction of natural resources. As a final element, the state also tends to intervene in crisis moments – often in favour of the dominant economic and political forces.

This is why many political struggles are struggles over state and governmental power (which, we will see, are not the same thing). This is also why political parties and struggles within and among them play an important role – in countries with single parties such as China, of course, struggles within the party are decisive (and in times of dictatorship, parties usually do not play any role).

This is why the emancipatory left – state-centred or, for good reasons, state-critical – needs to engage with the state. Even an emancipatory politics thatis distant from the state has something to do with this really-existing phenomenon.

The role of critical thinking and left strategising is to reflect on the manifold experiences which emancipatory forces have had, and still have, in engaging the state. Cases in point would include the historical experiences of anti-colonial movements and what Antonio Gramsci would have called their 'becoming-state'; the limits to socialist politics in countries with a well-developed welfare state; or the recent experiences of progressive governments in Latin America.[1] Scrutinising these barriers to radical change, exploring the contradictions of dominant patterns that reproduce capitalist social relations but also entry points for social-ecological transformations – this is the strength of critical thinking that avoids the state-centric view which characterises most social-scientific and philosophical approaches and instead focuses on the societal context that embeds and enables the state and is also in part structured by it. Critical thinking develops arguments and concepts to better understand this vague and ambiguous entity that we call the 'state'. It allows us to assume a societal 'totality' of societalisation (including its relationships with nature). This can be never fully grasped, but it does help us, for example, to locate the concrete forms of existing states within the historical, societal and international contexts (which mainstream state theory rarely does).

Understanding the state

Of course, reflecting on 'the state' is difficult because the historically concrete manifestations of the state are very different. The states in Bolivia, China, Germany, Russia, or Tanzania are difficult to compare. This is even more true when we look at them from a critical perspective where the state is not considered as a more or less neutral regulator and framework-setter for the economy and society, but interwoven with societies and economies. But despite these differences, which do need to be acknowledged, historical-materialist state theories help us to understand some central features of the capitalist state and its ambiguities.

To start with, the state is a relationship of domination, separated from but intrinsically linked to the capitalist economy and society. Its 'general function' – as Nicos Poulantzas put it[2] – is to secure the conditions of the capitalist mode of production: the conditions for accumulation such as the availability of wage-earners, natural resources, infrastructures, money, and a certain order and stability. For all this, the state is not the instrument of capital (because capital usually acts under conditions of competition with monopolistic tendencies) but it maintains a certain 'relative autonomy' to secure capitalism as such – not individual capitals per se. But this should not be read as meaning that the state per se secures capitalist reproduction – this process is always uncertain, full of tensions and contradictions, and the product and object of constant societal and political struggles.[3]

The state is not a neutral regulator but is permeated by manifold social relations. This becomes particularly clear when we think of the material basis of the state, which consists largely of taxes and tariffs stemming from capitalist commodity production and the direct and indirect taxes of wage earners. The state is, therefore, not an autonomous entity 'above' the rest of society, but an integral part of it. It also does not embody a social 'general will' that exists a priori; for social interests are far too incompatible. There are social struggles for certain interests to become generalised, to make them accepted by other interests as well, and to be promoted, actively organised and secured through state policies. One topical example is the tendency towards a selective greening of capitalism.[4] This does not necessarily take place explicitly, i.e. the actors do not always act cconsciously to make capitalism greener, but they pursue their business, workplace, or other interests.

Moreover, capital is not a homogeneous actor, but is full of tensions and conflicts. For instance, because accumulation strategies might contradict each other and, say, be oriented more towards the world market or towards the internal market. Another central function of the state is therefore to organise capital politically – and in a certain way to disorganise the subaltern classes. However, the interests of the wage-dependent people or subaltern are also partially and asymmetrically inscribed into the state.

The state is also dependent on a functioning capitalist economy, whether through the production of absolute or relative surpluses, or through rents, e.g. the selling of concessions to mining or oil companies. The actually existing states are part of the dominant capitalist growth regime, which enacts class-based, gendered, and racialised, as well as global forms of domination and exploitation.[5]

Historical-materialist approaches emphasise how the core structural principle of global capitalism permeates and shapes state structures and processes. On the most fundamental level, these core structural principles of capitalism as an economic and social system are characterised (among other things) by private ownership over the means of production, implying competing and antagonistic social interests, as well as an inherent drive of capital towards accumulation through profit-maximisation, owing to competitive pressure. This corresponds with an inherent growth imperative, which is, in principle, indifferent to its ecological consequences. Under neoliberal economic globalisation, transnational corporations compete on a global scale, and maintaining and increasing international competitiveness has become one of the primary policy goals of nation-states – often at the expense of stricter environmental regulation.

In the 1970s, the Marxist state theorist Claus Offe pointed out that modern states are restrained between two imperatives that may also contradict each other.[6] On the one hand, the imperative to secure ongoing accumulation, which means to privilege capital; and, on the other, the imperative to secure a kind of political legitimation which is mainly done through distributive policies, and which may itself affect the dynamics of accumulation. During the coronavirus pandemic the state's constrained position between these two imperatives became quite obvious.

Questions of legitimacy or agreement with the existing social conditions – even with one's own exploitation – were also dealt with by Antonio Gramsci and his idea of hegemony. Gramsci[7] focused on how in advanced capitalist countries mechanisms of coercive exploitation step back in favour of ones seeking to create consensus among the dominated. He argued that this consensus is not just formed by the state in a narrow sense (as a state apparatus) but also within what he called 'civil society' as part of the 'integral state'. When it comes to the materiality of the state, i.e. its apparatuses, an insight from Nicos Poulantzas is of utmost importance. He, and many others after him, conceptualised the state as a 'material condensation of a relationship of forces between classes and class fractions' which expresses itself within the state in a specific form.[8] From this perspective, the state is not just a neutral problem-solver or one actor among others, but the focal terrain of societal power-relations, in which the dominant social forces organise themselves by conducting their conflicts in a rule-guided manner. As a consequence, power relations among social forces and specific political actors are historically inscribed into the political structure of the state, that is, as a 'material condensation'.

This is also an entry point for emancipatory forces and demands, which must be understood without any innocence. Emancipatory demands and the related conflicts over particular policies or the general orientation of politics are fought out on a pre-structured, asymmetrical institutional terrain. This means that specific strategies and interests enjoy historically developed and entrenched privileged access to key decision-making areas (so-called structural and strategic selectivities).[9]

However, the state can also be understood as an asymmetric terrain of struggles and as a system that can possibly block powerful interests and give a certain durability to emancipatory demands and achievements:[10] leaving the oil in the soil, stopping the operation of nuclear power plants and the use of GMOs, enabling the expansion of sustainable public transport and democratic energy transitions, creating an education system that is part of the transformations we are talking about, introducing a tax system that supports them, and so on. This can be promoted by creating binding rules, limiting destructive dynamics driven by existing power structures, and dedicating resources to promote social-ecological processes such as the establishing of social-ecological provisioning systems and infrastructures that are not guided by profit.

Critical state theory also highlights an aspect that we may observe in everyday life, but which is often underestimated in analyses of the state: the various state apparatuses are in a relationship of tension with each other, even contradicting each other in part. It is therefore a political task to commit the various actors and organisations to one line or to formulate and implement a reasonably coherent and realisable 'state project'.[11]

As I argued, the state as an abstract real-object is assumed to be present, as form and logic, in all historically concrete states.[12] But the latter, of course, differ. Tilman Evers[13] argued almost five decades ago that a characteristic of the capitalist periphery – or of 'dependent determination' as René Zavaleta called it[14] – is its structural heterogeneity and the orientation of its economy towards the world market and its largely subaltern dependency. Joachim Becker[15] called this latter its 'passive extraversion' (in contrast, for instance, to an 'active' extraversion of the German economy). The state here plays a role, for instance, in coordinating the exploitation of labour and natural resources, in accepting or even imposing certain trade agreements or organising 'hard' currencies via credits and debts. And the countries of the periphery are characterised by a strong presence of international capital through foreign direct investment. Under particular conditions, foreign capital can be used for industrialisation processes, as was historically the case in some Latin American countries, or Turkey, and recently in China.

An important difference between the countries – and thus their states – of the global North and the global South is that in the latter there are more spaces that are not capitalistically organised, such as subsistence economies. That is, beside the capitalist mode of production, other modes remain important. Dependency theory called this coexistence of capitalist and non-capitalist forms of reproduction – and hence the different class structures – 'structural heterogeneity'. When it comes to political authorities, the capitalist state may coexist with other, often indigenous, authorities.[16] This is the reality behind the principle of 'plurinational states'.[17]

The concrete form of political economy has consequences for the state. Its material basis often comes from concessions and rents; in such cases, the state bureaucracy and the jobs that create loyal followers are based on rent-incomes, and strengthen a tendency towards clientelism.[18] In general, the state plays a greater role in the economy. The influence of foreign capital is strongly inscribed in the state apparatuses, in what Cardoso and Faletto called an 'internalisation of external interests'.[19] In sum, its more difficult for (semi-)peripheral states to formulate ambitious development and state projects that will be independent from foreign interests.

The state as a multi-scalar social relation – the internationalisation of the state

My argument so far holds that the national state (and its mechanism as a nation-state) is an especially crucial level for securing capitalist, patriarchal, racialised, and inter-national social relations and society-nature relations, which are highly unequal and shaped by domination. Moreover, it argues that the state is a highly asymmetrical terrain of contestation, which constitutes the entry point for emancipatory demands and forces.

However, what also needs considering is the multi-scalar character of the state. This is quite obvious and politically important when we look at sub-state levels, i.e. regions and provinces, cities, and administrative areas of the countryside. And there are state structures, too, bureaucracies which have more or less decision-making and fiscal power. In the last years, many progressive and emancipatory experiences occurred at the city level – with Barcelona as a prominent case – or in (semi-)rural regions.

But we could also talk about a state at the international level, seeing as particular norm-setting, conflict-resolution, and bureaucratic modes have become increasingly internationalised. The same applies to certain state functions, particularly the securing by political means of the conditions to reproduce capitalism, e.g. foreign investments or intellectual property rights.

Historical analyses show that the emergence of the capitalist world-system and of national states as the primary scale of political organisation was a contingent process.[20] And in fact, since the beginning of the existence and then dominance of the capitalist mode of production, empires and colonies long existed parallel to capitalist nation-states. One could even argue that it took until 1991 – with the disappearance of the Soviet Union – for the nation-state to become the almost exclusive form of capitalism's political organisation.

Interestingly, in the historical moment (the 1990s) when the nation-state became the almost exclusive form and scale to organise capitalist relations politically, the dominant forces sought to transfer political power to the international scale. Of course, the European Economic Community since the 1950s and the European Union were important precursors. But the process of capitalist globalisation and the 'unilateral moment' (Charles Krauthammer) of strong US global dominance at the beginning of the 1990s led to what critical scholarship calls the 'internationalisation of the state'.[21] The creation of the World Trade Organization (WTO) but also the enhanced role of the World Bank and the IMF were an expression of this.[22] But there is also an extensive international creation of environmental law. In November 2020, the International Environmental Agreements Database Project listed 1,300 multilateral and 2,200 bilateral agreements.[23]

Within scholarly debates at this time there were growing arguments against the perception that globalisation led to a decline or 'retreat of the state'.[24]

Globalisation and the internationalisation of the state is not something that simply *happens to* nation-states. It is a process which the dominant nation-states, in particular, actively shape, establishing international state apparatuses, such as international organisations, regimes, or governance networks.[25] Based on the notion of the state as a condensation of a societal relationship of forces, these international state apparatuses can be interpreted as a 'second-order condensation'.[26] That is, they are a condensation of forces between nation-states (which are themselves condensations of forces) as well as between nation-states and other actors operating on a global scale. A crucial benefit of this approach is that it allows us to take into account power asymmetries and competition between nation states in global (environmental) governance, including the postcolonial legacy of North–South asymmetries.[27] Moreover, the concept of second-order condensation also facilitates a nuanced perspective on the politics of scale, which focuses on why specific actors decide strategically where and how they engage in struggles and which level or fora of decision-making they strengthen or undermine.[28]

State transformations

The state cannot be a fixed entity in a society that is dynamically developing and profoundly transforming over time and often confronted with manifold crises. In the 1970 and 1980s many countries experienced a neoliberal transformation of economies and societies and a correlated transformation of the state which Joachim Hirsch called a 'competition state'.[29]

As early as the 1970s, Poulantzas argued that the state is internationalising, and yet remains essentially a nation-state. The nation-states, as condensed relations of forces, thus intervene in a field 'already permeated by the intra-imperialist contradictions, and in which the contradictions between the ruling fractions within the social formation are already internationalised'.[30] Its interventions thus do not clearly work in favour of a national bourgeoisie as against international capital.

Today, in those countries where 'green' capital and technologies are sufficiently developed and internationally competitive, we may experience a transformation towards an 'eco-capitalist state'. This does not at all mean that the deepening ecological crisis and related injustices are resolved, but rather than significant fractions of capital, workers and their organisations, the dominant science, the public, consumers, and also the state intend to deal with aspects of the ecological crisis. But this transformation tends to take place under conditions set by the dominant forces, a constellation that Gramsci called 'passive revolution'.[31]

Current debates and policy strategies around a 'European Green Deal' or a – more leftist - 'Green New Deal' (GND) suggest – despite very significant differences – that the state could (re-)assume a far more prominent role by massively investing in infrastructure and renewable energy or by introducing emission-related border taxation.[32]

Emancipatory transformations

The political ideas guiding Green New Deal proposals in the global North are often rather (eco-)Keynesian-oriented. In particular, the state or EU institutions are mostly understood as regulators, policymakers, and as redistribution mechanisms that advance social-ecological transformation processes under corresponding left-wing political and governmental conditions. The recent revaluation of the state to which we have referred is mostly limited to the level of policy proposals – sometimes with reference to the capital-friendly and/or repressive side of the state. In this context, a critical understanding of the state (including the EU) still needs to be developed; for in general its domineering, structurally selective, and multi-scalar character is not acknowledged, and the political economy of the capitalist growth imperative is rarely questioned.

The fact that the state is a major addressee also for emancipatory social-ecological concerns constitutes a paradox that needs to be understood. First of all, it needs to be acknowledged that the state is a major factor in the ongoing escalation of economic growth and unsustainable patterns of production and consumption. This capitalist growth imperative is not just an outcome of more and more production, consumption, and capital valorisation. The growth imperative is also secured by and deeply embedded in the state's structures.[33] So to think about, approach, and realise emancipatory alternatives, we need to understand the state not as one actor beside others – even if this is what it is assumed to be in most social-science debates where the concept of the state has since the 1990s been replaced by the fancy buzzword 'governance'.

Developing adequate political responses to the multiple crisis is not simply a question of overcoming the abstract logic of path dependence and finding cooperative, techno-scientific solutions. It also means confronting vested and highly organised interests, in order to transform deeply rooted social relations of production and consumption.

This implies that the very structure of the capitalist, imperial, patriarchal, and racist state needs to be entirely transformed, and that this struggle will also happen within the state.[34] But this will only happen in conjunction with social movements, conscious and engaged people, a critical public, and progressive businesses – and with a more or less rapid transformation of the mode of production and life. Some forms of apparatuses are needed to administer things and to establish certain rules for social life – and a certain stability will be important.[35] This is particularly the case if we also consider the global scale, i.e. the need for some kind of democratic and transparent coordination mechanisms. In that sense, in a social–ecologically transformed society, a 'state' also remains important as a label for a societal body that is an important part of such emancipatory transformations and – as a result of social struggles – secures them.

In the recent coronavirus pandemic, we have seen that the state is the crisis manager that guarantees certain, though unequal, forms of public interest and coherence where private capital cannot and is not willing to do so. But probably the most important argument for making use of the state is the need for massive investment, which in large parts will be public (or private investment with strong rules) and require a strong involvement of the wage earners and the public. Many people who see the deep problems and may be willing to actively contribute – or have at least passively accepted the need for far-reaching changes – expect a form of leadership from the state. This is, at least, true in many countries of the global North where we still have the experience of the state not acting exclusively in favour of the oligarchy and transnational capital.

In that sense, a transformed state that provides structure, personnel, and policies is necessarily part of changing societal power relations and pursuit of social-ecological transformations, sought by a successful broad movement. The state apparatuses in the global South and also in the global North need to be decolonised.

A highly contested issue – also for the left and progressive trade unions – will be the reduction of harmful production and branches of industry.[36] This is a plausible perspective when it comes to resource extractivism, but it must go hand in hand with a drastic reduction of the production of vehicles for individual(ised) mobility, of industrialised agriculture and food, or the production and sale of clothes as mere commodities (given new impetus by fast fashion).

Decisively, strategies that aim at societies and a global economy beyond a renewed – now labelled 'green' – colonialism and the imperial discourse of a largely Northern 'just transition' need to rethink and remake the internal and international divisions of labour. I think that a diversification of economies under strict social-ecological conditionalities is key. This is not just about trade but about the very material forms and modes of (re-) production of societies, and it includes a remaking of material infrastructures, e.g. for transport, energy provision, and water. More than that, it requires a rethinking and remaking of social infrastructures that, in principle, enable good living for all, not at the cost of others and of nature.

NOTES

1   Edgardo Lander, *Crisis Civilizatoria: Experiencias de los Gobiernos Progresistas y Debates en la Izquierda Latinoamericana*, Mexico City: Universidad de Guadalajara, CALAS, 2019.

2   Nicos Poulantzas, *State, Power, Socialism*, London: Verso, 1978.

3   Bob Jessop, *State Power: A Strategic-Relational Approach*, Cambridge, 2007.

4   Ulrich Brand and Markus Wissen, *The Imperial Mode of Living. Everyday Life and the Ecological Crisis of Capitalism,* London: Verso, 2021, chapter 7.

5   For a feminist perspective, see Birgit Sauer, 'Der Staat als Geschlechtsspezifisches Gewaltverhältnis. Eine (neo-)marxistisch-feministische Perspektive', Alexandra Scheele Stefanie Wöhl (eds), *Feminismus und Marxismus*, Weinheim, Basel: Beltz, 2018, pp. 202-217.

6   Claus Offe, 'Structural Problems of the Capitalist State: Class Rule and the Political System; on the Selectiveness of Political Institutions', Klaus von Beyme (ed.), *German Political Studies* Vol. 1, London: Sage, 1984, pp. 31-57.

7   Antonio Gramsci, *Selections from the Prison Notebooks*, London: Lawrence & Wishart 1971.

8   Poulantzas, *State, Power, Socialism*.

9   Jessop, *State Power*.

10   Miriam Lang et al., 'Dimensiones de la Transformación Social y el Rol de las Instituciones', Miriam Lang, Belén Cevallos, and Claudia Lopéz (eds), *Cómo transformar? Instituciones y Cambio Social en América Latina y Europa*. Quito: Abya Yala, Fundación Rosa Luxemburg, 2015, pp. 7-32.

11   Jessop, State *Power*.

12   On the historical phases of state development and its theorisation in Latin America, see Miriam Lang, 'El rol del Estado en la Transición hacia una Sociedad Post Extractivista: Aportes para un Debate Necesario', *Ecuador Debate*, 117 (2022), 143–170; Tobias Boos et al., 'State Transformation', Olaf Kaltmeier, Anne Tittor, Daniel Hawkins, and Eleonora Rohland (eds), *The Routledge Handbook to the Political Economy and Governance of the Americas*. London: Routledge, 2020, pp. 221-30. On the still-prevalent Eurocentric thinking on the state in Latin America, see Oscar Vega Camacho, 'Al sur del Estado', Grupo Comuna – Álvaro García Linera, Raúl Prada, Luis Tapia, and Oscar Vega Camacho (eds), *El estado: campo de lucha*, La Paz: Muela del Diablo, 2010, pp. 127-165.

13   Tilman Evers, *Bürgerliche Herrschaft in der Dritten Welt. Zur Theorie des Staates in ökonomisch unterentwickelten Gesellschaftsformationen*, Cologne: Europäische Verlagsanstalt, 1977; Spanish: *El estado en la periferia capitalista*, Mexico City: Siglo XXI, 1979.

14   René Zavaleta Mercado, *Lo Nacional-popular en Bolivia*, Mexico City: Siglo XXI, 1986.

15   Joachim Becker, *Akkumulation, Regulation, Territorium. Zur kritischen Rekonstruktion der französischen Regulationstheorie*, Marburg: Metropolis-Verl., 2002.

16   Cristóbal Kay, *Latin American Theories of Development and Underdevelopment*, London: Routledge, 1989; Fernanda Beigel, 'Dependency Analysis: The Creation of New Social Theory in Latin America', Sujata Patel (ed.), *The ISA Handbook of Diverse Sociological Traditions*, Los Angeles: SAGE, 2010, pp. 189-200.

17   Alberto Acosta et al., *Plurinacionalidad, Democracia en la Diversidad*, Quito: Abya-Yala, 2009.

18   Joachim Becker et al., 'Mechanisms of Dependence: Conceptualizing the Latin American Dependency Research Program for the Analysis of European Capitalism', Aldo Madariaga and Stefano Palestini (eds), *Dependent Capitalisms in Contemporary Latin America and Europe*, London: Palgrave Macmillan, 2021, pp. 75-99.

19   Fernando Henrique Cardoso et al., *Dependency and Development in Latin America*, University of California Press, 1979.

20   Kay, *Latin American Theories of Development and Underdevelopment*; Heide Gerstenberger, *Market and Violence: The Functioning of Capitalism in History*, Leiden: Brill, 2022; Benno Teschke, *The Myth of 1648. Class, Geopolitics, and the Making of Modern International Relations*, London: Verso, 2011.

21   Ulrich Brand et al., 'Second-Order Condensations of Societal Power Relations: Environmental Politics and the Internationalization of the State from a Neo-Poulantzian Perspective', *Antipode* 43,1 (2011): 149-175; Alex Demirović, 'Materialist State Theory and the Transnationalization of the Capitalist State', *Antipode* 43,1 (2011): 38-59; Birgit Sauer et al., 'Feminist Perspectives on the Internationalization of The State', *Antipode* 43,1 (2011): 108-128.

22   Quinn Slobodian, *Globalists: The End of Empire and the Birth of Neoliberalism*, Boston: Harvard University Press, 2018.

23   IEADP, International Environmental Agreements Database Project, 2020. <https://iea.uoregon.edu/>.

24   Susan Strange, *The Retreat of the State: The Diffusion of Power in the World Economy*, Cambridge: Cambridge University Press.

25   Christoph Görg et al., 'Is international democracy possible?', *Review of International Political Economy* 5,4 (1998): 585-615.

26   Brand et al., 'Second-Order Condensations of Societal Power Relations'.

27   Okereke Chukwumerjie et al. 'North-South Inequity and Global Environmental Governance', Agni Kalfagianni et al. (eds), *Routledge Handbook of Global Sustainability Governance*, London: Routledge, 2021, pp. 167-179.

28   Markus Wissen, 'Contested Terrains: Politics of Scale, the National State and Struggles for the Control over Nature', *Review of International Political Economy* 16,5 (2009): 883-906.

29   Joachim Hirsch, 'Globalization of Capital, Nation-States and Democracy', *Studies in Political Economy* 54 (1997): 39–58.

30   Nicos Poulantzas, 'Internationalisation of Capitalist Relations and the Nation-State', *Economy and Society* 3,2 (1974): 145–79 (quote translated from the German version).

31   See also Magnus Ryner, *Passive Revolution/Silent Revolution: Europe's Recovery Plan, the Green Deal, and the German Question*, Helsinki Global Political Economy Working Papers no. 5, 2021.

32   European Commission, *The European Green Deal*, COM 640 final, Brussels: European Commission, 2019.

33   Ulrich Brand, 'Emancipatory Social-ecological Transformations: Degrowth and the Role of Strategy', Nathan Barlow, Livia Regen, Noémie Cadiou, Ekaterina Chertkovskaya, Max Hollweg, Christina Plank, Merle Schulken, and Verena Wolf (eds), *Degrowth & Strategy. How to bring about social-ecological transformation*, Mayfly Books, 2022, pp. 22-33.

34   Lang, 'El rol del Estado en la Transición hacia una Sociedad Post Extractivista'.

35   Lang et al., 'Dimensiones de la Transformación Social y el Rol de las Instituciones'.

36   Maristella Svampa, *Development in Latin America: Toward a New Future*, Black Point, Nova Scotia: Fernwood Publishing, 2019.

Repressive State Mechanisms and Biopolitical Practices in the Age of Covid-19: The Example of Greece

Panos Ramantanis

The great pandemic crisis that has impacted societies in the last three years, as well as the different ways of addressing it, brought to the fore a series of political and other concerns which not only involved the pandemic directly, but also the relationship of this crisis with capitalist modernity in the current context. This created a de facto framework of theoretical approaches, within which contradictory positions and views emerged on a series of issues related to the biopolitics of power, sovereignty, and the state and its mechanisms. These approaches drew on theoretical tools from different traditions – from Marxism to social liberalism and neoliberalism, from the relational view of power to the view of power as pure domination.

Seeking a more limited focus, albeit without neglecting the big picture, the present analysis takes the perspective of biopolitics and the state – and, more specifically, the state's repressive mechanisms. It examines specific concepts mainly by applying Marxist theoretical tools, and then discusses the relationship between these repressive mechanisms and the biopolitical practices observed in Greek society during the period of the Covid-19 pandemic. In short, we will try to analyse this particular period by examining the operation of the state's repressive mechanisms and the level of biopolitical processes, as well as considering the practical choices of political power in the spatiotemporal juncture.

On the question of biopolitics: a theoretical approach

Biopolitics is a Foucauldian analytical concept. We need therefore first to understand Michel Foucault's sense of the biopolitical process and its relationship with state policies, in order to then highlight its negative (meaning inversely proportional) relationship to the intensity of the state's repressive mechanisms in the current juncture of the pandemic crisis.

As Michel Foucault showed us in his work *The History of Sexuality: 1: The Will to Knowledge,*[1] an important feature of the transition from feudal despotism to capitalist modernity was the transformation of the concept of power, from the right of death to the power over life. This latter now appears through two basic forms: an anatomo-politics of the human body and a biopolitics of population. Thus, the Foucauldian perspective on the new form of power, that is, the biopower that appears in capitalist modernity, can be understood as a methodological codification of the Marxist materialist analyses of capital (without only being this).

Indeed, if we look at the Foucauldian connection of biopower with the development and consolidation of capitalist relations – a connection that goes beyond the perspective of legal sovereignty in relation to power, while at the same time promoting the 'productive' confluence of knowledge and power – we could argue that biopower was ultimately a necessary condition for the development of capitalism itself. Only through the new technology of biopower could capitalism integrate bodies into the mechanism of the production process. And this process worked on multiple levels. On the one hand, at the 'macro' level the large (state) mechanisms of power ensured the maintenance of production relations, and, on the other, at a 'micro' level the techniques of power (in a context of anatomo-political and biopolitical interventions), invented as early as the eighteenth century, operated at all levels of the social formation and permeated social institutions.[2]

The Foucauldian conception of the new form of power, which appears in capitalist modernity, assigns the state a 'positive', i.e. productive, role. We would say that this follows as a logical consequence of the relational view of power and also of the anatomo-political/biological processes that operate at all levels of the social body. And, of course, the development of large state mechanisms already at the end of the seventeenth century facilitated the development of the above processes.[3] In short, Foucault does not see the state as playing a restrictive, prohibitive, repressive, and essentially 'negative' role. This would reproduce a juridical conception of the state. And it is precisely this process of a 'positive' (productive) state, which regulates/ ensures the biopolitics of the population, as, of course, a necessary element for the development and reproduction of capitalism itself, that constitutes a salient characteristic of the modern world, mainly during the twentieth century.[4]

The above productive thought of Foucault has a clear basis in Marxian thought, as it unfolds in the first volume of *Capital*. Moreover, Foucault not only did not deny this, but emphasised it often in several of his positions.[5]

So, the Foucauldian 'completion' of Marxian thought lies mainly in the question of the 'productive subject'.[6] As Kyrkos Doxiades notes, 'Marx's great discovery, even quite early, was that he identified the authoritative effect of matter, matter as the object of natural sciences and technology, in the process of constructing new power relations, which built a corresponding system of socio-economic organisation largely autonomous from the state and dominant over it'.[7] Almost a century later, Marxist thought, mainly in terms of how power relations are constituted, was complemented by Foucauldian approaches through the analysis of the biopolitical process. And precisely within this specific analytical framework we could see that during the twentieth century, or, more precisely, from the second half of the twentieth century onwards, the level of biopolitics itself is what determines the capitalist economy.[8]

Even if the above relationship seemed to — and in fact did — place limits on capitalist relations, it was also the one that defined the intensity of these relations. So, to use a mixture of Foucauldian and Althusserian tools, it is this restriction but also the changing intensity of power relations that ultimately defined — and continues to define — class struggle, which continues to shape the dynamics and the mechanisms of the state in this case, but also the corresponding context of class relations at each level of the social formation.

The question of the state's repressive mechanisms: The current situation

Leaving aside for now the analysis of biopolitics as an evolutionary/multi-layered process of the bourgeois regime itself and thus of capitalism as a socio-economic system, it would be interesting to see how the mechanisms of the state, and especially the repressive mechanisms within the social formation, work, focusing mainly on the case of Greece.

This specific framework of analysis of the state requires a multi-layered perspective which delimits the state both as a machine and as a condensation of class relations. This may seem contradictory, but it is not: the partial autonomy of the state can appear both in the form of a state of emergency and each time in a certain form of the state, in a certain context of class aggravation. This means that the state, either through its repressive mechanisms or through its ideological mechanisms, appears to be a machine that is partially autonomous, to the extent of course that it can maintain the ruling group in a hegemonic position. Louis Althusser, in his various texts, developed the idea of how these mechanisms operate; Nicos Poulantzas developed it in detail in his *Fascism and Dictatorship: The Third International and the Problem of Fascism*,[9] in which he formalised Marx's insight in *The Civil War in France*.[10]

Regarding the state's repressive mechanisms, we can say that they are structural in every system of dominant relations, and thus also in the bourgeois regime, and that they are innate since they develop in the context of the power relations (that is, the class struggle) of the social formation. Thus, we can claim that the repressive mechanisms take part in the class conflict both internally[11] – in a continuous process in which the state, and the state machine by extension, can appear partially autonomous – and externally, that is, mainly through the state's interaction with portions of the dominant classes as fractions of these rotate in and out of office at this superstructural level.[12] Even if the classes are unable, as historical experience has shown, to limit the nature of the repressive structural functions of the mechanisms themselves, they can, depending on the level of development of the class struggle, have an effect especially on the level of intensity with which these mechanisms are put to use.

Transferring this theoretical framework to the case of Greek society during the pandemic crisis and the first quarantine after March 2020, and also a little earlier, we can make some observations about the nature of the state's repressive mechanisms and especially the police – ones that point to certain continuities but also certain differences.

First of all, we could argue that the low-intensity repressive measures regarding the evacuation of refugee settlements that began in mid-2016, continued after the change of government in July 2019 but with much greater intensity. This shows the direct impact of the new conservative government on the intensity of the repressive mechanisms. In this case, the state's repressive mechanisms seem to interact with political power more as a relation of externality. We should also emphasise that this new political power gave the 'signal' to increase the intensity of the state's repressive mechanisms, just a few days after it came to power, by presenting a bill to abolish university asylum. This constitutes a particular intersection of authoritarianism, which also represents a movement towards a new type of authoritarian state, the characteristics of which are rather distant from the traditional image of bourgeois democracies. However, this movement, above all, seems to respond to the level of class struggle at this particular moment.

By contrast, in two typical cases – the invasion by the Units of Reinstatement of Order of a central Athens cinema during the screening of the movie *Joker* and, still more flagrantly, the police's invasion of a private residence without a warrant during the violent termination of a nearby occupation – the repressive mechanisms seem to have operated in a relation of 'interiority' to the field of conflict. More precisely, the repressive forces of the state in these particular cases are operating as a (relatively) autonomous machine or as part of a machine[13] that is trying to protect the 'sacred and true' of dominant relations (on the political, cultural, or the broader cultural level) against something it considers dangerous for their stability. With its repressive mechanisms, the state machinery may in this case appear to act autonomously, but in fact it is operating within a framework of relative autonomy, precisely because the pursued goal of its action has to do with the preservation and reproduction of the dominant social relations.[14]

Biopolitical processes and repressive mechanisms of the state: A negative relationship

There can be no doubt that the coronavirus crisis initially, but also the countermeasures that followed, brought to the surface a structural problem of urban economic relations. This structural problem, however, which appeared in essence through the biopolitical crisis of the pandemic, seems to involve a series of functions of the state machinery itself. In this relation we should point out a particularity of the Greek state in relation to other EU states: the ten-year crisis preceding the pandemic, in which the public health system was crushed. This points to the crisis of biopolitics that Greece had already entered in the early 2010s. At the same time, the dependencies, mainly in terms of economic relations, which often evaded the area of national political/governmental interventions, revealed a semi-instrumental character of the state which at this particular moment seemed to have a limited scope of action. This, of course, is not entirely true, since the state machinery, apart from certain short periods of time, has never, in fact, ceased to function in harmony with the urban regime itself, at almost every level of its structures.

However, to return to the issue of the biopolitical crisis, we should underline that the first lockdown decided by the Greek government, in March 2020, is directly related to it. The quarantine, that is, is a consequence of the inability of the state formation to maintain a level of biopolitics, meaning the level of care for living beings, sufficient for the smooth functioning of the dominant capitalist productive relations, but also the broader functioning of the social formation, with everything it includes.[15] With the so-called 'social state' disintegrated, the result of a chronic anti-biopolitical process, restrictive quarantine seemed to be the only option. The politics of containment – which clearly includes both the question of discipline and the question of surveillance as structural elements of modern capitalism – has come to replace, in a sense, the problem of biopolitical crisis.

This particular practice could only be effective in playing for time. In other words, for the political government to strengthen the public health system in order to deal with the coronavirus pandemic. In practice, this would mean a transfer of resources to the public health system (the construction of ICUs, the direct supply of medical and pharmaceutical material, etc.). The specific political evolution could, of course, mean a shift of the general political-economic model from neoliberalism to an unconventional social liberalism, always in the context of the dominant relations of production. But this would also mean accepting/understanding the importance of biopolitical practices in ensuring the health of the population and by extension the 'smooth' reproduction of the dominant economic relations as a whole.[16] Instead, Greece's conservative political government preferred a policy that transferred the problem of the biopolitical crisis to the area of individual responsibilities. In so doing, this transference, in fact, adopted an anti-biopolitical[17] approach for the entire response to the pandemic crisis, to the point where one could say that the biopolitical management of the pandemic crisis turned into 'death politics'.[18] These repressive policies, which even included incarceration, were continually reproduced.[19]

This whole process created a negative relationship between biopolitical processes and the intensity of repressive practices. As the level of biopolitics decreased, through the neoliberal choices of the government, the intensity of the violence exercised by the state's repressive mechanisms grew. In fact, the intensity of violence in policing the pandemic was observed across Europe.[20] This increase in the intensity of repressive mechanisms was fuelled both by relations of externality on the part of political power by increasing the intensity of repression, with the pretext of maintaining the restrictive options (lockdown), and by relations of internality, that is, through the operation of the state machine as a guardian of the dominant relations, over and above the political framework of bourgeois democracy and the 'rule of law'.

There is, of course, a particular question motivating this inquiry. It involves the analysis of the dominant relations resulting from the operation of the repressive state mechanisms and its intensity, but also from the way the biopolitical process is analysed, at least in the present juncture. In terms of the latter, the analysis of the restrictive policies of political power is of particular interest. It is crucial that this analysis is situated in the context of the materiality of power relations within a materialist approach largely drawing on Marxian theoretical tools. In other words, the lockdown must be seen primarily as the result of the absence of biopolitical practices at a certain level of development of bourgeois democracy itself, but also as a result of the action of political power, which leads not just to the cancelling of the biopolitical process – which we define as anti-biopolitical practices – but also to the transference of its function to the realm of individual responsibility. It would be a major theoretical error to consider the police-democratic and restrictive framework of the pandemic crisis as a pure assertion of the state's sovereignty. For this would make it impossible, at this level of analysis, to understand the relational aspect of power. But still more crucially, it would be impossible to understand the state's positive role in producing the mechanisms and functions of power – even if the latter act like a machine with internal relations of its own, in parallel with relations of externality, condensing the class balance of power of the specific conjuncture.[21] Thus it is clear that the anti-biopolitical framework, as a neoliberal political choice, cannot work outside of the violent use of the state machine. In this condition, the state – and this is a crucial point – may appear as an authoritarian/repressive state, with characteristics that, in some cases, not only depart from the framework of a typical bourgeois democracy, but appropriate something of the image of a totalitarian regime.[22]

In conclusion

In sum, what needs to be observed is that as the intensity of the use of the state's repressive mechanisms increases, its biopolitical practices (mainly through the so-called 'social state' and its effects on public health, education, etc.) decrease. But, as we have seen, this is not a natural evolution, as if the deterministic consequence of a natural equation. Rather, it is the result of political choices and practices involving the interaction of political power and the repressive mechanisms of the state.

This perspective sheds light on the unique nature of the state's repressive mechanisms, which becomes especially evident when we focus on its actual operations, taking into account both the partial autonomy they exhibit in any given moment and the instrumental use we see in their external interaction with political power within a fluid field of class relations. Here we see fluctuations in the intensity of deployed violence. Thus this function of repressive mechanisms substitutes for biopolitical practices that historically appeared mainly through state welfare policies, ultimately transforming biopolitics and by extension social care (protecting the population from pandemics) into repression. As we have pointed out, in the Greek case but not only, this process is particularly evident. We have tried to highlight the relationship between political power and the state's repressive mechanisms, but also how this relationship is inverted to become an essentially negative relationship between state repression and the biopolitical process.

Finally, in highlighting the above relationship, we attempted to understand not only the power relations but also how they manifest themselves in the context of the class struggle, with the operation of the repressive state mechanisms, in the current circumstances. The latter is particularly crucial in order to understand – beyond the present conjuncture – the issue of the state, political power, and political practices, mainly and above all in a materialist rather than idealistic analytical framework.

NOTES

1   Michel Foucault, *The History of Sexuality: 1: The Will to Knowledge,* London: Penguin, 2019.

2   Foucault, *The History of Sexuality*; Pierre Macherey, *Le sujet des normes*, Paris: Éditions Amsterdam, 2014.

3   Foucault, *The History of Sexuality*; Kyrkos Doxiades, *O Foucault tis philosophías kai tis Aristerás*, Athens: Nísos, 2015.

4   Doxiades, *O Foucault tis philosophías kai tis Aristerás.*

5   Michel Foucault, Colin Gordon, and Paul Patton, 'Considerations on Marxism, Phenomenology and Power. Interview with Michel Foucault', *Foucault Studies* 14 (September 2012): 98–114.

6   Pierre Macherey, *Le sujet des normes.*

7   Kyrkos Doxiádis, *Neophilelefiherismós kai Neoteriki Exousía: Kapitalismós, Viopolitiki, Akrodexiá*, Athens: Nísos, 2021.

8   Doxiádis, *Neophilelefiherismós*

9   Nicos Poulantzas, 'I simeriní metaskhimatismí tou krátous. I politikí krísi kai i krísi tou krátous', in *I krísi tou Krátous*, Athens: Papazísis, 1990, pp. 19-55; see also his *State, Power, Socialism*, London: Verso Books, 2000.

10   Karl Marx, *The Civil War in France*, Karl Marx and Frederick Engels, *Collected Works*, vol. 22, New York, International, 1986,

11   Michel Foucault, *Για την εξουσία και την ταξική πάλη, Αθήνα: Εκτός Γραμμής*, 2016.

12   *Νίκος Πουλαντζάς, 'Οι σημερινοί μετασχηματισμοί του κράτους. Η πολιτική κρίση και η κρίση του κράτους'*, in Νίκος Πουλαντζάς (ed.), *Η κρίση του Κράτους, Αθήνα: Παπαζήσης*, 1990, pp.19-55; Nicos Poulantzas, *State, Power, Socialism*, London: Verso, 2000.

13   Louis Althusser, *Σημείωση σχετικά με τους Ιδεολογικούς Μηχανισμούς του κράτους (ΙΜΚ)', Θέσεις, τ.* 21 (1987): 37-49.

14   Nikos Poulantzas, 'The Crisis of the Parties', *Situations*, IX, 1–2 (1979): 31-35.

15   Doxiádis, *Neophilelefiherismós.*

16   Doxiádis, *Neophilelefiherismós.*

17   The reduction of ongoing expenditures on health in the midst of the pandemic crisis is seen in the 2021 and 2022 state budgets. See <https://www.minfin.gr/web/guest/proupologismos/-/asset_publisher/qmvb5pyzdGAQ/content/kratikos-proupologismos-2021> and <https://www.minfin.gr/web/guest/- /kratikos-proupologismos-2022>.

18   The term 'death politics' may sound melodramatic; however, the report by Professor Thodoris Lytras on the deaths of intubated patients outside the ICU, brings home

the magnitude of the tragedy and the responsibilities of political power for it. See
<https://www.medrxiv.org/content/10.1101 /2022.09.25.22280326v1>.

19   Nikolaos K. Kouloúris, 'Asti(a)nomía', Institoúto Éna, 2021; Giorgios Papanikoláou, ,
'I astinómefsi tis pandimías kai i epómeni méra', Institoúto Éna, 2021.

20   Diethnís Amnistía, 'Astinomévontas tin pandimía: Paravásis anthropínon dikaiomáton
katá tin epivolí ton métron yia ton koronoïó stin Evrópi', *Diethnís Amnistía* 2020.

21   Poulantzas, *State, Power, Socialism.*

22   Paul Breines, 'Introduction to Horkheimer's "The Authoritarian State"', *Telos*
15 (1973): 2

Who Cares? Neoliberalism, Informal Labour, and Life-Making

Ankica Čakardić

Neoliberal abolition of society and the role of reproduction

Doubtless one of the more brilliantly formulated principles of neoliberalism is that found in Margaret Thatcher's iconic statement: 'There is no such thing [as society]! There are individual men and women and there are families [...].'[1] Referencing Friedrich Hayek's idea that 'society' is simply a 'spontaneous order' which should promote entrepreneurialism and personal responsibility,[2] Thatcher, almost programmatically, signals that every form of social solidarity or of the state's social roles should be abolished in favour of individualism, private initiative, and conservative family values. In this same interview, she goes on to say that 'our lives will depend upon how much each of us is prepared to take responsibility for ourselves' – thus encapsulating a neoliberal understanding of self-care and care for others as private, personal responsibilities.

Given the necessarily limited scope of this article, it would be impossible to comprehensively work through all the problems in Thatcher's canard about the sanctity of private initiative or the neoliberal conception of individual responsibility. But we will try to make one Marxist feminist intervention into the phenomenon of informal labour and life-making, as seen through a social reproduction lens. In order to approach these issues in a more coherent manner, we will structure our line of argument in two parts. After a few necessary theoretical and methodological notes on neoliberalism and social reproduction theory, in the second part we will elaborate the problem of informal labour and link it to the recent crisis of care work. We assert that this 'care crisis' arises from the neoliberal need for a reconfiguration of reproduction, deepened by the reassignment of care responsibilities from the welfare state to personal initiative and charity. 'The point is', as Emma Dowling has critically emphasised, 'that helping others must be voluntary and informed by an ethics of charity or other forms of moral obligation, such as those conferred by kinship. What it must not be is public – that is, organised, managed and funded collectively …'[3]

Our suggested thematic inclination may evoke the concept of the ideological formalisation of family as a fundamentally 'anti-social unit', as formulated by Michèle Barrett and Mary McIntosh at the height of Thatcherite politics.[4] As for context and method, we start from the basis that economic liberalism, grounded in individualist premises, represents an ideological expression of capitalism,[5] and that family, as a system for governing social reproduction within households, depends not only upon naturalisation, but also upon individuation.[6] Equally, we consider the phenomenon of 'reprivatisation' to be of key importance for analysing the issue of informal labour, since it explains the neoliberal processes of reducing and abolishing social-welfare services.[7]

When we talk about neoliberalism or neoliberal political economy, we are usually referring to the financialised, predatory, and technocratic form of capitalism seen in the last forty years, which strives to sweep away the social obligations of the state and democratic administrative procedures.[8] It advocates a free and non-regulated market, while also focusing on redefining the shape and roles of the state.[9] Wendy Brown treats neoliberalism in a Foucauldian way, that is, as a governing rationality through which everything is 'economised' in a very specific way: 'human beings become market actors and nothing but, every field of activity is seen as a market, and every entity (whether public or private, whether person, business, or state) is governed as a firm.'[10] While analysing the relationship between neoliberalism and social reproduction, we should take into account the reality that it simultaneously affects three spheres: the macro (world market and world policies), the meso (institutions: state, market, family) and the micro (individual).[11] It also relies on 'free choice ideology', which suggests that everything is possible with sufficient individual effort and personal entrepreneurial engagement.[12] Neoliberalism sees the individual as a locus of endless possibilities for actualising the entrepreneurial spirit and as a multi-use bundle of human capital. It counts on the interests of the individual always changing in accordance with the market and its values. This is the foundation of entrepreneurial individualism and a position in which the individual self is supposedly always attuned to personal metamorphoses, improvement, and innovation. Analysing Thatcher's economic reforms in Great Britain, David Harvey concludes that the process of neoliberalisation necessitates a great deal of 'creative destruction', not only in terms of previously built institutional frameworks and powers, but also in terms of the division of labour, social relations, care work, forms of living, and everyday reproductive activities.[13]

However, even if Thatcherite individualism, understood as a freedom of personal choice, may seem appealing on the surface, individuals in and of themselves cannot replace society. On the categorical level, an individual is a mere abstraction without flesh and blood, a metaphysical idea that owes its real form to specific political and legal relations of power. To use more Hegelian terms, the abstract manifestation of the individual actualises its subjectivity only through self-consciousness, but its concrete manifestation is shaped by its relations to others, which result in the individual's consciousness of its own freedom within the social order. Thus, society cannot exist without some form of relation – political, ideological, productive, sexual – between at least two individual subjects.

Contemporary sociality is based on social relations inherent to a particular mode of production, within which people are allocated certain roles and positions according to their class. In the capitalist mode of production, social relations are necessarily based on exploitation and conflict-ridden. For the class relations thus established to survive in a bourgeois society, they, as well as the productive capacities they utilise, must be reproduced. One of the key units that ensures the reproduction of social relations and productive forces within capitalism – besides a series of public services that are being systematically suffocated in neoliberalism – is family. This somewhat unromantic fact about family, which was already alluded to by Friedrich Engels,[14] as well as multiple subsequent traditions of social reproduction theory,[15] reveals the specific role allocated to the family, namely that of a focal point for social reproduction, which absorbs the problems that arise and accumulate in society. But what exactly are we referring to when we talk about social reproduction theory? Why is it a necessary tool for an analysis of informal labour within neoliberalism?

Social Reproduction Theory (SRT) is all about life-making. Its core tenet is the fact that the accumulation of surplus value is not possible without informal and unpaid labour that generates healthy labour power, either through maintenance of direct producers, or by taking care of non-labouring members of the subordinate classes (children, the elderly and the unemployed), or through generational renewal of workers and their lives (birth taken for granted as the biological reproduction of new labour force).[16] In recent times, SRT has been used as a characteristic Marxist-feminist tool, a theoretical and critical framework, and a political strategy for tackling the relationship between oppression and exploitation, as well as waged and unwaged labour. It departs from Marx's understanding of reproduction within the capitalist mode of production[17] but expands upon Marx's theoretical outlines and redirects the analysis from the logic of capital toward labour power.[18] It poses the question already formulated by Tithi Bhattacharya: 'If workers' labor produces all the wealth in society, who then produces the worker?'[19] Thus, SRT locates the 'hidden' processes that enable production, and it seeks to investigate the existential conditions of the worker and analyses the phenomena of life-making and produced gender reality. Nancy Fraser sums up this issue:

> Non-waged social-reproductive activity is necessary to the existence of waged work, the accumulation of surplus value and the functioning of capitalism as such. None of those things could exist in the absence of housework, child-rearing, schooling, affective care and a host of other activities which serve to produce new generations of workers and replenish existing ones, as well as to maintain social bonds and shared understandings. Social reproduction is an indispensable background condition for the possibility of economic production in a capitalist society.[20]

In addition, SRT sharpens the analytical tools we use to make existing theories of labour more thorough, to better understand the historical phenomenon of the gendered and racial division of labour, and to grasp the issue of class and class struggle more precisely. Capitalist societies have separated the social reproduction of labour from that of economic production and have 'remunerated "reproductive" activities in the coin of "love" and "virtue", while compensating "productive labour" in that of money'.[21] Since capital needs socially reproductive labour to produce and reproduce the labour force it is determined to secure the appropriate amount of this very valuable resource at the lowest possible cost. Neoliberalism does this by informally assigning the responsibility for social reproduction to women, families and communities. In so doing, it degrades reproduction, shrunken to the forms most suitable for the maximisation of capitalist profit.

As noted by the proponents of the Wages for Housework Campaign in the 1970s, family is still one of the most fundamental units of social reproduction and life-making, of heterosexual religion and private property, which simultaneously produces coercion and violence to further strengthen its basic economic role.[22] By the same token, it secures the unpaid care work for family members, domestic labour, and what Silvia Federici has called 'a labour of love'.[23] Despite the fact that family represents an 'ideological mystification and a political project',[24] that not all families are the same, that the idea of men as 'providers' is undergoing a serious crisis, and that not all families are even heterosexual, the legal and political project of 'familialisation' has never been stronger. This is not to be ascribed simply to religion or traditionalist conservatism, but to 'the morals of the market', as expressed by Jessica Whyte. What she means with this concept is a radical re-rolling back of the social, along with the neoliberal practice of outsourcing the burden of social responsibility to families.[25] It is precisely in this context that we should examine the Thatcherite canard about the primacy of family and individualism over society, and about the abolition of social responsibility.

The morals of the market presuppose the radical abolition of social roles of the state, reassigning them to the family as supposedly the only unit accountable for the subsistence of its members. Therefore, its moral role is to secure a shelter, a safe space, an isolated 'anti-social' island that is supposed to protect us from all social crises and economic insecurity. Exactly in this line of argument, Richard Seymour notes:

> When society is either hostile or indifferent, when public provision is etiolated, when institutions of solidarity are shrivelled and demoralised, the anti-social family can provide a range of services: free transport, help with spiralling debt, financial support against unemployment, care in the event of illness, or shelter against racism.[26]

The family thus becomes a shelter, expected to put in immeasurable effort, and to do it all out of love, because this is understood as a naturally given and necessary moral sacrifice. Neoliberalism literally turns the home into a physical shelter that allows the worker to rest before the next day's labour, a place that gives them a roof above their head and a bed to rest when rest is needed.[27] Rather than having the state and employers ensure socially conscious and sustainable housing, widely available and free public transport, public healthcare and education, as well as community services and decent wages and pensions, the morals of the market take on the role of a mediator between the state and the family and charge the family with all the duties of the state. This means making the family responsible for all the consequences of social crises, poor living conditions, and poverty.

However, the socially reproductive capacities of the family are not infinite. We are continually witnessing not only economic crises, but reproductive crises as well, systemic exploitations of individual and collective abilities for regeneration of people and relations between them, as well as a systemic 'care crisis'. 'In that case,' writes Fraser, 'the logic of economic production overrides that of social reproduction, destabilizing the very processes on which capital depends – compromising the social capacities, both domestic and public, that are needed to sustain accumulation over the long term.'[28] Furthermore, it appears that the ongoing global pandemic brutally intensified the care crisis and underscored the fact that the economy of so-called 'essential work' disproportionately exploits women,[29] especially women of colour,[30] and makes life intolerable and unhealthy for millions of people.[31]

Informal labour and 'care crisis'

The last report of the European parliamentarian (MEP) Katalin Cseh, published on 15 February 2022 with 524 favourable votes, 33 in opposition, and 143 abstentions, explored the crisis that urban areas face in post-pandemic times. It determined that 80% of care work for family members in the European Union is done informally.[32] Informal care workers are people providing continuous care for a partner, relative or friend who needs assistance with personal care and everyday tasks.[33] In other words, they are not paid professional caregivers or medical nurses; rather, here is a 'welfare mix' resonant of the 1990s.[34] This 'mix' pertains to the neoliberal idea of 'public-private partnership', which demands that families and 'volunteers' take care of others 'out of love', and/or on religious or moral grounds, and do so in their own free time and at their own expense.[35] Furthermore, the numbers of informal care workers are undoubtedly rising due to a combination of the increasing need for them and the neoliberal reconfiguration of reproduction.

The rise in the number of informal care workers has been more pronounced since the 2008 crisis, when the toxic cocktail of austerity policies and recession significantly destabilised the material and social rights of workers and the unemployed, and especially those of the elderly, children and chronically ill. To illustrate the extent of the global need for care work, we can draw on a couple of recent figures. In 2015 there were an estimated 2.1 billion people worldwide in need of care, predominantly children and the elderly.[36] By 2030, as reported by the International Labour Organisation, the total number is expected to reach 2.3 billion.[37] Another consequence of the increasing erosion of the state's social responsibilities and the related commodification of reproductive labour is the growing proportion of the world's population that cannot access care.[38]

However, the crisis of reproduction is not only reflected in the decreasing availability of care work for those who require it on an everyday basis; in parallel to this, the number of the world's population unable to satisfy basic need is growing across societies. On the one hand, the global north – after abolishing and commodifying medical, palliative and social services, and thereby mostly exploiting female migrant labour[39] – is becoming increasingly reliant on informal and voluntary care work,[40] which includes religious volunteers as well.[41] On the other hand, developing countries are faced with the disastrous situation in which a basic lack of healthcare infrastructure, food security, and safe housing daily destabilise social reproduction. Hence, capitalism creates class polarisation and a crisis of reproduction not only within societies, but also across societies, as was pointed out by Marxist studies of imperialism already over a century ago.[42]

Since we have raised the problem of the neoliberal reshaping of the social roles of the state – as well as the geopolitical fact that informal labour and life-making become increasingly complicated due to imperialist centre-periphery dynamics – we should not forget the already implied third factor of the care crisis – gender. The previously referenced report by Katalin Cseh notes that informal and unpaid labour in the EU is primarily performed by women. In fact, as much as 75% of its burden is carried by the female 'informal caregivers'. The situation in other parts of the world is even more dire: women and girls do more than 75% of unpaid care work in the world, they perform most chores in 89% of households, and 42% of women cannot secure paid jobs because they are busy with caregiving.[43]

As is common in neoliberal discourse, which manipulatively reduces real-life difficulties and political-economic struggles to 'personal challenges', in her report Cseh proposes financial measures and policies supposed to address the growing predicaments of female care work. Her suggestions may be read as drop-in-the-ocean remedies of long-term structural and ideological problems which formalise and strengthen the idea of the nuclear family as a shelter and assign women the role of informal care workers and life-makers responsible for all the urgent emotional, palliative, social, and financial issues of their family members. Cseh concludes that it is necessary to ensure additional financial support and part-time employment contracts to women that are staying at home to take care of their loved ones.[44] The policies suggested by Cseh correspond entirely to those of neoliberal regimes, which, according to Fraser, promote state and corporate disinvestment from social welfare and offload care work onto families and communities, all the while diminishing their capacity to perform it.[45] The unequal distribution of unpaid care work between women and men represents an infringement of women's rights and jeopardises their economic empowerment.[46] Unpaid care and domestic labour make a substantial contribution to countries' economies, and the total value of unpaid care and domestic labour is estimated at between 10% and 39% of gross domestic product.[47] This means that it contributes more to the state economy than sectors like manufacturing, commerce, or transportation.[48]

After considering these data, we should not be overly surprised to realise one of the logical consequences of such a state of affairs – namely that, during the period of the pandemic and remote working, the gender gap related to care work and informal labour widened tremendously. Indeed, it widened at the expense of women, and took gender equality a step back.[49] The pandemic delivered a series of blows to many women working from home, because they suddenly had to face a broader scope of work-related responsibilities. Moreover, the lines between work and free time were blurred, especially when it came to care of children and their remote schooling.[50] The OECD's survey *Risks that Matter* presents cross-national evidence indicating that, when schools and childcare facilities shut down during the pandemic, mothers took on the burden of additional unpaid care work and correspondingly experienced labour market penalties and stress.[51] It is in reference to this phenomenon that the recession accompanying the Covid-19 pandemic has frequently been labelled a 'shecession', implying a disproportionately negative effect it had on women. Alessandra Mezzadri notes that Covid-19 has reorganised world inequalities, revealed the centrality of social relations and confirmed the key reproductive role that informal – unpaid or poorly paid – labour relations may play in sustaining life during times of emergency.[52]

In the past two years of the pandemic, female workers have felt increasingly exhausted at home. No less than 46% have reported feeling burnt out and not being able to unwind at home.[53] The Deloitte report indicates that more than half of women are more stressed nowadays than they were the previous year (in 2021), and those who work flexible hours report poorer mental health. An example of this issue is the problems encountered by female scientists and teachers.[54] When working from home, they suffer typical neoliberal neuralgias, like having less time for research, writing and lecturing, constantly being interrupted while attempting to focus on delicate scientific work, and having disrupted, spontaneous, and flexible working weeks.

Feminists are alarmed every time women are pushed back into the domestic sphere, because they see the ideology of 'familialisation' as jeopardizing women's social and economic status. And feminists are rightfully outraged, because what might be the long-term consequence of the collective remote work? Firstly, flexible employment contracts and formal duties related to work will prompt women to spend more time at home and perform routine domestic labour. They will do the work they are paid for from their kitchens, spend an unknown number of hours each day replying to e-mails, and do all this under all manner of unforeseeable time dynamics. At the same time, they will have to take care of the children, elderly and chronically ill, and they will still have to do most of the unpaid reproductive labour like cooking, cleaning, shopping, ironing, washing the dishes, and similar features. And as both history and experience have mercilessly demonstrated, where women's world is being confined to household and care work, they are inevitably becoming more dependent on their husbands and partners. These are the exact conditions in which the rate of male violence against women has risen. The pandemic has revealed this problem and, indeed, aggravated it. Harassment and microaggressions against women have increased in recent years: 59% of women have experienced at least one instance of non-inclusive behaviour in the past year, compared with 52% in 2021.[55] Bhattacharya stresses: 'The real material need for food and shelter combined with the highly ideological expectation that women are responsible for meeting that need within the home, provide the conditions of possibility of gendered violence'.[56]

By simultaneously considering various issues generated by the problem of informal labour, the care crisis and life-making, including the neoliberal role of family as a 'shelter', instead of drawing a conclusion, we should rather pose a very alarming question: are there any progressive responses to the neoliberal abolition of the social roles of the state, as well as to the flourishing care crisis? The shortest possible answer would be the socialisation of reproductive labour. This Marxist-feminist, substantially anti-capitalist demand proposes the unification of various struggles from the bottom up. It encompasses the struggles for sustainable future, public and affordable healthcare, kindergartens, and nursing homes, for safe and socially conscious housing, for food security, for women's labour and reproductive rights, for safety at work, reduction of working time, and for campaigns to unionise service sector workers in for-profit nursing homes, hospitals, and child-care centres. As Fraser puts it:

> Taken together, these claims are tantamount to the demand for a massive re-organization of the relation between production and reproduction: for social arrangements that could enable people of every class, gender, sexuality and colour to combine social-reproductive activities with safe, interesting and well-remunerated work.[57]

If we took a step further and advocated a radical abolition of the Thatcherite idea of family, which is encoded in the morals of the market, where would that take us? Definitely not in the direction of abolishing close and intimate relationships, negating the importance of care for vulnerable family members, or destroying the concept of mutual life altogether. In fact, it would do the exact opposite. The idea of abolishing the nuclear family calls for expanding, socializing, and denaturalising current forms of life-making, care work, and reproduction.[58] If we define family as a household unit that relies on kinship and in which women bare the moral responsibility for care and reproductive labour that could be socialised, then we should strive to abolish such a nuclear family, expand the realm of free choice, and remove coercion from familial co-dependence. In so doing, we can explore new and different forms of living that may lead to greater emotional satisfaction and more sustainable alternatives to the classical family and its morals of the market. The abolition of the nuclear family in neoliberalism is a creative, collective process of building new forms of survival every day. As a simple alternative to family reform, the abolitionist project aims, in the words of Barrett and Mary McIntosh, to 'transform not the family – but the society that needs it'.[59]

NOTES

1   Margaret Thatcher, 'Interview for *Woman's Own* ("No Such Thing as Society")'. *Margaret Thatcher Foundation: Interviews and Other Statements*, 1987, available at: https://www.margaretthatcher.org/document/106689. Accessed 30 July 2022.

2   Friedrich Hayek 'Justice and Individual Rights: Appendix to Chapter Nine', in *Law, Legislation and Liberty: A New Statement of the Liberal Principles of Justice and Political Economy, 2: The Mirage of Social Justice*, London: Routledge, 1998, pp. 101–102.

3   Emma Dowling, *The Care Crisis. What Caused It and How Can We End It?* London: Verso, 2021, p. 9.

4   Michèle Barrett and Mary McIntosh, *The Anti-Social Family*. London: Verso, 2015 [1982].

5   Ishay Landa, *The Apprentice's Sorcerer. Liberal Tradition and Fascism*. Chicago: Haymarket Books, 2012, p. 19; Domenico Losurdo, *Liberalism. A Counter History*. London: Verso, 2011 [2006].

6   Kathi Weeks, *Abolition of the family: the most infamous feminist proposal. Feminist Theory*, online edition, 2021. Available at: https://journals.sagepub.com/doi/10.1177/14647001211015841. Accessed 31 August 2022.

7   Nancy Fraser, *Fortunes of Feminism. From State-Managed Capitalism to Neoliberal Crisis*. London: Verso, 2013, p. 68.

8   Here, it is worth remembering that, in contrast to neoliberal political economy, classical neoliberalism comprises doctrines and philosophies arising in the 1930s and 1940s among European liberal economists who attempted to revive and restore the central ideas of classical liberalism. In 1947 the Mont Pèlerin Society was founded in Switzerland and gathered liberal intellectuals from a dozen countries, most notably Walter Eucken, Friedrich A. von Hayek, Milton Friedman, Wilhelm Ropke, Ludwig von Mises, Karl Popper (see Philip Mirowski and Dieter Plehwe (eds), *The Road from Mont Pèlerin: The making of the neoliberal thought collective*, Cambridge, MA: Harvard University Press, 2009).

9   Philip Mirowski, *Never Let a Serious Crisis Go to Waste: How Neoliberalism Survived the Financial Meltdown*, London: Verso, 2013, p. 436.

10   Wendy Brown, 'What Exactly Is Neoliberalism?', interview conducted by Timothy
      Shenk, *Dissent*, 2015, <https://www.dissentmagazine.org/blog/booked-3-what-
      exactly-is-neoliberalism-wendy-brown-undoing-the-demos>.

11   Isabella Bakker and Stephen Gill, 'New Constitutionalism and the Social
      Reproduction of Caring Institutions', *Theoretical Medicine and Bioethics* 27,1 (2006), pp.
      35–57.

12   Ankica Čakardić, 'Down the Neoliberal Path: The Rise of Free Choice Feminism',
      AM Journal of Art and Media Studies 14 (2017): pp. 33–44.

13   David Harvey, *A Brief History of Neoliberalism*, Oxford: Oxford University Press, 2015,
      p. 3.

14   Friedrich Engels, *The Origin of the Family, Private Property and the State*. London:
      Penguin Classics, 2010 [1884].

15   Feminist approaches to the issue of social reproduction vary, and it is impossible to
      claim that there is one comprehensive theory. The discussions on domestic labour
      and wages for housework, articulated in the 1970s, represent only one approach to
      the problem of social reproduction. Starting with Margaret Benston, 'The Political
      Economy of Women's Liberation', *Monthly Review* 21,4 (September 1969), pp. 13–27,
      the text 'L'ennemi principal' by Christine Delphy, translated as 'The Main Enemy',
      Feminist Issues, Summer 1980: 23–40, and finally 'Donne e sovversione sociale' by
      Mariarosa Dalla Costa from 1971 (Mariarosa Dalla Costa and Selma James, *The Power
      of Women and the Subversion of the Community*. Bristol: Falling Wall Press, 1975) there
      began a period of more systematic and thorough feminist research into the theory
      of social reproduction, which became even more fruitful in the recent versions of
      unitary theory. See, on this, Lise Vogel, *Marxism and the Oppression of Women: Toward
      a Unitary Theory*. Chicago: Haymarket Books, 2013 [1983]; Cinzia Arruzza, *Dangerous
      Liaisons: The Marriages and Divorces of Marxism and Feminism*, Pontypool: Merlin
      Press, 2013; Tithi Bhattacharya (ed.) *Social Reproduction Theory: Remapping Class,
      Recentering Oppression*, London: Pluto Press, 2017; Martha E. Gimenez, *Marx, Women,
      and Capitalist Social Reproduction: Marxist Feminist Essays*. Leiden: Brill, 2018; Susan
      Ferguson, *Women and Work: Feminism, Labour and Social Reproduction*, London: Pluto
      Press, 2020; Aaron Jaffe, *Social Reproduction Theory and the Socialist Horizon: Work,
      Power and Political Strategy*, London: Pluto Press, 2020. In parallel to this, the queer
      theory of social reproduction has been honed by the respective scholars: Jules Joanne
      Gleeson, 'An Aviary of Queer Social Reproduction', *Hypocrite Reader*, 94, February
      2019; Noah Zazanis, 'Social Reproduction and Social Cognition: Theorizing (Trans)
      gender Identity Development in Community Context', in *Transgender Marxism*, edited
      by Jules Joanne Gleeson and Elle O'Rourke, London: Pluto Press, 2021, pp. 33–47;
      Nat Rana, 'A Queer Marxist Transfeminism: Queer and Trans Social Reproduction',
      in Gleeson and O'Rourke, pp. 85–116; Kate Doyle Griffiths, 'Queer Workerism
      Against Work: Strategising Transgender Labourers, Social Reproduction & Class
      Formation' in Gleeson and O'Rourke, pp. 132–56. However, it is important to note
      that the idea of social reproduction and wages for housework had been proposed well
      beforehand, most importantly in the struggles of the welfare rights movement, led
      mainly by welfare mothers (most of them African-American) in the 1960s United
      States and the 'unsupported mothers' in Britain (Louise Toupin, *Wages for Housework:
      A History of an International Feminist Movement, 1972–77*, London: Pluto Press and
      UBC Press, 2018, p. 41). Some of these ideas were first articulated in Claudia Jones's

seminal 1949 essay, 'To End the Neglect of the Problems of the Negro Woman', where she coined the idea of the triple oppression of working-class black women (*Political Affairs*, June 1949). See also my thesis on 'early social reproduction theory' in which I detect the initial premises of social reproduction theory already present in the texts and speeches of socialists and feminists such as Clara Zetkin, Rosa Luxemburg, Nadezhda Krupskaya, Alexandra Kollontai, and Eleanor Marx (Ankica Čakardić, 'Marx and Social Reproduction Theory: Three Different Historical Strands', in *Marxist-Feminist Theories and Struggles Today*, edited by Khayaat Fakier, Diana Mulinari and Nora Räthzel, London: Zed Books, 2020, pp. 105–24, see pp. 110–13).

16   Vogel, *Marxism and the Oppression of Women*, p. 150.

17   Čakardić, 'Marx and Social Reproduction Theory'.

18   Jaffe, *Social Reproduction Theory and the Socialist Horizon*, pp. 6–7.

19   Bhattacharya (ed.) *Social Reproduction Theory*, p. 1.

20   Nancy Fraser, 'Contradictions of Capital and Care'. *New Left Review* 100 (Jul/Aug 2016). Available at: https://newleftreview.org/issues/ii100/articles/nancy-fraser-contradictions-of-capital-and-care. Accessed 6 September 2022.

21   Fraser, 'Contradictions of Capital and Care'.

22   Giovanna Franca Dalla Costa *The Work of Love: Unpaid Housework, Poverty and Sexual Violence at the Dawn of the 21st Century*, Brooklyn: Autonomedia, 2008 [1978].

23   Silvia Federici, 'Wages against Housework', in *Revolution at Point Zero: Housework, Reproduction, and Feminist Struggle*, Brooklyn, NY: Autonomedia, 2012 [1975].

24   Richard Seymour, 'Abolition: Notes on a Normie Shitstorm', *Salvage*, <https://salvage.zone/abolition-notes-on-a-normie-shitstorm/>.

25   Jessica Whyte, *The Morals of the Market. Human Rights and the Rise of Neoliberalism*, London: Verso, 2019.

26   Seymour, 'Abolition: Notes on a Normie Shitstorm'.

27   Tithi Bhattacharya, 'Explaining gender violence in the neoliberal era', *International Socialist Review* 91 (2013–14), <https://isreview.org/issue/91/explaining-gender-violence-neoliberal-era/>.

28   Fraser, 'Contradictions of Capital and Care'.

29   Alessandra Mezzadri, 'Social Reproduction and Pandemic Neoliberalism: Planetary Crises of Life, Work and Death', *Organization* 29,3, (2022): 379–400.

30   Catherine Powell, 'The Color and Gender of COVID: Essential Workers, Not Disposable People', *Think Global Health*, 2020. <https://www.thinkglobalhealth.org/article/color-and-gender-covid-essential-workers-not-disposable-people>.

31   Jordan Kisner, 'The Lockdown Showed How the Economy Exploits Women', *PM Press Blog*, 2021, <https://blog.pmpress.org/2021/02/17/the-lockdown-showed-how-the-economy-exploits-women-she-already-knew/>.

32   Katalin Cseh, 'Report on the challenges for urban areas in the post-COVID-19 era', *European Parliament*, 2021, <https://www.europarl.europa.eu/doceo/document/A-9-2021-0352_EN.html>.

33   Dowling, *The Care Crisis*, p. 84.

34   Adalbert Evers and Helmut Wintersberger, *Shifts in the Welfare Mix: Their Impact on Work, Social Services and Welfare Policies*. Abingdon: Taylor and Francis, 1990.

35   Since the institution of family underwent numerous transformations with the neoliberalisation of society, over some decades the male-breadwinner model has been eroded (Gretchen Livingston, 'Fewer than half of U.S. kids today live in a

"traditional" family', *Pew Research Center*, <https://www.pewresearch.org/fact-tank/2014/12/22/less-than-half-of-u-s-kids-today-live-in-a-traditional-family/>; the role of the housewife has lost its importance (Dowling, *The Care* Crisis, p. 78) and it has been acknowledged that not all families are either nuclear or heterosexual (Seymour, 'Abolition: Notes on a Normie Shitstorm'). Neoliberalism introduced the 'welfare mix' as a creative innovation that relies on voluntary work. Dowling notes: 'The family may not be the only locale of unpaid reproductive labour, but the requirement of capitalism to draw on unpaid reproductive labour in different ways remains' (*The Care Crisis*, p. 78). As cuts in services reinvigorate the need for care, neighbourhoods, communities, NGOs, churches, and charities pick up voluntary care work either in the form of private initiatives or institutions.

36   Dowling, *The Care Crisis*, p. 4.

37   International Labour Organisation, *Care Work and Care Jobs for the Future of Decent Work*, Geneva: ILO, 2018, p. xxix.

38   Lourdes Beneria, Günseli Berik, and Maria Floro, *Gender, Development and Globalisation: Economics as if all People Mattered*, London: Routledge, 2015.

39   Eleonore Kofman and Parvati Raghuram, *Gendered Migrations and Global Social Reproduction*. London: Palgrave Macmillan, 2015; Salazar Parreñas, *Servants of Globalization: Migration and Domestic Work*, Stanford: Stanford University Press, 2015; Sara Farris, *In the Name of Women's Rights: The Rise of Femonationalism*, Durham, NC: Duke University Press, 2017, pp. 119–31.

40   Veerle Miranda, 'Cooking, Caring and Volunteering: Unpaid Work Around the World', *OECD Social, Employment and Migration Working Papers*, No. 116, OECD Publishing, 2011, <https://www.oecd.org/berlin/47258230.pdf>.

41   Andrea Muehlebach, 'The Catholicization of Neoliberalism: On Love and Welfare in Lombardy, Italy', *American Anthropologist* 115,3 (2013): 452–465; Antonio Maria Pusceddu, 'The Moral Economy of Charity: Advice and Redistribution in Italian Caritas Welfare Bureaucracy, *Ethnos* 87,1 (2022) 168–87; Piotr Krakowiak, Katarzyna Skrzypińska, Iwona Damps-Konstańska, and Ewa Jassem, 'Walls and Barriers. Polish Achievements and the Challenges of Transformation: Building a Hospice Movement in Poland', *Journal of Pain and Symptom Management* 52:4, October 2016, pp. 600–4; John Wilson and Thomas Janoski, 'The Contribution of Religion to Volunteer Work', *Sociology of Religion* 56,2 (Summer 1995): 137–152.

42   Rosa Luxemburg, 'The Accumulation of Capital: A Contribution to the Economic Theory of Imperialism', in Peter Hudis and Paul Le Blanc (eds), *The Complete Works of Rosa Luxemburg. Volume II: Economic Writings 2*, translated by Nicholas Gray and George Shriver, London: Verso, 2015 [1913].

43   Leah Rodriguez, 'Unpaid Care Work: Everything You Need to Know'. *Global Citizen*, 2021, <https://www.globalcitizen.org/en/content/womens-unpaid-care-work-everything-to-know/>.

44   Clara Bauer-Babef, 'Unpaid, undervalued: Women shoulder three-quarters of the burden of EU caregiving', *Euractiv, 2022*. <https://www.euractiv.com/section/health-consumers/news/unpaid-undervalued-women-shoulder-three-quarters-of-the-burden-of-eu-caregiving/>.

45   Fraser, 'Contradictions of Capital and Care'.

46   United Nations, *Report of Sepulveda Carmona, M., the Special Rapporteur on Extreme Poverty and Human Rights: Unpaid Care Work and Women's Human Rights*, 2013, available at SSRN 2437791.

47   United Nations, *Commission on the Status of Women. Women's economic empowerment in the changing world of work. Report of the Secretary-General*, <https://www.un.org/ga/search/view_doc.asp?symbol=E/CN.6/2017/3, 2016>.

48   Rodriguez, 'Unpaid Care Work'.

49   Deloitte, *Understanding the pandemic's impact on working women*, 2020, <https://www2.deloitte.com/content/dam/Deloitte/global/Documents/About-Deloitte/gx-about-deloitte-understanding-the-pandemic-s-impact-on-working-women.pdf>.

50   OECD, *Caregiving in Crisis: Gender inequality in paid and unpaid work during COVID-19*, 2021, <https://www.oecd.org/coronavirus/policy-responses/caregiving-in-crisis-gender-inequality-in-paid-and-unpaid-work-during-covid-19-3555d164/>.

51   OECD, *Risks that matter 2020: The long reach of COVID-19*, 2020, <https://www.oecd.org/coronavirus/policy-responses/risks-that-matter-2020-the-long-reach-of-covid-19-44932654/>.

52   Alessandra Mezzadri, 'The Social Reproduction of Pandemic Surplus Populations and Global Development Narratives on Inequality and Informal Labour', *Development and Change*, <https://onlinelibrary.wiley.com/doi/full/10.1111/dech.12736?fbclid=IwAR02aJFev-8ZJ-menOWI6xd-yvUWQOLpC_TFSUohYM7WKUP7NkpsBklmSy4>.

53   Deloitte, *Women at Work 2022: A Global Outlook*, 2022, <https://www2.deloitte.com/content/dam/Deloitte/global/Documents/deloitte-women-at-work-2022-a-global-outlook.pdf>.

54   UNESCO, *Covid-19 pandemic disproportionately affecting women in science and engineering*, 2021, <https://en.unesco.org/news/covid-19-pandemic-disproportionately-affecting-women-science-and-engineering>.

55   Deloitte, *Women at Work 2022*.

56   Bhattacharya, 'Explaining gender violence in the neoliberal era'.

57   Fraser, 'Contradictions of Capital and Care'.

58   Sophie Lewis, *Full Surrogacy Now. Feminism Against Family*, London: Verso, 2019; Michelle Esther O'Brien, 'To abolish the family', *Endnotes #5: The Passions and The Interests*. October 2019, <https://endnotes.org.uk/articles/to-abolish-the-family.pdf>; Weeks, *Abolition of the Family*.

59   Weeks, *Abolition of the Family*.

The Extreme Right and the State: What Should the Left Do?

Steven Forti

'In order to fight it is necessary to know the enemy's forces deployed in the field and also the reserve forces camped in the rear,' wrote the Italian Communist leader Palmiro Togliatti. The evidence for this came in Togliatti's *Lectures on Fascism*, which he gave in 1935. Antonio Gramsci had been convinced of this since the early 1920s, as shown by his reflections published in *l'Ordine Nuovo* and *l'Unità* or, later, collected in his *Prison Notebooks*. In short, without knowing and studying a phenomenon, it is impossible to understand it and, consequently, to fight it.

One of the main existing debates on the new extreme right is the terminological one, which is directly connected to its relationship with interwar fascism. Both in academic publications and in the media we have read different and distant definitions for Donald Trump, Giorgia Meloni, Marine Le Pen, Viktor Orbán and Santiago Abascal: from radical and populist right to far right, extreme right, national populism, post-fascism, neo-fascism or even fascism. This is not, as it might seem, a trivial debate: to understand things properly, it is essential that we know what to call them.

My perception is that we face two major obstacles – the concepts of fascism and populism – which do not allow us to arrive at a satisfactory solution to this question. First, the new extreme right is something different from historical fascism. As Emilio Gentile explains, fascism was a political movement and an ideology that had a series of characteristics that we do not find in Trumpism, Fratelli d'Italia, Fidesz or the Rassemblement National: from the use of violence as a political tool to the desire to establish a totalitarian one-party regime, from the project of organising the masses into large organisations to its self-presentation as a palingenetic revolution aimed at radically transforming society and creating new men and women.[1] This does not mean that there are no elements of continuity between those experiences and the present ones: however, fascism was simply something else. Neo-fascist and neo-Nazi groups still exist today – think of CasaPound Italia or the Blood & Honour network – but, without underestimating the influence they can have, we can say that they are ultra-minoritarian.

In short, the new extreme right has stopped giving the Roman salute, shaving its head and tattooing swastikas on its arms: it now wears a jacket and a tie. It has made itself more presentable. Moreover, today the extreme right speaks the language of ordinary people, rejects the label of fascist or extremist, and accepts the democratic framework. What there has been, rather, is an *aggiornamento*, i.e. an updating, of fascist ideology that began at least between the 1960s and 1970s. One of the key figures is undoubtedly Alain de Benoist who, together with the French Nouvelle Droite group, has allowed a rethinking of neo-fascist political culture based on a re-reading of Antonio Gramsci. The extreme right decided to put aside the struggle for the conquest of political power and focus on the Gramscian war of position to gain cultural hegemony.

Second, the term populism is of little use in defining and understanding the new extreme right. Over the last two decades, rivers of ink have been spilled on this concept, which has become a kind of catch-all term for everything that does not fit in with traditional political ideologies. Perhaps the only consensus that has been arrived at is precisely the 'protean nature' of populism and its being 'an essentially controversial' and 'politically controversial' concept.[2] There are those who consider it an ideology, albeit a thin one that can be juxtaposed with others, such as nationalism or socialism, and those who consider it a rhetoric, a style, a language or a political strategy.[3] In the absence of a doctrinal corpus, I believe that this second interpretation is more accurate. Add to this the fact that we are living through a phase in which populism permeates everything. If Le Pen, Mélenchon and even Macron are populist, how useful is this concept in understanding politics today? Rather, it is the mark of the era in which we live and we would more properly speak, as Marc Lazar and Ilvio Diamanti pointed out, of *popolocrazia* ('populocracy').[4] In short, the extreme right uses the rhetorical and linguistic tools of populism, but populism in itself does not help us to define and understand it.

In defining the 'radical right', Cas Mudde has managed to overcome both of the aforementioned pitfalls.[5] However, his proposal is itself problematic. On the one hand, is it correct to define with the same adjective – radical –, as if there were a kind of symmetry, the formations of the new extreme right and those of the left such as Podemos, Syriza or La France Insoumise? Personally, I think this is a mistake: the radical left, in fact, criticises the existing liberal systems, focusing mainly on the neoliberal model and economic issues, and calls for their reform, but does not call into question the democratic gains and rights guaranteed by these systems. Rather, it calls for a broadening and deepening of these rights, along with a reduction of inequalities. As Beatriz Acha Ugarte asks, 'can we conceive of a non-pluralist democracy? Can we describe as democratic – although not in its "liberal version" – forces which, in their treatment of the "other" (immigrant, foreigner), show contempt for the democratic principle of equality?' One should therefore be 'cautious when considering [them] democratic formations, since they defend an *ideology of exclusion* that is incompatible, even with [the] merely procedural version of democracy'.[6]

Understanding the extreme right 2.0

Based on these considerations, I have proposed the definition of extreme right 2.0.[7] With this concept, I want to emphasise not only that Trump, Salvini and Le Pen are a phenomenon different from historical fascism, with radically new elements compared to the past, but also that new technologies have played a crucial role in the rise of these political formations. I would also like to underline the usefulness of a macro-category in which we can include all these political formations: for beyond some divergences, there are more things they have in common, both from the point of view of ideological references and from that of their political and communicative strategies.

All extreme right 2.0 formations have some lowest common denominators, i.e. common ideological references. Among these, we can mention a marked nationalism, identitarianism or nativism, the call for the recovery of national sovereignty, a deep criticism of multilateralism – and, in Europe, a high degree of Euroscepticism –, anti-globalism, the defence of conservative values, law and order policies, Islamophobia, condemnation of immigration as 'invasion', criticism of multiculturalism and open societies, anti-intellectualism and anti-progressivism. There are also other common elements: a exacerbated tactical bent, with the aim of setting the media agenda; the ability to use new technologies and social networks to make their messages go viral, profile citizens' data and further polarise society with culture wars; and the desire to present themselves as transgressors and rebels against a system supposedly hegemonised by the left, which they claim has established a progressive or politically correct dictatorship.

The new extreme-right forces have not only become more 'presentable', but are also trying to appropriate progressive and left-wing banners – think of the concept of 'freedom' or phenomena such as homo-nationalism or eco-fascism – in a historical moment marked by ideological confusionism.[8]

Moreover, all these political forces share the same objectives. In the first place, to move the Overton window by making acceptable discourses and narratives that were not acceptable until a few years ago. Secondly, to radicalise the mainstream right-wing parties so that they adopt their discourse and forge governmental alliances. Third, to come to power – alone when possible or alternatively in coalition with the mainstream right – to establish an illiberal democracy along the lines of Viktor Orbán's rule. Hungary today is not a full democracy, but 'a hybrid regime of electoral autocracy'.[9]

However, there are also differences and divergences between these political formations. These range from their economic programmes –those like Vox or Chega who are ultra-liberal, and those who, like Le Pen, defend so-called welfare chauvinism – to their values – in the south and east of Europe the position is much more ultra-conservative than the extreme right in the Netherlands or Scandinavia, which are a little more open on issues such as LGBTQI rights and abortion – or geopolitics, in which there are Russophile parties and others that are Atlanticist. Perhaps the declension of the concept of extreme right 2.0 needs to be in the plural: to paraphrase the historian Ricardo Chueca, who studied the Falange during Franco's regime, each country gives rise to the extreme right that it needs. And, we can add, each extreme right is the fruit of the political cultures existing in each national context. Hence their peculiarities, which do not prevent them from being considered part of a large global family, since there are also transnational networks that strive to strengthen existing ties, draw up a common agenda and finance these parties.

Compared to the past, moreover, in the last two decades the extreme right 2.0 has advanced everywhere. They have parliamentary representation in all European countries – except Malta and Ireland – and, for the first time, they have reached government in different countries: in Hungary in 2010, in Poland in 2015, in the United States in 2016, in Brazil in 2018, and in Italy in 2022. If we add the cases in which the extreme right has either been (or is) a partner in the governing coalition or has influenced (or influences) government policies by supporting the executives from outside, we should add at least another half a dozen countries, such as Austria, Belgium, Sweden, Denmark, Norway and the Czech Republic. This list is, in reality, an understatement. It would be easier to list the countries where the extreme right has so far had no institutional responsibilities. Indeed, as Mudde notes, with the new millennium the far right has become a 'pathological normality', and has de-marginalised, established its presence and radicalised the positions of democratic political systems.

The causes of the advance of the extreme right 2.0

But to fight the new extreme right, we must also understand why they achieve such levels of support among citizens. In short, three main causes have been identified to explain the advance of these political forces across the Western world.

Firstly, the increase in inequality, as well as the precariousness of work, the weakening of the welfare state and the shrinking of the middle class, have pushed part of the electorate, dissatisfied with neoliberal economic prescriptions, to choose political formations that criticise the existing order. This would also include the shift towards the centre in the economic policies of the traditional parties, starting with social democracy, whose positions have often been similar to or hardly distinguishable from those of the centre-right. This cause could be summarised under the formula of the *forgotten man*.[10]

Secondly, we find what has been called *cultural backlash*, i.e. the cultural reaction to liberal globalisation. Our societies have gradually become multicultural and many demands labelled as post-materialist have become rights, from divorce and abortion to gay marriage. This has led, according to various specialists, to a reaction from sectors of the population who see their position in society and even their identity threatened. Hence, they vote for parties that reject immigration, criticise what they see as progressive excesses, and defend the traditional family. If we had to choose a formula to sum up this cause, the most appropriate would probably be that of the *angry white man*.[11]

Thirdly, liberal representative democracies are undergoing a deep crisis: our societies are frayed, political parties no longer fulfil their function as a transmission belt and an escape valve between territories and institutions, trade unions are finding it extremely difficult to adapt to a fully post-Fordist reality, and public distrust is on the rise. In such atomised societies where trust in institutions seems to have disappeared, it is not unreasonable to imagine that part of the electorate is opting for parties that claim to want to overturn everything or, at the very least, oppose the establishment and criticise the functioning of democracies that they consider disconnected from the will of the people.

To these three causes, we could add a fourth, which has even more to do with the perceptions of the population. The demand for safety and security has increased in a liquid world that is hard to understand: what will become of my job in ten years' time, with artificial intelligence? What will happen in our neighbourhoods if migrants continue to arrive from other continents? What will become of the concept of the family in which many have grown up, if homosexual couples are allowed to adopt children? What will become of our social relations in times of virtual reality with projects such as the Metaverse? In its own way, the extreme right knows how to offer security and protection to many people who live in dread of what the future may hold, giving simple answers to complex problems.

There is no doubt that many answers offered by the extreme right are based on incessantly repeated falsehoods. But what are the responses offered by the left? Perceptions and fears can be irrational and exaggerated: indeed, they often are. This does not mean that they do not exist and do not influence citizens' political decisions. Sometimes there is no lack of progressive responses to the challenges of our time: what is lacking is empathy and the ability to communicate with those who think differently. This is also how hegemony is built.

A multifaceted and multilevel response

As we have seen, there is no single factor that explains the advance of Meloni, Trump, Orbán and Le Pen: their – not only electoral – successes are due to a set of causes that are not mutually exclusive, but combine and overlap. And they may not be just the same everywhere: again, context matters. In one country, region or city, the advance of the extreme right may owe to the closure and relocation of a factory or the rise of unemployment; in others to the presence of a large community of foreigners; in others to the fear of losing one's job or status in society. Or there may be a bit of one and a bit of the other, in different proportions varying over time.

So, in order to defeat, or at least weaken, the extreme right 2.0, it will be necessary to confront and resolve these problems. Or at least acknowledge that they exist. It will not be enough just to raise wages or to fund more public health and education. Nor will it be enough just to pull together the broken threads to rebuild our societies. Or, indeed, just to make progress on civil rights or to restore the centrality of schools and culture. Of course, these are all crucial issues, but they are not enough on their own. We must face up to the complexity of the liquid world in which we live. It is time to develop a multifaceted response that takes into account the fact that, since the reasons for the rise of the extreme right are multiple, the responses must also be plural. There are no magic wands or miracle solutions.

So let's not fool ourselves: it is not enough to act at one level either, be it institutional, political, social, economic or cultural. We need a multi-level strategy that addresses different areas. Effective responses must be provided at different levels at the same time. As Julia Ebner points out, speaking more generally about extremism, 'we need a holistic approach that considers long-term solutions, based on an alliance of different sectors and political parties. Politicians as well as tech companies, social workers and civil society'.[12]

The state and the extreme right

Another issue of paramount importance also needs mentioning. While the extreme right's penetration into institutions is not new, the last decade has seen an acceleration of this process. The extent to which the extreme right has worked its way into some state apparatuses can be seen by looking at three areas in particular: the police and the army; the state bureaucracy, and the judiciary.

Large sections of the police, and in some cases the army, are close to or inclined towards the positions of extreme-right parties. This has led to the infiltration of neo-Nazis into army units and the cover-up by police of the actions of extreme right-wing parties, as has been seen in Germany. Added to this is the control of police representation by extreme right-wing trade unions, as has happened in, among other countries, Spain with Jupol, a union close to Vox. Likewise, various military officers, most of them retired, have expressed themselves publicly by signing manifestos and letters of support for extreme right-wing parties, showing a climate of opinion that exists in certain sectors of the army. Symptomatic of this are the cases of France and Spain, where even Vox has put forward several retired military personnel as candidates in parliamentary elections. Finally, it is worth recalling the support that Trumpists and pro-Bolsonaro supporters received from sectors of the police and armed forces in the their respective assaults on Capitol Hill in January 2021 and on Planalto in Brasilia in January 2023. The police and armed forces are undoubtedly the weakest link in democratic states.

This phenomenon of gradual and silent penetration can also be seen in the state administration and the judiciary. There are considerable differences between European countries, but in various cases the extreme right has been working for years to gain influence in key state apparatuses or to co-opt members of these same apparatuses. In countries where it has come to power, such as Hungary and Poland, it has proceeded directly to control the judiciary from the executive, eliminating its independence and, consequently, the separation of powers. In Italy, since the days of the Berlusconi-led governments, the extreme right has been able to appoint leaders of the top state administration, a process that has been implemented exponentially after the formation of Giorgia Meloni's government. Likewise, in Spain, the mostly conservative judiciary has in various cases taken a sympathetic view towards the causes defended by Vox, while in different countries, starting with Italy, existing laws against the apology of fascism or hate crimes have not been applied with due resolve.

The strategy of penetration carried out by the extreme right in recent decades brings us once again to the teachings of the French Nouvelle Droite: the metapolitical strategy understands that the cultural battle is crucial. This implies, therefore, the ability to penetrate not only the media, but also universities, schools and the state administration in order to spread its discourse and achieve cultural hegemony.

What should the left do?

As far as the left is concerned, I think there are at least two levels to consider: that proper to parties and that proper to social movements. On the one hand, social democracy must shake off the weight of neoliberalism by returning to social policies and the fight against inequality. On the other hand, the radical left must know how to build a project that breaks out of irrelevance and does not seek self-indulgent purity. It must prove itself able to bring together the different existing struggles, giving them unity, without falling into sterile debates only meant for the already initiated and incomprehensible to a large part of society.

At the same time, the left must at all costs avoid buying into the discourse of the extreme right, even if only partially and tactically, mistakenly believing that the attention paid in recent years to struggles such as feminist, LGBTQI or migrants' rights has allowed the extreme right to penetrate into the working classes. Obviously, the left must be concerned about the material conditions of the 99%, but it cannot imagine that the defence of the material conditions of those who were once called proletarians or working class is not compatible with the other struggles. A woman who works as a cashier is at the same time a poor worker and a woman. A foreign day labourer is at the same time a farm worker and a migrant. Identities are multiple. As Colin Crouch reminds us, multiple identities 'should become a series of concentric circles that enrich each other with roots anchored in a cooperative subsidiarity, or a kind of Russian matryoshka with a succession of dolls of different dimensions comfortably contained inside each other'.[13]

In addition, there is a profound misunderstanding and ignorance of what the concept of class is and how it has been transformed since the time of Marx and Engels. As Sandro Mezzadra and Mario Neumann point out,

> the New Left, the feminist movement and the struggles of migrants are not the opposite of political struggles, but have historically been at their core and have also helped to overcome the objective limits of traditional Marxism and its conception of class. We believe, in fact, that those struggles that are too

often downplayed as identity politics have not only emerged in the realm of labour, but have even anticipated and politicised transformations in the world of work. What is at issue here, then, is not the disjunctive "this or that", but the systemic conjugation, the "and", the political and theoretical recomposition of past and present struggles – and not just their superficial reunion.[14]

The proposal must therefore be inclusive. Anything else implies the suicide of the left, not only electorally, but also ethically and morally. So-called national Bolshevism, or red-brownism, is nothing other than paving the way for the extreme right, and people always prefer the original to the copy. The left, in short, has to again take up the cultural battle that, over the last two decades, has been won by the extreme right. This cannot be done in a day: we will have to roll up our sleeves and hack at the coalface for a long time. Political schools must be set up, and time and money must be devoted to training, debate and communication skills. At the same time, precisely in order to halt the process of penetration of the state apparatus by the extreme right, it is also necessary to develop a strategy aimed at co-opting cadres from the administration and the bureaucracy, as well as members of the police and the army, and training and inserting new cadres who defend left-wing positions. In short, it is a question of not giving the extreme right a free hand in these sectors and of understanding that the struggle for cultural hegemony also takes place in this way.

The left must also have the courage to step out of its comfort zone, trying, for example, to forge broad alliances to protect democracy with politically distant parties and sectors of society. Electoral alliances? When necessary, this should be done, too: look at the Italian elections of 2022, where the division of the centre and left-wing parties allowed the extreme right to win a large absolute majority, thanks to an insane electoral law. However, it is not always necessary to go that far: it would be enough to propose specific anti-fascist agreements to at least prevent the extreme right from entering the institutions. It is possible to go beyond the cordons sanitaires which, today, are only a distant memory in most countries. It is hard work where everyone will have to make concessions – not only the left, obviously. But it is the left, I believe, that must take the first step and show its clear determination to defend a higher good – pluralist democracy – than any party affiliation or sympathy.

In 1936 the Communists abandoned the suicidal theory of social-fascism and joined the Popular Fronts in Spain and France, electoral alliances with socialists and even timidly progressive republicans. Three years earlier it was unthinkable: but the German events – with the tragic division of the left and Hitler's rise to power – showed that avoiding the establishment of a totalitarian dictatorship was the highest priority. Would it be so difficult today to reach agreements with the liberals or even with sectors of the democratic right to prevent the latter from falling into the ultras' embrace? This point demands attention, because this is indeed the main objective of Meloni, Orbán and Morawiecki: to bring the European People's Party and, when necessary, even the liberals into their own camp. No one would lose their identity or their political projects through such arrangements. It would simply be a matter of agreements to protect the rule of law and prevent the establishment of electoral autocracies. A pluralist democracy also needs a democratic right wing.

As for the second level, that of social movements, it should be made clear that most of them – from anti-fascist and anti-racist collectives to feminists – have long warned of the extreme right threat: in many cases, their actions have been crucial. Consider the work of the *Unitat contra el Fascisme i el Racisme* (Unity against Fascism and Racism, UCFR) in Catalonia and similar organisations in other countries, inspired by Britain's Rock Against Racism and Unite Against Fascism. The UCFR has advocated an "anti-fascism of the 99%", i.e. collaboration with all sectors of society to develop a united fight against the extreme right and racism.[15] As historian and activist Marc Bray points out, the approach of an organised anti-fascism should be combined with that of a 'broader, everyday anti-fascism', i.e. an 'anti-fascist perspective that does not tolerate "intolerance"'. According to Bray, 'militant anti-fascism alone is necessary but not sufficient to build a new world on the ruins of the old one'. For, as one of the anti-fascist militants interviewed for his book confirms, with the emergence of extreme right parties winning millions of votes, 'we cannot hope to defeat such an electoral project in the same way as we would a fascist street movement. Instead, we have to put forward better policy proposals than theirs.'[16]

In short, the left, understood in a broad sense, must continue to encourage actions of this kind, promoting the creation of networks from below to prevent the settlement of extreme right forces in our cities and the recruitment of young people – and not only young people. It must take to the streets and talk to the people, strengthening community ties, especially in the neighbourhoods and peripheries. So, more useful, in the current context, than a combat anti-fascism, is an anti-fascism that creates spaces of mutual support and that can stop the social penetration of the ideas of the extreme right.

In all this, the feminist movement can and must play an important role.

As María Eugenia Rodríguez Palop has explained, this obviously cannot mean the liberal or classist version of feminism – also well represented by far-right leaders such as Meloni or Le Pen – but the feminism of difference or relational feminism that 'proposes contagion, contact, recognition of the other and the construction of the "you"' and that 'promotes the shared experience and the continuous politics of bodies', calling for 'a much broader and more inclusive community of care'.[17] A feminism, in short, that goes out of its comfort zone, that is empathetic with other struggles and that also knows how to explain to men that feminism is a project for them too, so that they do not feel rejected or 'afraid'.[18]

However, we cannot expect activists alone to salvage the situation. There must be a responsibility incumbent on all of us, each with our own possibilities and capacities. We cannot look the other way and then complain when our democracies become empty shells and the rule of law a distant memory. The far right is also growing because many people feel lonely and abandoned in increasingly individualistic societies: the response of the extreme right to these people is to feel part of a (national) community with strong values (God, country and family). They allow them to be and feel part of something 'common', even if it is in most cases fictitious and mythologised. How can this dynamic be countered? By rebuilding the ties that have been broken in recent decades, by participating in political and associative life, starting with our neighbourhoods and our cities. By being empathetic with our neighbours, listening, talking, understanding the fears and anxieties of others even if we cannot share them, involving others in initiatives, associations and collectives. In short, by ensuring that this loneliness and these fears find a collective network and spaces of mutual support to prevent them from turning into frustration and anger. In this, the left has much to contribute, and municipalist experiences, such as those of Barcelona en Comú ones in other cities in Europe and America, are an example worth considering.[19]

Democracy can be lost very quickly, but it can take years or even decades to recover it. We should not forget this. This is precisely why it is necessary for the left to get down to work, fighting the cultural battle, building an inclusive project that draws a future of hope and rebuilding community ties, without being afraid to step out of its comfort zone. Is this simple? Obviously not, but it is necessary and urgent.

NOTES

1   Emilio Gentile, *Chi è fascista*, Rome-Bari: Laterza, 2019.
2   Paolo Graziano, *Neopopulismi. Perché sono destinati a durare*, Bologna: Il Mulino, 2018, p. 13.

3   See, for example, Cas Mudde & Cristóbal Rovira Kaltwasser, *Populism. A Very Short Introduction*, Oxford: Oxford University Press, 2017; Ernesto Laclau, *On Populist Reason*, London: Verso, 2005; Benjamin Moffitt & Simon Tormey, 'Rethinking Populism: Politics, Mediatisation and Political Style', *Political Studies* 62/2 (2014), pp. 381-397.

4   Ilvo Diamanti & Marc Lazar, *Popolocrazia. La metamorfosi delle nostre democrazie*, Rome-Bari: Laterza, 2018.

5   Cas Mudde, *The Far Right Today*, Cambridge: Polity Press, 2019.

6   Beatriz Acha Ugarte, *Analizar el auge de la ultraderecha*, Barcelona: Gedisa, 2021, pp. 43, 44, 58.

7   Steven Forti, *Extrema derecha 2.0. Qué es y cómo combatirla*, Madrid: Siglo XXI de España, 2021.

8   See Pablo Stefanoni, *¿La rebeldía se volvió de derecha?*, Buenos Aires: Siglo XXI, 2021 and Philippe Corcuff, *La grande confusion. Comment l'extrême-droite gagne la bataille des idées*, Paris: Textuel, 2021.

9   'Existence of a clear risk of a serious breach by Hungary of the values on which the Union is founded.' European Parliament, 15/09/2022: https://www.europarl.europa.eu/doceo/document/TA-9-2022-0324_EN.pdf

10   See, for examples, Roger Eatwell & Matthew Goodwin, *National Populism: The Revolt Against Liberal Democracy*, London: Penguin, 2018.

11   Pippa Norris & Ronald Inglehart, *Cultural Backlash. Trump, Brexit and Authoritarian Populism*, Cambridge: Cambridge University Press, 2019.

12   Julia Ebner, *La vida secreta de los extremistas. Cómo me infiltré en los lugares más oscuros de Internet*, Barcelona: Planeta, 2020, p. 281.

13   Colin Crouch, *Identità perdute. Globalizzazione e nazionalismo*, Rome-Bari: Laterza, 2019, p. 6.

14   Sandro Mezzadra & Mario Neumann, *Clase y diversidad. Sin trampas*, Pamplona: Katakrak, 2019, p. 20. In German: *Jenseits vo Interesse & Identität. Klasse, Linkspopulismus und das Erbe von 1968* Hamburg: LAIKA verlag, 2018.

15   David Karvala, *El antifascismo del 99%. La lucha unitaria contra el racismo y la extrema derecha*, Barcelona: Ediciones La Tempestad, 2019.

16   Mark Bray, *Antifa. El manual antifascista*, Madrid: Capitán Swing, 2018, pp. 271-280.

17   María Eugenia Rodríguez Palop, 'Antifeminismo y extrema derecha', *Espacio Público*, 22/04/2021: https://espacio-publico.com/antifeminismo-y-extrema-derecha.

18   See Clara Serra, Cristina Garaizábal & Laura Macaya (eds), *Alianzas rebeldes. Un feminismo más allá de la identidad*, Manresa: Bellaterra, 2021.

19   See, for example, *Fearless Cities. Municipalist Politics in Action*, Barcelona: Fundació Sentit Comú, 2022.

Rivalries at the International Level

Download our e-publications at the website
www.transform-network.net/publications

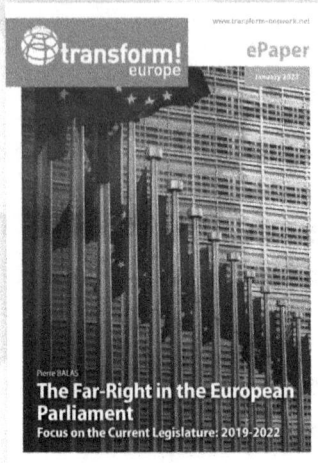

The influence of the far-right has globally been rising in every aspect of society (street mobilisations, political discourses, public debate, etc.). The European Parliament is not immune from this shift. Media and political commentators even feared a far-right tidal wave during the 2019 European elections campaign (9th legislature). Even if it did not occur, far-right political forces are doing well in the European Union and in extenso, in the EP.

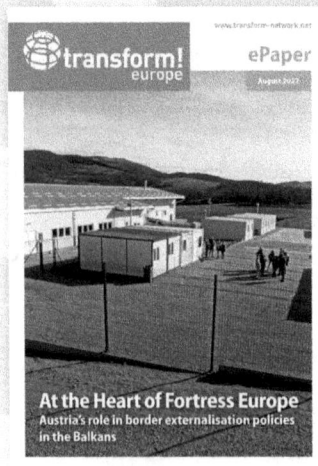

The study provides a broad mapping of Austrian-based multilateral cooperation, actors, and organisations that are heavily involved in EU border externalisation policies far beyond Austrian borders – and therefore in the violent and sometimes lethal approach to people on the move.

Subscribe to *transform! europe's* monthly newsletter to stay informed about the transform! network's activities and current events.

www.transform-network.net

[f] /transformeurope   [🐦] @transform_ntwrk   [▶] @transformeurope

The Left, the State, and International Institutions

Antonios Tzanakopoulos

In a volume on the left grappling with the state, I was called upon to contribute a note on the state and international institutions. A lot of further clarification is required here, at least to try and define what we intend by 'international institutions'. Actually, one might entitle this contribution 'The Left Facing the State Facing International Institutions', considering that the left today is normally once removed from the government of any given state – with few exceptions. And even if this is not the case, it is still 'states, not classes or other social forces, which are the fundamental contending agents of international law'.[1]

In what follows, I will discuss how the state, using legal tools at its disposal, can react to an international organisation that is allegedly violating the law. But first it will be crucial to offer some terminological clarifications and provide a brief introduction to the peculiarly decentralised international legal order. I will then provide a couple of examples of states having 'faced up' to an international organisation which they perceived to be acting wrongfully (that is, in violation of the organisation's own constitutive instrument or 'constitution', as well as in violation of general rules of international law applicable to it). The examples relate to 'sanctions', that is, non-enforceable measures taken by the Security Council under Chapter VII of the UN Charter to maintain or restore international peace and security.

In those cases, the reacting states managed to successfully react to the organisation and, to some extent, to force it to reverse its course, not only because they had a more or less strong legal footing, but also because they could form an alliance of like-minded states that was strong either in numbers or at least in political clout. Even then, the reaction had to build over a rather long period before it could produce effects. There are also cases, however, in which a state may have an equally strong legal argument against an international organisation but is unable to successfully react to the organisation due to insufficient support. Finally, I will demonstrate that it is not the strength of the legal arguments that defines the outcome of such clashes, but simply the relative power (both political and economic) of the relevant actors. This is especially so when there is no time for the reacting state to hold on while trying to build an alliance that will take up the cause.

This will certainly not come as a surprise, but in an age of increasing legalism it is on occasion useful to recall that the law is not very good at bringing about transformative change. It can be used now and then to fight rearguard actions, but you will hardly ever bring down the master's house by using the master's tools.[2] In that sense, the left faces a double-uphill battle; not only does it have to 'win over' the state – through electoral success or, dare I say, revolution, or in a much more limited manner by forcing a particular position upon the state – but it also has to win over other states in order to face down the international institutions, which – in their vast majority – constitute socialisations of the power of the dominant class (the capitalist class) at the international level.

Overview of the international legal order and terminology

Unlike the domestic legal order, to which all of us are more or less accustomed, the international legal order is highly decentralised and thus, to most people, seems a strange beast. What this means is that while in the domestic legal order the functions of lawmaking, law-determination, and dispute resolution, as well as law-enforcement are essentially centralised and assigned to specific organs (the legislature, the judiciary, and the executive, respectively), in international law no such centralisation has taken place at a general level. States make law by consent, which can be explicit or implicit (roughly corresponding to signing treaties or creating customary law through practice); resolve their disputes by consent, which may include consent to submit the dispute to an international court or tribunal; and enforce the law by themselves, mainly through taking countermeasures (often referred to as 'sanctions', which is a non-technical term in this context) against other states they perceive to be acting in violation of the rules of international law.

'International institutions' do of course exist and have been created initially as fora for debate and eventually as instruments for the collective action of states, leading to a (small) degree of centralisation at the international level. What is understood as 'international institutions' in the context of this contribution are 'international (intergovernmental) organisations', such as the United Nations, its specialised agencies, other organisations belonging to the UN family, as well as any international organisation that is established on the basis of an international treaty, has been given organs to operate through, and possesses some degree of international legal personality.

Most international organisations have no powers to legally bind states to their will, and those few that do, only possess such powers in the most exceptional circumstances, but in such cases these powers tend to be significant. More importantly, as entities with their own separate (if more or less limited) international legal personality, international organisations can also enter into binding agreements with states and thereby create obligations incumbent upon those states (to which of course the latter consent).

As examples, let us take the United Nations and the European Union. While the UN in general cannot impose obligations on its member states — for example the resolutions of the General Assembly are without binding character — the Security Council of the UN does have the power to bind members when it decides what non-enforceable (economic or other) measures are to be taken to respond to a situation which the Security Council has determined to be a threat to the peace.[3] Any refusal by the member states to comply with such measures, also commonly called 'sanctions',[4] will constitute a breach of their obligations under the UN Charter.[5]

The European Union is an international organisation that produces a significantly higher level of centralisation, even if only at the regional level. At the most basic level, the EU can not only impose binding obligations on its member states but can adopt acts (Regulations) that have direct effect in the domestic legal order of its member states. Disputes as between EU organs and member states can be resolved only by recourse to the EU's own courts. Further, the EU has shown considerable versatility in contracting with non-member states, other international organisations, and even member states and other international organisations, thereby creating binding rules between itself and those other actors. Of particular interest in this connection are the 'bailout packages' of 2010-2018 between the Commission, the European Central Bank, the International Monetary Fund, and Greece, and later between the European Stability Mechanism, another international organisation, and Greece (the 'Economic Adjustment Programmes' which were international agreements accompanied by Memoranda of Understanding detailing the conditions for the disbursement of bailout funds).

How can (member) states challenge the decisions of an international organisation, or the obligations that have been imposed on them, if they perceive these to be unlawful, for example as going beyond the competence of the organisation or as violating the human-rights obligations of the organisation? They can of course raise such legal arguments; however, in most cases they will have no access to an international court or tribunal which could adjudicate such claims. Can they go at it alone? Let us try to answer this question.

Facing up to an international organisation as an alliance[6]

The UN Security Council remained deadlocked for the better part of its life since the establishment of the United Nations until the end of the Cold War. With the collapse of the Soviet Union, however, the Security Council, no longer blocked by the reciprocal vetoes of the two superpowers, began to operate with, and thus demonstrate, the enormous power with which it had been vested. The crippling measures taken against Iraq in the aftermath of the latter's invasion of Kuwait have been well documented and discussed in the literature. Similar measures were taken on many other occasions in the 1990s and provoked considerable reactions both on the part of states and on the part of civil society, particularly due to their significant negative effect on the civilian population of targeted states.

The Security Council did in turn heed some of that criticism, seeking to target its measures more precisely (considering, for example, that the initial measures against Iraq were comprehensive trade-blocking measures that led to serious food and medicine shortages affecting the civilian population). This is how 'targeted sanctions' were born. Initially targeted either to specific goods, considered to be fuelling a conflict (for example, arms embargoes, oil embargoes, and even diamond and timber embargoes), or to specific individuals belonging to the government or the governing elite of the target state, these measures then evolved to target individuals who were not necessarily connected to the government of any state. But we are getting ahead of ourselves. Let us first consider a Security Council measure that provoked considerable reaction, and ultimately massive disobedience on the part of (at least part of) the UN's membership.

You may be familiar with the Lockerbie incident. This refers to the destruction of Pan Am flight 103, the transatlantic leg of a multiple stop-over flight between Frankfurt and Detroit on 21 December 1988. The Boeing 747 operating the flight exploded over Lockerbie in Scotland, during the London to New York leg of the flight. The explosion was caused by a bomb in the hold of the aeroplane, contained in a suitcase that was loaded onto the aeroplane during its stopover at Heathrow Airport.

The US and the UK accused Libya of destroying the aircraft, and in late 1991 demanded that Libya turn over the two agents that they had identified as responsible in order to face trial in the US and the UK respectively. Libya noted the lack of extradition treaties with either of the two states and invoked its rights under the 1971 Montreal Convention for the Suppression of Unlawful Acts against the Safety of Civil Aviation. In accordance with the treaty, Libya has an obligation to either prosecute those alleged to have committed an offence within the scope of the treaty and present in its territory, or to extradite them to a state that will prosecute them. In this instance, Libya was insisting on its right to prosecute rather than extradite the alleged offenders.

In January 1992, the US and the UK managed to 'convince' the Security Council to issue a non-binding resolution 'urging' Libya to cooperate with the 'requests' that had been directed to it. The handwriting was on the wall and Libya read it: In March 1992, it launched proceedings against both the US and the UK before the International Court of Justice, the principal judicial organ of the UN, which has jurisdiction to resolve any disputes which may arise under the Montreal Convention. In its Application to the Court, Libya asked the Court to find that it had complied with its obligations under the Montreal Convention, and that, conversely, the US and the UK had violated the Convention and should cease and desist from making threats against and applying pressure to Libya to turn over its accused nationals. At the same time, Libya asked the Court to indicate provisional measures requiring the US and the UK to stop trying to coerce or compel Libya to turn over the accused while the case was pending.

Between Libya's application and the Court's decision on the provisional-measures request (which took less than a month and a half), the US and the UK had 'convinced' the Security Council to use its Chapter VII powers to impose sanctions on Libya for its failure to 'comply' with the 'requests' made of it – in short, for failing to turn over the accused. What followed was a long period in which Libya, being subjected as it was to considerable sanctions which all members of the UN had to enforce, sought some negotiated way out of the difficulty. Using both the (then) Organisation of African Unity (now the African Union) and the (then) Organisation of the Islamic Conference (now the Organisation of Islamic Cooperation) as conduits, Libya offered various compromise solutions, including the trial of the accused before an international tribunal, or even their trial by a Scottish tribunal that would sit outside of Scotland. All compromise solutions were rejected by the US and the UK, who could maintain their pressure on Libya via the still-in-force sanctions imposed by the Security Council.

To cut a long story short, at some point the Organisation of African Unity had had enough. That 'some' point was not soon – it was in August 1998, when eventually the then 53 member states of the Organisation declared that the Security Council measures against Libya were not lawful, and that they would cease to comply with them in September 1998. Faced with the prospect of massive disobedience on the part of what was almost one third of the total membership of the United Nations, the Security Council (and the US and the UK) promptly backed off and accepted that the two accused be tried by a Scottish Court that would sit in Camp Zeist, outside The Hague in the Netherlands. The Security Council suspended its sanctions against Libya, and the trial went ahead (which is an extremely interesting story whose details would exceed the length of this article).

There are further examples of such (threats of) mass disobedience by states forcing the Security Council to redress concerns. One such, which I will touch on here very briefly (greatly simplifying it), is the reaction, in particular by EU member states, to Security Council 'targeted sanctions' against Al-Qaeda and the Taliban, measures that later evolved to include ISIS sanctions, while separating the regime of sanctions applicable to the Taliban. Again cutting a very long story short, in 1999 the Security Council adopted sanctions against any person 'associated with' Al-Qaeda and the Taliban, which was extended post-9/11. A number of individuals were included in a 'blacklist' prepared by the Security Council, on the basis of information available to it but to no one else, and all members of the UN were required to comply with the obligation to freeze the assets and ban travel, etc, for those named individuals.

These individuals had no way to complain to the Security Council, while any challenges against the measures in domestic courts were, at least at first, predictably dismissed by those courts for lack of jurisdiction over the United Nations and its decisions. Eventually, and given the length of the sanctions, domestic courts did start to react, striking down domestic implementations of the sanctions (that is, the domestic administrative decisions that were required for freezing assets or for travel bans to take effect), forcing their own states to disobey the Security Council. When the Court of Justice of the European Union adopted a similar line,[7] forcing mass disobedience on the part of (then) 28 member states, including some very powerful ones and some that were also permanent members of the Security Council, those states had to do something. They were caught between a rock and a hard place: Should they disobey their own courts, laying waste to their own incantations about the rule of law, or should they try and force the Security Council to offer some redress, so as to avoid having to disobey it? They opted for the latter, and so the Security Council had to establish a process of delisting of individuals targeted by those sanctions, which involved a quasi-obligatory decision by an independent and impartial 'Office of the Ombudsperson'.

What these examples show is that states, in and of themselves quite powerless against an international organisation controlled by powerful states and with binding powers at its disposal, can 'face up' to it in exceptional circumstances which lead them (or force them) to unite against it, either in significant numbers or in a situation where powerful states are included among their number. Of course, the conflict does not take place in terms of naked power (although that is always a possibility). Rather, in the cases described above, the conflict was clothed in legal terms. According to the Organisation of African Unity in the Libyan case, the Security Council had misinterpreted the concept of 'threat to the peace', which Libya quite clearly did not represent at the time that it was bending over backwards to find a compromise solution for bringing the alleged perpetrators of the Lockerbie bombing to justice. And according to the EU courts and the courts of various states, Security Council anti-terrorist sanctions could not eliminate the basic human right of accessing some effective remedy in case a country found itself 'blacklisted' by the Security Council. Things, however, are quite different when no such (occasional) alliance of states is forthcoming, no matter how strong a legal argument one is able to put forward.

Facing an international organisation alone[8]

'Maybe there are perfectly obvious and feasible responses to the ills of the global economy that states cannot implement because these responses are resisted by other, more powerful states whose own interests argue against them.'[9] This resistance may of course also be actuated by international institutions that such powerful states control, precisely in order to do their bidding.[10] And the odds of a lone state faced with such institutions are not particularly good. International legal arguments will not necessarily help in such circumstances, although – as sketched out in the previous section – they may be good instruments through which to articulate a basis for disobedience.

The example of Greece during the economic crisis that began in 2008 and led to Greece seeking a bailout and entering its first 'Economic Adjustment Programme' in May 2010 is instructive. Again, it would be impossible to do justice here to both the developments over the years in which Greece was subject to the 'Economic Adjustment Programmes' (2010-2018), or to supervision by the EU (2010-2022), and the complexity of the programmes and their legal implications. However, in broad outline, the following occurred: Greece voluntarily turned to the EU to seek a bailout to avoid a sovereign default in 2010 and voluntarily signed on to both the first and the second 'Economic Adjustment Programme' with the 'Troika' of creditors, namely the European Commission, the European Central Bank, and the

International Monetary Fund. These 'Economic Adjustment Programmes' involved the assumption of obligations on the part of Greece to take specific measures to restructure its economy (including serious austerity measures slashing wages and pensions, cutting public services, and accelerating privatisation).

Legal arguments were raised at the time that these measures led to violations of human rights – but it is the Greek state that is under an international obligation to respect and protect human rights obligations within its jurisdiction, and not any third state or international organisation. And in any event the government(s) of Greece between 2010 and the end of 2014 did not seem particularly interested in making any such arguments against the European Union or the International Monetary Fund, which were bailing Greece out at quite considerable cost to the Greek population.

Be that as it may, the electoral success of Syriza in January 2015 led to the formation of a government with the stated purpose of releasing Greece from the unconscionable burden that had been imposed on it in exchange for the bailout. This in turn precipitated a showdown with the European Union and the IMF. However, the battle was clearly unequal; no amount of brilliant or even disingenuous legal argument about human rights, coercion, odious debt, and what have you, was going to tip the scales, especially since Greece seemed to stand alone against a more or less united European Union and an unrelenting IMF. When Syriza sought to negotiate with the creditor institutions based on the anti-austerity platform on which it had been elected, the institutions progressively turned off the liquidity tap, pushing Greece against a wall of sovereign default. Eventually, Greece had to impose capital controls at the end of June 2015 in order to stop capital flight. As a last ditch effort to consolidate a negotiating position, the Greek government called a referendum on the outstanding offer of the institutions (an offer that was immediately rescinded) in early July, but was forced to submit (although not without considerable gains) after a 17-hour negotiation session on 12/13 July 2015, eventually signing on to a third 'Economic Adjustment Programme', which came to an end in July 2018.

The enormous pressure that the creditor institutions brought to bear on Greece and its government in the first half of 2015, culminating in the eventual agreement of July/August 2015, may have been widely seen by (at least a part of) civil society as a coup attempt – with #ThisIsACoup trending on social media, especially during the 17-hour negotiations in July. And plausible arguments could be made that such enormous pressure may have amounted to coercion, which is prohibited under international law. But the plausibility – and more importantly, the eventual success – of such arguments, especially in a decentralised legal order, as is the international legal order, is determined by whether states accede to the arguments, take up the cause, and form a more or less united front of pressure against the relevant institutions. This did not happen. Greece stood alone, and had to submit, even if with some concessions.

Conclusion

International law is made and constantly remade by states through patterns of action, reaction, acquiescence, and objection. When pitted against international institutions, especially powerful ones such as the UN Security Council acting under Chapter VII of the UN Charter, the IMF and World Bank, or the European Union, the plausibility or strength of any legal argument is alone never enough to determine the outcome of a confrontation between a lone state and the international institution. What matters is the creation of a sufficiently strong coalition of states backing up their international legal argument with a threat to the operation of the international institution that has the credibility to lead to a more or less equitable resolution of the confrontation. In this, the overdetermination of the position of the state before international institutions is laid bare for all to see.

What can the left facing the state facing international institutions do in such a case? The answer is, unsurprisingly: little. The left has to win a dual political struggle: 1) to win over the state, and 2) to win over (potentially as the government of the state) other states to its cause. If it is successful in doing so (which is in itself a great challenge), then of course it can face up to a strong international institution with some prospect of success. And it can employ legal arguments in doing so, as it would have a possibility of backing its interpretation with enough of a political or economic threat to make that interpretation prevail in the instance in question. But any such legal argument, no matter how brilliant or compelling, will never be enough to win a battle without a strong political alliance behind it. Thus, it may be that the left needs to focus more on 'winning over' enough states through political struggle than on fighting rearguard actions through legal arguments.

NOTES

1   China Miéville, *Between Equal Rights: A Marxist Theory of International Law*, London: Pluto Press, 2006, p. 317.

2   See Audre Lorde, chapter 'The Master's Tools Will Never Dismantle the Master's House', in Audre Lorde, *Sister Outsider*, London: Penguin, 2019 (1984), pp. 103ff.

3   Or 'breach of the peace', or 'act of aggression'. See Articles 41, 39, and 25 of the United Nations Charter.

4   Unilateral measures taken by states to respond to perceived breaches of international law are also commonly called 'sanctions'. As we have said, this on occasion causes great confusion even among international lawyers. However, unilateral action in response to breaches (countermeasures) is conceptually distinct from collective action decided by the United Nations in response to a threat to the peace.

5   Article 25 of the UN Charter provides that '[t]he Members of the United Nations agree to accept and carry out the decisions of the Security Council in accordance with the present Charter'.

6   See generally Antonios Tzanakopoulos, *Disobeying the Security Council: Countermeasures Against Wrongful Sanctions*, Oxford: Oxford University Press, 2011, passim with further references.

7   In the Kadi cases, on which see further Antonios Tzanakopoulos, 'The *Solange* Argument as a Justification for Disobeying the Security Council in the *Kadi* Judgments' in Matej Avbelj, Filippo Fontanelli, and Giuseppe Martinico (eds), *Kadi on Trial: A Multifaceted Analysis of the Kadi Judgment*, London: Routledge, 2013, pp. 121ff.

8   See generally Antonios Tzanakopoulos, 'The Right to Be Free from Economic Coercion', *Cambridge International Law Journal* 4 (2015): 616ff., with further references.

9   Anthony Carty, 'Marxism and International Law: Perspectives for the American (Twenty-First) Century?' in Susan Marks (ed.), *International Law on the Left: Re-Imagining Marxist Legacies*, Cambridge UK: Cambridge University Press, 2008, pp. 169, 178.

10   In fact, this is increasingly the case since the second half of the twentieth century, with the 'physical violence of western intervention' being 'replaced by the economic violence of structural adjustment and the debt crisis, mediated by the [IMF] and the World Bank (Balakrishnan Rajagopal, *International Law from Below – Development, Social Movements and Third World Resistance*, Cambridge UK: Cambridge University Press, 2003, p. 34.

The Capitalist State and the Looming Endgame of Western World Domination

Göran Therborn Interviewed by Haris Golemis

Haris Golemis: Capitalism in its various forms is responsible for climate, health, and economic crises, creates huge economic and social inequalities within all countries and among them, limits freedom and democracy, and contributes to, if not causes, wars, which especially in the present period could lead even to the extinction of humanity. All these are being carried out through the actions or inactions of states, especially those of big countries. It is for this reason that in the past, since the nineteenth century and until recently, at least before the fall of the soviet-type regimes, the radical left political and social forces (but also the social democratic left of the Second International), as well as radical intellectuals all over the world, in their aim to transcend capitalism used to have a strategy for the capitalist state: to overthrow or transform it in various ways. Do you think that this has changed in the 21st century and if yes, in what ways?

Göran Therborn: We should not forget that there once was a significant current of the labour movement that was not focused on winning the state, one way or the other: the anarchist and anarcho-syndicalist tendency. Before World War I it was an important tendency in Latin Europe generally, in Spain in particular, and in parts of Latin America. And also in the USA, where alongside the revolutionary Industrial Workers of the World, with their industrial focus, there were the moderate craft unions of the American Federation of Labor, which similarly were not oriented towards winning the state. Anarchism was also the major source of inspiration for the first modern rebels of Japan and Korea.

The subsequent overwhelming turn to a state-centred focus of both the revolutionary and the reformist wings of labour and the left has been vindicated by experience. What major progressive transformations have been achieved through the dialectics of industrial capitalism have been achieved through some kind of control of the state, in the welfare states as well as the anti-capitalist revolutions. Neither industrial action, nor cooperatives, not to speak of anarchist 'direct action' against individual power holders and exploiters, have any comparable record of social achievement, although the first two courses of action also have left enduring accomplishments.

Within the 21st-century left, after the end or relative marginalisation of the class dialectic of industrial capitalism, and in the face of apparently solidly fortified capitalist states, neo-Anarchist and cooperativist ideas have returned. Militant movements of the early 21st century, like the Occupy and Indignados movements, saw themselves, in their formally leaderless participatory action, as prefigurations of a different, new social world – more or less communist in the classical Marxian sense – rather than as a means to power.

Theoretically, a new argumentation in this direction has been developed by the late Erik Olin Wright. He first drew our attention to 'society' with the state bracketed, by raising the novel question, 'What is social in socialism?' He saw it as 'social power', as 'rule by the people collectively organized into voluntary associations ... parties, communities, unions [...]'.[1] In his last strategic publication he presented a perspective of 'eroding capitalism' through a variety of social action without a central state-power focus, escaping, resisting, taming, and dismantling capitalism.[2] He saw this kind of complex, gradual social transformation as similar to the rise of capitalism out of feudalism.

These practices and theorisations have enriched the left. However, the structures and institutions of power and exploitation persist, while the inspiring radical movements of the first two decades of this century have left us with little more than their memory. Wright's theory of erosion opens up a wider vista of left-wing thought, and combines a spectrum of time horizons, from escapes in the here and now from capitalism, like Wikipedia, communal living, or basic-income projects, to a multi-generational shrinking of the space for private capital accumulation. But his historical parallelism of capitalism and socialism underestimated the role of state violence and power in the rise of capitalism, not only of bourgeois revolutions but even more the role of political power and violence in the dispossession of collective communities, in colonial exploitation, in inter-state wars with their historically crucial outcomes, and in maintaining labour discipline.

Moreover, we have to recognise today's much increased significance of the state for the dynamics of capitalism, compared to a century ago. The digital revolution, for instance, developed out of the US military. Today's financial capitalism is kept going by state and state bank policies and interventions.

Tax-financed healthcare and education have now become 'asset classes' for corporate capital accumulation. The mitigation of, now unavoidable, climate disasters crucially depends on state and inter-state action.

HG: According to Nicos Poulantzas, whose relational state theory 44 years after his death I still consider valuable, the capitalist state is 'the material condensation of the relation of forces between classes and class fractions'. Do you think that this definition is conceptually valid, and useful for the establishment of the potentially new revolutionary or transformative subject of our times? In this framework, do you agree with the 'left populist' strategy towards the state encapsulated in the slogan 'we (the people) are the 99%, while you (the elites) are only the 1%', when this 99% consists of antagonistic social forces? Could the entrepreneurial so called 'middle classes' (i.e., the owners of capitalist medium-sized and small enterprises which aim to maximise their profits) make the same demands on the national state as even their own precarious workers? This, of course does not mean that the transformative left shouldn't have a strategy of ad hoc and time-limited social and political alliances. As you have also dealt in the past with state theory (I have in mind your book *What Does the Ruling Class Do when it Rules?*, but also several of your articles), I would appreciate your view on this issue.

GT: I have always thought, and still do, that Poulantzas's definition was brilliant and an excellent starting-point for understanding and analysing the state. It implies, for instance, that a capitalist state is not necessarily just 'a committee of the ruling class', and could very well be impacted by a strong working-class movement. But I think this should be, on the one hand, generalised, and, on the other, specified.

Generalising, the contemporary state cannot be conceived *only* as a capitalist state. States are also parts of a historically evolved geopolitical state system, and rooted in national history and culture. So, I would say, states are, or need to be seen as, the material condensation of the relation of social forces within a specific territory, of class forces and forces of class fractions but also of territorial culture and history, with their forces and movements, e.g. secularist or religious, feminist or patriarchal – and as material refractions of their positions and history in the pertinent geopolitical system of states. All this means that studying how a state is organised and its everyday functioning – best done in a comparative framework – is an important path to understanding a society's layered social, cultural, and geopolitical history.

In terms of specification, the material condensation and refraction of states are embodied in an organisation, the state apparatus complex. As such, the state is an actor, in a sense more directly than a class is, because the latter is not an organisation but a networked social force. Therefore, between a social imprint of condensation and refraction and an acting formal organisation, there is always the possibility of a considerable social indeterminacy, i.e., organisational autonomy.

What power is manifested when the state acts? Is it state power or class power, or, more generally, social power? This was a question much discussed in Poulantzas's time and after. The contest can in a way be seen as one between choices of perspectives. From a liberal perspective, the distinction between state and non-state power is central; from a Marxist one, the specificity of class power, bourgeois or working-class, is crucial. More generally speaking, a focus on the social character of power is motivated by an interest in an often neglected question of power: the power to do what? To answer that you have to look at the social and geopolitical matrix – including the character of the state apparatus – of a state government/political leadership. In this social matrix, the relations between, and the relative weight of, the state apparatus and voluntary organisations of class and other social groups are significant.

State analysis and populist strategy are to me two quite different topics. The relational state theory highlights the social character of the state, which it is always good to have a grasp of, regardless of your political goals and strategy. Left populism is a strategy for breaking up the socio-political carapace of a political landscape, where a working-class majority is a distant, unlikely reachable future – as in Latin America – or a thing of the past, as in Europe. Its claim to speak for the 99% is, of course, a rhetorical device, no more. In Latin America, ambiguous figures and regimes like those of Vargas in Brazil and Perón in Argentina, managed to break the oligarchic grip on their countries. European attempts have been less successful, and attempts to reach the non-left have made little headway. Class interests in Europe are more crystallised and articulated than in Latin America. Nevertheless, European left populism has widened the left's appeal, with Syriza in Greece, Podemos in Spain, and with Jean-Luc Mélenchon and La France Insoumise. A pure class strategy is not viable in post-industrial societies, and even under industrial capitalism successful labour movements had to broaden their appeals beyond the working class.

HG: What is the influence of class and class fractions, international organisations like the IMF, the World Bank, and regional integration like that of the EU on the policies of the contemporary capitalist states?

GT: That is a new and important question, post-dating the Marxist state debates of the 1960s-70s. A set of inter-state bourgeois organisations has developed as significant pillars of the capitalist world order, which in the last instance, of course, rests on the military might of the USA. There are several of them, but the EU, NATO, the World Bank, and the IMF are the most important. They all weigh heavily on most capitalist states, except on the USA, which stands on top of them all. In NATO, France under de Gaulle asserted some independence, and currently Turkey under Erdoğan is refusing to participate in the economic war against Russia. In the EU, France and Germany can more or less do what they want. The World Bank and the IMF weigh only on poor or weak countries.

In the late 20th and early 21st centuries, the IMF was the International Brigade of neoliberal capitalism. Its 'structural adjustment programmes' caused painful damage to many vulnerable economies and societies, including excess deaths from respiratory diseases and tuberculosis.[3] The World Bank is much larger and more diverse, but it is also a powerful force of international capital. In the 1990s, the Bank launched a vicious campaign for privatising pensions with a view to boosting financial capitalism. Inspired by the example of privatisation by the Chilean military dictatorship – in turn under the spell of Chicago economics – the Bank campaign concentrated on Latin America and Eastern Europe, to begin with. (It soon backfired, had to be stopped, and has largely been undone.)

In recent years both the IMF and the World Bank have moved towards more enlightened bourgeois positions, concerned with inequality as potentially socially destabilising. Last autumn, the IMF even criticised a major Western country, the UK, and its Truss-Kwarteng budget, not only for its inflationary implications but also for 'increasing inequality'.

The EU is a grand liberal project, of free trade, free movement of capital, and free movement of residents within the union, which has to pay some attention to the social concerns of the population. After all, the member-state governments have to be re-elected. On solemn occasions it is presented as a peace organisation. When tested, it was unwilling or unable to prevent the wars of secession in Yugoslavia, to commit itself to an implementation of the Minsk Accord of autonomy for eastern Ukraine, and to stopping the US drive for NATO and military-base expansion in Eastern Europe. In response to the ensuing Russian invasion, the EU has decided to become a party to the war, becoming a geopolitical-economic war machine of ever escalating 'sanctions'.

NATO was founded as an anti-communist Cold War military organisation, which never has had to defend any nation from external attack, but which has taken part in the invasions of Afghanistan and Libya. It developed a US-led international secret apparatus to deal with possible internal threats to the capitalist order, as well as to operate as a stay behind force in case of a Soviet attack: 'Operation Gladio'.[4] Gladio was officially dissolved in 1990, but the NATO-alignment with the US superpower has generated Pentagon and CIA-oriented and -guided 'deep states', under the radar of democracy, of military, security police, spies, surveillance agents, 'security analysts', and some selected politicians. Deepest of all perhaps are the members of the Nuclear Planning Group, planning, under US oversight of course, which parts of Russia and China should be annihilated in a future nuclear war. Sweden's NATO application was characteristically accompanied by a new law giving the state the right to close TV and radio channels deemed unacceptable to national security, and a change of the Constitution, making it possible to indict people for espionage in case they release information damaging allied powers and relations to them.

HG: Despite the dominant discourse about 'globalisation' that was born of 'technical change' and/or an autonomous change in relations of production which resulted in a reduction of the role of the national capitalist state and its gradual disappearance, the latter was, is, and will continue to be present in societies for the indefinite future. It is the big states, mainly the US, which established and imposed neoliberal globalisation through national legislation, authoritarianism, international institutions, imperialism, and war. Moreover, it is true that during and after the Covid pandemic, following forty years of neoliberal policies, there is a return of the capitalist state's intervention also in economic and social policy. Do you consider this development to be a defeat of neoliberal capitalism that could, in the long run, benefit the left's emancipatory anti-capitalist cause, or as a victory of mainly right-wing and extreme right-wing nationalism?

GT: Capitalist globalisation is being overrun by the geopolitics of Western supremacy. Free trade, free capital movements, and global supply chains are now being trumped by national security, national non-dependence, and national power. In the 2010s, the US elite found out that the Chinese were winning the game of globalisation. China became the world's largest economy measured in purchasing-power parities. Therefore, the US regime resurrected the old game of imperial geopolitics. Everything now has to be subordinated to the maintenance of US technological and military superiority.

The end of liberal capitalist globalisation should be seen as the beginning of the end of the 500 years of Western world domination, the incipient decline of a Euro-American White Christian dynasty which has governed the world for almost half a millennium. The US elite is realising that it can no longer aspire to dominate the whole post-Cold War world, and is implementing a strategic retreat. Instead of ruling economically through a universalistic 'rule-bound' market order, the US is retreating to what liberal economists hitherto have called 'crony capitalism', that is, to a fortified sub-global circle of friends. Treasury Secretary Janet Yellen (on 13 April 2022) called it 'friend-shoring'.

The US grip on the world is likely to continue loosening, and Asian, not only Chinese, influence to continue rising. But neither the manner nor the timing of the end of US world domination can be predicted, nor what will take its place. It is not to be excluded that the Western dynasty might be succeeded by a global republic.

The neoliberal variant of capitalism has taken two major hits, the pandemic, and the geopolitical challenge. The state is no longer 'the problem', as Reagan once proclaimed, but the solution to big problems, pandemics, war mobilisation against Russia and China, and climate change. This is clearly a defeat of neoliberalism, but certainly not a victory for extreme right-wing nationalism.

Towards the end of the pandemic, it looked as if it might lead to ecological change and social reform. In the UK and the US ideas of a 'Green New Deal' were gaining traction, the EU was preparing a major funding of reforms in the member states, and the enlightened bourgeoisie, as exemplified by the editors of the *Financial Times* and the manager of the Davos Economic Forum, Klaus Schwab, were proposing and (Schwab) predicting radical egalitarian social change. However, the Anglo-Saxon New Deals were stymied by domestic politics, and the international reform agenda was overwhelmed by the geopolitical ice age accelerated by the Ukraine war.

What is instead on the rise is not so much extreme right-wing nationalism as it is *right-wing and centrist extreme internationalism*, expressed in the growing all-Western Sinophobia and pan-European Russophobia, in the EU's High Representative for Foreign Affairs and Security Policy's dividing the world into the European (and allied) 'garden' and the 'jungle' of the rest of the world,[5] and in the Biden administration's frantic efforts to establish two global blocs, one of allies-cum-partners and another of inimical sanction targets. Benefits for an emancipatory anti-capitalist course are nowhere to be seen.

HG: Judging mainly from the quite recent experience of the Syriza government in Greece – a small, highly indebted eurozone country – but also from old and new cases of radical left parties' participation in coalition governments as junior partners (the French CP in France in the 1980s and, during the present period, Unidas Podemos in Spain and some parties in the Nordic countries), can the radical left in governments of Western small or medium-sized countries transform the state in order to gradually transcend capitalism, or is the transformation of the party itself into a harmless political force more probable? Could the situation be different in big countries, or in countries of other regions, for example Latin America?

GT: For the foreseeable future, there are no prospects of radical progressive transformations in any part of Europe. On the contrary, the whole continent is being rolled back – by militarisation, xenophobia, censorship, and by a sado-liberal punishment mission. The progressive forces who remain have to fight for their survival. In Latin America a certain space for social reform, and for a non-aligned foreign policy, has opened up. But the social space is clearly smaller than that of the first decade of this century. Both Africa and Asia are getting free of the grip of the USA and of the European former colonial powers.

However, the social prospects for Africa and Asia are very unclear. Nowhere are any important, enduring, and unambiguous movements of social emancipation in sight. The huge farmer-labour movement in India in 2020-21 did stop a policy change with respect to farm produce sales, but achieved no new reforms. The large and broad Indonesian protest coalition in 2019 against a neoliberal anti-labour investment law failed. But both Africa and Asia harbour plenty of frustration, anger, and protest, as well as fragile systems of power.

HG: Are capitalist states intertwined with financial and digital capital? And can the left break this connection?

GT: Yes they are, indeed. State policies and state funding have enabled and pushed for the digital revolution, opened the sluices for financial speculation, stepping in to bail out the speculators during crashes. Financial and high-tech capital make up the core of contemporary capitalism, and their bond with their state protector is unbreakable under capitalist conditions. But a powerful left digital infrastructure and left social media networks could develop and question capitalist power. Digital mobilisation has in this century been a very important instrument of both power and counterpower. In democratic countries it has so far been used most successfully by the far right, such as Trump and Bolsonaro.

HG: Can the left in government challenge a state's subordination to the will of the financial markets and face climate crisis?

GT: Standing up to the financial markets is very difficult, because it is very costly, in terms of currency depreciation and the greater cost of credit or exclusion from it, all leading to a short-term decline of living standards. You have to have the stamina of a Lenin or Fidel Castro, and their support, to stand up to this, and/or a bloc of states behind you.

However, the relation of financial markets to the climate crisis complicates the issue. Finance is not necessarily a defender of fossil fuels. There is no intrinsic link of interests between them, although many asset managers have investments in hydrocarbon corporations. A significant segment of financial capital has expressed support for a transition to a fossil-free capitalism. Capital's pressure against climate-change adaptation is more likely to come – and is already coming – from fossil-fuel corporations than from finance. Domestic employment interests will be mobilised.

The adaptability of capital to a zero-emission economy remains to be seen. But the left had better be aware that a green capitalism is not inconceivable, and that it is the aspiration both of social democracy and of the enlightened right. It will not be easy to bring about, and therefore there will likely be several opportunities for left forces to press for alternatives combining economic transformation and energy transition.

NOTES

1   Erik Olin Wright, *How to Be an Anti-Capitalist in the 21ˢᵗ Century*, London: Verso, 2019, p. 69.
2   Wright, pp. 59ff.
3   Elias Nosrati et al., 'Structural adjustment programmes and infectious disease mortality', PLOS ONE 17,7 (2022), <https://journals.plos.org/plosone/article?id=10.1371/journal.pone.0270344>.
4   There is a good summary at <https://en.wikipedia.org/wiki/Operation_Gladio>.
5   In his speech of 13 October 2022 at the opening of the European Diplomatic Academy, Josep Borrell laid out his worldview: 'Europe is a garden […]. Most of the rest of the world is a jungle, and the jungle could invade the garden […] your duty will not be to take care of the garden itself but the jungle outside.' At Jovan Kurbalija's blog: <https;//www.diplomacy.edu/blog/Borrell>.

National Self-Determination and European Integration Are Not Mutually Exclusive

Walter Baier interviewed by Haris Golemis

Haris Golemis: As you know, this 2023 yearbook deals with various aspects of the left's relationship with the state. So let's start by talking about the ability of radical-left parties in the EU and especially eurozone countries to carry out a meaningful social transformation that would gradually overcome capitalism. Some of these parties, as well as important intellectuals, scholars, and researchers of European integration, consider such a perspective impossible by definition. So, as the Greek political scientist Gerassimos Moschonas said in his interview for the 2022 yearbook, this means that either 'our' left has to abandon its radical visions and embrace social democracy, or fight for a Lexit (left exit) of their country from the EU, since this bloc cannot be changed. What is your view on this crucial strategic issue? Can we remain radically in the EU – and how?

Walter Baier: Firstly, I dislike the notion of 'by definition' – because in social and political life, actually nothing is defined. If you look at the history of the European integration process, you will find that in different stages, the European Union and its predecessor institutions – the European Community of Coal and Steel and then the European Communities – had very different functions. Initially, it was about subordinating French and German heavy industry to a common administration in order to do away with the sources of the eternal German-French cleavage. Then in the second phase, it was a free-trade agreement, trying to create the framework for the stabilisation of European welfare state arrangements. And in another phase after the fall of the Berlin Wall, the neoliberal turn came. So, what we see now is a neoliberal integration process. But that doesn't justify the misleading dilemma – either European integration or national self-determination. The EU does constitute a sort of democratically deficient constitutional treaty. But like any treaty or constitution, it can be changed and can even be written anew. I personally don't see the nation-state and the national feelings of the European people disappearing. Nor do I believe in a socialist transformation in one country only. We can think of socialism only in a European, most probably even global scope.

That's why I think, and this is not an ideological but a political, pragmatic matter and not a theoretical one, that our goal should be ecological transformation, energy transition, and European industrial policies for all. To achieve all these goals, we need an intelligently designed European frame. We need European minimum social standards; something which is not easily achieved, because of the objective differences in the economic potential of member states. This is not – as nowadays – about creating a level playing field for companies, but the establishment of common social and tax policies. So, for this reason, I believe we need to come up with a design for European integration which carefully balances the democratic self-determination of the people in the nation-state with transnational democracy.

To open a parenthesis: as we see nationalisms rising all across Europe, we also have to admit that even the nation-states which currently form the European Union consist of different peoples. So, integration is not only a problem of the supra-state level, it's also a problem within the states. My view is that the European level might be the appropriate frame to address the many national conflicts which we see within European states.

Haris Golemis: Those who support the view that a radical social transformation isn't possible often cite as an example the case of the Syriza-led government in Greece formed in January 2015. In that case the Troika of the country's lenders (European Commission, European Central Bank, International Monetary Fund) didn't allow Syriza to implement its electoral programme, and insisted that it should follow the lines of the two adjustment programmes, or Memoranda as they use to call them in Greece, agreed by the previous governments. After six months of hard negotiations and following a referendum in which the Greek people rejected the Troika's final proposal by 61.3%, the government, threatened with an expulsion from the eurozone and possibly from the EU, was forced to succumb and sign a third painful Memorandum. It is this disregard for the democratic will of a sovereign people (both in elections and especially in the referendum) that underlies the argument of those who support Lexit, let alone the fact that the programme of the Greek government was only a mild Keynesianism, not a socialist experiment. They have a point, don't they?

Walter Baier: I do not neglect either the necessity or the possibility of expressing the will of the people through national governments. The problem I would like to address is that it's not about the European Union per se, but about the dominance of the international financial markets and the financial institutions. And if you look carefully into the Greek case, it was less about the European treaties or the European institutions, as much as these latter executing the pressure and the demands of the international financial institutions, for which Syriza had to be subdued.

So, in practical terms the European integration process adds a political frame to the spontaneous effect of the power relations on the financial markets. I think the political frame can be changed – while the power relations on the international markets would continue to exist, even if a country decided to leave the European Union. Everything is about power relations. Of course, it is a different matter if France is disobeying rather than Greece. But at the same time, in the 1980s, Mitterrand also tried to disobey the international financial markets and had to accept that even a strong country is forced to adapt and adjust. Indeed, this is why Jacques Delors decided to invest himself in the deepening of European integration. So, the problem which we face is that on the one side we have a neoliberal construction of the European Union, and on the other the economic dominance of the financial markets and the financial sector. In this situation the only leverage that I see for us is, in fact, changing the political construction of Europe.

Haris Golemis: But how? Can we rely only on the European Parliament, for example, can we rely on some kind of first move coming from a big EU member state? It is easy to give prescriptions of what should be done – and here I agree with you that getting out of the EU is not a solution – but we don't know how to do it.

Walter Baier: The problem is less in the recipe. The problem is in the fact that on the European level our left represents on average only 5%, that we are represented with minorities in some governments of small countries, and where we did achieve a majority it was in an economically weak country, in the year 2015 and the years that followed. This is the problem which we need to address.

Speaking about European unity and European integration generally, I think we should abandon a teleological approach to the problem. It is more about having an orientation, i.e. one of admitting that states exist and will continue to exist, and at the same time that the traditional idea of transforming our societies through governing the state or assuming power in one state is not sufficient to address the problems of ecological crisis, globalisation, and security.

Haris Golemis: This brings us to the next question. The war in Ukraine has developed into a conflict between the West and Russia, which is very dangerous for world peace. In this situation, there has been a serious blow to the concept of 'European sovereignty' and strategic autonomy with regards to the United States and NATO, an autonomy in the past supported not only by the Eurocommunists, such as Enrico Berlinguer, but even by Charles de Gaulle. Then it was about autonomy in between the two blocs. Now, during the war, it has to do with not following the US and the West in their antagonism to Russia and China.

So do you think that achieving this vision requires the transformation of the European Union into a normal federal state with a constitution, a central government with a large budget, extensive executive powers, including those relating to fiscal policy, a true European Parliament, a European Central Bank and a single currency valid throughout its territory, a European Court of Justice – and finally, a federal police force and European Army? Is this feasible, and desirable from a radical left point of view?

Walter Baier: Firstly, I would say that the allegiance or rather the subordination of the European states to the US during the war was a political choice and does not result from the constitutional order of the EU, or from structural constraints. It was politically decided by the major states, although you easily get the feeling that none of the heads of these states were really happy with it. But after all, they joined in the confrontational policies of the United States and that's very bad for Europe. Secondly, I am not part of the federalist camp. So, when we are talking about industrial policies, mobility policies, the energy transition, we talk about a grand design on the European level and the huge amounts of money which ought to be raised, but also about even important changes in the habits and mindsets of the people. All this can only be done under the conditions of democratic decision-making. Of course, I'm in favour of a common budget, much bigger than the 1.2% which the EU currently disposes of. But at the same time, I would reiterate that economically, socially, and politically it is important to find the right balance between spaces, so that, so to speak, national self-determination is realised. And on the other hand, what is defined as common spaces, or common policies must be placed under a system of transnational democracy. This means, of course, that we need to transform the European Parliament into a fully-fledged parliament constituted by representatives of fully-fledged European parties. It must have the right of electing the executive, passing laws, and controlling the European Central Bank. But I don't think that this necessary balance between national self-determination and democracy on the European level can be conceived in terms of conventional constitutions, civil law. There is the Austro-Marxists' argument that there are no readymade recipes for designing national arrangements in conflicting and contradictory societies. If it's about finding names, I would prefer to define this European model, which we have to develop, as a 'common', possibly as a Commonwealth, but certainly not as a European federation. Is this an abstract perspective? I don't think so, at least if we don't think of Europe in a teleological way – meaning we want to achieve a European federation with a European president, about 2050 – but rather as a continuous political transformation.

For example, we should oppose a European army, of course, because it would be nothing other than the European pillar of NATO. From a leftist point of view, we cannot accept the way of thinking that goes 'first, let's demand an army and let's, later on, discuss its political and strategic purposes'. So, I would say things ought to proceed the other way around. And this leads again to the question of the necessity of thinking outside the box of conventional constitutional theories, because as a matter of fact, European integration must have a security dimension. Obviously, the security dimension means to have structured and institutionalised relations to states and countries which do not belong to the core of that what is now called European integration. So, what we ideally want to see is a common home of Europeans, consisting of a variety of institutional and political arrangements. I think this is the direction which we should take steps toward.

Haris Golemis: Is the only reason you are against a European army the fact that it will be part of NATO, or is it because in our view of international politics what we need is another kind of security in Europe, another kind of handling matters than war, because when you have an army, you are involved in wars. If the vision is a Commonwealth, as you said, there is no need for a common army.

Walter Baier: Exactly. It's a very principled position. We are against armies and wars. It's as simple as that. But in real political terms, being against NATO is not only, so to say, the conclusion which we draw from the life experience of our generation. It also has the dimension of a search for peace, because this latter tells us that military blocs are actually impeding common security. Replacing military blocs through common security means achieving situations in which the level of armaments is reduced, in which trust-building measures and schemes are introduced. Again, it's not about abolishing armies, but a process of reducing their importance. But forming a new army isn't a good step in that direction, since even simply for technical reasons, in the first phase at least, it would not replace existing armies but add to them.

Haris Golemis: Since we're talking about armies, what about Frontex, which is a kind of military force whose task is to protect the borders of Europe.

Walter Baier: It's the emblematic case of the shame of the European Union. Because if you seriously think about human rights and adequate asylum and border politics, you should firstly think of safe pathways for an orderly, organised immigration. You should secondly not create an armed unit, but you should attach these policies to social ministries and not to the police and the military. So, also with Frontex you see that if you make certain structural arrangements, they lead to a certain policy. And if you do want to avoid these policies, then you have to avoid creating structures such as a European army.

Haris Golemis: We are in a period of war between Ukraine and Russia – and in fact, we know, between the West and Russia. What do you think should be the attitude of the left in Europe and the Party of the European Left (EL)?

Walter Baier: Well, I think the Party of the European Left has taken a very good decision in its Congress in Vienna by focusing on three elements: ceasefire, negotiations, and the withdrawal of Russian troops. These three elements are, of course, not the formula for a diplomatic process, but symbolise our attitude, namely that we demand peaceful and diplomatic means to end the war.

Without any doubt it was the Russian Federation who started the war unjustifiably in breach of international law, unacceptably. There is no question about this. But we also know that NATO could have prevented the war by having delivered to Russia the security guarantees it was demanding. If we are honest, we must say both sides wanted this war, and that's why it's an imperialist war, possibly the prelude of a more dangerous standoff between China and the United States. Tragically, Volodymyr Zelenskiy, seduced by nationalism, has offered his country as the theatre of this war and is sacrificing his people. That's why ceasefire, negotiations, and the withdrawal of the Russian troops are so essential, because we require conflict resolution according to the rules of international law and in the framework of the international institutions.

My personal attitude is that there is no reason, not even a need, to justify a pacifist attitude.

Haris Golemis: In the EU there are enormous and widening economic and cultural differences between its core states and the states of some of its other regions – Southern European states, the majority of Central and Eastern European states (CEE), the Baltic states, and the Balkan states. Should the radical political and social left of these countries strengthen and 'enhance' their cooperation, to put it in EU language, or will this disturb their unity with the corresponding forces in the core EU countries? This question, of course, applies to the Party of the European Left. Do you favour this kind of regional left cooperation of social and political forces?

Walter Baier: Well, I'm very much in favour of this cooperation because it fits perfectly into this idea of a variety of arrangements within the European space – not only on the state level, but also on that of political parties and social movements. If the European Union was a real advanced democracy, alliance building would be a very normal process that would be happening in the European Parliament, and indeed between social movements.

I don't think that left-wing political and social alliances on the level of the regions you mentioned would disturb the unity with the corresponding political forces in the more privileged EU countries. I know that these kinds of tensions, for example, exist in the European trade-union movement. The core idea of political parties is class-based, and this implies also that alliances are class based. The idea of uniting the peripheries does not stop us from acknowledging that even there, as well as in the privileged societies of the EU, huge cleavages between classes and social strata exist. Meaning, if we speak of alliances between the European peripheries, we are talking about alliances between common people, workers, the precarious, and women. I cannot see any reasonable argument why that should disturb the unity of the left, or create problems for the EL.

Haris Golemis: In a recent *Jacobin* interview you said that when describing the European Left, you prefer the term 'socialist Left'. May this cause confusion between our radical left, which seeks to overcome capitalism, and the social democracy of the Party of European Socialists?

Walter Baier: In the past, I have written that there exists a terminological confusion because in CEE, including Germany and Austria, we use the word 'socialist' for a particular current which situates itself to the left of social democracy, almost a 'left socialism'. Simultaneously, the term 'radical left' has different connotations in different countries. In Germany or in France, it more or less refers to the Trotskyist end of the political spectrum. Sometimes, I smile because often the politics of our parties are rather moderate and rightfully so, since we accept the constitutional frame of liberal democracies.

So, what would be our distinctive characteristic? I would say it lies in the assertion that the people must emancipate themselves from the dominance of private capitalist property, and of the uncontrolled financial markets. To put it differently, ecological transformation, overcoming patriarchy, creating a society of care and of peace require not only a cultural change – including consumer habits which many left-minded people, even liberals, would agree with – and go beyond even political change. A change in the productive and property relations is needed. And this, in my opinion, is, so to say, the essence of what socialism is about.

Haris Golemis: What are your hopes and expectations for the 2024 European elections, for the Party of the European Left and beyond?

Walter Baier: I think that we can expect a considerable strengthening of the far-right parties in their different nuances. If they were able to form a common group, from open neofascist currents to far-right nationalism in the style of Viktor Orbán, they could really form a very powerful group. There are many reasons for this, and now isn't the time to discuss the far right. But politically speaking, this largely reflects the fact that the so-called traditional right, the conservative right, is adopting and justifying the far right's agenda. This is very troubling. As for us, if we could unite all the forces which belong to our family in the broad sense, i.e. the European Left and the parties with which it shares a large portion of its agenda, there could be a growth in the number of MEPs. But the question of whether we are really able to unite will be decided in the coming months. My own ambition is to do the utmost to create such a unity; it is, we might say, the emblematic slogan of my current term as president of the Party of the European Left.
The strongest sign of hope, actually, is the series of social struggles which we are seeing now in Europe. It's in France, it's in the UK, it's in Belgium, it's in Greece, it's in Germany. It's an open question if the left can respond to this new situation by creating unity.

I would think we have to understand that these are class struggles. All the rhetoric that 'class does not matter anymore' is, in my opinion, obsolete in light of these recent experiences. Of course, it is class struggle in a modern and new way, but it is about class. It's also a struggle to break with the neoliberal historic bloc which is in power in the main European countries. This historic bloc includes the billionaires of the finance industry, Big Pharma, the military industrial complex, the politicians, the media tycoons. And that's why I think it's justified to speak of an elitist layer in our societies. I think we have to oppose this layer with a strategy which I would like to call 'class populism'. That is, turning to the popular layers of society, while at the same time keeping the conclusions which we draw from a class analysis. And again, the criterion, if such a strategy can be implemented, lies in our capacity to create unity amongst the different forces which belong to our political family. We say 'family' instead of 'radical-left parties', because it's more accurate in sociological terms.

Haris Golemis: It seems to me that any kind of radical change in individual states – big or small, in Europe, but also in the world – requires political and social alliances, operating at the national, European, and world scale. What initiatives do you think the Party of European Left should take in this direction?

Walter Baier: I think that firstly we should elaborate on our own characteristics – social justice, ecological sustainability, feminism, democracy – and try to unite the family on the basis of them. I believe that what applies here is Polanyi's argument that what is required is that societies take back, so to say, the competence of managing societal development through changing the property order. Secondly, it's obvious that change requires dialogue and alliance building both on the national and the European level. We have to do both. Then we should see that there are parties which, in a certain way, belong to our political family and at the same time to the broader left. The Greens in Italy, for example, are part of the Alleanza Verdi e Sinistra, and Yolanda Díaz's Sumar movement is supported by both the European Left Party and the European Greens. Instead of looking at this situation with suspicion we should try to take advantage of it in order to create common goals and objectives on the European level. The EL's efforts at this level include the Forum of Progressive Forces in Europe, which this year will be held in Athens, hopefully with the very broad participation of different progressive forces in the largest sense. This has also a more international dimension. We are cooperating with the São Paulo Forum, which is also a very broad and diverse organisation. Transform! europe, the European Left's political foundation, cooperates with Clacso, which corresponds to the São Paulo forum. I would hope that we could find links to comparable fora in Asia and Africa. Not to forget the Christian-Marxist dialogue which we have initiated, aimed at a broad audience. Defining our own characteristics must not by any means contradict our willingness and our determination to create dialogue and broad alliances.

Authoritarian Capitalist States

The State and Restoration

Boris Kagarlitsky

There is a well-known saying by Friedrich Engels that revolution, by dint of political and social inertia, extends beyond its historical tasks. In a certain sense this can also be applied to reaction. As it gains momentum, a given political process transforms into a force of inertia, according to which each subsequent step is predetermined not even by specific social, economic or political tasks, but by the logic of previous events, earlier decisions, and the new interests which emerged as a result. The evolution of the Russian state at the beginning of the twenty-first century is a vivid illustration of this thesis.

The Promise of Democracy

The basic institutions of political democracy were introduced in the USSR thanks to the policy of perestroika initiated by Mikhail Gorbachev. The changes did not take place without hiccups, but by 1990, Russia already had a multiparty system, competitive elections, a press free of state censorship, and courts which were beginning to show signs of independence. Of course, many democratic processes and structures were still in their infancy, and society itself was far from having mastered the new rules of political behaviour. Nonetheless, a significant part of the Soviet country's population had every reason to expect a successful continuation of democratisation, which, although initiated from above, was taking place under serious pressure from below.

Yet, three decades later, it is difficult to name a single republic of the former Soviet Union that could serve as an example of a successfully functioning democracy. Even the three Baltic states that joined the European Union lag far behind their Western neighbours in this regard. Discrimination against the Russian-speaking population in voting rights and education remains a fundamental political principle there. The persecution of leftist politicians and prohibition of communist parties are not regarded there as an attack on civil liberties since the struggle against the totalitarian past and the Russian threat serves as a justification for all of it. The persecution of leftists and physical reprisals against dissidents have become common practice in Ukraine since 2014, and corruption scandals have shaken Moldova. In Georgia, Kyrgyzstan and Armenia, the democratic order is maintained through periodic popular uprisings and mass protests. Other countries are ruled by open dictatorships or else by 'hybrid regimes', which allow some freedoms, but even the possibility of peaceful transitions through free elections.

Against this backdrop, Russia at the beginning of the twenty-first century did not look like the worst example. However, throughout the post-Soviet period, the political system evolved not towards the expansion and development of democracy, but in precisely the opposite direction. The authoritarian evolution of the state reached its climax in Russia in 2020-23, when the 'hybrid' regime of 'managed democracy' was replaced by an open dictatorship. To understand why it turned out this way, it is pointless to seek an answer in the analysis of political institutions. The deeper reasons for this process lie in the realm of economics.

On the one hand, the dismantling of the welfare state, which has taken place more or less wherever neoliberalism has prevailed, has increased inequalities and exacerbated the contradictions already existing in society. In theory, of course, market ideology assumed that expanding economic freedom would enable people to earn their own money to solve their problems without becoming dependent on bureaucrats to provide 'public services'. In practice, however, the number of people whose lives were made worse, or at least substantially more difficult, by the elimination or reduction of social protections increased sharply. The growing spontaneous discontent was counterbalanced by a strengthening of the state's organs of repression.

On the other hand, there were also specific problems on the territory of the former Soviet Union that worked to strengthen authoritarian tendencies. The issue stems from the nature of Soviet industrial enterprises, which were not only structures of production, but also part of the state, with its entire complex of institutions – social, political, ideological, etc. They were tightly integrated into the system of state administration and directly interacted with administrative bodies, solving many problems together with them.[1] Privatisation and the destruction of the enterprises which followed created an administrative and political vacuum at the local level. This could not be filled with institutions of formal democratic representation imported from the West, and no one even tried to replace them. The vacuum was mostly filled by new practices of administrative paternalism and informal arrangements between bureaucracy and local business. Citizens were excluded from participation in decision-making, losing even those channels of influence and feedback that existed in Soviet times, when it was possible to solve personal and collective issues through party, Komsomol, and trade union committees.

Authoritarianism and oligarchy

Growing social tensions created a natural demand for authoritarianism at the top of society. However, the evolution of state structures was gradually influenced by several differently directed tendencies. Although Boris Yeltsin in 1993 did not hesitate to order tanks to fire at the first freely elected parliament, and did so to the applause of Western politicians, there was no talk of establishing a dictatorial regime. On the contrary, for Russia's ruling circles, as well as for their partners in the West, the preferred option was a state system which combined elements of authoritarian and democratic rule. This, not only because it was better for Russia's reputation, but also because the Russian elite itself was not consolidated.

In the history of Russia's new capitalism, we can clearly distinguish three phases. The first was the phase of oligarchic privatisation, when there were a number of more or less organised groups associated with the state, which simultaneously seized and divvied up national property, competing with each other. Each group formed its own media, financed its own politicians, and often directly competed for power. Democratic institutions, preserved formally though not substantively, created a favourable environment for this competition. Moreover, the seized property had to be legalised in the West, and the companies emerging on this basis had to be integrated into the global economy. The presence of Western-style political institutions in Russia made it easier to solve these problems.

And yet it is pointless to speak of democracy in 1990s Russia. Oligarchic groups controlled the press and television and directly influenced elections. Corruption became the most important aspect of state institutions and played a role in all kinds of decisions. Moreover, both for the bureaucracy and for private companies, their business rationality was based on corrupt interests. The oligarchic groups themselves were not yet formed along industry lines or on the basis of common business interests; they were formed around individuals who had achieved political influence and were able to convert this influence into capital, such as Boris Berezovsky, Vladimir Gusinsky, Mikhail Khodorkovsky, and so on. President Yeltsin had to strike a balance between the struggling factions and defend them all together against the bulk of the population, who got nothing from this feast of carved-up property.

The order that emerged from this could be called *authoritarian pluralism*.

The system was authoritarian, but there was a diversity of interests and open competition at the top of society, which led to an inability to consolidate the authoritarian model of power (the state functioned in a similar way in Ukraine, the only difference being that there, the conditions Russia experienced in the late twentieth century continued into the early 2020s). Robert Dahl uses the term *polyarchy* to describe such political models: there are several oligarchic groups that share power, while the people are not allowed to participate in politics.[2]

Putin No. 1

The situation began to change with Vladimir Putin's first rise to power. This, of course, is not only due to the personality of the new president whom Boris Yeltsin chose as his successor. The collapse of the rouble in 1998 led to the departure of several oligarchic groups from the scene. At the same time, the sharp depreciation of the national currency increased the competitiveness of Russian products and created incentives for economic growth, and the equally sharp increase in world oil prices allowed the state to pay off its foreign debt and accumulate resources. It also provided an opportunity for state paternalism to use its largesse to ease social tensions. In the 2000s, Russian capitalism entered a new phase in which the oligarchic groups, earlier formed on a random basis, were reconstructed into more or less rationally organised corporations with their own stable bureaucratic structures, strategies, and conscious long-term interests. The 'first wave' oligarchs who failed to fit into the new relations were removed from power and pushed out of business. Their place was taken up by representatives of the new corporate elites, replenishing their ranks from among government officials and high-ranking functionaries of the secret services, who are much more capable of coping with the challenges of governing in the new environment.

This was Vladimir Putin's golden age. And the Russian president himself was not at all like what he would become after spending more than two decades in the Kremlin. This 'Putin No. 1' was not just younger and healthier, but also much more rational. As the leader of the Russian bourgeois class, he was perfectly suited to the new challenges of the times. The stage had arrived when all the most valuable property had already been seized and divided, and its new owners were interested in stability. They needed to build their business reputations, promote corporate brands, and increase their business capitalisation. This demand automatically led to an ideological reassessment of the past. In the 1990s, when enterprises were being taken over, everything that remained of the USSR was devalued, but now there was a need to increase the value of acquired assets. The capitalisation of Russian companies was growing rapidly, and so on the ideological level there was a partial rehabilitation of the Soviet heritage. If, before, the discussion of the company being privatised had focused on its gross inefficiency, then, now that its shares needed to be sold, the subject of discussion became its brilliant history and traditions.

The Soviet past began to be used to justify and legitimise the capitalist present. But what was borrowed from the Soviet heritage, here, was not the belief in social progress, enlightenment, or friendship between the peoples and equality, but rather the USSR's authoritarian, conservative, and imperial elements. They were quite successfully incorporated into the ideology of new capitalism.

At first, this reconstruction of the state and economic system was successful. Under Putin No. 1 an important change took place: The interest in stability within the elite put an end to the war of all against all. A sharp increase in state revenues not only made it possible to save the remnants of social programmes – they were even expanded.

Society could be consolidated using not only repressive measures. In the 1990s, a large part of the lower strata of society already had hopes of benefiting from the neoliberal reforms. And their hopes were not entirely without foundation. Although factories were closing down, small businesses were opening, and whole new industries were springing up: mass international tourism, private banks and insurance companies, and a burgeoning service sector. Those who wished to study abroad were free to leave, and after 2000 many families had the money to pay for a foreign education. The opportunities for social mobility for young people were, despite the problems and risks, much greater than in the late Soviet era. With this, support for the government increased dramatically. At the same time, however, the system, having reached social and political equilibrium, would become more and more closed. Social mobility began to fall and the cadre of ruling circles stabilised. The ruling groups were categorically unwilling to share power with the majority of society, let alone access to the decision-making process.

The 2008 crisis

In the 1990s, proponents of neoliberal reforms attributed the failure of individuals and entire social groups or industries to the fact that they 'did not fit into the market'. However, this situation changed in the 2000s when the situation became more favourable for the export of Russian raw materials. The corporate capitalisation grew by leaps and bounds, completely independently from the quality of management or the technological level of production. Everything changed dramatically in 2009, when the waves of the global crisis, dubbed the Great Recession, broke in Russia. It was clear that, on a global level, the neoliberal model of capitalism had reached its limits, yet the ruling circles of the leading countries were not only unwilling to make any serious changes, but, on the contrary, they used the crisis as an excuse to further curtail the social rights of working people. Specifically for Russia, this meant that its economy first fell sharply due to a steep decline in the demand for raw materials, and then began to recover quite successfully because the US Federal Reserve and then the European Central Bank, bailing out the financial institutions of the West, literally flooded the market with liquidity. Excess funds went into speculative markets, including investments in oil futures, which boosted the revenues of Russian oil corporations and the budget. However, as Russia exited the crisis, both its economy and social policy changed dramatically. The oligarchy no longer recognised the possibility of continuing social handouts to the general population. In 2010, huge resources were needed to save the corporations. The funds were provided by the budget and later returned, but from that moment on both the government and private companies began to actively accumulate new foreign currency reserves, fearing a new wave of the crisis. Having restored the level that existed before the Great Recession, the Russian economy failed to reach its former growth rate and began to stagnate. The real incomes of the population no longer continued to rise, while household debt grew, and many regions of the country could no longer balance their budgets as normal.

The peripheral commodity economy that then emerged in Russia as a result of neoliberal reforms simply had no internal sources of growth that could shore it up against a weak – and most importantly, unstable – external environment. There was still demand on the world market for Russian raw materials, but prices fluctuated wildly. This increased the need for companies and the treasury to accumulate reserves, perceived as the only way to solve the problem. In parallel, there was a partial reorientation to China as a more stable growth machine. But all was not well here either. The growth rate of the Chinese economy was slowing. Beijing's leadership was not so much interested in obtaining large quantities of raw materials, as in the maximum reduction of prices for them, because it was a question of maintaining the competitiveness of production in changed and deteriorating conditions. Thus the Chinese 'engine' turned out to be capable of keeping the Russian economy running, but it did not allow it to increase its pace of development – the shift that would allow it to solve the problems it has accumulated.

Putin No. 2

Against the backdrop of the changed economic situation, the nature of domestic politics was also changing. The quality of management was sharply falling, and at the forefront was a desire to strengthen connections with power, which had saved companies in 2010 and could save them in the event of a new crisis. Personal relationships within the elite became the most important factor of stability for all participants in the process. The bureaucratic rationalisation that characterised the early 2000s gave way to the personalisation of politics and business, resulting in a rapid return to the oligarchic model that existed in the 1990s. The fundamental difference from that period being, however, that while under Boris Yeltsin's rule the oligarchs fought against each other directly, now they lobby their interests by strengthening ties with the top political leadership.

It is noteworthy that the transition from the 2000s model of governance to the new order that emerged during the 2010s took place in a context of a political interlude, when Vladimir Putin temporarily ceded the presidency to Dmitry Medvedev and sat in the prime minister's chair. Of course, real power still remained in his hands, but the reshuffles that took place, especially by the time Putin returned to the Kremlin as president, led to a very serious readjustment of the system.

This process was not without its difficulties, since in 2011-12 the government faced strong protests provoked by the rigged parliamentary elections. Still, it was able to limit street unrest to the major cities, and then suppress them. By the summer of 2012 the contours of the new governing system had more or less taken shape. 'Putin No. 1' was replaced by 'Putin No. 2'. Power came increasingly to resemble Yeltsin's order, in the sense that it was organised around certain individuals and groups, and the level of access to the body of the president determined the extent of economic influence. The difference was that now the clans were acting not in competition, but in coalition, and able to negotiate the constant redistribution of resources. Therefore, the function of Putin as the principal mediator became crucial, as he would provide a balance between the oligarchic groups interested in grabbing everything for themselves. The president's personality took on an increasingly important role in the system's everyday functioning, with elites afraid that if he left there would be no one to manage their relations. The system thus became less and less orderly and stable. It could no longer purchase the support of the population through a generous social policy, as the accumulation of funds in the Stabilisation Fund had become a kind of *idée fixe*. Now, the primary emphasis would instead fall on propaganda and repression. It is characteristic of this period that the presidential administration fixated constantly and almost maniacally on Putin's popularity ratings, which gradually declined and had to be sustained artificially. There was no natural mechanism of maintaining trust in the authorities. While in the past the state propaganda machine could successfully compete with the independent media (if not on equal terms), now, despite huge investments (including technological ones), it was beginning to lose out. The only answer was a gradual strangulation of independent media. But in the new technological environment, it is not so easy to do this. Before, it was enough to simply maintain control over television, but with the advent of the Internet it has become increasingly problematic for the Kremlin to retain a loyal audience. The revelations of corruption by Alexei Navalny's Anti-Corruption Foundation showed that the Internet can be used as a channel for influencing public opinion and political mobilisation, and successfully compete in this with censored television. The ruling circles discovered a solution in fighting not only against the opposition media itself, but also directly against the people who created that media. More and more repressive laws were adopted, and in many cases, the authorities did not limit themselves to the rules of legal sanction.

Nevertheless, discontent grew, as did the conflicts at the top. That part of the bourgeoisie that did not enter into Putin's inner circle was also unsatisfied with its position. In turn, the reliance on informal networks as a mechanism for sorting out and solving any and all conflicts and problems resulted in a ruling group that was increasingly self-contained. It was already becoming very difficult, almost impossible, to replace leading ministers and government officials, even if they had completely failed in their work. Removing such a person could cause the entire informal system of connections, all the arrangements and agreements between the various groups, to collapse. The knot of informal ties and mutual obligations turned out to be impossible to untangle. They became more and more complicated and opaque.

The Opposition

Alexei Navalny's opposition activity has been an attempt to challenge the system from outside, from that part of the bourgeoisie that had not joined the elite. But just as in 2011-12, his protest was quashed using repressive methods. The authorities also ignored the protests against pension reform in 2018. Public discontent initially found an outlet in voting for the candidates of official opposition parties, some of whose representatives even developed a kind of taste for politics. In 2018-19, candidates of the pro-government United Russia party failed in elections again and again, with opposition governors winning leading positions in major regions such as

Irkutsk and Khabarovsk Krai. In response, the Kremlin was forced to act. Unruly governors were removed (Sergei Levchenko resigned in Irkutsk Oblast, and Sergei Furgal was arrested in Khabarovsk Krai). The electoral laws were radically revised to make rigging as easy as possible. It can be said that the Russian election laws passed in 2020-21 represent a unique case in which rules were specifically adopted to streamline and prepare for election fraud, making it into an institutional framework for the process itself. These include rules restricting the rights of observers, three-day voting in which uncounted ballots are kept at night in an area where access is prohibited to all but government-appointed election commissioners, and non-transparent 'remote electronic voting' that simply allows votes in any quantity to be attributed to the 'right' candidates.

Along with the reform of the electoral legislation, measures were taken to tighten control over the Duma parties. Even before this, they had only relative autonomy, but now they would finally be placed in the position of junior partners to the government, without any ability to make independent decisions. Politicians who did not agree with the new rules were either marginalised or pushed out of their parties. With respect to especially recalcitrant members of the Communist Party of the Russian Federation, the authorities resorted to direct repression, and the party leadership not only failed to protect their own activists but, on the contrary, stood in solidarity with the authorities.

The Covid epidemic that began in 2020 was an extremely convenient excuse for stepping up control and repression. Under the pretext of fighting the spread of the disease, protests and marches were banned – that is, for everyone but the authorities themselves, who went on staging parades and the like as if nothing had happened. After the medical restrictions on Covid were lifted, the ban on street protests for the opposition remained in place. Changes to the electoral law were also attributed to the epidemic but were not repealed once it was over.

Amendments to the constitution, adopted in 2020 and approved by a rigged 'popular vote',[3] gave Vladimir Putin the opportunity, as an exception, to hold his post until 2036, effectively securing his position as president for life. But whatever rhetoric might be used to cover up such decisions, they were a consequence and a vivid illustration of the institutional weakness of a regime that could neither ensure presidential succession nor nominate a single politician from its ranks who could claim both the trust of the elites and the respect of the people. Neither prohibition nor propaganda could conceal the growing tensions in society. Most importantly, the personalisation of political power was becoming a factor of vulnerability. Rumours of problems with

Putin's health, which had been circulating in political circles for a long time, were becoming a real threat to stability. Various factions of the oligarchy began to work out their own plans in the event of a possible change in the chief executive. And here it was not so important how ill the president really was. The fact that there was a discussion about a possible change in the head of state was itself changing and destroying the existing balance of power: once the question of the transition of power is raised, it will not go away. And it is not surprising that in the minds of top officials there emerged an idea to strengthen power and consolidate elites and society by achieving foreign policy successes. Ukraine seemed the most convenient field for achieving this. After all, in 2014, when a political crisis arose in the neighbouring country, Russia was able to annex Crimea without much trouble, and this certainly contributed, albeit not for long, to an upsurge in patriotism and a strengthening of the authority of the government in the eyes of society. The 'Crimean consensus' that emerged at the time was short-lived and finally evaporated after Putin's extremely unpopular pension reform in 2018. But the idea of the importance of foreign policy and patriotism in stabilising the domestic political situation was firmly planted in the minds of officials. An offensive operation against Ukraine, repeating on a larger scale what had already happened eight years earlier, seemed a very simple and convenient solution. However, things turned out quite differently.

Reactionary Caesarism

The theoretical question that inevitably arises, for the researcher trying to understand the nature of the political regime that emerged in Russia at the beginning of the twenty-first century, is that of its place in the general process of historical development. The system of personal power established during Putin's presidency is not a historical anomaly, let alone a result of the personal qualities of the president and his entourage. It is useless to look for the causes of what has happened in the 'cultural codes' of the Russian state, which are supposedly doomed to reproduce authoritarian models from its previous history.

In the late 2010s, sociologist Grigory Yudin described the Russian state order as a 'plebiscitary democracy' comparing it to the regime of Napoleon III in nineteenth-century France.[4] Of course, even in the golden years of Putin's rule it was possible to speak of 'democracy' in Russia only with very serious reservations (even the authorities' supporters used the terms 'managed democracy' or 'sovereign democracy'), but the comparison of early twenty-first century Russia to Second Empire-era France is eminently valid. It is not only a question of the formation of a system of personal power legitimised by popular vote (which was, indeed, systematically falsified). More importantly, these forms of power emerge as the product of a crisis of social transformation, whether progressive or reactionary. Classical Bonapartism (a variant of which we might also consider the protectorate regime of Oliver Cromwell in seventeenth-century England and Stalin's regime in the USSR) was a product of revolution that had lost its potential and produced its own new elite, who were interested in the preservation of revolutionary achievements, but not in their development.

The restoration of capitalism in Russia at the beginning of the twenty-first century produced a similar situation, since the new elite that emerged during the reforms needed political and social consolidation at the expense of even those elements of social mobility that were born of the changes of the 1990s.

Here, it is impossible not to recall Antonio Gramsci's statements about reactionary Caesarism, which reproduces a form of progressive Caesarism, but exactly opposed to it in content. According to Gramsci, such regimes emerge at the moment when struggling forces reach a 'catastrophic equilibrium' (*si equilibrano in modo catastrofico*), when no single class can establish effective hegemony. Then the state apparatus and its leader do not only acquire autonomy – they acquire the ability to become the decisive force in society. Politically and socially, however, this 'does not always have the same historical meaning'. The author of *The Prison Notebooks* gives examples of progressive Caesarism, which includes the regimes of Julius Caesar and Napoleon I, and reactionary Caesarism, which is exemplified by the regime of Napoleon III. Gramsci interprets the difference between these regimes through the dialectic of 'revolution and restoration'. No matter how radical a policy of restoration may be, it can never make a 'complete return' to the past (*in tutto*).[5] Thus, reactionary regimes are forced to make considerable use of the legacy of the progressive period that preceded them (which perfectly explains Putinism's ambivalent attitude toward the Soviet past).

Gramsci also notes that the anchor for Caesarist regimes is provided by the cult of the 'heroic' personality, but that this is no longer necessary under contemporary conditions. In this sense, the cult of Vladimir Putin, which has been artificially created by propaganda against the background of a complete lack of significant personal achievements, and which is already acquiring completely grotesque and absurd forms, is a vivid illustration of the Italian philosopher's thought. But what, according to Gramsci, is an obligatory feature of modern Caesarism, is that it relies not only on the resources of the military and police, but also on society's weakness.[6]

The evolution of Putin's regime vividly confirms that society's U-turn from the perspective set by the revolutionary upheaval of the early twentieth century toward the restoration of bourgeois order has, by virtue of its own internal logic, undermined the conditions for the development of democracy and freedom in the name of which, it would seem, the communist regimes were rejected. And if this anti-democratic logic has not fully prevailed in the countries of Eastern Europe outside the former Soviet Union, this is partly due to the presence of a stronger and more organised civil society there, and partly due to integration into the structures of the European Union. The only question is to what extent the evolution of Western societies against the background of the crisis of neoliberalism corresponds to the logic of democratic development. After all, the emergence in the West of right-wing populist movements led by dubious individuals proves that old European democracies are not immune to such trends, either.

The steady strengthening of authoritarianism in Russia at the beginning of the twenty-first century was the natural and logical result of its neoliberal economic policies, and the resulting Caesarist regime is as prone to military and political adventures as the personalist dictatorship of Napoleon III in nineteenth-century France. The more power is concentrated in the hands of a national leader who claims not only infallible judgment, but also a 'heroic' image, the greater the need to periodically confirm this image with at least some victories. This becomes part of the regime's legitimisation. Paradoxically, the adventurism born of such ideological logic in turn threatens to bring such regimes to their end, as Napoleon III discovered in 1870.

The overaccumulation of capital

Rosa Luxemburg, in her book *The Accumulation of Capital*, written before World War I, clearly demonstrated how the contradictions of capitalist development create imbalances which cannot be solved within the framework of an ordinary market cycle.[7] The use of foreign policy not only as an instrument of capital competition but also as a factor in stabilising the system is a natural consequence of this state of affairs.

The contradiction inherent in the bourgeois order between the social character of production and the private character of accumulation leads to the situation in which resources are accumulated where it is not most profitable for all society. This results in the effect of capital over-accumulation when it is more profitable to invest funds in speculation or to use them in the most irrational way than to invest them in production. For the Russian economy, capital overaccumulation has been a constant problem since the mid-2000s. The state moved money into the Stabilisation Fund, oligarchs bought villas in Nice and Miami, or built unbelievably large yachts. The bureaucrats would simply steal money and stack piles of bills in specially purchased or converted apartments (in this sense, corruption was not so much of a problem as much as – on the level of political economy – a way to solve the problem).

It is revealing that, while economising on pensioners and socially necessary measures, refusing to build roads between regional centres and reducing the number of hospital beds, the authorities have been extremely generous when it came to large, expensive projects. Significant sums were spent on prestigious projects, such as the Winter Olympics in Sochi. After the annexation of Crimea in 2014, a similar super-project was the construction of the Kerch Bridge, which, in addition to its economic importance, acquired military significance.

The growth of Putin's foreign policy ambitions and attempts to pursue an imperialist policy at the regional level are also closely linked to the process of capital accumulation. Excess funds, having found no use inside the country, stimulated foreign expansion. One of the most convenient and profitable uses of surplus resources has been to buy up assets in the former Soviet republics. Ukraine, with its still functional but obsolete and capital-intensive industry, was the ideal territory for the expansion of Russian oligarchic business. Along with businesses and real estate, local politicians who were supposed to protect these investments were bought, since the level of corruption in Ukraine was off the charts even compared to what was going on in Russia. But by meddling in Ukrainian affairs, the Russian elite was stepping into a political quagmire from which it would become increasingly difficult to escape.

The Ukrainian catastrophe

Economic, cultural, and family ties between the societies of Russia and Ukraine have always been so close that even becoming separate states could not break them apart. In the new situation, however, the mutual involvement of Russian and Ukrainian societies in each other's affairs was not only positive but also negative since any political conflicts and processes in one state automatically affected the other. The political crisis that broke out in Ukraine in 2013-14 led to a temporary paralysis of power, and it is quite natural that Russian elites, already actively involved in the affairs of the neighbouring state, took advantage of the opportunities that presented themselves. It is important to note, however, that a significant part of the Ukrainian population, at least in the south-eastern regions of the country, pinned their hopes for improved economic horizons on growing Russian influence, and also saw in the Kremlin an ally who would strengthen the

198 FACING THE STATE

position of these regions in the numerous cultural, political, and economic conflicts that were tearing the country apart. The annexation of Crimea in 2014 was welcomed by much of the peninsula's population. How unanimous that support really was is another question. The opponents of annexation had no ability to participate in the referendum held after the territory was occupied by the Russian military. But for a large part of the residents of Donbass and other regions displeased with Kyiv, Russia's intervention in Crimea was an important signal, and it stimulated decisive action.

The unrecognised republics proclaimed in Luhansk and Donetsk initially relied on spontaneous grassroots protest, which the Kremlin politicians tried in every way to exploit and bring under their control. By 2015, they had succeeded: the Donetsk and Luhansk people's republics had become puppet regimes completely dependent on Moscow. The popular leaders who had led the protests from the start were either removed or died under mysterious circumstances.

In deciding to invade Ukraine in February 2022, Putin and his entourage clearly hoped to repeat the success of eight years prior. Since then, however, the situation had changed in both states. After Volodymyr Zelenskiy's victory in the 2019 elections, the crisis of power in Ukraine, if not completely overcome, had at least become less acute. It was obvious that the new president, who had won his victory in a competitive election, was legitimate. Ukraine's armed forces, which had been in a state of complete decline in the early 2010s, had been brought up to fighting strength and partially modernised.

The Russian ruling circles were also influenced by poor intelligence, overseen by corrupt generals, and by the incompetence of people who had lost touch with reality after holding power without accountability for twenty years.

It is illustrative that Zelenskiy's rule in Kyiv largely repeated the path of the early Putin. He tried to consolidate the elites and streamline the workings of the state under his personal control. In essence, the same personalisation of power was taking place, but the process was at a much earlier stage, and therefore it was impossible to speak of its results. The outbreak of a full-scale war dramatically increased the authority of the president and his team, allowing Zelenskiy to achieve the concentration of power and real powers that he did not have in the early years of his rule. Thus, Putin's Russia was no longer confronted by a failed state, as in 2014, but by a fully capable, though not particularly effective, state. Of course, one cannot speak of Ukraine as a model of democracy, but the minimum level of governability and political consolidation necessary to resist the invasion had been achieved.

Unable to win the war, Putin's regime faced an insurmountable political and moral crisis, the way out of which could be either the radical reform of the state or its revolutionary transformation. In either case, it is clear that, in order to solve the accumulated problems, the system that has developed over the years of Putin's rule must be dismantled.

Restoration, in terms of social dynamics, is a kind of shadow of revolution. It goes through similar stages, gaining the same inertia, going beyond its historical tasks and material possibilities. In this way, the restoration regime is entering a new round of destruction, overcoming not only the social institutions that emerged as a result of the revolution, but also undermining the objective conditions of its own existence. This is exactly what we have been seeing in Russia in the 2020s.

The logic of political and social reaction naturally leads it to self-negation, creating an objective need for a new cycle of revolutionary change. The only open question is whether the society that has survived a long period of degradation – economic, cultural, and political – is capable of successfully coping with the challenges that arise on this basis. But this is, as Karl Marx liked to say, not a theoretical question, but a practical one.

NOTES

1   See I.V. Glushchenko, B. I. Kagarlitsky, and V. A. Kurenny (eds), *SSSR: Zhizn' posle smerti*, Moscow: Izd. Dom Vyssheishkoly ekonomiki, 2012.

2   See Robert A. Dahl, *Polyarchy: Participation and Opposition*, New Haven: Yale University Press, 1971.

3   The authorities did not dare call it a referendum, the organisation of which requires compliance with certain rules. There was a ban on criticising the project and no observers or rules that would have been guaranteed by law in an actual referendum.

4   See G. Iudin, 'Rossiia kak plebistsitarnaia demokratiia', *Sotsiologicheskoe obozrenie* 20,2 (2021): 9-47.

5   Antonio Gramsci, *Quaderni del carcere*, vol. 3, Turin: Einaudi, 2007, p. 1623.

6   Gramsci, *Quaderni*, p. 1624.

7   See Rosa Luxemburg, *Die Akkumulation des Kapitals. Ein Beitrag zur ökonomischen Erklärung des Imperialismus*, Berlin: Vorwärts, 1913.

The Left and the Changing Authoritarian State in Capitalist Poland

Gavin Rae

Little over three decades ago, the countries of Central and Eastern Europe (CEE) were regarded as being at the head of a new wave of political and economic liberalism sweeping the globe. After the populations of these countries had thrown off the yolk of 'communism', they were believed to be forging a new path of democratic and economic reform that would herald an era of stability and prosperity in Europe and beyond. Nevertheless, the neoliberal transformations, from 'socialism' to capitalism, undermined the prospect of liberal democratic orders stabilising in the CEE countries. Moreover, rather than history ending in 1989, a new neoliberal, socially conservative and militaristic international order rose out of the ashes of the Cold War. In this article I will examine the rise of authoritarianism in Poland, by deploying Karl Marx's theory of primitive accumulation and Antonio Gramsci's understanding of the state and civil society. In doing so, I shall consider the ongoing difficulties and challenges facing the Polish left.

The freedom of accumulation

The restoration of capitalism was presented as a great civilisational leap forward for the CEE countries. The accepted neoliberal wisdom of the time was that the economic role of the state had to be diminished as rapidly as possible, in order for the private market to grow. In turn, this would instigate the flourishing of a robust civil society that would protect these countries' burgeoning democratic systems and help to instil liberal values throughout society. Liberals essentially regarded civil society as being synonymous with the growth of a new middle class, who would naturally embody the values of individualism, self-reliance, entrepreneurship, democratic accountability, and so forth.

Despite such proclamations, the CEE countries were not transforming into mythical liberal market economies but were rather being incorporated into the world capitalist economy. Marx took from Adam Smith the notion of primitive accumulation in order to explain the origins of capitalism, which Marx understood as the often violent practice of separating producers from their means of production. The emancipation of producers from the bonds of serfdom and guilds also involved expropriating their previous means of production, making them 'free labourers' dependent upon selling their labour power to the owners of capital. Therefore, 'the expropriation of the mass of the people from the soil forms the basis of the capitalist mode of production, creating the social relations needed for capitalism to develop.[1] Rosa Luxemburg famously elaborated Marx's conception of primitive accumulation, seeing it as a continuous element of capitalist development ('untrammelled accumulation'), through expanding into pre-capitalist countries, regions, and branches of production.[2]

Despite historical differences, the notion of primitive accumulation can still be applied in order to understand the creation of capitalism in the 'post-socialist' countries. During the 'socialist' period, a class of labourers existed that had a largely decommodified existence, upheld by such things as the policy of full employment and the state's monopoly control over production and trade. In order for capitalism to consolidate in the 'post-socialist' countries these barriers had to be removed, compelling workers to sell their labour power to the owners of private capital. Whilst a coherent bourgeois class had not evolved in 'socialism', the shock-therapy reforms paved the way for large foreign capital or oligarchs to take over major sections of the 'post-socialist' economies. In Poland, foreign capital quickly monopolised much of the Polish economy, with the foreign ownership of banks rising to 70 per cent and industry to 35 per cent by the end of the 1990s.[3]

The primitive accumulation of capital in CEE resulted in one of the greatest falls in living standards in peacetime history. Millions of workers were made redundant, poverty and social inequality soared, the existing social welfare system collapsed, and life expectancy slumped. This was most pronounced in the former states of the Soviet Union and Yugoslavia, where capitalism was often reborn through wars, coups, and dictatorships, whose repercussions the world still feels today. In the Central European countries these effects were less severe. Although, Poland's GDP fell by around a quarter during the first three years after the fall of 'socialism', it had recovered its pre-1989 position by 1996 and enjoyed economic growth every year until the Covid-19 pandemic. However, the social effects of the shock-therapy reforms were long-lasting, with millions of workers exiting the labour market. In 1988, 83.5 per cent of the working-age population were in paid employment, a percentage which fell to just 56 per cent 14 years later, with around nine million Poles neither working nor in full-time employment. This contributed to a sharp rise in poverty, which grew (according to the social minimum level of existence measurement) from 14.8 per cent to 57.3 per cent between 1989 and 1994.[4]

The Undemocratic Shock

No proposals for shock-therapy style neoliberal reform were approved at the round-table talks held between the former government and the Solidarity trade union in 1989. Rather, these negotiations concluded with the agreement to build a 'social-market' economy, which would include such things as the workers' self-management of enterprises. This settlement, based on a broad social consensus, was then simply abandoned by the new Solidarity-led government, which introduced a package of neoliberal economic reforms based upon the IMF's recommendations. The government rushed a total of 16 laws through parliament, without any social consultation or public debate, which helped to entrench anti-democratic features into the new political system. According to the left-wing economist, Tadeusz Kowalik:

> The events in Poland between 1980 and 1992 were another tragicomedy. Europe's largest mass labour movement led a social upheaval from which one of the most unjust social regimes in post-war Europe emerged. It is not true that it was only the large industrial working class, employed in outdated 'socialist mammoths', that lost out. Such a claim is a new form of ideological legitimacy. The losers include workers in the private sector, the vast majority of farmers, craftsmen, nurses, and teachers. Their fall in living standards and even status has been somewhat compensated by some regained freedoms. But for these social groups – with the possible exception of teachers – freedoms have been severely limited by the shattering of the foundations of their material existence.[5]

This huge transfer of wealth and ownership was facilitated by the strengthening of unaccountable institutions, such as the courts, state bureaucracies, and media. The courts, for example, enabled the privatisation of property and the forcible removal of tenants from their homes, outside of public scrutiny. The media complied obediently, with almost 80 per cent of the press owned by foreign media conglomerations by the early 2000s and the German press giants (including Axel Springer Verlag, Passauer Neue Presse, Bauer, and Gruner+Jahur) holding over 50 per cent of the colour magazine market and owning numerous national and regional daily newspapers.[6] The Catholic Church received generous subsidies and grants of land, constructing an extensive network of schools, universities, and media outlets and regaining its status as one of the country's major private landowners, amassing extensive wealth and political clout. Simultaneously, participation in the democratic process declined, with turnout in the parliamentary elections consistently averaging less than 50 per cent, and fewer than 1 per cent of the Polish electorate belonging to any political party.[7] Furthermore, trade unions now represented just 1 in 10 workers, meaning that the countermovement of the working class was virtually extinguished in the homeland of the historical Solidarity trade union movement.[8]

Therefore, a form of 'undemocratic liberalism' consolidated itself, with non-elected authorities ensuring that the neoliberal reforms were continued. This political and institutional arrangement undermined the possibility of constructing a robust civil society that could uphold the new democratic system. This can be understood by returning to Gramsci's understanding of the relationship between the state and civil society. According to Gramsci, the capitalist class has historically been able to maintain its political hegemony through consensus, by the state intervening to take on 'the 'protection' of the working classes against the 'excesses of capitalism'. In doing so, the state, according to Gramsci, becomes the 'outer ditch' behind which the 'fortresses' of civil society lie. The educative, interventionist, and protective activities of the state help to create a sturdy, well-formed civil society, meaning that the coercive elements of the state are tempered and the democratic consensus reinforced.[9]

The first form of authoritarianism faced by the Polish left in the early 'post-socialist' era was the non-democratic liberal order established after 1989. However, the majority of the left accepted this new situation, and generally continued the course of neoliberal reform when in office. This was particularly the case when the second centre-left government (2001-2005) deepened the country's neoliberal path in order to meet the accession criteria laid down by the EU, which further stunted economic growth. This government also supported the disastrous US wars in Afghanistan and Iraq and did not challenge the power of the Church by failing to fulfil its election promise to liberalise the abortion law. This led to a collapse in support for the social democratic left in Poland, from which it has never recovered.

Right-wing hegemony

From this time on, two right-wing blocs have dominated Polish politics: the Law and Justice Party (PiS) and Citizens' Platform (PO). These two political formations have been controlled by Jarosław Kaczyński and Donald Tusk respectively, who both derived from the opposition movement in Gdańsk and jointly participated in the extreme neoliberal right-wing coalition government from 1997 to 2001. These parties seemed to be converging during the early 2000s, sharing a common attachment to social conservatism, anti-communism, and Euro-Atlanticism. However, after emerging from the 2005 elections as the largest party, PiS chose to form a governing coalition with two right-wing nationalist and agrarian populist parties. During the electoral campaign, PiS had promised to increase social spending, pledging, for example, to build three million homes. However, once in power, PiS followed the normal script by ditching its economic programme and continuing the established neoliberal economic line. The failures of this government opened the door for PO to win power, with Tusk elected Prime Minister in 2007.

PO won power at a time of economic recovery. After entering the EU, Poland enjoyed a decade and a half of increased economic growth. Companies gained access to the EU single market, unemployment decreased as millions of workers moved abroad, and most importantly billions of euros flowed into the country through EU funds and subsidies, financing a surge in government-led investment. For the first time since the 1970s, the central and local governments were able to invest in parts of the country's infrastructure. Poland became the only EU country that did not fall into a recession following the 2008 financial crisis, whilst the populations in other 'periphery' economies in Ireland and southern Europe bore the cost of the eurozone crisis. This improvement in economic and social conditions ensured that in 2011 PO became the first party in 'post-socialist' Poland to win two successive parliamentary elections.

Yet, whilst Tusk with one hand was increasing public investment through utilising EU funds, with his other he was deepening Poland's neoliberal course. During its second term in office, PO increased its assault on public services by shutting down over 150 hospitals and thousands of primary schools, halving the construction of public housing, and raising the pension age to 67. The precarity of workers (including the burgeoning middle class) grew, with over a quarter of the workforce employed on temporary contracts by 2012 and the proportion of young Poles with a higher education in casual jobs increasing to 39 per cent. The government maintained the state's right-wing conservative stance on issues of abortion, LGBT+ rights and history, not challenging the overwhelming power of the Catholic Church. Meanwhile, it increasingly became tainted by a string of corruption scandals and ostentatious displays of wealth. As large sections of the Polish population were not sharing in the country's growing prosperity, dissatisfaction with the undemocratic liberal political system increased. By the end of PO's second term in office, trust in the country's governing institutions had slumped, with just 13 per cent expressing trust in in the parliament, 20 per cent in the government, and 34 per cent in the courts.[10] At this point, undemocratic liberal rule had reached its end in Poland.

Illiberal Democracy

With the left still marginalised, PiS stood as the main political opposition to the PO government. Kaczyński's party promised to cleanse the Polish state of corruption and represent the people against the interests of the corrupt elite. The party used patriotic rhetoric of standing up for the country's interests against a government and state that were subservient to foreign owned banks, corporations, and media. PiS pledged to raise taxes on large foreign companies and financial institutions, increase welfare spending, and restore the previous pension age. It promised all this whilst whipping up hostility to refugees and refusing to comply with the EU's demand to accept its quota of refugees coming to Europe. PiS won both the parliamentary and presidential elections in 2015, beginning a new chapter in Polish politics.

Once in power, PiS broke the political mould by actually carrying out many of its electoral promises. Most famously, it introduced a new universal child benefit (500+) that led to the halving of child poverty, whilst also lowering the retirement age and raising the minimum wage. Despite dire warnings from the representatives of European and international capital, the Polish economy did not enter a new crisis but continued to expand whilst many of the poorest and socially excluded saw their living standards rise. However, the new government did not directly challenge the power of international capital. It quickly ditched its policy of taxing large supermarkets and maintained the country's regressive business and income tax rates. Two years into the PiS government, Kaczyński appointed Mateusz Morawiecki as Prime Minister, who had previously worked as an economist for financial institutions in Poland and Germany. Despite grumblings about the government's 'pro-social' policies, the institutions of financial capital gave the PiS government their stamp of approval, with Poland becoming the first CEE country to be ranked as a 'developed' country by the FTSE Russel Index.

The PiS government has introduced a range of measures to assert its influence and control over various 'independent' institutions, including the constitutional court, supreme court, and public media, whilst simultaneously seeking to reduce the level of foreign ownership in the press and media. The government has therefore partly curbed the power and interests of powerful domestic and foreign elites, which has at times brought it into conflict with the centres of power in Brussels, Berlin, and Washington. If a progressive left-wing government had been formed in Poland, it would also have had to reform such institutions. However, PiS did so in a way that entrenched its authoritarian right-wing rule, using such institutions to build a new conservative-nationalist political hegemony in the country. Furthermore, the government actually strengthened the political role of one of the most powerful institutions in Poland: the Catholic Church. This political alliance not only further eroded the secular structure of the state but was also deployed to launch a new attack on the rights of women and the LGBT+ community.

Although the PiS government has not seriously challenged the power structure and the major privileges derived from the period of primitive accumulation, nevertheless its takeover of parts of the courts and media has been enough to raise concerns abroad, particularly inside the EU where Tusk worked as President of the European Council from 2014 to 2019. Alongside the Fidesz administration in Hungary, Poland became the black sheep of the European Union and has regularly been threatened with sanctions and fines for its actions. In turn, the PiS government has often resorted to Eurosceptic and 'anti-German' rhetoric, drawing on deep justifiable historical grievances within Polish society.[11] PiS deploys a form of 'cultural nationalism', which challenges the influence of the EU and Germany at a superstructural and ideological level but without questioning the economic structure of domination that underpins it. Meanwhile, although the EU uses the language of liberal democracy and tolerance, its main concern is to return to the status quo where it could better exert its influence through the institutional structure of 'undemocratic liberalism'.

Majoritarianism and opposition

The partial reversal of the previous economic and political course in Poland cemented the social base of support for PiS. Sections of society saw how governments could implement some form of social redistribution and stand up to the powerful lobbies opposing it. Many liberal critics of the PiS government have accused it of 'majoritarianism' – i.e., using the political majority that it has gained through elections to erode the democratic structures of the state. There is some truth in this accusation. However it is also true that the PiS government has won democratic elections fairly, through mobilising a section of the electorate that had effectively been disenfranchised, with turnout at the 2019 parliamentary elections around 10 per cent higher than in any previous election since 1989.

Nevertheless, the PiS government had only partially broken with the past. Its 'pro-social' policies have primarily been based on handing out benefits to certain groups of the electorate, such as pensioners and families. This has firstly enabled it to promote a new conservative *Bismarckian* form of welfarism, as part of its wider campaign of promoting 'traditional Polish' and 'family' values. Secondly, by concentrating on social benefits, the government has prioritised supporting individuals and families financially, whilst continuing to run down public services such as the health service and education. To a large extent this is therefore a continuation of the individualistic neoliberal policies of the past.

The right-wing conservative turn in Poland led to a wave of protest in the country. During its first term in office large demonstrations have been organised against the government's proposals to reform the courts and media. These protests were largely attended by supporters of the previous liberal order, mainly relatively privileged sections of society form the large cities. Parts of the left, it is true, often attended these demonstrations, although liberal politicians, parties, and organisations led them politically. After retaining power in 2019, the PiS government opened up new offensives against the LGBT+ community and women, which resulted in a wave of social mobilisations against them. Far broader layers of society participated in these demonstrations (particularly those against new restrictions on the already draconian abortion law), spreading well beyond the metropolitan centres. The left was able to play a more central role in these protests and partially rebuild its support in society, particularly amongst younger people.[12] In turn, the PiS government used its control over institutions such as the police, courts, and public media, deploying symbolic and physical violence against the demonstrators and opposition.[13]

Despite centre-left forces coalescing into a single electoral coalition (which we will refer to by its Polish name Lewica), it still struggles to gain over 10 per cent in the opinion polls.[14] Lewica has found itself caught between both liberal and conservative authoritarianisms that have overlapped during the past couple of decades. Whilst it rightly opposes many of the conservative authoritarian policies of the PiS government, it has failed to construct a robust alternative pole of opposition independent from PO and the 'liberal centre'. This is becoming clearer as living standards fall in Poland and opposition to the PiS government rises.

Pandemic and inflation

The Covid-19 pandemic exposed the incapacity of the PiS government to correct the systemic failures of Poland's transition to capitalism. In 2021, the average number of deaths in the country rose by nearly 96,000 compared to 2019, with the total number of excess deaths recorded in the country, since the beginning of the pandemic, exceeding 200,000. A total of 506,000 people died in Poland in 2021, the greatest number since the end of the Second World War, when 520,000 deaths were recorded in 1945. Life expectancy has also fallen. In 2020, men in Poland lived on average for 72.6 years, and women for 80.7 years, a decrease of 1.5 and 1.1 years respectively, compared to 2019. The number of recorded births also fell sharply, down by around 155,000 in 2020 alone. In September 2021, the Polish population was recorded as 38,151,000 – a drop of around 200,000 people from the previous year, meaning that the population of Poland is now smaller by around 400,000 than in 2010.[15]

The human cost of the pandemic was much greater in most CEE countries compared to richer nations to their west, partly due to the ongoing weakening of the state's welfare services, particularly the region's public health systems. Whilst average health spending in the European Union equals almost 10 per cent of GDP, this is much lower in most CEE member states (which also have lower levels of GDP per capita) – for example Romania 5.5 per cent, Latvia 6.0 per cent, Poland 6.7 per cent, Hungary 6.9 per cent. Also, the provision of social benefits for children in Poland has not been enough to compensate for the deterioration of health and child-care public services and exploitation of workers on the labour market, which discourage people from having more children.

The Covid-19 pandemic contributed to a sharp rise in inflation, which is eating into living standards. Inflation soared from around 8 per cent to 18 per cent in the year leading up to October 2022. The Polish economy has also been severely hit by the economic fallout from the war in Ukraine at its eastern borders, contracting by 2.4 per cent in the fourth quarter of 2022. The strain on Poland's public services is increasing due to the knock-on effects of the war in Ukraine. This includes facing the challenge of integrating around two-thirds of the estimated 3 million refugees to have fled Ukraine since the start of the war. Around 1.38 million of these have sought temporary protection in Poland and an estimated one million remain in the country.[16] As the war extends deep into the winter, the possibility of a new wave of refugees coming into Poland remains. At the beginning of the war, the Polish population mobilised impressively to help Ukrainians, with huge numbers of refugees accommodated in private homes. However, the Polish government has placed the main burden of housing refugees on individuals, rather than providing more sustainable structural solutions. Also, the arrival of large numbers of refugees has further exposed the underfunding of public services. Around 200,000 Ukrainian children have started attending Polish schools since the start of the war, at a time when Polish schools already faced a severe shortage of teachers.[17]

The Polish government is also beefing up military expenditure. Spending on national defence is set to soar in 2023 to 20.7bn euros, up from 12.3bn euros in 2022, bringing the military budget to above 3 per cent of GDP. A further 8.4bn euro will also be allocated to the Armed Forces Support Fund, organised by the Polish national bank. This would add up to a combined sum of 29bn euros, twice that spent in 2022 and five times greater than that allocated in 2015.[18] In conditions of an economic downturn and rising inflation, this will put further pressure on public finances and lead to curtailed spending on other public and social services. It will weaken the protectionist arm of the state and, as living standards fall and social dissatisfaction rises, raise the prospect of the repressive branch of government coming further to the fore.

Authoritarianism and the left

For the first time, PiS is governing whilst living standards are falling. Yet, despite these difficulties, it has remained the largest party in the opinion polls throughout 2022, ahead of parliamentary elections scheduled for Autumn 2023. As things stand, PiS will emerge from these elections as the party with the largest number of seats in parliament but will lose its overall majority and be unable to form a governing majority. One potential ally has been the far-right Confederation party, which combines neoliberalism with extreme nationalist and xenophobic policies. However, since the Russian invasion, support for Confederation has slumped below the 5 per cent threshold needed to enter parliament due to the party's opposition to actively supporting Ukraine. Confederation will be hoping that they can rebuild their position if war-weariness grows inside the Polish population. Sections of the party have been trying to whip up hostility towards Ukrainian refugees, building on historical resentments and social frustrations in order to scapegoat Ukrainians for the economic difficulties faced by Poles. The party is close to some of the most right-wing and authoritarian sections and personalities of PiS, such as the current Minister of Justice Zbigniew Ziobro. A coalition government of these two parties would represent a convergence of neoliberal and conservative authoritarianism and open up a new more dangerous phase in Polish politics.

In the summer of 2021, Tusk returned to mainstream politics in Poland, becoming leader of the Citizens' Coalition (KO).[19] Although KO's standing in the polls has improved, it still trails PiS by a few percentage points. However, if things remain as they are, it would be able to form a coalition government with the liberal 2050 party and Lewica. Over the past year, Tusk has attempted to change his party's image, recognising that its potential electorate has shifted to the left. KO has announced that it now supports a woman's right to abortion and Tusk has expressed his personal support for same-sex marriages. The former President of the European Council and leader of the European People's Party has also said that if KO forms the next government it will seek to reduce the work week and raise public-sector salaries by 20 per cent.[20] This move has been welcomed by sections of the left, who are now in a de facto alliance with Tusk and KO. At the feminist Womens' Congress, in October 2022, Tusk was given the first special award for men who have contributed to gender equality.[21] Around the same time, the leader of Nowa Lewica, Włodzimierz Czarzasty, declared it had come to an agreement with KO: 'I am informing you that the opposition is agreed, that the opposition is planning together for the future, that the opposition is going to form a government together, and the opposition is not going to be quarrelsome.'[22] And then, remarkably, the left-wing trade union confederation (All-Poland Alliance of Trade Unions – OPZZ) appointed Tusk as one of the public faces of its campaign to protect workers' rights and raise salaries.[23] Although the most left-wing party in the Polish parliament, Razem, has opposed such alliances with KO, it has also stated that it will continue to stand on the joint Lewica electoral slate and will therefore also be drawn closer towards cooperation with KO and Tusk. For Lewica to go along with Tusk's cynical manoeuvres is symptomatic of its political weakness and highlights how it has been subsumed by one side of the PiS-KO divide.

PiS has responded, quite understandably, by pointing out the hypocritical nature of Tusk's political reinvention and reminding voters of PO's neoliberal record in government. Although, increasing sections of society are growing dissatisfied with the PiS government, many are unwilling to hand back power to those who had previously attacked their livelihoods and blatantly shifted wealth and power further to the top. Simultaneously, PiS is opening up a new attack on the LGBT+ community, declaring that it is defending Poland's traditional values against the moral depravity imported from the west.[24] During the next year PiS will continue to remind voters about the previous PO government's policies, whilst opening up new right-wing conservative attacks on different oppressed groups of society. As the military conflict continues in Ukraine, PiS will also increase the atmosphere of militarism and claim that Poland is threatened militarily from Russia and morally and financially from Germany and the EU.

Despite its rhetoric, KO has no solutions to the socio-economic crisis facing Poland. Both KO and Lewica are committed to the PiS government's position on the war in Ukraine and have supported the hike in defence spending. Although Lewica has rightly supported protecting the rights of Ukrainian refugees in Poland, its unconditional support for the government's position on the war means it is unable to craft an independent position on peace, security, and increasing economic and social spending. If KO forms the next government, it will undoubtedly revert to its previous neoliberal positions, save for some minor symbolic pro-social gestures. As Rosa Luxemburg reminded us, primitive accumulation is a permanent feature of capitalist expansion and particularly in times of economic difficulty capital will seek to take over those parts of socio-economic life that remain outside of commodified relations. In such conditions, especially if Lewica is in coalition with KO, forces to its right will coalesce to first blame the liberal-left for the country's problems and then try to construct a new even more right-wing authoritarian political alternative.

NOTES

1   Karl Marx, *Capital A Critique of Political Economy Volume I*, Karl Marx and Federick Engels, *Collected Works*, vol. 35, New York: International, 1996, p. 755.

2   Rosa Luxemburg, *The Accumulation of Capital*. London: Routledge, 2003.

3   Władysław Szymański, 'Przyczyny I Skutki Nadmiernego Uzależnienia Gospodarki Od Kapitału Zewnętrznego', in *Polska Transformacja Ustrojowa*. Warszaw: Fundacja Inowacja, 2005, pp. 394–423.

4   Gavin Rae, *Poland's Return to Capitalism: From the Socialist Bloc to the European Union*, London: Tauris, 2012.

5   Tadeusz Kowalik, 'Kłopotliwy Sierpień '80', *Przegląd Tygodniowy*, 2009.

6   European Federation of Journalists, 'Eastern Empires: Foreign Ownership In CEE Media', 2003, <http://subsol.c3.hu/subsol_2/contributors3/efjtext.html>.

7   Czesław Kulesza, Katarzyna Piotrowska, and Gavin Rae, *Left-Wing Non-Voters in Poland*, Naprzód, no date, <https://www.transform-network.net/en/blog/article/left-wing-non-voters-in-poland/> and <https://www.academia.edu/37367512/Left_Wing_Non_Voters_in_Poland>.

8   Cleverway (2021) Trade unions, Worker Participation, <https://www.worker-participation.eu/National-Industrial-Relations/Countries/Poland/Trade-Unions#:~:text=Trade%20union%20density%20is%20low,and%20the%20somewhat%20smaller%2C%20FZZ>.

9   Antonio Gramsci, A. (2011) Prison Notebooks. New York: Columbia University Press.

10 Gavin Rae, 'Polish Mirror', *New Left Review* 124 (2020).

11 One such example has been Poland demanding in October 2022 that Germany pays it €1.3 trillion in reparations for losses incurred during the Second World War.

12 The social group in Poland that most defines itself as left wing are young women. Over 40 per cent of women under the age of 25 declare themselves to be left wing, compared to 22 per cent of men from the same age group (CBOS: Z lewicą Utożsamia Sięaż 40 proc. Młodych Polek (2021) Gazeta Prawna.pl., <https://www.gazetaprawna.pl/wiadomosci/kraj/artykuly/8111172,lewica-mlodziez-mlode-polski-cbos.html>.

13 However, the level of violence used by the police at demonstrations, whilst often excessive, is not unusual by European standards. The actions of the police in many

western European countries have often been more violent and repressive than those applied in Poland.

14   The main left-wing party in Poland has been the Democratic Left Alliance (SLD). Before the 2019 parliamentary elections it formed a coalition with the liberal party Wiosna (Spring) and the left-wing party Razem (Together): Lewica. In these elections, Lewica won 12.56 per cent of the vote, gaining 49 seats in parliament (24 SLD, 19 Wiosna and 6 Razem), and these three parties then formed a joint parliamentary group. Then in October 2021, the SLD and Wiosna fused to form a new party Nowa Lewica (New Left).

15   Gavin Rae, 'Facing the COVID-19 Crisis in Poland', Transform (UK) Journal, No. 8 (2022), <https://prruk.org/facing-the-covid-19-crisis-in-poland/>.

16   Daniel Tilles, 'Around one million Ukrainian refugees remain in Poland, estimate experts', Notes From Poland, 14 October 2022, <https://notesfrompoland.com/2022/10/14/around-one-million-ukrainian-refugees-remain-in-ukraine-estimate-experts/>.

17   <https://serwisy.gazetaprawna.pl/edukacja/artykuly/8526376,uczniowie-z-ukrainy-szkola-oddzialy-przygotowawcze.html#:~:text=Na%20koniec%20ubieg%C5%82ego%20roku%20szkolnego,631%20tys>.

18   Jarosław Ciślak , 'Polska Planuje Gigantyczne Wydatki na obronność W 2023 Roku', Defence24, 30 August 2022, <https://defence24.pl/polityka-obronna/polska-planuje-gigantyczne-wydatki-na-obronnosc-w-2023-roku>.

19   Citizens' Platform (PO) changed its name to Citizens' Coalition (KO) before the 2018 local elections, after formally merging with the small liberal party Modern.

20   Agata Szczęśniak and Dominika Sitnicka, 'Co W Po Sądzą O Socjalnych Pomysłach Tuska? "Donald Przesterowuje partię. Mało Kto ma takie cojones"', Najważniejsze informacje, oko.press, 16 July 2022, <https://oko.press/co-w-po-sadza-o-socjalnych-pomyslach-tuska-donald-przesterowuje-partie-malo-kto-ma-takie-cojones>.

21   Daniel Tilles, Polish opposition leader Tusk's award at feminist congress stirs controversy, Notes From Poland, 10 October 2022, <https://notesfrompoland.com/2022/10/10/polish-opposition-leader-tusks-award-at-feminist-congress-stirs-controversy/>.

22   Katarzyna Przyborska, 'Co Obieca Nam Lewica, Czego Nie Obiecał Tusk?', Krytyka Polityczna, 12 October 2022, <https://krytykapolityczna.pl/kraj/kongres-lewicy-kobiet-donald-tusk/>.

23   Piotr Lewandowski, 'Pomroczność jasna w OPZZ?!', Nasze Argumenty, 7 November 2022, <https://nargumenty.pl/index.php/poglady/polityka/73-opzz-tusk>.

24   For example, at a speech in November 2022 Kaczyński said: 'We don't want, ladies and gentlemen, a country – and unfortunately such things are already spreading in Poland – where 12-year-old girls declare themselves to be lesbians. This is madness, ladies and gentlemen, and this madness must be opposed.' Referring to the situation in universities, he claimed: 'some boy, two metres tall, 120 kilograms, with a beard, says that he is Zosia [a female name], lecturers have to refer to him that way or face "repression".' '[...] we don't want a country where 12-year-old girls declare as lesbians', says Polish leader, Notes From Poland, 12 November 2022, <https://notesfrompoland.com/2022/11/12/we-dont-want-a-country-where-12-year-old-girls-declare-as-lesbians-says-polish-leader/>.

Country Case Studies

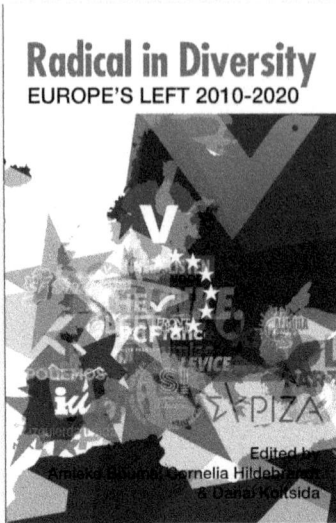

Radical in Diversity. Europe's Left 2010-2020

edited by Amieke Bouma, Cornelia Hildebrandt, Danai Koltsida

Publisher: Merlin Press / Rosa-Luxemburg-Stiftung (November 2021)
Language: English
ISBN-10: 0850367697
ISBN-13: 978-0850367690

What is the role of the radical left in Europe? How can regional groups parties and groups contribute to a common European left?
Scholars and activists from 22 countries explore radical left strategies:

- How best to struggle against chauvinism and right-wing extremism?
- How to respond to economic, financial and migration crises?
- How to combine traditional left interests - social welfare, workers' rights, medical care and education, with new left concerns such as the social inclusion of migrants and the protection of the environment?
- How can left parties contend with new bourgeois and green left-of-center parties?
- And importantly, how to forge a European left that transcends national interests, reigning in corporate interests and promoting social, gender and racial emancipation?

State vs. Government –
The Experience of Unidas Podemos in Spain[1]

Alberto Garzón

The main question – one which history never resolved because it cannot be resolved once and for all – was whether the bourgeoisie would respect its own legal order in case of an electoral triumph of socialism.
Adam Przeworski[2]

In January 2020, the first coalition government since the Second Republic took form in Spain. For the first time since the return of democracy, political forces to the left of traditional social democracy were included in the government. However, it took four general elections to achieve this result, even though it would have been arithmetically possible from the first of these. The main cause for this delay was the resistance that reactionary forces put up to the possibility of Podemos joining the government; this expressed itself in a combination of interventions aimed at wearing down and neutralising this political force, including through illegal operations that involved state institutions such as the police and the judiciary. This whole experience, still ongoing at the time of writing, has allowed us to explore some of the traditional left's hypotheses regarding participation in the government of a state.

★ ★ ★

Early socialists were sceptical about using the institutions of representative democracy under a capitalist system. Already in the nineteenth century, the debates in the First International revolved around the usefulness of participating in bourgeois institutions; while the anarchists flatly refused, the communists accepted joining in the electoral game. However, even they suspected that, in the event that they won a majority of votes, reactionary forces would not respect their own legality and would respond to socialist victories with military coups.[3] History has seemed to bear out this suspicion on all too many occasions, such as in Chile in 1973 or in Spain in 1936.

Today this response by reactionary forces does not necessarily have to be of a military nature, since there are other, less costly mechanisms for destabilising political forces and even whole countries. In recent decades, *lawfare*, i.e. the use of judicial channels for the political persecution of left-wing parties and/or candidates, has become widespread, especially in Latin America. This method is characterised by the combination of judicial operations with the media, in order to cohere public opinion against the target, and this with a particular timing aimed at influencing the electoral process. This type of operation has recently been deployed in countries such as Brazil, Ecuador, Bolivia, Argentina, and Colombia, among others.[4]

In what follows, we analyse the Spanish experience in relation to Podemos – renamed Unidas Podemos after it formed an alliance with Izquierda Unida. After emerging in 2014 and then topping national polls in 2015, this political force has suffered a virulent campaign against it, essentially a political, media, and judicial plot aimed at wearing down the organisation and its representatives. Yet such operations are not only spurred on by business or political interests, which of course do exist; rather, they are rooted in the reactionary ideology that contaminates much of the actually existing state and are products of the country's specific history.

To analyse this phenomenon, we will first review some definitions of the state that provide us with a useful first approach. Next, we briefly review the historical development of the state in Spain. We then address the crisis of the Spanish political regime that opened up the opportunity for the electoral rise of an alternative left. Finally, we analyse the response of the most reactionary sectors to the possibility of the left governing in Spain.

The definition of a state

One of the most complex and controversial questions concerns the definition of the state: it is not clear whether it is an (appropriable) thing, a subject (with intentions), or a relation (of articulation). Indeed, some conclude that we are really dealing with an institution of an entangled, polymorphic, and polycontextual nature that is, above all, a social relation.[5]

Karl Marx himself never developed a theory of the state; different definitions, which are not always mutually compatible, can be found in his texts. However, in one of his most fruitful approaches to this issue, Marx interpreted the state as an instrument of class rule. From this point of view, the state could be used by any social class for its own benefit, although it was taken for granted that under the capitalist system 'the executive of the modern state is but a committee for managing the common affairs of the whole bourgeoisie'.[6] Following in his and Engels's wake, Lenin asserted (quoting Engels) that the state 'is, as a rule, the state of the most powerful, economically dominant class', such that the proletarian revolution would have to use the state itself until it withers away under communism.[7]

However, Marx also introduced some nuances by understanding that the state is not a monolithic entity, but more precisely a set of institutions which have specific effects on the class struggle. This is the kind of interpretation he made in his works analysing the political conjuncture, in order to try to explain which social fraction or class controls which part of the state's institutional structure.[8] Thus, in complex societies the state can appear as a mediating force that stands above the contradictions in civil society and acquires a specific autonomy that allows it to introduce reforms that do not necessarily respond to the needs of the dominant class.

Taking these complexities on board, Antonio Gramsci also conceived of the state as an instrument of class domination, but identified two distinct modes of domination: coercion or force, and consensus or hegemony. In his view, the bourgeois class not only maintains its domination through the violence exercised by the repressive state apparatus against the subaltern classes, but also through ideological practices that are introduced, expanded, and reproduced throughout the sinews of civil society: churches, trade unions, media, political parties, etc. Consequently, Gramsci attached great importance to moral and intellectual leadership, i.e. to the capacity to construct and maintain a common vision of the world that suits the needs of the social and economic reproduction of the dominant mode of production. In Gramsci, the national-popular project for the state is a key vector that condenses the worldview shared by a collective subject – in this case the nation-people – and which allows the reproduction of values and principles through the illusion of the idea of nation.[9]

Nicos Poulantzas went a step further, as he defined the state as a set of institutions whose main role is to give coherence to a class-divided society, and moreover underlined its nature as a complex social relation. Thus, on this reading hegemony serves not only to secure the consent of the dominated class, but also to unify the fractions of this class into a coherent power bloc; for prior to this state intervention, they do not form a cohesive whole. Consequently, the state can be defined as the condensation of the struggle between social classes and their fractions, throughout the whole set of institutions.[10]

Following in this tradition, Bob Jessop concluded that the state should not be considered as a substantial and unified thing or as a unitary subject; rather, the most useful way to analyse the state is through the *strategic relational approach*, i.e. by contemplating:

> [...] not just the state apparatus but the exercise and effects of *state power* as a contingent expression of a changing balance of forces that seek to advance their respective interests inside, through, and against the state system [...] The changing balance of forces is mediated institutionally, discursively, and through governmental technologies.[11]

This approach allows us better to understand the role that different state institutions can play. For our purposes, it is useful to highlight four of its conclusions.

The first is that the state does not exercise power, but that 'the exercise and impact of state power (or, better, state powers) are activated through changing sets of politicians and state officials located in specific parts of the state apparatus, in specific conjunctures',[12] meaning that the government is both one more institution within the state and a reflection of the correlations of forces in a given moment. The second is that state-driven strategies are never coherent, since they are criss-crossed by the struggles between different factions within the state and relations with other non-state actors. There is no such thing as *the Spanish state* acting in a unified manner in pursuit of certain given objectives. The third is that these state powers are activated under the inspiration of an ideologically constituted state project, which is especially fertile if it appears in the trappings of nationalism. If it is hegemonic, this state project privileges certain particular interests and passes them off as general interests, thereby undervaluing or disregarding other (class, national, etc.) interests. The fourth is that these state projects are embodied and crystallised in power blocs, i.e. alliances of state and non-state political actors that compete for the control of the state.

Having given ourselves these tools, we will try to expand on the idea that in Spain over the last decade various class fractions have been uniting around a conservative-reactionary state project that calls for a radical response to what it considers serious challenges to the *Spanish nation*. These class fractions form a power bloc that emerges and operates throughout the body of the state; in fact, it both directly and indirectly, legally and illegally, confronts the pro-independence movements, the progressive political forces – in particular Podemos – and the progressive coalition government itself. All of these elements represent, according to its own narrative, an anomalous element in the nation, a kind of 'anti-Spain'. This narrow idea of nationhood is itself hardly new, but has its roots in Spanish history, which has been characterised by the stranglehold of reactionary Spanish nationalism.

A historically conservative state

In Spain, the power of reactionary forces and the weakness of oppositional ones (i.e. first liberal, then republican and socialist forces) has historically marked the very unfavourable correlation of forces for the consolidation of radical changes. Throughout the entire nineteenth century, liberal currents governed for only fifteen years, while reactionary forces governed for sixty-six, albeit often in contexts of enormous difficulties and with little or no effective capacity to carry out their political projects.[13]

In fact, it was only after the first third of the nineteenth century that the capitalist mode of production was consolidated in Spain, through a long process of liberal reforms. As Fontana has explained, after the failed liberal *trienio* (or three-year spell) from 1820–23, the absolutist monarch Fernando VII realised that the best way to hold back social revolution was to begin to implement a reformist programme. It was precisely during this period that important liberal reforms took place; they both brought about and symbolised the transition from a predominantly feudal model to a predominantly capitalist one, through measures like the confiscation and sale of church properties, the abolition of the feudal regime, the abolition of a system of inheritance favouring only the eldest son, and the abolition of the tithe, as well as the definitive abolition of the Inquisition. But these changes, directed from above, took place without the direct intervention of the bourgeoisie, to the point that we can speak of a revolution without a bourgeoisie in Spain.[14] The old feudal landowners became capitalist entrepreneurs overnight, but they brought with them their political culture and their generally reactionary ideology. Here, we are not talking about a new, enterprising and dynamic social class, as suits liberal narratives, but about a transmutation of the old oligarchic class that ultimately continued to be the one holding most political and economic power in Spain during the nineteenth century.

As if that were not enough, history continued along the same path during the twentieth century. The – economically, politically, and socially – modernising experience of the Second Republic (1931-1936) was interrupted by a coup d'état, with the ensuing civil war (1936-1939) and a fascist-inspired dictatorship (1939-1978). Franco's state project, in its ideological aspect, was characterised by the essentialist idea of an indivisible, Catholic, and ultra-conservative Spanish nation. Spanish nationalism had already in the past been a vehicle for alliances among reactionary forces, based on the idea of Spain as a historical Catholic nation and the sole sovereign subject, thus rendering inadmissible any secession, even a peaceful and democratic one.[15] Consequently, this ideological framework allowed reactionary forces to identify the enemy within in Catalan, Basque, and Galician nationalism, Freemasonry, liberalism, and, especially after 1918, communism.

The way out of that long night was only possible thanks to the so-called Transition, although it did not prove to be a canonical break with the previous regime either. During the dictatorship, the Communist Party of Spain (PCE) had been the main opposition party. After the death of Francisco Franco in 1975, the PCE was the force that had best understood the economic transformations and had adapted to them in order to continue to build its forces. But all this was not enough to overthrow the Franco regime, nor was it enough to impose a democratic break with the dictatorship. The only possible way forward was to negotiate a transition agreed with the reformist forces from within the Franco regime. The PCE's then-general secretary, Santiago Carrillo, would later say in his memoirs that 'the *agreed rupture* was a formula born of the conviction that the democratic opposition had neither the power nor the will to put an end to the system by producing a rupture using its own forces'.[16]

The 1978 constitution was, consequently, the result of what Manuel Vázquez Montalbán called a 'correlation of weaknesses'.[17] The democratic framers of the constitution had to negotiate with the regime-reformist framers under the watchful eye of the most reactionary sectors, particularly the military. Thus, for example, Article 2, which established the 'indissoluble unity of the Spanish nation', was drafted directly by the military,[18] which was not enough to prevent the attempted coup in 1981. The truth is that things did not change much even with the arrival of the Spanish Socialist Workers' Party (PSOE) in government in 1982. As has been pointed out, 'out of fear, neither the UCD [Union of the Democratic Centre] nor the PSOE governments ever endeavoured to thoroughly clean out the former dictatorial administration. The army, the state security forces, and the judiciary were mainly made up of Francoites, and remained so'.[19] Much of the media powers that had served the dictatorship were also actors in the Transition, becoming the country's new democratic media overnight.[20]

However, the reform promoted by Franco's regime itself owed to the fact that – as Fernando Claudín had rightly foreseen – 'for an increasingly decisive sector of the ruling classes, of their political, economic, and military personnel, the need to transform the political regime in order to preserve the social regime became obvious'.[21] That social regime was the one cemented by the class fractions that had mounted a military uprising against the Second Republic's modernising project, and whose privileges would be preserved for the future thanks to an agreed process – i.e. the Transition – that would not fundamentally alter the country's power structure.

That new political regime born of the Transition, and above all its incorporation into the European Economic Community – later the European Union – brought Spain closer to the economic and social standards of the rest of Europe. However, this went hand in hand with multiple and serious processes of corruption, as well as an intense liberalisation and privatisation process that weakened the government's power to implement public policies and reconfigured the business system to the benefit of those with close connections to conservative governments.

Regime crisis

The economic crisis of 2008 revealed the fragility of Spain's model of economic growth and prompted a political and cultural rupture with the institutions that had been inherited from the Transition. The depth of the economic crisis led to an organic crisis that made the ruling classes lose their hegemony; this crisis also brought a crisis of political representation and of all the socio-cultural variables that sustained it. This was also an opportunity for other political forces and other state projects to contest state power itself.

Indeed, Spain's economic growth model was sustained by a real-estate bubble and high domestic consumption underpinned by very high levels of private indebtedness. These bases were too weak and dependent on a European model that exacerbated the centre-periphery dynamic.[22] Contrary to the liberal narrative, by the time the crisis erupted, public debt levels were very low, and it was private debt that sustained consumption and, therefore, economic growth. External financing came from foreign banks that recycled the trade surpluses of the countries of origin, including Germany, forming a symbiotic pattern in European relations. But when the tap was turned off, and priority was given to debt repayment, the burden of neoliberal adjustment fell on the Spanish economy and families.

As could have been expected, the onset of the economic crisis did not lead to an immediate delegitimisation of the political and social regime. In the early years, citizens trusted the PSOE in 2008 and the Partido Popular (PP) in 2011. As in Gramsci's conception, it was the persistence of the crisis, combined with the cycle of social and political mobilisations, that undermined confidence in the system and the electoral support of the two major parties. Indeed, the data reveal that the deepening of the economic crisis triggered distrust in Spanish institutions as a whole. Data from the *European Social Survey* show that in 2006, coinciding with the peak of the housing bubble, the percentage who had no confidence at all in parliament and political parties was 6.5% and 16.3% respectively. By 2014 these percentages had risen to 18.6% and 33.7% respectively.

On the other hand, the emergence of Podemos in 2014 contributed significantly to the re-politicisation of Spanish society. In October 2013, the percentage of people who declared that they had no sympathy for any political party was 62.1%, but just a few months later, in January 2014, this percentage had dropped to 44.7%. Finally, the results of the European elections in May 2014 provoked a huge political earthquake, and the King of Spain was forced to abdicate in a process agreed with the PP and PSOE. There was fear – and the most reactionary sectors of society began to mobilise.

The deep state

The regime crisis created an opportunity for new state projects, but this also triggered a response from the most reactionary sectors. In this process, the state apparatus would be crucial, especially the repressive and administrative apparatuses. Moreover, their capacity to intervene was backed up by previous experience, both in terms of practices during the dictatorship and the abuses that had taken place during the democratic era, such as the dirty 'war against terrorism' waged from the Ministry of the Interior.

The starting point of this reactionary response was itself solid. In matters sensitive for the reactionary state project, including the question of national identity and the unity of the nation, the state institutions had made a lot of headway already. With regard to Spain's territorial structure, the Constitutional Court, through its interpretations, set itself up 'from day one as a constituent power trying to correct the Constitution'.[23] Perhaps the most significant case occurred in 2010, when the Court challenged most of Catalonia's statute of autonomy, which had been approved by the national and regional legislatures and had entered into force four years earlier. This milestone marked a turning point in the strategy of actors pushing for Catalan independence, who radicalised their agenda, reaching its culmination in the 2017 referendum on self-determination.

In the last two decades, 'the most democratic interpretations of the 1978 text have been pushed into a corner, perhaps irreversibly'.[24] In fact, the conservative interpretation of the Constitution by the Constitutional Court in 2013, in the midst of the crisis, prevented progressive regional governments from passing housing laws. On the other hand, from 2011 to the present, dozens of trials have taken place for supposed crimes linked to offence against religious feelings or the crown and national symbols, and in some cases the penal code and articles reserved for the fight against terrorism have been used to prosecute singers and rappers. In practically all cases, the complaints originate in reactionary civil-society organisations, sometimes finding judges who tackle them amidst a wave of media acrimony.

There have also been direct operations by the state apparatus against political forces that defended different models of the state or even simply represented an opposition. Thus, the practice of *lawfare* has been increasingly common in Spain as an instrument against political parties and left-wing and pro-independence social movements.

Perhaps the paradigmatic case was that of the operation orchestrated by the Interior Ministry during the last conservative government. The minister was Jorge Fernández Díaz, an ultra-Catholic who had claimed that Pope Benedict XVI himself had told him that 'the devil wanted to destroy Spain because the devil knows the service that Spain provides to the Church of Christ'.[25] It has been proven that the ministry used public resources to obstruct the investigation of corruption scandals concerning his party, but also deployed them for the monitoring, investigation, and persecution of political opponents. This was, in fact, established by the parliamentary commission of enquiry in 2017 that investigated what had happened. However, we know an important part of the plot because at least one of the main actors in these irregular operations, police commissioner José Manuel Villarejo, recorded several or all of the conversations and leaked them to the media as he saw fit for the criminal case that ultimately landed him in jail. At the time of writing, the trickle of leaked recordings continues.

The para-police institution created by the conservative government to carry out its political objectives is known as the *patriotic police*. But the party's general secretary and other high-ranking conservative politicians also appear prominently in the recorded conversations.[26] However, it should be kept in mind that this plot does not stop at the relationship between the conservative government and certain high-ranking police officers. On the contrary, these operations could not have been carried out without the participation of other state apparatuses such as the media and the judiciary.

The modus operandi could be summarised as follows. First, the *patriotic police* constructed false evidence or looked for accomplices who would do this. Then they used the media to leak this false information and spread public contempt for their adversaries. This gave rise to private entities or individuals, usually on the ultra-right, denouncing in court the alleged irregular dealings of those who were in fact the victims. In the end, some judges gave credence to suspicions and kept cases open for extraordinarily long periods of time, thereby inflicting extremely serious reputational damage on the victims. All the cases have now been closed, but some have been kept alive in the media for up to eight years, with a continual stream of headlines.

As far as Podemos is concerned, the aim of all these operations was not primarily legal – to jail some of its leaders – but rather to wear it down politically. In the 2014 European elections Podemos burst onto the scene with 8 per cent of the vote, but by the end of the year polls showed the party already above 20 per cent. It was then that Commissioner Villarejo noted in his diary the first meetings with high-ranking officials of the conservative government to discuss this new political formation.[27] In January 2015, Podemos was already topping the national polls, and the manoeuvres to erode the party's support intensified. The operations of the conservative and reactionary sectors of society converged.

Precisely at the beginning of 2015, a new national political formation called Ciudadanos also burst onto the scene, in what was an operation by the big companies of the Spanish stock exchange (Ibex-35) to confront the threat posed by Podemos at the time. In June 2014, the president of Banco Sabadell and then president of the board of trustees of FEDEA, a think tank financed by the big Ibex-35 companies, publicly stated that 'a kind of right-wing Podemos should be created'.[28] Senior Ciudadanos officials acknowledged that the party's main concern was in 'distancing [the PSOE] from its natural ally, Podemos'.[29] The media push was not minor and, in fact, the former editor of the country's main progressive newspaper, Antonio Caño, has publicly acknowledged that 'four years ago we at *El País* tried to avoid [PSOE leader Pedro] Sánchez's pact with populists and separatists because we believed that this was bad for the left and for Spain'.[30] To a certain extent, the operation was successful because it caused Podemos's support to fall very quickly, to the point that it went from an average of 28 per cent in January 2015 to 17 per cent in June of that same year.

However, at the end of 2015 the general election took place and the results gave more votes to the sum of the left-wing parties – Podemos, 5 million; Izquierda Unida, 1 million – than to the PSOE alone, with its 5 million. It was time to negotiate a left-wing government, but the negotiations failed. The result was that the elections would have to be repeated in June 2016. It was then that the lawfare and attrition operations were stepped up, with the dissemination of fake news, the launching of unfounded police and judicial investigations and the media bombardment which spread this misinformation through the country's main political outlets. The timing was perfect.

Indeed, in January 2016, Operation PISA was launched, in which the *patriotic police* falsely accused Pablo Iglesias of having received close to €2 million from Iran. According to conversations recorded by Villarejo and broadcast years later, the false information had been created by a high-ranking police official.[31] That information was published by the ultra-right-wing newspaper *Okdiario*, which receives huge amounts of money from conservative governments,[32] and gave rise to multiple legal complaints that were all eventually shelved.

Also in the same month, the SIM card of a close collaborator of Pablo Iglesias, whose mobile phone had been stolen a few months earlier, reached a media outlet. Although this was an act of theft from a Podemos leader, some media published sensitive content damaging to Iglesias. In an utterly irrational move, the judge in the case, García-Castellón, who is closely linked to conservative governments, changed the status of Iglesias from victim to defendant. Despite the judge's requests, the Supreme Court ended up refusing to charge the Podemos leader. However, the storm of media reports on this case did not cease and the damage was never repaired.

Three months later, in the middle of the election campaign, the *patriotic police* launched another operation against Podemos. This time they accused Iglesias of receiving more than 200,000 euros from the Venezuelan government. Once again, the ultra-right-wing newspaper *Okdiario* published a document that theoretically accredited these facts but which turned out to be a shoddy fabrication by the police itself. It has been proven that during those years senior officials of the conservative government met with former ministers and former representatives of the Venezuelan government to encourage them to provide evidence of irregular financing of Podemos, as well as any other information that could undermine it. The subsequent investigation has revealed that the Venezuelan witnesses were pressured by the police and the ministry to fuel the dirty war against Podemos, in exchange for residence permits and other administrative benefits. One of the recordings reveals that a high-ranking police official urged a supposed witness to collaborate in the following terms: 'if you help us to prevent Podemos from reaching [the government], it is better for everyone.'[33]

In short, between the general election in December 2015 and the one in June 2016, there was a series of political and media operations that, notwithstanding other factors, contributed to Unidas Podemos losing a million votes and failing to overtake the PSOE. However, a coalition government was not possible this time either; a palace coup within the PSOE managed to oust its general secretary Pedro Sánchez, who was, according to some, ready to form a government with Unidas Podemos. Sánchez himself acknowledged a year later that powers in the world of business had been deeply involved in ensuring that there would be no left-wing government.[34] Even so, the attacks would not stop there, either against Unidas Podemos or against Pedro Sánchez himself, though he regained his position as general secretary after internal elections.

In this continuous onslaught against progressive political forces some judges have overstepped their functions to such an extent that, as in the case of Judge Alba, they have ultimately been struck off and imprisoned, having been convicted of prosecuting Podemos MPs using false evidence.[35] Another case resulted in the loss of Alberto Rodríguez's standing as an MP, after he was convicted for an alleged assault on a policeman eight years earlier. This was only reported once the accused had obtained his parliamentary status, and without any solid evidence. Despite this, a minor conviction was enough to remove a seat from the parliamentary group of Unidas Podemos.[36] Similarly, the party spokesperson in Madrid, Isabel Serra, was also disqualified for two years for having participated in a rally to block an eviction.[37]

Despite the seriousness of what has been described thus far, in most cases judges have not even received the reprobation of their superiors, who are organised in the CGPJ (General Council of the Judiciary), which has a majority of members elected by the right and whose last president was a high-ranking member of a conservative party government. The reconstitution of this governing body has been delayed for more than four years, coinciding with the last time the right-wingers had control of the parliament that chooses some of its members.[38] There have thus been multiple occasions on which this governing body has raised public complaints against the statements of left-wing political leaders, as part of the same strategy of political attrition. The control of judicial bodies by the right has even been acknowledged by conservative leaders, such as when it became known that the PP justice spokesperson assured his colleagues that they controlled the criminal chamber of the Supreme Court – the one that judges corrupt politicians – 'from behind the scenes'.[39]

In the light of these facts, it is very difficult not to conclude that a substantial part of the judiciary and the media, central apparatuses of the state, are attempting to harass and demolish Unidas Podemos – or rather, at least this party's strength, and, on more than a few occasions, the government of which they form one part. This is, in all probability, an attitude driven by the belief that, ultimately, they are *saving the nation* from the anomalous elements which – in their opinion in accordance with the whole reactionary tradition in Spain – must be extirpated from public life.

Conclusions

In September 2017, a few days after the independence referendum in Catalonia, which resulted in heavy police repression and the arrest and imprisonment of those who promoted the vote, Unidas Podemos convened an assembly for dialogue and the non-judicialisation of politics. With the lone exception of the PSOE, this involved all the political forces that, two years later, would support the progressive coalition government. The reactionary mobilisation resulted in a siege of the assembly's venue and even assaults on its participants,[40] as well as a lawsuit against two left-wing leaders that was admitted by a court.[41] All in all, that assembly was the first crystallisation of a new power bloc that defended a state project – one with a republican and plurinational parameter – that confronted the hegemonic reactionary state project.

This alternative power bloc, which remains unstable, is largely made up of political and trade-union organisations and defends another way of understanding the state and its institutions. Although it is made up of highly diverse forces, since 2019 its political practice has been consistent in its support of the progressive coalition government. However, this government, as we have argued here, is besieged by other state institutions and by a power bloc that brings together those who defend the reactionary state project, with a much greater institutional grip and a longer historical tradition.

Indeed, many state institutions in Spain are permeated by a reactionary ideology that sees the unity of the nation as its fundamental pillar, although not the only one. Inspired by this ideological framework, state apparatuses such as the judiciary, the police, and the media have mounted legal and illegal operations to wear down political opponents who their narrative casts as enemies of the unity of Spain. Among these enemies are, paradigmatically, the independence movement and Podemos as a political force. In the latter case, between the 2015 and 2016 general elections, an avalanche of actions was set in motion, aimed at preventing Podemos from reaching the government and, with this, the possibility of launching any other state project.

The underlying idea that justifies these reactionary forces' activity is that they are *saviours of the nation*. Such a notion is crucial to understanding these recent phenomena. It has sometimes served to unify the reactionary bloc, allowing the entire opposition to explicitly join forces in mobilisations against the coalition government.[42] Indeed, even a corrupt policeman like Villarejo has defined himself as a patriot working in defence of Spanish democracy. This means that we are talking about operations that, although they go beyond the legal framework, their protagonists consider necessary to serve a very specific state project. As journalist Pedro Vallín has stated, 'patriotism in Spain has never consisted of protecting the country, but rather the state, its secrets, and its sins'.[43]

In any case, the strong roots of this reactionary ideology among state institutions is clashing head-on with the popular sovereignty that has been systematically expressed in recent general elections, giving rise to a confrontation between the democratically elected government and the state apparatus, which, moreover, continually tries to escape from popular legitimacy. In the case of the judiciary, all right-wing political forces defend the full autonomy of judges to govern themselves outside the legitimacy emanating from parliament – something that should be highly controversial, in light of the liberal tradition and the separation of powers.

These tensions within the state express the conception of the state as a complex institutional whole, as a condensation of the class struggles taking place throughout the social body. Indeed, the regime crisis has led to a redefinition of the state project, and this is the subject of fierce political dispute on all fronts.

This article is intended as a modest first contribution to the debate on the strategies of left participation in contemporary governments. At the time of writing, the coalition government still maintains an attitude of resistance against the siege mounted by the institutions controlled by the reactionary bloc, while Unidas Podemos and pro-independence forces continue to be the prime target of the lawfare operations directed by that bloc. There is still not a full understanding of the necessary unity of an alternative bloc – which could well simply be called a democratic bloc – from which to build a different state project. So far, there is more intuition than there is strategy.

Nevertheless, the left's participation in the government has made it possible to locate some notable contradictions in the reactionary bloc. For example, the work of Unidas Podemos in the Ministry of Labour, headed by Yolanda Díaz, has made it possible to reach a dozen important social dialogue agreements on labour issues that have had a very positive effect on the labour market, but have also ensured that big finance capital and big productive capital have not sided with the reactionary bloc in its political manoeuvres. Indeed, the efforts of the reactionary bloc to win the favour of the bosses of the big companies, especially the most technologically dynamic ones, has so far met with little success.

NOTES

1   Article finished on 12 December 2022. This text reflects the state of affairs in December 2022 and represents the views only of the author and not necessarily those of the government of Spain, in which he serves as Minister of Consumer Affairs. The author is grateful for the comments on an earlier draft provided by Javier Moreno, Ángel de la Cruz, Daniel Ayllón, and Eduardo Garzón. He would like to dedicate the article to Pablo Iglesias Turrión in recognition of all the political work he has accomplished over the last decade.

2   Adam Przeworski, *Capitalism and Social Democracy*, Cambridge, UK: Cambridge University Press, 1985, p. 79.

3   Przeworski, *Capitalism and Social Democracy*.

4   Silvina M. Romano (ed.), *Lawfare. Guerra judicial y neoliberalismo en América Latina*, Madrid: Mármol Izquierdo, 2019.

5   Bob Jessop. *The State: Past, Present, Future*, Cambridge UK: Polity Press, 2016.

6   Karl Marx and Friedrich Engels, *The Manifesto of the Communist Party*, in Karl Marx and Frederick Engels, *Collected Works*, vol. 6, New York: International, 1976, p. 486.

7   V. I. Lenin, *The State and Revolution*, in V. I. Lenin, *Collected Works*, vol. 25, Moscow: Progress Publishers, 1964 (1974), pp. 397 and 402.

8   Karl Marx, *The Class Struggles in France, 1848-1850*, in Karl Marx and Friedrich Engels, *Collected Works*, vol. 10, New York: International, 1978.

9   Antonio Gramsci, *Prison Notebooks* [critical English edition], translated and edited by Joseph A. Buttigieg, New York: Columbia University Press, 1992 – 2007, 5 volumes projected, 3 completed. See anthologies edited by Quintin Hoare, Geoffrey Nowell-Smith, David Forgacs, and Derek Boothman.

10 Bob Jessop, *Nicos Poulantzas: Marxist Theory and Political Strategy: State, Class and Strategy*, Basingstoke: Palgrave, 1985: Nicos Poulantzas, *State, Power, Socialism*, London: New Left Books, 1978; Nicos Poulantzas, *Political Power and Social Classes*, London: New Left Books, 1978 (original 1968).

11 Bob Jessop, *The State. Past, Present and Future*, Cambridge, Polity, 2016, p. 54.

12 Jessop, *The State*, p. 20.

13 Josep Fontana, *La época del liberalismo: Historia de España*, vol. 6, Barcelona: Crítica, 2015.

14 José Antonio Piqueras, 'De la burguesía sin revolución a la revolución sin burguesía', in *Historia Social* 24 (1996): 95-132.

15 Xosé M. Nuñéz Seixas, *Suspiros de España. El nacionalismo español 1808-2018*, Barcelona: Crítica, 2018.

16 Andrea Donofrio, *El fracaso del eurocomunismo: Razones y reflexiones sobre el giro del movimiento comunista en occidente (1975-1982)* [The failure of Eurocommunism: reasons for and reflections on the turn of the communist movement in the West (1975-1982)], Ph.D. dissertation, Universidad Complutense de Madrid, 2012, <https://core.ac.uk/download/pdf/19719008.pdf>.

17 Manuel Vázquez Montalbán, interviewed by Begoña Aranguren and Isabel Verajáuregui in the programme *Epílogo*, 2003, <https://www.youtube.com/watch?v=_4ueSwSyyvs>.

18 Jordi Solé Tura, *Nacionalidades y nacionalismo en España: autonomías, federalismo y autodeterminación*, Barcelona: El viejo topo, 2019 (1985).

19 José Luís Villacañas Berlanga, *Historia del poder politico en España*, Barcelona: RBA, 2014.

20 Gregorio Morán, *El precio de la Transición*, Barcelona: Akal, 2015.

21 Fernando Claudín, *Eurocomunismo y socialismo, Madrid:* Siglo XXI, 1977.

22 Alberto Garzón, 'Las relaciones centro-periferia en la Unión Europea después de la covid', *El Trimestre Económico,* 89,356 (October-December 2022).

23 Villacañas Berlanga, *Historia del poder politico en España*.

24 Gerardo Pisarello, 'La Constitución española y las trampas del reformismo imaginario', 2013, <http://www.sinpermiso.info/textos/index.php?id=6492>.

25   *Lavanguardia.com*, 'Benedicto XVI le dijo a Jorge Fernández Díaz sobre Catalunya: "El diablo quiere destruir España"', 12 June 2020, <https://www.lavanguardia.com/politica/20200612/481720647421/benedicto-xvi-fernandez-diaz-catalunya-diablo-destruir-espana.html>.

26   *Lavanguardia.com*, 'Cospedal, a Villarejo sobre un tema "de la hostia" contra Podemos: "Yo eso sí lo quiero"', 2022, <https://www.lavanguardia.com/politica/20220707/8391760/cospedal-villarejo-sobre-tema-hostia-quiero.html>.

27   Villarejo's diary reveals that the PP's political brigade attacked Podemos right from its first emergence.

28   *El Periódico*, 2016, <https://www.elperiodico.com/es/politica/20140625/josep-oliu-propone-crear-una-especie-de-podemos-de-derechas-3329695>.

29   *Tercera Información*, 'Begoña Villacís: Ciudadanos pactó con el PSOE para "alejarle de su aliado natural, Podemos"', 2016, <https://www.tercerainformacion.es/articulo/actualidad/28/08/2016/begona-villacis-ciudadanos-pacto-con-el-psoe-para-alejarle-de-su-aliado-natural-podemos/>.

30   Antonio Maestre, 'Cronología de una guerra sucia contra Podemos', 2022, <https://www.eldiario.es/opinion/zona-critica/cronologia-guerra-sucia_129_9160022.html>.

31   Óscar López-Fonseca, J. J. Gálvez, and Fernando J. Pérez, 'Interior costeó con dinero público el viaje de la "policía patriótica" a EE UU para recabar datos contra Podemos [Interior paid with public money for the trip of the 'patriotic police' to the USA to collect data against Podemos], 4 April 2019, <https://elpais.com/politica/2019/04/03/actualidad/1554278400_131510.html>.

32   Yago Álvarez Barba, 'Ayuso inyectó 300.000 euros de publicidad a *OkDiario* solo en 2021', *El Salto*, 2 December 2022, <https://www.elsaltodiario.com/comunidad-madrid/ayuso-inyecto-300000-euros-publicidad-eduaro-inda-okdiario-2021>.

33   J.J. Gálvez and Óscar López-Fonseca, 'Ocho testigos sitúan a la "policía patriótica" de Rajoy detrás de la guerra sucia contra Podemos', *El País*, 14 November 2022, <https://elpais.com/espana/2022-11-14/ocho-testigos-situan-a-la-policia-patriotica-de-rajoy-detras-de-la-guerra-sucia-contra-podemos.html>.

34   20minutos, 'Sánchez admite presiones para no pactar con Podemos y que való abstenerse ante Rajoy', 30 October 2016, <https://www.20minutos.es/noticia/2876142/0/pedro-sanchez-entrevista-salvados-jordi-evole-rajoy-podemos/>.

35   Guillermo Vega and Óscar López-Fonseca, 'El exjuez Salvador Alba ingresa en prisión para cumplir una pena de seis años por conspirar contra Victoria Rosell', *El País*, 18 October 2022, <https://elpais.com/espana/2022-10-18/el-exjuez-salvador-alba-ingresa-en-prision-para-cumplir-su-condena-de-seis-anos-de-carcel-por-conspirar-contra-victoria-rossell.html>.

36   Paula Chouza and José María Brunet, '"Caso Alberto Rodríguez": un año sin escaño y sin sentencia en el Constitucional', *El País*, 22 October 2022, <https://elpais.com/espana/2022-10-22/caso-alberto-rodriguez-un-ano-sin-escano-y-sin-sentencia-en-el-constitucional.html>.

37   *Eldiario.es*, 'El Supremo ratifica la condena a 19 meses de cárcel de Isa Serra poratentado a la autoridad en un desahucio', 5 July 2021, <https://www.eldiario.es/politica/supremo-ratifica-condena-19-meses-carcel-isa-serra-atentado-autoridad-desahucio_1_8104722.html>.

38   Elena Herrera, 'Cuatro años de parálisis en el Poder Judicial por el bloqueo del Partido Popular', 3 December 2022, <https://www.eldiario.es/politica/cuatro-anos-paralisis-judicial-bloqueo-partido-popular_1_9765184.html>.

39   Óscar López Fonseca, 'Cosidó admite el mensaje de WhatsApp en el que presume de un futuro control del PP sobre el Supremo',19 November 2018, <https://elpais.com/politica/2018/11/19/actualidad/1542630134_616500.html>.

40   Irene Castro, 'Cientos de ultras cercan la asamblea de Unidos Podemos sobre Catalunya por escasez de Policía, según la organización', 26 September 2017, <https://www.eldiario.es/politica/concentracion-pabellon-convocada-unidos-podemos_1_3173572.html>.

41   *Eldiario.es*, 'Alberto Garzón y Pablo Echenique, citados por llamar "nazis" a los ultras que rodearon la asamblea de Zaragoza', 8 November 2017, <https://www.eldiario.es/politica/alberto-garzon-pablo-echenique-zaragoza_1_3082734.html>.

42   Lucía Tolosa, 'La foto de Colón cumple dos años con la derecha y el centroderecha fragmentados', *El País*, 1 February 2021, <https://elpais.com/espana/2021-02-10/la-foto-de-colon-cumple-dos-anos-con-la-derecha-y-el-centroderecha-fragmentados.html>.

43   Pedro Vallín, *C3PO en la corte del rey Felipe: La guerra del Estado Profundo español contra la democracia liberal*, Barcelona: Arpa, 2021.

The Greek State: Theory, History, Policies[1]

Aristides Baltas

What follows is an effort to come to terms with our, and my, experience of participation in the socio-political 'experiment' of Syriza in power. We all know, of course, that Syriza characterises itself as a political party of the radical left; and so it follows that its practices ought somehow to relate to a broadly Marxist theoretical orientation. Nevertheless, the elements of such a theory, the premises and lemmas that could effectively guide the actual implementation of Syriza's policies when in power, have been sorely missing. And I confess that in fact we did feel the lack. It is because I think this lack needs to be directly addressed that I propose conceiving of our experience as an experiment, which might form some kind of initial basis for formulating this still missing but necessary theory. I should, however, add that the policies in question could not but relate to the state since political power, as such, crucially involves governing the state. What I have in mind here is not the state in general but the Greek state in particular, which is a state with a relatively short history, exhibiting stark idiosyncrasies and peculiarities that became conspicuous when governing it. However, this does not mean that the lessons learned from it are only relevant to Greece. It is my firm belief that comrades and friends living and struggling outside our borders can find our experience useful; although they are facing situations that are necessarily different, we do have in common our major opponent, namely the neoliberal (and final?) form of the capitalist mode of production.

Let me expand on the last point. All social experiences are singular. Each takes place at some fixed time and unfolds at a particular location; each is constrained by idiosyncratic factors at work both inside and outside of it; each is dependent on specific conditions, social as well as historical. No single one of these can be exactly replicated and serve as a prototype. Yet some may claim to have more general relevance; a particular social and/ or political experience can be especially instructive when it transforms power relations and other factors at more than one level, thus directly or indirectly affecting analogous experiences at different times and places. Moreover, such an experience can be instructive insofar as it demonstrates the possibility of breaking new ground and opening new vistas, vistas that allow the experience to generate novel ideas as well as pinpoint entrenched fallacies that have consistently led to impasses or dead ends.

A social and/or political experience cannot automatically reach a theoretical level. Before doing so, before generating well worked out concepts, the experience has to be discussed as such. Its salient features have to be singled out in their own right, become both connected to and differentiated from the salient features of analogous experiences, and be thought through by everyone involved.

Clearly, the publication of the present text in the *Transform!* yearbook suggests I believe that the experience we call 'Syriza in power' is worthy of a broader discussion. But my impression is that in relation to this experience I am still limited to a pre-theoretical level of reflection, for I am still in the process of identifying different parameters and dimensions of the experience, in particular those that might be of general interest to the international left.

Syriza has published an evaluation of its experience of governing Greece for four and a half years in the form of a 125-page document that has been discussed more or less thoroughly inside the party and approved unanimously (with one abstention) by the party's Central Committee. This document, entitled *Account of Syriza 2012-2019*, is in the process of being translated into English. In addition, the Nicos Poulantzas Institute has initiated a more detailed discussion of Syriza's government experience.

I will not attempt to summarise this document nor elaborate the first steps that could enable a deeper discussion. Instead, I will raise only a few points that are particularly relevant.

To begin with, I will propose a theoretical framework that would, at a minimum, be necessary for understanding the contours of this experience, at least as I have come to understand it and its context – a framework that I believe is general and inclusive enough to embrace the views of most people involved in *Transform!*. I believe it is the kind of common ground on which we all stand. In saying this I nevertheless view each one of its tenets as well as their interconnections as elements that can be elucidated, elaborated, interpreted, critically evaluated, or even rejected. Despite the necessarily sketchy formulation of this framework my hope is that it may help in lending a modicum of theoretical discipline to the discussion.

Theoretical precepts

In an interview given to a Greek newspaper (*Εφημερίδα των Συντακτών*,

12-13 February 2020) the South Korean film director Bong Joon-ho was asked why he thought that his film *Parasite* won the Academy Award (Oscar) for Best Picture in 2019, despite the fact that it was set in Seoul and its dialogue was largely in Korean. The reply was disarmingly simple: '*We live in a gigantic capitalist nation.*'

With its metaphor of 'the nation', the reply spotlights the obvious: nowadays official borders and dominant languages cannot be impenetrable barriers to ideas or sensitivities coming from anywhere in the globe. Concern for social (and political) issues can cross these barriers and circulate throughout the 'gigantic nation' in which attitudes and modes of action can become generally known and, at times, inspirational for others. This is to say that the fate of a film and generally of a work of art, or of any and all of us individuals, has become interdependent, determined to some extent by what happens in any other, even remote, part of the 'nation' we all inhabit. Put succinctly, the 'capitalist nation' no longer has an *outside*.

This is not to say that capitalism is our inescapable destiny: manifold struggles against its diverse manifestations have been waged ever since its beginnings. Even though this gigantic 'nation' covers the entire globe, without there being a foreign territory that functions, or so we imagined, as a lever from which we can launch and support our struggle and confront the system as a whole – and without our being able to confront it as individuals unshaped by capitalist relations, that is, as mentally 'outside' of it – we can criticise it and struggle against what it has been doing to the peoples of this earth and to earth itself. We have started to realise that we are living in the devastating *anthropocene* era; we can unravel capitalism's modes of operation; we can understand how it emerged, evolved, and managed to overcome its crises; we can even guess where it is leading: the destruction of the planet as we have known it for millennia. But at the same time we have to admit that all the valiant efforts to overthrow it, despite the sometimes staggering successes that have inspired and emboldened us in the past, have all ended in capitalism landing back on its feet. The vantage point that seemingly allowed us – even if only in our imagination – to confront capitalism as a whole and from the outside has evaporated. And so we must realise that all that we are and are doing – what we eat, what we consume and what we discard or waste, what we work on and how we do it, where and how we live or die, what clothes we manufacture and wear, how we entertain ourselves and how we move and travel, what we think and imagine – has an indelible capitalist stamp. It is in this sense too that the gigantic capitalist 'nation' has no outside.

On the other hand, the fact that we are all inside the 'nation' also means that we are all its 'citizens'. It means that our demands, our actions and our struggles against capitalism's manifestations and symptoms, as well as our critical ideas about it, are interconnected in multiform ways and therefore can be shared by all who suffer from the system in all countries and in all continents of the 'nation' – and shared *inside* capitalism but also *in opposition to capitalism*. This is then how we should characterise the condition of the international Left: not outside capitalism but *inside* and *against* it. *Dentro e contro*. These two unassuming little words made famous by the Italian movement and highlighted by the theoretical work mainly of Étienne Balibar among others, fittingly plot where we now stand as well as how we got there. For we realise, with a bit of reflection, that the principle indicated by these two little words – were always just as applicable in the 'short' twentieth century as they are today.

Let me explain. Relatively early in the past century, the struggle within capitalism and the struggle against capitalism were essentially separated and went in two divergent directions: reform or revolution. This has been the fundamental dilemma characterising and dividing the left for most of the twentieth century. But we have to admit that in the era of globalisation – the era of the 'making of global capitalism' as Leo Panitch and Sam Gindin have put it in their key work – neither reform nor revolution lived up to their original expectations. This has led to what has been dubbed by Enzo Traverso 'left melancholia'. Which is to say that, on the one hand, reformism – or, if you like, social democracy – became gradually absorbed without too much difficulty into the political arsenal of capitalism, while, on the other hand, successful revolutions fell back on capitalist relations of production and the associated values, even if with qualifications of one sort or another. The central examples of the latter are the collapse of the Soviet Union and the complex evolution of China after Mao. These are the political landmarks of capitalist globalisation, which show that thinking of capitalism from the outside and trying to confront it as a whole has led us astray. In more abstract terms, we now appreciate that we had been silently renouncing the idea of immanence in favour of some kind of imaginary, external standpoint of transcendence. And paid for it.

Politically speaking, the left has slowly begun in recent decades to realise that such strategic failure has deeper roots, for the dilemma as such had been mostly papered over after the First World War and the stabilisation of the Soviet Revolution or even initially misconstrued. The requisite subtle distinctions, the need to pay attention to the different embodiments of capitalism in time and space and to correctly handle this in varying circumstances, had been for the most part undervalued and theoretically ignored or dismissed. In other words, we have by now 'discovered' that neither extreme – non-transformational reformism or total systemic opposition 'from outside' – can nourish and sustain successful social resistance. It became evident that left theory cannot appeal to inexorable historical laws in order to cheer up those suffering and brighten the prospects of a happier future. By now we have come to realise that historical laws simply do not exist. What 'governs' history throughout is what Althusser has called '*l'aléatoire*' – which means that it is tendencies rather than mechanical laws on which the left can rely socially, historically, theoretically and politically.

I am referring in particular to a tendency that has always been inherent in society and proper to society as such, a tendency that represents something like a historical constant. This is a tendency that has been manifested in history under different names, a tendency that has become more or less explicit in the differently worded programmes of those who have risen up against exploitation and repression throughout the ages, always professing the values of freedom, equality, and justice: from the slaves rebelling with Spartacus to Münzer's peasants and from the Paris Commune to the successful revolutions or major uprisings of the twentieth century, and up to today's Black Lives Matter, lives that should have mattered since and before the beginnings of colonisation.

This tendency can be called the tendency to communism, to honour the *Communist Manifesto*, the womb from which most of us originate in one way or another. But its names vary: Benjamin calls the horizon of this tendency 'redemption' and Derrida calls it 'democracy-to-come' or 'infinite justice' – where 'infinite justice' is the horizon that brings together freedom and equality (both social equality and equality before the law), with the two thus ceasing to be at odds with one another as they often have been even in the 'best' democracies that have existed in history. Hence the term 'democracy-to-come', which is analogous to Balibar's 'equaliberty'.

To this we may add that we humans *do possess* the *experience* of justice, and this from infancy: children in all cultures and through all historical periods distinguish whether they are being justly or unjustly reprimanded or praised. If this is true, then the tendency to communism – seen in all acts of unselfish solidarity – is a historical and quasi-anthropological constant, unceasingly at work within our societies, which overrides the dilemma we have been talking about. What Benjamin calls 'heliotropism' of the past towards the present amounts, I believe, to the double nature – historical because anthropological and anthropological because historical – of this constant. There is no space to go further into the concept, but I hope the idea is clear enough for present purposes.

Turning to the second principle of the framework I am proposing, I would emphasise that the experiment of 'Syriza in power' was mainly a *political* experiment. According to Poulantzas, the political instance is the instance integrating, condensing, and representing the forces at play within any given social formation, and it is the decisive instance: this is, *pace* Foucault, where the decisive power over the social formation's reproduction or transformation resides. Given this, we cannot endorse the more or less standard formula that the political as such amounts to the administration of the feasible. From the vantage point of the left, political action cannot but aim at *enlarging* and *deepening* the feasible: a *directed* and *engaged* enlarging and deepening that unwaveringly points the compass toward the horizon of communism.

Nevertheless 'feasible' remains a key word for us since we must take into account the specific circumstances and the power relations actually at play in any given conjuncture – realistically and with *sang froid*. This is to say that we must always tread a narrow path between inspired but thoughtless voluntarism, on the one side, and cautious but over-thoughtful adjustment to the forces at play, or actual capitulation, on the other. We are obliged to walk, that is, between the twin 'temptations' that are always at work and eager to destroy our efforts and drown our aspirations. The name of this narrow path is, of course, Gramsci's 'pessimism of the intellect' – for in most cases the dominant power relations are fundamentally hostile to an enterprise such as ours; but at the same time 'optimism of the will' – as an unflinching will is always prepared to muster the necessary force to overcome such hostility, forces which always lie in readiness if the tendency to communism is indeed a historical constant, forces which are practically invincible if mobilised.

Here, however, an additional question arises. And this leads to the third and last principle of the framework I am proposing. For, how can we effectively walk along the path illuminated by the inherent tendency to communism if even our richest theories are in this respect inadequate by definition? If, that is, they cannot predict or harness the unexpected – Althusser's *l'aléatoire* – which is always lurking in the shadows of the future and can thus derail even our best efforts – or at times enhance them through a totally unexpected 'event'? Since we cannot answer this theoretically, we can appeal to '*ποίησις*' – not just in the current but also in the original sense of the word, which means that we should not take poetry to be our only sanctuary, although it is a fundamental inspirational source in its own right, but also always assume responsibility for the *naked deed*, the deed that, as

Goethe has taught us, is always in the beginning: *Am Anfang war die Tat.* For '*ποίησις*' originally means doing, performing, creating. In our case it means doing and creating while at the same time assuming the relevant responsibility even if not supported by theory. It means doing by replying each time specifically and *by way of deeds* to Lenin's classic question: *what is to be done?* There is no other way, as Antonio Machado makes limpidly clear:

> 'Caminante, no hay camino,
> se hace camino al andar.'
> 'Wayfarer, there is no path,
> you make the path as you walk.'

The path here not being any path but the path we make in walking toward the horizon of communism.

Transition

To summarise. 1) Capitalism has no outside, we can only struggle inside and against it. 2) Our political struggle amounts, each time, to enlarging and deepening the feasible through walking toward the horizon of communism, being aware that at the same time the tendency to communism is constantly at work and indelibly inscribed within our societies. 3) The path we have to walk on is not subject to laws or even theoretically describable as such but is just made as we walk it. These are the basic principles of the framework I am proposing, which have emerged from the experiment of 'Syriza in power' – at least in so far as I have participated in and understood the experience, and have helped compose the document presenting it.

Certainly, these principles as well as their interconnections have not been worked out thoroughly. All sorts of questions can and should be raised; disagreement and criticism of all kind is to be more or less expected. However, recognising this is not a token of modesty or mere politeness; rather, I recognise the insufficiency of what precedes, and a clear sign of it is the proliferation of references and allusions to a disparate array of historical figures, authors, and their works, who are rarely, if ever, thought to be related – namely, Spartacus, Münzer, Marx, Lenin, Gramsci, Mao, Althusser, Poulantzas, Balibar, Benjamin, Derrida, Foucault, Panitch and Gindin, Bong Joon-ho, Machado, and Goethe.

What I would like to suggest with this series of apparently incommensurate names is that the inadequacy of theory ought to be compensated by serious efforts to *connect*, as far as possible, the work produced by these people (as well as the works created by many others from equally disparate fields).

I am aware that some are already doing so in one way or another. But I believe that there is too much emphasis placed on the superficial differences between such figures, and too little on their deeper affinities, affinities that show that all these personalities actually envisioned the path I have indicated. Some of these works are even key to uncovering the reasons why, and how, previous efforts to chart and walk this path have failed. Bringing such works together would amount to a difficult long-term collective project. However, to my mind at least, this task increasingly appears indispensable: the globe we all inhabit, especially after the outbreak of war in Ukraine, is approaching the limit where a radical change of the whole world order appears to be the only prospect for the survival of the human species. Even if this is an exaggeration, the bleak situation we are presently experiencing makes it imperative to assume the full responsibility of starting to walk, in a completely conscious way, the path to communism *right now*. At the same time, while we continue in the various struggles in which we have been engaged on different fronts, the long collective project of building the necessary theory could start illuminating the beginning of the path. For, as the famous saying goes, even the longest march starts from a first step.

In the case of Greece, this first step consists in trying to make explicit the salient features of the experiment 'Syriza in power' and offer them up for discussion. In this sense I will in what follows single out and limit myself to only one such feature – some aspects of the Greek state as they came into full view through Syriza's coming to power.

History

The Greek state is a relatively new creation. It was founded after 1827 when the naval forces of Britain, France, and Russia defeated the Ottoman fleet at Navarino, thus obliging the Ottoman Empire to grant independence to a number of provinces forming part of historical Greece. The Greek War of Independence – the Greek Revolution – had been declared in 1821 and passed through various difficult stages before finding its resolution in that decisive victory.

The Greek state's evolution from that time to the present saw many changes. Without trying to describe them all, one remark may suffice: the fact that Greek independence was achieved through the victory of the great powers of the time has left a lasting mark on the course followed by this state. To begin with, these powers thought it self-evident that Greek society was too immature to govern itself. Consequently, they appointed as a fully empowered Governor of Greece Ioannis Capodistrias, an ex-foreign minister of the Russian Empire of Greek origin. And after the assassination of Capodistrias, they appointed as a fully empowered king the young Prince Otto of Bavaria. After a revolt in 1843 King Otto granted a very defective constitution – with the country formally becoming a constitutional monarchy – but dependence on the great powers had already left an enduring stamp on Greece's political evolution and particularly on the prevailing mindset. Among other things, Greek political parties of the time had taken the cue and aligned with these powers even by name. Thus we had the 'British', the 'French', and the 'Russian' parties whose antagonisms determined much of the political life of the country for decades. The net result has been that the Greek state appeared and mostly acted from its very beginning as something foreign to Greek society, as an all-powerful arrogant institution, contemptuous if not actually hostile to the 'natives' and to their needs and demands. In the last analysis, Greece has remained 'immature' in this sense ever since.

Since then, waves of modernisation have occurred from time to time with many important changes. However, the DNA, so to speak, of the Greek state remained relatively stable. The deeper reasons for this have become obvious – the state was not built by the practices and reflective efforts, however divided internally, of a people having gained independence by its own efforts alone as happened, say, in the US. Nor has it evolved to post-absolutism through the kind of *internal* transformations, however moderate, disruptive, or radical, that led to the modern states of most major European countries. To repeat, the Greek state was concocted by foreign interventions, not taking into account popular aspirations, popular expectations, and the popular will. And since this inheritance has never been effectively confronted head on, the Greek state is still felt as standing above Greek society, as a self-interested, haughty and domineering instance, turning mostly a deaf ear even to the most legitimate of popular demands. Family-based political dynasties that control electoral enclaves run it, nepotism in terms of public posts is the rule rather than the exception, labyrinthine bureaucracy reigns unchallenged, corruption at various levels and in various forms and guises has been continuously at work in its interstices and, as it has almost never been defied and punished, has continued to thrive. Greece's 'immaturity' has been and continues to be quite profitable for the happy few: Greece's capitalism is fundamentally state-dependent.

The establishment of the Greek state by foreign intervention and the attendant absolutism have endowed it from the start with disproportionately great power as well as with a dynamic aimed at encompassing and regulating everything social from above. Which means that civil society rarely gained a real purchase. Control of the state as such, or participation at its higher echelons, has instead been the main goal for practically all involved in public life. Given the financial means and other privileges at the state's disposal, such control has constituted the coveted trophy of all political parties (and of each of its factions or 'families'), for their power bases have been formed and shaped by promises to be honoured through dispensing state positions and state funds. Even if elections were at times lost to the benefit of some competing party (with its own factions, 'families', and electoral basis), there were always the next elections to look forward to. Eventually, alternating between different parties in government through rapidly succeeding elections became a more or less stabilised political 'habit' in which the power base of each party (and faction and 'family') acquired characteristics of traditional property. The unity of the political system as a whole was thus assured even if ideological differences and political agendas had to be filtered by such traditions and accommodated correspondingly.

In such stable conditions, profitable to all parties involved, no interest in transforming the state and changing its role and function, and hence no political will to do so, has ever materialised: the rules of the political game were set and no political force was keen to change them. Excepting of course the Communist Party. But this has been either outlawed or banned from the state for the greater part of the twentieth century. It follows that, with the political instance formed in such ways, grassroots movements rarely appeared or, if they did, they either remained extremely weak or soon became mere extensions of the political parties at play. In other words, political parties reigned undisturbed over everything social while their internal connection to the state (excepting again the parties of the left, either communist or those critically valuing their communist heritage) offered a clientelist handle for individual – or family – aspirations. To make a (very) long story short, it is this kind of state that Syriza inherited and had to govern.

Policies

Poulantzas has taught us that the state is not just an instrument of the ruling class; it is itself traversed by class struggle in its various forms and guises even if most of these have been consistently underplayed in the popular perception. In any case, the experience of Syriza in government has surprisingly verified the hypothesis that quite a few of those working in the public sector could turn out individually, if not collectively, to be something other than dull bureaucrats, servile to those above them, imperious towards those below them, and arrogant towards the public at large. Instead, they quite often were eager to change their 'habits', shed the bureaucratic 'aura', promote honesty and oppose corruption, and participate in initiatives embodying the idea that a ministry, for example, is there to serve a particular sector of society, not dominate it. In short, what was revealed is that they had previously been obliged rather than willing to conform to the 'standard' rules of state functioning and thus were quite eager to change entrenched habits and attitudes and thus recover real meaning in their work.

In view of this situation an obvious policy was initiated: Those who assumed the political responsibility to run a governmental agency (a) treated right from the start all those working in it as responsible and proud citizens, willing to fulfil their assigned tasks and serve public interest to the best of their abilities irrespective of political preferences or even affiliations; b) encouraged the free expression of ideas, proposals, and initiatives irrespective of hierarchical constraints while appreciating well-defined hierarchies that are run justly and efficiently; c) helped create an open atmosphere of freedom and solidarity across the board; and d) set the example by working in this way themselves while relinquishing unjustifiable privileges, symbolic, material, or otherwise, no matter how well tradition had entrenched them. In short, insofar as such a policy was implemented, experience showed that many – perhaps most – of those working in the agency were all too ready to embrace a renovating spirit in respect to their tasks at the same time as practically everybody started to literally enjoy her work.

Is this a big deal? Perhaps such a policy sounds trivial, as practically all MBA programmes teach as much. However, in a country like Greece and with a state and a whole political system jealously defending the characteristics I outlined, the policy in question does indeed have the potential to stimulate important changes. For it may lead to a situation in which a governmental agency opens up, becomes directly acquainted and connected without intermediaries with what happens in the sectors of society for which it is responsible, can assist and enhance initiatives undertaken in a similar spirit outside its walls, and finally become a *social subject* in its own right, a subject aspiring to equality, freedom, and justice for all. In the longer run, society at large can thus come to feel and act as if it *owns* a state that should be there only to serve its members while the state itself starts to be dissolved within society. This is indeed a major transformation, and the path leading there is certainly untrodden – despite Lenin's precepts, injunctions, and efforts. But nothing forbids a left government, particularly in Greece, from starting to walk on such a path, deepening and enlarging the feasible by each step taken, correcting its policy when necessary and thus making the path by its very walking. Popular support and the attendant initiatives from 'below' might then deepen the transformations and accelerate the pace.

The document *Account of Syriza 2012-2019* roughly describes this path and gives some examples. However, it also indicates that the overall surrounding conditions were not particularly propitious for such an undertaking, and time proved insufficient for the initial steps to bear visible fruit. There is no space here to detail these conditions and their effects.[2]

Nevertheless, it should be pointed out that very few people or agencies outside Greece, either on the left or the right, seem to have taken into serious consideration the historically entrenched features of the Greek state I have tried to sketch. They notice its purely formal characteristics (quite 'up-to-date' in their own right) and thus tend to perceive it as more or less a modern state like others. If seen in that way, the policy outlined above cannot help appearing bland and self-evident, as just another policy of further modernisation with no left political bite to speak of. Needless to say I disagree completely – without implying, however, that we have 'first' to pass through some 'stage' of 'further' modernisation so as to put forth 'socialist' demands only afterwards. On the contrary, the untrodden path I have been speaking of is a path oriented *directly*, with *no* intermediate stages, to 'infinite justice' or 'democracy-to-come' – that is, to communism.

The only forces that have understood that such a policy is not just more of the same modernisation are the Greek political forces struggling to wipe Syriza off the political map. And this for very good reasons. Although they are obliged to admit that the social reforms implemented by Syriza were both necessary and mild while its programme could not be understood as promoting ostensible 'socialist' goals, Syriza's very coming to power has been perceived by them as endangering the real interests vested in the way the Greek state has been functioning for two hundred years. Defending the status quo by all means, legitimate or illegitimate, is in the vital interest of these forces; hence the unbridled fury they have unleashed against Syriza since 2012.

Closure or opening

That Syriza came to power in the first place appeared as a kind of miracle even to us who participated actively in the process. What the forces were that brought this about, how they did so and have been faring ever since are major issues in their own right, full of vital lessons that require deep examination. However, it is not only we in Greece who face a difficult situation but the world as a whole. The pandemic has been changing everything; the climate catastrophe has reached gigantic proportions; continuously growing waves of the victims of war, oppression, and hunger encircle the wealthy countries of the political West; a deeper economic crisis looms on the horizon; the political elites in almost all countries appear to be fully immersed in their

244   FACING THE STATE

neoliberal fantasies, incapable of addressing any of these major challenges; the war in Ukraine seriously threatens the whole geopolitical order; a perfectly destructive world war has become a matter of 'when', not even of 'whether or not'. What the next day will be like and how each individual, each class or group of people, each country, big or small, each international institution, will fare is, as we are speaking, up for grabs. Struggles around all such issues do mobilise the international left, but its responses cannot but appear largely inadequate, even if we do not yet know what needs to be done to make them adequate. We cannot predict what will happen. But our experiences, our values and our ideas, if exchanged systematically in solidarity, discussed thoroughly and elaborated carefully, can enable us to withstand most shocks and prepare us to effectively face the oncoming challenges. Once again, optimism of the will and the 'poetic principle' are our best counsellors.

NOTES

1   The present paper relies heavily on my contribution 'Ο Σύριζα στην εξουσία: διδάγματα διακυβέρνησης και το Ελληνικό κράτος' ('Syriza in Power: Lessons on Governmentality and the Greek State') to the volume *Αριστερή Κυβερνησιμότητα: Η εμπειρία του ΣΥΡΙΖΑ 2015-2019* (*Left Governmentality: the Experience of Syriza 2015-2019*), edited by Kostas Douzinas and Michalis Bartzidis, Athens, 2021, Nissos: Nikos Poulantzas Institute – at times translating passages almost *verbatim*.
2   See, however, Aristides Baltas, *Within a parenthesis? Governing Radical Left, first period, (25 January 2015-21 August 2018)*, Athens: Patakis Editions, 2019 (in Greek).

Finland's Left Alliance in Government

Jukka Pietiläinen

Among all radical left parties in Europe, Finland's Left Alliance has had the longest period of participation in coalition governments. The Left Alliance was founded in 1990 but its predecessor, the Finnish People's Democratic League (FPDL), had already participated in coalition governments many times, namely in 1944-1948, 1966-1971, 1975-1976, and 1977-1982. In all these governments, the FPDL participated together with the Social Democrats and the Centre Party (former Agrarian League) and occasionally with some other leftist or centrist parties. The period of these people's front coalitions, which realised important social reforms, created an atmosphere on the Finnish left in favour of governmental participation. However, from 1968 the Finnish Communist Party, which was the FPDL's most important member organisation, was split between reformists and traditionalists, and the question of governmental participation was one of the key stakes of their divisions. The traditionalist, pro-Moscow minority did not support joining the government and usually voted against government proposals in parliament. Conversely, among the reformist, Eurocommunist majority, governmental participation was also seen as a way to be a part of the political consensus. But there was also a change over time: while in the late 1960s taking part in government was justified in the name of achieving important social reforms, 'in the later seventies justifications have been more of the "lesser evil" type'.[1]

The internal split, together with social change and the decline of the traditional working class, led to a fall in FPDL's popular support, from 21.2% in 1966 to 13.5% in 1983. It remains uncertain how far governmental participation per se was a factor in this development.

In December 1982, the party left the government because its MPs voted against the weapons spending which had been proposed in the budget. This was expected to lead to a long period in opposition for the FPDL. Even so, the party was ready to take part in government after the parliamentary elections in 1983 but the Social Democrats (SDP) and Centre Party did not even seriously consider such a prospect.[2]

The political and economic bankruptcy of the Finnish Communist Party led to the founding of Left Alliance in 1990 with the aim of gathering various leftist forces together. The willingness to participate in government remained strong within its ranks. Since 1995 Left Alliance has been in government over half of the time, amounting to around 14 years and 9 months (up to the parliamentary elections of 2023). This is a clear record among the radical left parties in Europe. So, what has the Left Alliance's experience been – and what does it have to tell us about the state today?

The Finnish political system as the background of government participation

The Finnish party system is in many ways distinct, in particular due to the following features: 1) the party system has been fragmented and a large number (usually 8-9) of parties gain representation in parliament, 2) the absence of a party that is decisively larger than its main competitors, 3) the increased weakness of parties on the left, 4) the strength of a Centre party that is historically an agrarian party, 5) the absence of a liberal party.[3] Since 1987, Finland has followed a more clearly parliamentary system in which it is the parliament that elects the prime ministers (formerly, they were nominated by the president).

Since 1977 Finland has had nothing but majority coalition cabinets and since 1962 the largest party has always been in a majority coalition. Since 1987 majority cabinets have always been based on co-operation between two of the three largest parties (Social Democrats, Conservatives, and the Centre Party).[4] The emergence of the right-wing populist True Finns, now one of four major parties, has not changed the situation: two out of three traditional large parties have formed the basis of the coalition. Sometimes, minor parties have participated in ideologically unorthodox coalitions, but the Left Alliance has not been (and perhaps could never be) in the government without the Social Democrats.

The Finnish system of government formation has been described in terms of 'a lack of bipolarised dynamics'; 'governments have been routinely formed "across the blocs", that is they have included both socialist and non-socialist parties'.[5] In contrast with other European countries, the Left Alliance has also participated in government with the main conservative, right-wing party, the National Coalition Party. In his memoirs, Ralf Sund, who was Left Alliance party secretary from 1995-2001, judges that left-wing parties had an easier time finding common ground with the National Coalition Party than with the Centre Party, because the latter has moved to the right and kept its conservative positions in policy areas such as gay marriage and the environment, where the National Coalition Party has instead modernised.[6]

Although the centre-right parties have received between 52% and 66% of votes in every parliamentary election since 1991, only twice has the government been formed without both Social Democrats and Greens. The Left Alliance has been included in governments four times, and only once have the Social Democrats been in government without the Left Alliance and Greens; the Greens, for their part, have been in government without the Left Alliance and SDP only once.[7] In fact, the Left Alliance has been in government with all the main parties expect the right-populist party today known as The Finns (ex-True Finns).

One of the reasons behind Finland's broad government coalitions and 'unholy' government alliances might be that in this country's local politics there is no government-opposition division; rather, all parties represented in municipal councils are equal, and even smaller parties can get their initiatives realised if they are capable of co-operating with other parties. Most Finnish politicians at the national level have a background in local politics. That fact is testified, for example, by Left Alliance MP Erkki Virtanen, who has said that he was critical of government participation but then changed his opinion after experience in local politics in which a smaller party can achieve its aims in exchange for concessions on other issues.[8]

Rainbow Coalition 1995-2003

In 1995, the Left Alliance participated in Prime Minister Paavo Lipponen's 'Rainbow' Coalition government together with the Social Democrats, the National Coalition Party, the Greens, and the Swedish People's Party of Finland. The Social-Democratic leader became prime minister after four years of bourgeois government, which contributed to the electoral victory of both the SDP and Left Alliance.

New in this government was that the Social Democrats' traditional partner, the Centre Party, had been replaced by the National Coalition Party. The Centre had suffered electoral setbacks but remained the second largest party; however, the Social Democrats had made gains in the elections and wanted budget cuts to agricultural subsidies, which Centre Party opposed. The fact that the National Coalition Party and not the Centre was included was also due to the personal antipathy of Social-Democratic leader and premier Paavo Lipponen towards this agrarian force. All government parties agreed on 20 billion FIM (€3.4 billion) in budget cuts but aimed to preserve the welfare state and to cut unemployment by half before the next parliamentary elections. The amount of budget cuts was at a level of 10% of the 1995 state budget.

Participation in such a government was difficult for the Left Alliance. Prime minister Paavo Lipponen visited the meeting of the Left Alliance party council and parliamentary group when it was deciding on participation and tried to convince it to approve joining the government.[9] The vote on the decision saw 47 delegates for and 25 against. Yet both participation and the government's programme were criticised from the beginning and even minister Terttu Huttu-Juntunen said that this would remain a difficult choice, especially because of cuts in social expenditure.[10]

An English-language publication by Left Alliance reports that 'the decisive reason to take part in the government was the readiness and willingness to do something concrete to overcome the enormous mass unemployment and save the Finnish welfare model and its financing'.[11]

However, this participation in government caused an immediate split in the Left Alliance's parliamentary group. Three MPs voted against cuts in student and child benefits as well as unemployment compensation, after which they were expelled from the parliamentary group and founded their own Left Group. One of them, Esko-Juhani Tennilä, criticised the Left Alliance. He insisted that it had participated in cutting social security, that other parties laid claim to even the positive decisions that were made, and that the Left Alliance had given up its political line in the name of being in government.[12]

Claes Andersson, the party chairperson at that time, reports in his memoirs that when he was giving May Day speeches in two left-wing strongholds, he was greeted by a furious response. In Nokia a group of protestors chanted 'Hang up Andersson, Hang up Andersson' and in Tampere eggs were thrown at him.[13] This came just after the coalition government had cut unemployment benefits.

In addition to Andersson, it was understood that the other minister for Left Alliance needed to be a woman and hail from Northern Finland. Among the Left Alliance's MPs only few fit these criteria and so the newly elected, first-term MP Terttu Huttu-Juntunen became minister of social affairs. She had worked in the local administration in the same field but was rather inexperienced in national politics. In 1996 an opinion poll deemed her one of the most unsuccessful ministers, while Andersson was among the most successful.[14] The whole government had poor ratings: in 1996 only 20% of Finns rated it as successful, and among Left Alliance supporters only 5% had such an opinion.[15]

The most problematic issue for the Left Alliance came in the fall of 1997 when it decided to ask its members if the party would approve Finland's membership in the European Monetary Union, thus organising an internal referendum in November 1997. With 67% turnout, 52.4% of voters approved EMU membership while 41.5% voted against; the rest preferred to leave the decision to the party leadership. According to party secretary Ralf Sund[16] the members did not vote primarily for the EMU but against the radicals: a victory for the 'No' camp would have left the party in the hands of the radical opposition and would have meant withdrawing from the government.[17]

Commenting in his memoirs, Claes Andersson stated that this vote was seen as necessary to participate in a government which aimed to improve employment, reduce public debt and take care of the future of the welfare state, and to deepen and democratise EU cooperation. For him, the government succeeded in its aims, except for that of cutting unemployment in half.[18] The Centre Party as the leading opposition party 'claimed that income disparities had grown, social exclusion increased, problems of regional imbalance worsened, and that the government had not halved unemployment'.[19]

The participation in this so-called Lipponen I government led the Left Alliance to approve budget shrinkage, but it was successful in making smaller cuts in basic social security than other parties would have liked. Other parties in government wanted to include 20% of housing costs in basic social benefits (in practice, cutting the basic social benefit by a similar amount) but the Left Alliance succeed in reducing this cut to only 7%. Meanwhile free day-care for the poor remained, although both the SDP and National Coalition wanted to remove it. Costs for medicine were also cut.[20]

Following its participation in this government, in the 1999 elections Left Alliance slipped back from 11.2% to 10.9%, losing two seats. Minister Terttu Huttu-Juntunen lost her seat although she got marginally more personal votes than she had in the 1995 elections (3,407 in 1999 and 3,383 in 1995), and the party increased its vote share in her constituency. Another candidate Unto Valpas, who had a more critical attitude to the government, got more votes and was elected. On the other hand, all the MPs who were expelled from the parliamentary group increased their percentages significantly.

In this same election, the SDP lost over 5% of votes and 12 MPs, while the conservatives gained 7 new MPs; because the Greens also won 2 MPs, the total loss for the government was a mere 5 seats out of 200. The SDP was still the largest party and the new government was formed on the same basis.

In the recent period, Left Alliance voters had become more gender equal and even had a female majority (55% in 1999, compared to 50% in 1995 and 29% in 1991) but were also less working class (70–72% in 1991 and 1995 but only 54% in 1999). Possibly this was because the working class and the poor were most directly affected by the cuts in public spending, for which Left Alliance was partly held responsible given its role in government.[21]

According to an opinion poll produced during the government negotiations, most Finns would like the red–blue (SDP and Conservatives) government to continue instead of one pivoted on an SDP-Centre pact. Moreover, among Left Alliance voters, 38% preferred a SDP-National Coalition government, while a SDP-Centre government was backed by only 27% of Left Alliance voters. The Centre Party was criticised because it had gone into the elections with a programme called 'Work reform', one of the cornerstones of which was to reduce the position of trade unions and centralised collective bargaining. 'In rebuilding the Rainbow Coalition in quick time, Lipponen declared the need for a solid base of co-operation and ministerial experience in view of the fact that the vital EU presidency was just around the corner'.[22]

Trade unionists in particular wanted the Left Alliance to continue in office, while the greatest risk was the formation of a completely bourgeois government. Both in 1995 and 1999 shortly after the government was formed 'the five main labour-market organisations, both employers and trade unions, issued a declaration of support for the new administration [...] Moreover, the existence of what might be called "summit-level corporatism" has been mirrored in a couple of exceptionally broad two-year income policy agreements in 1995 and 1997 which contributed significantly to holding down inflation'.[23]

In government negotiations, the Left Alliance 'was able to put together a more coherent set of priorities for coalition negotiations and secured itself more impressive portfolios'[24] than in 1995. In setting its aims it emphasised employment, actions against poverty and more balanced regional development.[25] The other parties largely agreed with these objectives, and Prime Minister Paavo Lipponen stated that after four years, full employment should be in sight. The smallest pensions were increased, and no new budget cuts were planned but the government aimed to reduce the state debt level, while capital income tax was also pushed up.[26] The ministerial posts taken up by the Left Alliance were considered rather stronger than in 1995: the party chairperson Suvi-Anne Siimes became second finance minister (focusing on tax policy) and the ministry of the environment also transferred certain housing issues to her purview. Martti Korhonen, the former chairperson of the parliamentary group, became minister of regional policy. Korhonen represented Northern Finland and therefore gave regional balance to the Left Alliance ministers.

This time around, the Left Alliance party council and parliamentary group made a much clearer choice to participate in government than in 1995, with 61 votes for, and only eight against. But of these eight, five came from the parliamentary group, showing that the party council, representing the broader membership, had become more favourable to governmental participation than MPs themselves. One of the delegates stated that support for governmental participation meant that the party's ministers and MPs could be trusted; if the party could not participate in government, it would not be useful even in opposition. Critics pointed to the difficulties they faced in going back to their own constituencies to defend government policy, and some especially noted a change in national-security policy: according to this criticism, the new programme was more compatible with NATO than earlier ones. [27]

The second Lipponen government 1999-2003 did not cause any permanent split in the Left Alliance parliamentary group, which unanimously voted for the government upon its initial formation. However, some MPs were critical of the government's actions and occasionally voted against it. In March 2001 three members of the parliamentary group were expelled for two weeks because they voted together with the opposition against the government's anti-poverty package, which was seen as inadequate. One MP each from the Social Democrats and the Greens also voted against the government.

But there were also differences from the Lipponen I administration. The economic situation was better,[28] most of the cuts to welfare spending had already been made, and the early years of Lipponen's second government saw progress in areas dear to Left Alliance. However, it seems that toward the end of its tenure it had lost the original spirit of 1995: from 2001 onward job creation stagnated and the government more often faced problems borne of its overly broad political composition.[29]

According to the future Left-Alliance chairperson Paavo Arhinmäki there was practically no ideological discussion during the period in government: every day political issues filled the agenda and needed to be solved, whereas ideological issues were left aside.[30] On a similarly pragmatic note, Claes Andersson stated in an interview in April 2000, 'no party can stay in opposition a long time without losing its credibility. One must occasionally be able to show that programmes, visions, and aims can be realised.'[31] Yet, outgoing party secretary Ralf Sund claimed in an interview in June 2001, the Left Alliance had been too eager 'to prove that we can be trusted' and to make compromises, without doing enough to emphasise its own message; however, doing so would have been easier if it had not been for the internal opposition.[32]

The left-wing newspaper *Kansan Uutiset*[33] summarised Left Alliance's performance in government by saying that it had provided its social conscience. Throughout, the Left Alliance had emphasised employment and the link between social security and employment, but in such a way that the poorest would not suffer. When it came to tax cuts, the Left Alliance focused on relief for the lowest incomes, while the right emphasised tax cuts for the highest earners. The government had good relations with the trade unions and three major collective agreements were reached during its term which raised workers' salaries. The lowest pensions were also boosted, health costs for pensioners were cut, unemployment benefits were raised, free pre-school was introduced for 6-year-olds, and maternity benefits were raised for the first time since 1993.

According to an opinion poll conducted before the 2003 parliamentary elections, Left Alliance voters were split exactly 50-50 on whether the government had been doing well. This opinion on the government was the poorest among all the main parties' bases; indeed, even supporters of opposition parties gave better assessments.[34]

The whole period of the Rainbow Coalition succeeded in creating over 300,000 new jobs and reducing the unemployment rate from 16% in 1994 to 9% in 2001. At the same time, the public finances were balanced, and capital and corporate taxes were raised from 25% to 29%. On the other hand, severe cuts to public expenditure were made, even if Left Alliance was able to soften them.[35]

After the Rainbow Coalition

However, in the 2003 elections Left Alliance lost more support than in 1999, dropping from 10.9% to 9.9% of the vote. Three of the five MPs critical of governmental participation also lost votes, implying that a critical attitude towards governmental participation no longer proved a means of rallying greater electoral support. The pro-government MPs also tended to lose rather than gain support in this election; seven of them got fewer personal votes, and six did better, but two pro-government MPs lost their seats.

One possible reason for the lower support was the election campaign's focus on the prime minister's post, which has in recent contests belonged to the largest single party. The Social Democrats increased their support but were nonetheless edged out of first place by the Centre Party, now in a position to appoint the prime minister. Before the elections, an SDP representative had criticised the Left Alliance as an unreliable partner in government and stated that the strength of the political left would depend on the SDP's support level alone.[36] After its election success, the Centre Party chose the SDP as its main coalition partner and without including the Left Alliance. Within the Left Alliance, there was considerable willingness to continue in office, with its confinement to the opposition producing the 'disappointment and surprise not just of its of leaders but also its activists and members, who were by then more reconciled than ever to the government role. Inevitably, the party's exclusion sparked a debate about whether it should Return to a harder line against Social-Democratic compromises in pursuit of votes or tone things down so as not to blow any chance of being invited back into government next time around.'[37]

This disappointment also heralded an internal crisis in the party. Suvi-Anne Siimes had difficulty finding her place as an opposition politician, and the editor of the party newspaper *Kansan Uutiset*, Yrjö Rautio, criticised the party's lack of a strong political line. In 2004, he quit both his editorial role and his party membership after having strongly criticised Siimes. According to Rautio, her oppositional politics was close to the position of those who had always been against governmental participation, only now this stance was taken up by formerly pro-government MPs: 'The only position is to oppose everything which the government is doing.' Rautio especially criticised the Left Alliance's negative attitude towards the SDP (which he later joined).

Party chairperson Siimes 'was determined to change party policy on participation in a common EU defence policy [...] as the key to an early return to government'.[38] This led to public confrontations with the party opposition. Although the ardent Eurosceptics were in a minority, there was not wide support for Finland's military integration in the EU or participation in military alliances, and this led to a conflict between the chairperson and the radicals inside the party. In March 2006, Siimes resigned the leadership of the Left Alliance and announced that she would not stand for election to parliament again.[39] Most especially, she would not help the former hard-line communist candidates such as Jaakko Laakso to become MPs: with her huge number of personal votes she had helped additional MPs win election for the Left Alliance in her district. Political commentators expected the Left Alliance slowly to decline to the condition of a minor party. In 2007, it again lost out in the parliamentary elections, mostly because of internal conflicts in the party.

Katainen government

A turning point came in 2011 when the right-populist The Finns scored a major breakthrough, becoming the second largest party with 19% support. But, with its large cohort of new MPs, it was unwilling to take part in government. This also made it more difficult for the traditional political coalitions to form a majority government. Moreover, the Centre Party had suffered a setback and was willing to stay in opposition. According to Arter 'the result of the 2011 general election meant that the "Finnish model", in which two of the three larger "old parties" comprise a parliamentary majority and proceed to form the nucleus of the new cabinet, was no longer sustainable'. Instead, the new coalition would have to represent 'a continuation of the Finnish tradition of "anything goes" governments'.[40]

The government negotiations lasted longer than any previous post-election period in Finnish history, with the programme for the new administration made up of different elements without a common basis. One particular sticking point, in this crisis period, was a bailout package for Portugal, opposed by the Left Alliance because the package would mean austerity measures for the people and support only large European banks. However, this difficult point for coalition formation was evaded, as the outgoing government took responsibility to approve the package on Finland's behalf in May 2011, before the new government was nominated and Left Alliance voted against the bailout package in the parliament.

This time the Social Democrats wanted the Left Alliance to participate in government. Incoming prime minister Jyrki Katainen, of the conservative National Coalition, pointed out that there were good memories of co-operation between his party and the Left Alliance in 1995-2003, when the country's economic situation was repaired after the economic collapse of the 1990s.[41]

Initial government negotiations based on a six-party pact were abandoned when Katainen pushed SDP and Left Alliance away from the negotiations, but he then needed to invite them back, given the failure of alternative attempts to form a majority. The Left Alliance had to change one of its negotiators, an MP who stood in opposition to such a coalition. Yet an agreement on the government programme was finally reached, and the Left Alliance party council and parliamentary group again voted for participation in government with 40 votes for, 23 against, and 3 abstentions. Party chairperson Paavo Arhinmäki insisted that there were real achievements for the Left Alliance, with the government programme including what he called the largest package for the poor in 40 years. Arhinmäki became the minister of culture, while MP Merja Kyllönen from northern Finland became the minister of transport.

Again, the Left Alliance's participation in government was criticised by hard-line leftists within the party and also by Left Youth. Two members of its parliamentary group voted against the government's policy in parliament and were thus expelled.

The first major crisis for the Left Alliance's participation came in fall 2013 when it again had to vote for continuing in the government. The critics of government participation pointed to the fact that EU policy was headed in the wrong direction and that state subsidies for municipalities in the fields of social and healthcare services and education had been cut. On the other hand, supporters of government participation pointed out that Left Alliance had made a real difference, including increases for pensioners, students, and basic social assistance.[42] Pro-government MPs feared what would happen if the poor were left without anyone to defend them within the coalition. The economic situation had become worse than expected and public finances were tighter than expected at the beginning of the government's term.

In November 2013 the party council and the parliamentary group decided to continue in government, with 43 votes for and 24 against. The division of votes was almost the same as in 2011 when the party decided to participate in government, although the party council had been renewed in the party congress in summer 2013. According to media, the critics of the government participation included both young radicals and old veterans who saw participation in a government with conservatives as inadmissible.[43] According to some commentators this meant a loss of the Left Alliance's political capital.[44]

Before the decision to remain in government, a wide discussion had taken place in the party newspaper *Kansan Uutiset*. According to critics, the Left Alliance had difficulty deciding if it was a serious democratic party or a utopian revolutionary one. On this reading, it ought not to have based its support on groups which are bound to end up dissatisfied with the outcomes of democratic politics, but should instead orient itself to those with a clearer appreciation of its possibilities and its limits. It was thought important, moreover, that the Left Alliance's positions also be respected among other parties.[45]

The final end of the Left Alliance's government participation came in March 2014 when the administration changed its line and decided to make cuts in the most basic benefits for the poor. This contradicted the agreed government programme and the Left Alliance's parliamentary group decided unanimously to leave the government. An irony of history is that in 1995 Left Alliance had accepted cuts in child benefits as part of the government programme, while in 2014 this had become unacceptable.

According to party chairperson Paavo Arhinmäki the basic principles of the Left Alliance in the government had been that 'income differences should be reduced and that the position of the poor should be improved. That had been the government policy during the first three years but in spring 2014 this policy had changed.'[46] Minister Li Andersson, at that time chairperson of the Left Youth and future chair of the Left Alliance itself, pointed out the incongruence in the party's economic policy: the Left Alliance had approved budget cuts of almost €7 billion but decided to leave the government because of incorrectly focused cuts of €310 million.[47]

The decision to leave the government did bump up the Left Alliance's opinion poll ratings, from around 7-8% to 8-9 %, but in parliamentary elections in 2015 it got its worst ever result, with its 7.1% score bringing the loss of four MPs. One incumbent MP opposed to governmental participation did not stand at all, while another lost about 25% of his votes, significantly more than Left Alliance as a party, though many pro-government MPs also scored worse than in 2011.

Rinne-Marin government

After four years (2015-2019) of a centre-populist-right coalition led by centrist prime minister Juha Sipilä, three opposition parties – the Social Democrats, the Left Alliance, and the Greens – won the elections. The SDP became the largest party, albeit just one seat ahead of the right-populist True Finns. Although the Centre Party suffered heavily at the polls – getting its worst result in 100 years – and even though 75% of its party council members favoured going into opposition,[48] the party ultimately opted to participate in government, following pressure from the Social-Democratic prime minister, Antti Rinne, a development which disproved political commentators expectations that the Social Democrats and the conservative National Coalition would be the backbone of the government. Rinne's coalition programme would represent a shift from austerity towards a more traditional social-democratic politics of distribution.[49] The government decided upon the abolition of a model that had sought to push the unemployed into work through the threat of cutting unemployment benefits, and also imposed stricter rules regarding the number of nurses per patient in hospitals and nursing homes. The government's programme also included Left Alliance's proposals for an increase in the compulsory education age, from 17 to 18 years, and the free provision of schoolbooks and other materials for secondary education. Abortion law and legislation on transgender issues were also renewed.[50]

The government negotiations were easier than in 2011 and one could say that the new government was also better. Its programme,[51] as measured in wordcount at least, was the longest in Finnish history, approximately three times longer than that of the outgoing government.

There was only one dramatic moment during the talks for the creation of the government, when the Left Alliance negotiators disagreed with the other parties on the matter of selling state assets to balance the budget.[52] The Left Alliance had a crisis meeting, accepted the sell-offs and returned to negotiations.[53] The government programme included the selling of state assets and did not include changes to the taxation of non-listed companies, from which the richest continued to get low taxed income. These were seen as the weakest parts of the government programme by a new Left Alliance MP Jussi Saramo, but the party accepted them as part of a document it considered mostly good.[54]

For Left Alliance the participation in this government was significantly easier than in 2011 and the decision was confirmed by an advisory referendum among the membership, as had been suggested by a grassroots party activist. The referendum produced a 97.2% majority in favour of governmental participation. The voting period was only a few days, and was organised online, while the turnout was very low (33.7%),[55] but most of the critics of the government participation certainly did vote. The clear result helped also to silence the internal opposition and this time there was no split of the parliamentary group, although some MPs were more critical than others. The party council and the parliamentary group decided unanimously to participate in the government.

The Left Alliance got more important ministerial posts than in 2011: the party chairperson Li Andersson became education minister and Aino-Kaisa Pekonen minister of social affairs and healthcare. After two years, Pekonen was replaced by Hanna Sarkkinen, as earlier agreed, in order to give a ministerial post to someone from Northern Finland. In 2020 Andersson was replaced for a few months of her maternity leave by party vice chairperson Jussi Saramo.

Prime Minister Antti Rinne came under attack from the Centre Party in the fall 2019; he resigned, for lack of trust, and was replaced by Sanna Marin, albeit on the same government programme.[56] The formal reason for the distrust was the labour conflict in the state postal service and statements of the prime minister concerning it[57] but it can be interpreted also as revenge for the 2003 machinations when the SDP had lost confidence in and sought the resignation of Centre PM Anneli Jäätteenmäki.[58] Marin was at that time the youngest prime minister in the world and all five parties in government were chaired by women.

Marin's government had to tackle two unforeseeable crises: first the Covid-19 pandemic and then the war in Ukraine. The Russian invasion led to a major change of Finnish public opinion, and NATO membership, which in the recent past was rejected by most Finns, within a few months received clear majority support. According to opinion polls, around half of Left Alliance supporters now favoured NATO membership.[59] The government decided in May 2022 to apply for NATO membership, a choice backed also by Left Alliance ministers. Among 16 Left Alliance MPs, nine voted for Finland's NATO application while the others opposed membership (six voted against and one was absent). In the Left Alliance party congress in June 2022 a clear majority accepted a new formulation in the party programme, accepting NATO membership as a reality.

An even more serious crisis for the Left Alliance's participation came in fall 2022 when the government decided to reduce healthcare workers' right to strike, through a Patient Safety Act. Earlier the trade union had planned to organise strikes also in emergency care. Only seven Left Alliance MPs voted for the law, while five voted against and four were absent because they were not willing to back the measure, although Left Alliance ministers could negotiate some positive amendments.[60] Oppositional MPs were punished with a warning in the parliamentary group but even this did not cause a split or visible problems for government co-operation itself.

In the Rinne-Marin government, the Left Alliance did not cause major political problems and the party remained united. The Marin government retained high levels of support and among Left Alliance voters its popularity was among the strongest. In spring 2021, some 94% of them were very satisfied with the government. Li Andersson was rated as third most popular government member after the prime minister Marin and foreign minister Pekka Haavisto (Greens). In mid-2020 Andersson's work was assessed as good by 52% and in December 2021 by 38% of poll respondents.[61] In spring 2020 two thirds of Finns (69%) were either very or somewhat satisfied with the government and this figure was 53% in the fall of 2022,[62] a record for that stage of a government.

The popularity was visible also among members of the Left Alliance party council: in summer 2021, 22 out of 35 members described themselves as very satisfied, and 10 somewhat satisfied. Only 2 members were dissatisfied with the government. According to the party council members, the Left Alliance had worked for the poor without causing much noise, stuck by its values, and been a responsible party in the government.[63]

The Left Alliance's 2014 decision to leave government has led many commentators to expect the party would do the same in the present. Yet despite the NATO decision and limitation on the right to strike, the Left Alliance remained in Marin's cabinet, being perceived as one of its cornerstones. The main problems inside the government have resulted from public spats with the Centre Party, which has tried to gain visibility due to its falling popularity rates. These have focused for instance on environmental protection, with the Centre (representing countryside and farmers) in conflict with the Greens. According to an opinion poll 38% of Finns believed that the Centre Party was responsible for the internal conflicts in the government, while Left Alliance went practically unmentioned (1%).[64]

According to Minister of Social Affairs and Health Care (2021-2023) Hanna Sarkkinen, Left Alliance had fulfilled 50% of its electoral programme in the government[65] and Left Alliance during the electoral campaign 2023 distributed a leaflet titled '50 decisions with which the government has improved your daily life'. Opinion polls were higher than election result in 2019 and the party was even expecting that it could win after participation in government.

However, Left Alliance lost in the parliamentary elections of April 2023 and got its worst result, 7.1% and 11 MPs, although the result in 2015 was almost the same (7.2% and 12 MPs). The loss in support was rather typical for Left Alliance after a government participation but it was aggravated by tactical voting: a significant number of voters who might prefer Left Alliance (and the Greens) voted for the SDP in order to make it the largest party, which in the Finnish system usually becomes the prime minister's party. The SDP increased its support, which was unusual for a prime minister's party, but nevertheless remained the third largest party.

Impact on Finnish policy

In its government action, the Left Alliance has promoted issues such as decreasing poverty, improving the position of the poorest, and preserving public services and the welfare state. The reduction of unemployment and more stable regional development have also been priorities which Left Alliance has kept on the political agenda, as well as (especially pre-school and school-age) education.

It is less simple to identify what impact the Left Alliance has actually had on Finnish society through its historical governmental participation. First, it has been among the smallest parties in government and therefore its impact is not easily separated from the actions of other parties. The Left Alliance has usually participated in governments with Social Democrats and Greens and its successful initiatives are typically ones on which these parties can agree.

Moreover, factors other than government decisions have also played a role.

For example, because of the rise in capital incomes and the reduction of the taxes on them (realised by the bourgeois government in 1993) income differentials widened in times when the Left Alliance was in government. Left Alliance largely disagrees with other parties on taxation policy and has not been able to promote its views. According to official statistics, the Gini Coefficient measuring inequality increased from 22.2 in 1995 to 28.4 in 2000, while during the second Lipponen government it decreased to 27.2 in 2003. During the Katainen government the Gini coefficient was reduced from 28.2 in 2011 to 27.0 in 2014, while after the Left Alliance's departure it grew to 27.3 in 2015. During the Rinne-Marin government this figure first decreased from 28.1 in 2018 to 27.7 in 2020, but then increased to 29.1 in 2021, mostly because of the economic recovery after the Covid-19 crisis.[66]

The Left Alliance did not compromise on basic social-security benefits for the poorest, nor on the goal of creating new job posts. However, in the first Rainbow government it had to agree with budget cuts proposed by conservative finance minister Iiro Viinanen, who had the same post in the former bourgeois government. But while other parties sought to cut basic social subsidies by 20% Left Alliance negotiated a lesser, 7% reduction. Left Alliance also succeeded in preserving free day-care for the poorest, as against plans to equalise day-care fees, reducing medicine prices, and in creating jobs with public investments, for example for housing construction.[67]

Finland is a small economy, and consequently market forces and international economic developments play a more important role than the country's government in practical economic policy. As the *Kansan Uutiset* editor explained, 'every government has to pay attention to the conditions of the market economy' – adding 'would it be a left policy to cause economic bankruptcy?'.[68]

Equally, unemployment numbers are no mere function of government policy. During the first Rainbow government, 170,000 new jobs were created, mainly due to economic growth and lower interest rates. The government succeeded in stabilising the economy and public finances.

Impact on Left Alliance

In 1995 Left Alliance became a government party for the first time after 1982. In can be said that the party came to government unprepared: only three of its 22 MPs had been in parliament back in 1982, and two of those three criticised governmental participation. As recognised in the party council, everything was new and required a new attitude and new thinking. It was not easy to transform a party of permanent opposition to a party of government;

for some MPs this task was extremely difficult or even impossible. In 1995, the party council also noted that at the grassroots level, the transition away from a purely oppositional rhetoric had not taken place.[69]

The situation was different in 1999 when the Left Alliance had more experience as a government party, and because with a better economic situation budget cuts were no longer necessary. The decision to participate in government was easier and the parliamentary group remained united for most of the term.

In 2011 the party was hesitant even if this was not seen in the voting figures of the government participation vote by the parliamentary group and the party council. Left Alliance did not like to be treated as a support party for the Social Democrats.

In 2019 the membership referendum gave almost unanimous support for governmental participation, also quiet opposition voices inside the party. As mentioned above, in fall 2019 as many as 62% of the Left Alliance's supporters were very or somewhat satisfied with the government, while in spring 2020, during the onset of Covid-19, this score had grown to 87%; in spring 2022, some 85% of Left Alliance voters remained satisfied with the government.[70]

Political commentators and politicians from other parties have often taken a negative attitude toward the Left Alliance, raising doubts about its capability to participate reliably in a coalition government. In the 1970s and 1980s a radical minority of the party had regularly opposed participation in various governments and voted against their policies. The same was also true later in both Lipponen governments and in the Katainen government, which caused a split in the parliamentary group and, in this latter case, the Left Alliance's withdrawal before the end of the government's term. However, in the Rinne/Marin government Left Alliance was a reliable partner without a split in its parliamentary group.

Governmental participation has made the Left Alliance's political line less radical; this may have helped it to be a more reliable government associate and capable of realising its political aims. This may have facilitated the widening of its support potential to the middle-class, former Green and more highly educated voters. Left Alliance has been successful in changing its political support base from a shrinking working class to ideologically left-green voters and from declining industrial towns and the northern countryside to growing university cities. This has given Left Alliance a stronger political basis in population groups which are increasing in numbers while the former industrial and agricultural working class has been diminishing.

Left Alliance voters used to be loyal to the party and stick with it despite disagreements with its political line, but over the past decade generally voter behaviour has become more volatile. According to a Finnish election study, today the Left Alliance can only count on preserving 56-58% of its voters from one election to the next.[71] Therefore, the ability to take new voters from other parties has become more important and the party's capacity to realise its aims in government has become more essential. According to opinion polls, the majority of Left Alliance voters would like to see it in government; among the most important reasons why leftist voters would vote for Social Democrats or Greens instead is the risk of their vote being wasted because the party is not so willing to participate in government.[72]

Governmental participation has made the political aims of Left Alliance more realistic, although the concept of 'socialism' has returned to its programmes, having been largely excluded when the new party was founded in 1990. It may have also reduced the position of the more radical fraction which has occasionally been excluded from the parliamentary group.

Usually, the opponents of government participation have argued that an oppositional stance would rally increased support for Left Alliance. Yet periods in opposition have not produced any great success in elections: after parliamentary terms when the Left Alliance was in government its support decreased on average -0.9% while in opposition the result has been on average increased by only 0.1%. The largest fall in support occurred in 2007, when there was a 1.1% drop, although the Social Democrats had been in government with the Centre Party and the Left Alliance in opposition. In 2023 the drop was also 1.1% after a period in government.

Left Alliance participation in coalition governments has been promoted by trade unionists because the participation of both Left Alliance and the SDP in government decreases internal conflicts in trade unions and fosters left-wing policies. The role of the SDP has also been essential: Social Democrats have at times wanted the Left Alliance to participate in government but have also decided to leave it in opposition, as in 2003. The willingness of the SDP to include Left Alliance in government is due to its fear of losing voters to the left and because Left Alliance participation would support Social-Democratic legislation in a coalition government.

Governmental participation has also impacted the Left Alliance internally. According to former party chair Suvi-Anne Siimes,[73] the radical opposition followed a Leninist conception in which parliament was seen only as a tribune, and governmental participation possible only if the party itself had the leading position. When the Left Alliance was in government these issues were marginalised (partly because the radicals were expelled from the parliamentary group), but in opposition periods the situation inside the party reached a crisis point. Would the situation be different if Left Alliance had been in opposition all the time? Possibly the result would have been a more radical political line but coupled with declining popular support.

Public trust in Left Alliance has increased and more people see it in positive light. In February 1995 only 15% of the Finnish population had a positive attitude toward Left Alliance, while in May 1995 this had climbed to 22%. In 2019-2022 an average of 35% of Finnish voters had a positive attitude toward the Left Alliance and it has reached the approval level of other large and middle-sized parties. In 2022 as many as 23% of Finnish voters said they might possibly vote for Left Alliance, while this figure had been just above 10% in the 1990s. Yet this potential support has not materialised as electoral success, and the party tends to receive less than 10% of votes.

As former party chairperson Claes Andersson has stated, the Left Alliance's attitudes toward governmental participation and the European Union amount to a choice between co-operation with other leftist forces and trade unions, or else remaining bystanders, in a traditional role of opposing everything.[74]

For him, an opposition role should be a temporary state of affairs during which the party prepares for a place in government – a view not shared by some other Left Alliance leaders.[75] According to Andersson, 'too long a trek in the wilderness of opposition did not tend to increase the credibility of our party'.[76]

In the 1990s Left Alliance's electorate was divided between a traditional working-class and less educated electorate, and a new post-materialist one,[77] while a traditional hard-line group generally opposed governmental participation. In this sense, governmental participation has been a key factor in transforming Left Alliance from a traditional leftist, working-class party to a new party that has adopted post-materialist values. In comparison with the Social Democrats, the Left Alliance electorate is younger, more educated, and increasingly middle class. However, unemployment, precarious employment and poverty are linked to voting for the Left Alliance.

Left Alliance has also learnt to participate in negotiations for the formation of government and once in it to influence its policies. Its ministerial posts have become more important despite its reduced popular support.

* * *

Jarmo Lindén, a member of the Left Alliance's international committee, summed up in 2010 what could be learned from its experiences in government: 'A radical left party cannot preserve its political innocence if it wants to deliver at least some of its electoral programme; electoral programmes should not be unrealisable; the party should participate in government wholeheartedly, for it would be lethal if a minority of the party leads it to the opposition; and the party should demand ministries with serious portfolios and be very precise in its demands when the government programme is being prepared.'[78]

We can conclude that Left Alliance has indeed learned from its experiences – and provided important lessons in how a left-wing political force can be a party of government.

NOTES

1   Olavi Borg & Jukka Paastela, *Communist Participation in Governmental Coalitions: The Case of Finland*, Tampere: University of Tampere, Department of Political Science, Research Reports 59 (1981), p. 34.

2   Jukka Paastela, *The Finnish Communist Party in the Finnish Political System 1963-1982*, Tampere: University of Tampere, Department of Political Science and International Relations, 1991, p. 218.

3   Lauri Karvonen, *Parties, Governments and Voters in Finland. Politics under Fundamental Societal Transformation*, Colchester: ECPR Press, 2014, pp. 18-19.

4   Karvonen, p. 77.

5   David Arter, 'The Finnish election of 21 March 1999: Towards a distinctive model of government?', *West European Politics* 23,1 (2000), p. 185.

6   Ralf Sund, *Uhrataan puoluesihteeri*, Helsinki: WSOY, 2002, p. 214.

7   Here government coalitions have been counted at the beginning of the electoral period, disregarding the change of prime ministers without change of government coalition or midterm withdrawal of a party.

8   *Kansan Uutiset*, 22 November 2013.

9   Paavo Lipponen, *Murrosten aika, muistelmat 1979–1995*, Helsinki: WSOY, 2014, p. 532.

10   *Iltalehti* 13 April 1995.

11   Sirpa Puhakka and Rauno Merisaari, *The Left-Wing Alliance in Government*, Helsinki: Left-Wing Alliance Party Office (October 1996).

12   Esko-Juhani Tennilä, *Sateenkaaresta vasemmalla*, Helsinki: Otava, 1995.

13   Claes Andersson, *Mina tolv politiska år*, Helsingfors: Söderströms, 2000, p. 62.

14   *Iltalehti* 15 October 1996.

15   *Helsingin Sanomat* 16 December 1996.

16   Sund, p. 117.

17   See also Katja Tuokko, *From Left to West. The position of Vasemmistoliitto on European Integration in 1990–1998*, Master's thesis on Political History, Faculty of Social Sciences, University of Helsinki, 2012.

18   Andersson, 2000, pp. 115-116, 136.

19   Arter, 2000, p. 180.

20   *Kansan Uutiset* 16 March 1999.

21   Kim O.K. Zilliachus, '"New Politics" in Finland. The Greens and the Left Wing in the 1990s', *West European Politics* 24,1 (2001), pp. 41-43.

22   Arter, 2000, p. 184.

23   Arter, 2000, p. 185.

24   Tim Bale and Richard Dunphy, 'In from the cold? Left parties and government involvement since 1989', *Comparative European Politics* 9,3 (2011), p. 281.

25   Kansan Uutiset 30 March 1999.

26   Kansan Uutiset 14 April 1999.

27   *Kansan Uutiset* 15 April 1999.

28   Richard Dunphy, 'In search of an identity: Finland's left alliance and the experience of coalition government', *Contemporary Politics* 13,1 (2007), p. 45.

29   Jarmo Linden, 'Radical Left in Government – Finnish Experiences.' A speech at Socialist People's Party seminar, 25 April 2010, Odense.

30   Paavo Arhinmäki, 2006, *Punavihreä sukupolvi*, Helsinki: Otava, 2006, p. 12.

31   *Arbetarbladet* 27 April 2000.

32   *Suomen kuvalehti* 15 June 2001.

33   *Kansan Uutiset* 28 February 2003.

34   Matti Mattila and Risto Sänkiaho, 'Luottamus poliittiseen järjestelmään', in Heikki Paloheimo (ed.), *Vaalit ja demokratia Suomessa*, Helsinki: WSOY, 2005, p. 84.

35   Linden 2010.

36   *Kansan Uutiset* 29 January 2003.

37   Bale and Dunphy, p. 281.

38   Dunphy, pp. 50-51.

39   Dunphy, p. 51.

40   David Arter, 'Taking the Gilt off the Conservatives' Gingerbread: The April 2011 Finnish General Election', *West European Politics*, 34,6, 2011, p. 1294.

41   *Etelä-Suomen Sanomat*, 17 May 2011.

42   *Kansan Uutiset*, 15 November 2013.

43   *Helsingin Sanomat*, 24 November 2013.

44   *Iltalehti*, 25 November 2013.

45   Kalevi Suomela in *Kansan Uutiset* 8 November 2013.

46   *Iltalehti*, 27 March 2014.

47   *Kansan Uutiset*, 28 March 2014.

48   David Arter, 'When a pariah party exploits its demonised status: the 2019 Finnish general election', *West European Politics* 43,1 (2020), p. 270.

49   Arter, 2020, p. 271.

50   Yle (Finnish broadcasting company) 22 September 2022, <https://yle.fi/a/3-12635170>.

51   The government programme in English can be found at <http://urn.fi/URN:ISBN:978-952-287-760-4>.

52   Juri Mykkänen, 'Government Formation Amidst Increased Party System Complexity', *Scandinavian Political Studies* 42, 3–4 (2019), p. 198.

53   *Helsingin Sanomat* 15 June 2019.

54   *Kansan Uutiset* 22 June 2019.

55   *Kansan Uutiset* 5 June 2019.

56   Emilia Palonen, 'Finland: Political Developments and Data in 2019', *European Journal of Political Research Political Data Yearbook* 59, p. 133.

57   Jukka Pietiläinen, Finland: New Government, Same Programme, <https://www.transform-network.net/es/blog/article/new-government-same-programme/>.

58   *Yle News*, 4 December 2019, <https://yle.fi/a/3-11102130>.

59   Suomalaisten mielipiteitä ulko- ja turvallisuuspolitiikasta, *maanpuolustuksesta ja turvallisuudesta* 2022:4, Helsinki: Puolustusministeriö, p. 45, <https://www.defmin.fi/files/5568/MTS_Joulukuu_2022.pdf>.

60   'Despite leadership's hopes and assurances, vote on patient safety bill divides Left Alliance', *Helsinki Times*, 20 September 2022, <www.helsinkitimes.fi>.

61   *YLE*, 28 December 2021, <https://yle.fi/a/3-12248811>.

62   *Helsingin Sanomat*, 4 November 2022.

63   *Kansan Uutiset*, 9 July 2021.

64   *Helsingin Sanomat*, 7 December 2022.

65   Personal communication, 27 April 2023.

66   Statistics Finland, Income distribution statistics, <https://stat.fi/en/statistics/tjt>.

67   *Kansan Uutiset*, 9 March 1999.

68   *Kansan Uutiset*, 5 March 1999.

69   Left Alliance party council minutes, 31 August 1995.

70   Internal party barometer opinion polls 2019-2022.

71   Heikki Paloheimo and Sami Borg, 'Hallitus- ja oppositioaseman yhteys kansalaisten puoluevalintoihin', in Sami Borg, Elina Kestilä-Kekkonen, and Hanna Wass (eds), *Politiikan ilmastonmuutos. Eduskuntavaalitutkimus* 2019, Helsinki: Oikeusministeriön julkaisuja, Selvityksiä ja ohjeita, p. 142.

72   Jussi Saramo, 'Uusliberalismi ei ole joko päällä tai pois', *Peruste* 1/2013: 57.

73   Suvi-Anne Siimes, *Politiikan julkisivu*, Helsinki: Otava, 2007, pp. 86-96.

74   Andersson, Claes, 'Kohti punavihreää Eurooppaa – Vasemmistoliitto valitsee linjansa', in Jussi Okkonen (ed.), *Vaihtaa vai ei? Suomivasemmiston näkemyksiä Emusta*, Helsinki: KSL-opintokeskus, 1997, p. 141.

75   Andersson, 2000, p. 100.

76   Andersson, 2000, p. 129.

77   Kim O.K. Zilliachus, 'Development of the Finnish Left Wing: Trends of Old versus New Politics', in Sami Borg and Risto Sänkiaho (eds), *The Finnish Voter*, Helsinki: Finnish Political Science Association, 1995, pp. 232-233.

78   Linden, 2010.

The Left and the State –
The Case of the Portuguese *Geringonça*

Marina Mortágua

The election of 36 left-wing representatives in Portugal's 2015 parliamentary election put an end to the absolute majority for right-wing forces, while also preventing the Partido Socialista (PS) from being the single most-voted party. After the collective trauma of austerity under the Troika, the PS had two options: to come to an understanding with the biggest right-wing force (Partido Social Democrata – PSD), and thus run the risk of Pasokification on the model of its Greek sister party, or else turn to the left for support in Parliament. Rather than an ideological or political shift, the PS above all sought to save itself from the fate of several socialist parties in its European family, and it was on this basis that negotiations began.

In this highly particular context, the survival instincts of PS Secretary-General António Costa led him to break an eternal taboo in Portuguese politics that had long deprived left-wing parties of any kind of governmental influence. Costa's rupture with what was then called the 'governance arch' triggered a prolonged campaign of hostility from the right, headed by the President of the Republic, Cavaco Silva, and seconded by employers' representatives and opinion makers.

The man who had served as deputy prime minister in the right-wing coalition baptised the government arrangement that followed with the name of a strange and uncoordinated device – the 'contraption' (*Geringonça*). Yet its longevity and apparent successes would create a wave of enthusiasm around the Portuguese experience.

During a trip to Portugal in 2016, the leader of the Spanish Socialist Workers' Party (PSOE), Pedro Sánchez, who was at that time heading the opposition, declared his wish to 'be inspired by the Portuguese model', albeit pointing out that he would reject any agreement with those (i.e. Podemos) who 'questioned the unity of Spain'. In 2022, the recently re-elected president of Brazil, Lula da Silva, paid a visit to António Costa, declaring his wish to learn from that same Portuguese model that had ceased to exist years before. Even after the PS's absolute majority in the 2022 election, won at the expense of a heavy electoral defeat for the parties to its left, the myth of the *Geringonça* perdures.

Three years after the end of the *Geringonça*, now is a good moment to draw up a brief balance sheet of the agreements between the PS government and the left, as well as of the years that followed. It is my hope that a realistic analysis of the Portuguese experience (albeit one without regrets) can contribute to the ongoing debate on the role of the left in these times of deep political reconfiguration.

The *Geringonça* (2015-2019) was born from the defeat of the Partido Socialista

The public challenge to the PS to negotiate with the left had been launched by Catarina Martins (the Bloco de Esquerda coordinator) in a debate with António Costa before the 2015 elections. The PS at that time presented the most liberal electoral programme in its history, reflecting its difficulty in breaking with the hegemonic principles of austerity. For Bloco to participate in post-election negotiations, Catarina told Costa, the PS would have to withdraw from three programmatic proposals: the planned freezing of all pensions; measures to make firings easier; and the reduction in employers' contributions to the social security and pension system.

Once these preconditions were met, the negotiations began. The negotiations between the Partido Comunista Português (the Portuguese Communist Party, PCP) and the PS proceeded in parallel, thus resulting in two separate agreements. At the time, the priority was to break with the ongoing process of generalised impoverishment: cuts in wages and pensions would be reversed, as well as the extra tax levied on salaries. The agreement also prevented new privatisations and called for the reversal of the most recent ones (that is, in cases where such a move was legally possible). In the agreement with Bloco, a set of further initiatives was agreed for the duration of the parliamentary term, setting objectives to increase the minimum wage as well as other social and tax measures.

This agreement guided the new government's first State Budget, prepared shortly after the elections. In the following Budget, for 2017, this path continued with another increase in the minimum wage and an extra raise for the lowest pensions, as would be repeated until the end of this legislature. The new wage policy promoted by the left triggered a confrontation with the government, which sought to compensate employers by recovering the idea of a reduction in their Social Security contributions. However, the left took this measure to parliament and forced its reversal, making the government back down on the agreement that it had already signed with the main organisations representing employers.

During those four years, the conflicts between the left and the government were mainly centred around two themes: the labour code, given the PS's determination to maintain the 'reforms' introduced by the Troika; and the management of the banking sector, which involved the sale of two rescued banks under the new Banking Union regime. Banif and Novo Banco were then sold (or practically given away) to Santander and Lone Star (a North American hedge fund), respectively. Despite these growing difficulties, and the constant threats from the European institutions in 2015-2016, the increase in both labour income and social confidence allowed aggregate demand to pull the economy forward. Unemployment dropped below 10%, and contributions to social security were at their highest since 2008.

These numbers should, however, be interpreted with some caution. On the one hand, most of the new employment created in this period was precarious, indeed linked to the boom in tourism. On the other, the left was confronted with the strategic question of how to improve the conditions for the (much needed) social conflict. The fight against precarity in the private sector, the reversal of Troika's reforms of employment legislation, and the recovery of collective bargaining (which had hitherto been practically destroyed) were and are essential elements for the organisation of workers and the survival of the trade union movement.

The main challenge was, therefore, to transform a defensive political agreement – made to prevent new austerity measures and to stop impoverishment – into a process of accumulation of forces in which the left would gain influence and prepare the conditions to change the balance of power in favour of workers. Could the left, and Bloco in particular, again find itself in a position of power like when it scored 10% of votes against a weakened PS in the aftermath of a dramatic period of right-wing governance? Historically, in the European context, an agreement between a leftist party and a centrist government is a difficult process – one of permanent dispute with a likely unhappy ending.

Should Bloco have joined the government?

As part of the initial agreement, Bloco, the PS parliamentary group, and the government formed working groups on specific topics: public debt management, tax policy, and labour laws. Despite the already mentioned deadlocks regarding key aspects of labour legislation, these groups, which also included independent experts, searched for new ways to take forward the initial agreement.

In 2017, the working group published its conclusions on the sustainability of Portuguese debt. Their report addressed two types of measures: public-debt management decisions to alter the balance of payments in the short term by reducing the weight of interest payments; and a structural policy directed at the renegotiation and restructuring of the public debt, in addition to the monetisation of the securities held by the ECB. The combined effect of these measures would be to reduce Portuguese public debt from 132% to 91% of GDP.

While the PS *as a party* signed this report, the government distanced itself from the working group's agreement, and refused to present the proposal to the European authorities. In any case, this process, much like the refusal to revert the Troika's labour reforms, demonstrated both Bloco's capacity for initiative and coordination as well as our difficulty in having a decisive vote on major issues. Having one or two ministers from Bloco (or the PCP) in the government would not have changed the initial relative power of the left, or the nature of its relationship with the PS.

Neither did the PS want this to happen (it would make its relationship with the European authorities difficult, not to say impossible), and nor did the left accept it (the existing level of agreement did not justify a coalition government). The conflicts around the strategy for the banking sector showed that this decision was correct: if there had been ministers from the left, they would have opposed the decision to sell the banks and the coalition would not have endured. There were also other substantive differences that justified our non-participation in government. However, as was often acknowledged by the prime minister, 'neither party had to change their minds about the nature of the European Union, the euro or NATO' to sign an agreement that challenged austerity and impoverishment.

Did Portugal have a left-wing government?

The 'Portuguese model' to which both Pedro Sánchez and Lula da Silva referred benefited from three favourable conditions: cheap oil, low interest rates due to the unprecedented quantitative easing programmes, and some level of expansionary policies in the years before the pandemic. This evolution allowed, for the first time in the twenty years of the European Monetary Union, a real convergence with the European average in terms of GDP, a positive trade balance (positively influenced by the previous austerity measures) and an improvement in the balance of payments thanks to a steady decline in interest payments. The rise in tax and social security revenues, the fall in spending on unemployment benefits, plus a strategic drop in public investment by the government, brought the budget deficit close to zero. The endorsement of the fiscal compact and further improvements in the government's balance became central pieces of the Partido Socialista's electoral strategy, which ultimately led to the erosion of any political space left for new arrangements with Bloco or the PCP.

This is not to say that the left failed in pushing the boundaries of the very restricted nature of the initial agreements. This process of pressure and negotiation was key to extending some rights and to creating new solutions, like a social discount for energy tariffs, a special programme to guarantee stable work contracts to tens of thousands of precarious workers in the Public Service, extraordinary annual increases for the lowest pensions, and the reduction in tuition fees for undergraduate students in public universities.

In other areas, the conflicts with the PS grew in scope and severity, driven by the government's (restrictive) fiscal strategy. Such clashes emerged over the effort to restore the job security hitherto enjoyed by teaching staff; the call to improve the salaries of public officials; and the public-private management of public hospitals. In some cases, these conflicts and alternative solutions were carefully staged in order for the left to get symbolic wins with little practical results. The best example is that of the Health Bases Law. A former coordinator of Bloco de Esquerda, João Semedo, together with Partido Socialista founder and honorary president, António Arnaut, developed a proposal to reorganise the structure of the National Health Service. Their contribution had a notable impact, raising public awareness of the ongoing private predation of public-healthcare institutions in Portugal. The government, which had initially supported the proposal, entrusted the task of presenting an alternative text to a former PS minister, known for his right-wing ideas. This project was later abandoned, as the government sought an agreement with the left, but not on the basis of Semedo and Arnaut's initial proposal. Then, under the pressure from financial interests, a new agreement was attempted, this time with the main right-wing party. Finally, after the failures of all these manoeuvres, the Prime Minister ended up accepting a last-minute agreement with the left. The result was a progressive law that recognised the need to protect the public sphere from the permanent draining of resources to the benefit of private health groups. Nevertheless, in practice, the lack of investment in both infrastructures and working conditions is delivering the National Health Service over to a slow process of degradation, with ever more healthcare services being supplied by the private sector.

In sum, in the years 2015-2019 Portugal was governed by a minority government of a centrist party, PS, supported by a parliamentary majority which integrated left-wing forces, that managed to negotiate important progressive measures in a specific political and historical context.

2019-2022: No agreements, no negotiations, no *Geringonça*

The electoral results of 2019 did not bring dramatic changes to the previous parliamentary arithmetic, apart from a slight increase in the PS's votes, and the election of one MP for each of two new right-wing parties: the ultra-neoliberal Iniciativa Liberal, and the extreme-right Chega. However, unlike in 2015, there was a general understanding that the left should endorse the previous model, irrespective of the concrete negotiations. As the agreement became an end in itself, the pressure was transferred from the PS (to find the bases for parliamentary support) to the left (which was expected to keep supporting the government, no matter what).

This change in political perceptions was met by the PCP's unwillingness to sign a new written agreement for the course of the parliamentary term. While this party still preferred to enter into (annual) specific negotiations, Bloco proposed a new version of the initial model, updating its preconditions in order to start a negotiation: the elimination of the amendments the Troika had introduced to labour legislation (devaluation of overtime payments, reduction in the number of vacation days, reduction of the calculation base for severance pay from 30 to 12 days for each year of work, and other measures). The day after the meeting with Bloco, António Costa met with the employers' confederation and, at the door of the building, told the press that he would reject any agreement to reform the labour law. The minority government instead chose to navigate by sight, budget by budget, ever more openly threatening a political crisis by prompting early elections. It also exhibited contrasting attitudes towards the parties of the left: hostility towards Bloco, condescension as a strategy designed to subordinate the PCP.

Only weeks after the 2019 elections, the State Budget for 2020 was still approved with the abstentions of Bloco and the PCP (and of the three MPs from the animal-rights party PAN). In the following year, the government persisted in its unwillingness to alter the labour law and refused Bloco's proposals to deal with the consequences of the pandemic, namely: i) the improvement of the extraordinary benefits created for the emergency response; ii) the creation of a new anti-poverty social benefit that would reorganise the pre-existing policies, marked by arbitrary exclusions and a good dose of stigma; and iii) a remuneration scheme for the exclusive dedication of health professionals to the National Health Services to stop the drain of doctors and nurses to private hospitals. As a consequence, the budget for 2021 was approved only with the abstentions of the PCP (whose main achievement was the guarantee of basic salary payment to 100% of the workers in layoff programmes) and the PAN. At this stage, the PCP was still arguing that labour laws, not being strictly budgetary issues, should be negotiated only between the government and unions.

The PCP changed this position in the following budget negotiation, as the party began to call for the withdrawal of the Troika's labour laws, as well as an accelerated rise in the minimum wage. These demands justified the vote that eventually led the 2022 budget to be rejected. Faced with the unwillingness of both Bloco and the PCP to pass more budgets without actual negotiations or political gains, António Costa hurried to ask for new elections, hoping for an absolute majority that would free his Partido Socialista from the left's influence.

PS's subordination to the European canon and the large capitalist interests became more visible as the pandemic, the war in Ukraine, and surging inflation called for decisive measures to protect workers and salaries. Despite the suspension of the EU's fiscal rules, Portugal's budgetary efforts to confront the Covid-19 crisis were relatively small, compared to other member states. This alignment also blocked measures to counteract the housing crisis and curb speculation in real estate, to stop the advance of private health groups or to dismantle the rent-seeking rules benefiting electricity companies.

PS's absolute majority

After four years of a working agreement, António Costa managed to put the left between a rock and a hard place. With time, supporting the government without true negotiations or political gains would condemn the left parties to lose their credibility. In the short run, public opinion could be mobilised to blame Bloco and the PCP for burying the beloved *Geringonça*. And so it was.

The elections in 2022 gave the Partido Socialista an absolute majority, as the left suffered a significant defeat, dragged along by the spectre of polarisation emanating from the pre-election polls. Far from threatening Costa's government, the traditional right had another defeat, failing to concentrate its own votes and opening the way for the far right both new and the old: Chega (populist and racist extreme-right) and Iniciativa Liberal (radical neoliberals).

Given the polls a few days before the election, with the PS and PSD in a technical tie, and with PSD seducing Chega and Iniciativa Liberal, left-wing voters rallied behind the Partido Socialista. On that Sunday, these voters found out that the difference between the PS and PSD was 13 percentage points, enough to guarantee António Costa the first one-party absolute majority in almost twenty years.

Despite the results, Bloco embraced the new cycle as a left-wing opposition to the absolute majority, mobilising the social struggles that respond to the growing fractures in the country: the crises in healthcare and housing, workers' precarity and the environmental catastrophe. As for the government and the Partido Socialista, they have chosen confrontation with the extreme right as their main strategy to win over the left-wing electorate, irrespective of their own neoliberal policy turn.

On the right, the map has changed. It is easy for Chega and Iniciativa Liberal to use their momentum as opposition forces, without their policies being tested: their mixture of propaganda and aggression thus faces an open goal. The traditional right's change of orientation will also be influenced by this new political map. This also means that it is more likely that it will make approaches to these new radical expressions of the right, in turn intensifying the PS's strategy to occupy the Portuguese political centre ground.

There might be a temptation to see in these results a retroactive bankruptcy of the 'Portuguese model' (which, being Portuguese, was never intended to be a model), of autonomous parliamentary support without participation in government. However, to be precise, that agreement that lasted between 2015 and 2019 handed the left a victory in the elections in this latter year. The next day, António Costa rejected an agreement with the left and put an end to the Geringonça. The intransigence that led to the rejection of the State Budget, and the artificial political crisis that followed it, was a successful polarisation strategy to guarantee his party an absolute majority. Ultimately, this is the result of the ideological and political choices of Partido Socialista, and its unwillingness to move further into a left-wing agenda with radical elements.

The most difficult challenge

Political alliances depend on the relative power of each force to impose a certain outcome, and that balance can change over time, as public perceptions and social struggles evolve. Without the possibility of new gains and advances, or with the left in a secondary position relative to the political centre, pressure for the mere preservation of the status quo constitutes a major risk. In such situations, the long-term survival of a coalition/agreement may come at the cost of giving up crucial and even constitutive causes of the left. A similar kind of dilemma emerges from the experiences of left-wing governments in the face of the European Union's institutional design, which is tailored to ringfence the field of accepted policies. Especially in the case of smaller European countries, the Stability and Growth Pact, the Fiscal Compact and competition rules constitute radical constraints on any left-wing programme. In both cases, the left submitting to these designs would mean giving up not only on concrete social and economic transformations, but also on the revolutionary horizon that inspires the anti-capitalist movement. And here lies our most decisive and difficult challenge.

The Redistribution of the Common in Serbia

Giulia Russo

Welfare states play a crucial role in shaping modern capitalist states. Since the end of the nineteenth century, welfare has been progressively expanded to combat inequality, poverty, and various kinds of societal problems. After World War II, states increasingly invested resources in ever more complex welfare systems. On the one hand, socialist countries created comprehensive, centralised, and highly bureaucratised welfare states; on the other, capitalist liberal democracies had to counterbalance the risk of any socialist drift and prevent general discontent by compromising with workers' demands through balanced and generous welfare provisions. Welfare capitalism was then adopted almost everywhere, reaching its maximum spread at the peak of the Fordist–Taylorist capitalist paradigm. With the advent of neoliberalism, Fordism began to recede in the advanced capitalist countries, to the benefit of flexible production. Based on the pillars of social security and income support, pensions, health, education, and housing, welfare systems in capitalist states were able to redistribute and pre-distribute the results of collective production, counterbalancing excessive accumulation of wealth; these systems were therefore, until the late 1980s, strategic to capital accumulation in the realm of the distribution and redistribution of value(s).

In fact, capitalist welfare contributed to mitigating inequality and the hyper-concentration of economic power in the hands of capitalists, albeit in a market-based liberal capitalist framework of production and reproduction. Similarly, in the state socialist countries, wealth accumulation was considered unethical. So, the egalitarian provision of services, benefits, and assistance not only maintained low inequality but prevented accumulation in private hands. The neoliberal turn in the late 1980s, in combination with the collapse of the socialist alternative, reversed the trend. This led to the unchallenged hegemony of the capitalist model, characterised by a devastation of social welfare, further exacerbated during the 2008 financial crash and the subsequent debt crisis in Europe. By now, the neoliberal plundering at the expense of labour and welfare has been accompanied by renewed forms of valorisation in bio-cognitive capitalism which appropriate the commons, *de facto* valorising immateriality in addition to the material elements exploited and dispossessed in traditional industrial capitalism. Bio-cognitive capitalism (based on a 'life theory of value' – see p. [ASSIGN PAGE #AFTER TYPESET]) is used here as an analytical tool helpful in understanding the current worldwide developments of neoliberal capitalism, beginning with the abandonment of the Bretton Woods system and thus with the progressive financialisation of the capitalist mode of production and reproduction. These developments have allowed the opening up of new spaces of accumulation through the marketisation and commodification of sectors of society previously excluded from capital accumulation, in a process of increasing colonisation, extraction of value, and dispossession.[1]

Thus, welfare is here considered as a mode of both value production and value distribution. This article investigates the demise of social welfare in post-Yugoslav Serbia as a form of capitalist accumulation, namely a dispossession of the commons which proceeded through the adoption of a 'minimum state' approach, that is, through measures that limit public spending, systematically privatise collectively produced wealth, and commodify welfare, with devastating consequences in terms of income inequality.

Identifying the causes and consequences of the rise of neoliberal-cognitive capitalism in Serbia requires a comprehensive empirical historical investigation, approached in a dialectical manner. We will focus on the main turning points in welfare policies from the end of the 1980s, contextualising this within the process of Serbia's re-peripheralisation, with an extensive investigation of value production and (re- and pre-) distribution by means of welfare. Quantitative tools are needed to measure the impact of welfare provisions on income inequality and address the (lack of) redistributive potential of modern welfare in Serbia.

The analysis uses data included in official European surveys (particularly the EU – SILC Survey)[2] and in the publications of international agencies (the World Bank and World Inequality Database).[3]

The convergence towards neoliberal welfare

The Fordist-Taylorist paradigm of industrial capitalism was characterised by deliberate policies to manipulate liberal market forces in three main directions: (1) towards 'minimum income irrespective of the market value of labour power or property'; (2) 'narrowing the extent of insecurity' (3) offering ' a certain agreed range of social services' to all citizens regardless of their status.[4] Indeed, in the capitalist economy 'welfare is about the degree of market immunity'.[5] According to Esping-Andersen, welfare capitalisms were able to guarantee a certain degree of de-commodification thanks to social policies, *de facto* contributing to shaping class and the social order in terms of not only income distribution but also entitlements to (future and present) welfare.[6] Moreover, welfare offered a stability pact: it guaranteed industrial capitalisms a compromise between equality and growth, both directly and indirectly influenced by the structure and dimension of social welfare.[7]

The role of the state has oscillated between market fixing (in the capitalist European countries) and market shaping (as in Yugoslav market-socialism): in both cases, welfare needs to be understood in terms of value, in order to disentangle its complexity and relevance as an institutional pillar of modern societies. Despite the differences between various capitalist welfare regimes and the socialist welfare model in the post-World War II period,[8] in general there was a degree of redistribution guaranteed through social policies especially regarding healthcare, housing, education, and pensions. Inequality was mitigated through various provisions: different forms of income support, such as social transfers, allowances for the unemployed, benefits for disabled people or those unable to work, retirement pensions and family benefits, in addition to poverty-reduction measures in the form of price and rent controls, healthcare, housing, and schooling and other kinds of education.[9] At this level, what distinguishes socialist from capitalist welfare is the degree of minimal social rights – far more extensive in socialism – and the establishment of strong workers' entitlements guaranteeing the emancipation of labour, with stronger bureaucratic and centralised state control, and less market intrusion in the organisation of the forces of (re)production.[10]

Throughout the entire European continent, the multiple dynamics which characterise the capitalist structure have converged in the dominance of the neoliberal-meritocratic model.[11] Since the 1990s, both the Western and Nordic European social democracies (unable to satisfy growing demands for redistribution) and the ex-socialist regimes have followed similar paths in regard to inequality, both converging around the neoliberal consensus.[12] In particular, the extraordinary apparatus of welfare which performed as a device for value *pre-* and *re-distribution* has been subjected to liberalisation, privatisation, and retrenchment, in accordance with free-market dogmas. The 1990s saw mounting cuts in public spending on social provisions; the recalibration of social welfare, increasingly oriented to poverty-reduction instead of inequality-mitigation; and the attempt to construct a 'new welfare' incorporating market-oriented approaches into traditional programmes (especially in unemployment and healthcare). All this resulted in the preservation of part of post-war welfare and economic security for 'insiders' while developing fragmented welfare for 'outsiders'.[13]

Thus, the neoliberal turn at the end of the 1980s pushed towards a global model of the welfare state that is far more extractive of surplus-value, consisting of the externalisation and outsourcing of various services, the privatisation of once-public firms and of welfare provision, reduced public spending, and the re-calibration of welfare by adopting alternative models such as workfare or occupational welfare.[14] The overall result of these processes is heightened value accumulation by capital. What had been largely conceived – both within the Keynesian consensus and in socialist states – as common production turned out to be another basis for value extraction and accumulation. Not only did the financial crash of 2008 and the subsequent sovereign debt crisis further exacerbate the trend, but they pushed towards further retrenchment of public spending under the watchword of 'austerity' and the admonition to not 'live beyond our means'.[15] Less progressive taxation led to revenue shortfall, with the *de facto* shrinking of states' room for manoeuvre. The financialisation and capitalisation of welfare became widespread means of funding what were deemed the excessively high costs of maintaining these programmes, especially pensions and healthcare.[16] In addition, the socialist legacy in eastern and south-eastern Europe was largely dismissed by means of powerful external pressures; already before the 2008 crisis, the EU strongly recommended reducing public spending in social welfare for member states and for candidates as a condition for membership of the monetary union.[17]

But despite the commodification, privatisation, and financialisation of welfare that occurred with the rise of neoliberal capitalism(s), we should not overestimate the role of the market. In fact, welfare state institutions in their 'twofold function as systems of (*pre-* and *re-*) *distribution* and *production*'[18] play a new role in cognitive neoliberal capitalism – that of providing a new space for capital accumulation within (re)productive dynamics.

Welfare states in cognitive neoliberal capitalism

Clearly, the distributional inequalities exacerbated by the market need to be rectified by removing from it the allocation of goods, resources, and services which should be distributed (in kind) equally to all.[19] But, as we have said, even if in neoliberal capitalism free-market dogma does play a role in determining inequality, it should not be overestimated. In fact, the current development of capitalism is pushing it in a direction that is even more extractive of surplus-value, and which has much more to do with issues of *production* and *reproduction* of value than it does with (re- or pre-) distribution. The basis for surplus-value extraction in this new rentier model of capitalism, which a part of the neo-Marxist literature defines as 'bio-cognitive', is no longer exclusively the accounting of abstract labour-time embodied in products according to labour theories of value (LTV) but increasingly what can be described as a new LTV: a *life* theory of value.[20] This perspective, which I find helpful in describing the modern evolution of capitalism, argues that 'the production of wealth and value is no longer based solely and exclusively on material production, but is increasingly based on immaterial elements'.[21] Therefore, capitalism is more and more extractive of the entire complexity of human existence, from the relational and affective schemes of behaviour, through all activities included in the realm of 'social reproduction' and pertinent to the 'production of (wo)man for (wo)man', including welfare.[22]

Hence, welfare can be understood as a mode of value-production: it constitutes the 'primary productive force that has allowed the development and reproduction of the knowledge-based economy that feeds cognitive and financialised capitalism'.[23] It is clear that the two main structural pillars of both Beveridge-Keynes-style capitalist systems and socialist welfare systems (namely, (1) socialised wages such as pensions, unemployment benefits, and family allowances; and (2) services provided outside the free market such as education, health, housing, and community services)[24] play a crucial role in value-production in service economies, because they represent a growing share of what is collectively generated. Without welfare systems, there would not have been mass schooling, higher education, and research, with all of the consequences this has had for innovation and technology; consequently, there would not have been the resulting wealth.[25] Moreover, the economic stability guaranteed by means of welfare states has been crucial in determining the development of *capabilities*, with positive effects for communities and societies. Reclaiming the crucial role of 'the production of humans for humans', [26] jeopardises the hegemony of the private/public distinction: collectively produced value – deriving either from mechanisms of labour-capital interaction or from the jointly and multifaceted realm of 'social activities' – is essential in expanding and claiming the role of the Common.

In fact, welfare clearly falls into the category of reproductive activities: it involves a kind of labour not directly producing surplus-value; rather it anticipates and provides the necessary premises of production and accumulation.[27] Valorisation in neoliberal capitalism mainly occurs after reproduction via (formal and real) labour subsumption, in Marx's terminology, which is further extended in the current hyper-privatised property regimes. On the other hand, the lenses of bio-cognitive capitalism allow us to see how capital has been expanding the realm of subsumption to encompass all of humanity's production of the commons – first of all, welfare systems. The progressive expropriation occurs not only through pressure to privatise collective welfare services; the evolution of profit to become rent – an intrinsic characteristic of financialised capitalism – encompasses attempts to commodify social reproduction and put the latter 'to work', thus 'valorising' it.[28] The logic of the demise of the Common resembles a new sort of 'primitive accumulation'[29] occurring through forms of dispossession, capture, and/or extraction ('the ability on the part of capital to externally capture the self-valorisation capacity of social cooperation'),[30] appropriation,[31] subsumption of productive to financial capital, and imprinting[32] – in addition to other old and new forms of labour exploitation.

The progressive demise of the Common is evidently the modern form of 'accumulation by dispossession', corresponding to the progressive *enclosures* by the gigantic engine of the social production of value, in the attempt to enlarge market spaces by increasingly colonising welfare institutions.[33] Strategies of valorisation have underpinned privatisation policies, workfare models have replaced Keynesian welfare, and public spending on social services has been delegitimised. As Pierluigi Vattimo explains, modern *enclosures* consist in the progressive impoverishment of welfare institutions (in education, health, pensions, and culture), introducing the logic of private investment in the strategic sector of 'the production of humans for humans'. Moreover, the progressive demise of the Common involves depriving people of the results of social production: knowledge, languages, information and emotions – cognitive capitalism's regime of property excludes and exploits all these elements.[34]

Moreover, the demise of the Common occurs in a widespread relationship of asymmetric (neo- and post-)colonial (re-)peripheralisation. It can be argued that the convergence of capitalisms around neoliberal welfare has led to the dominance of the neoliberal-cognitive model throughout the entire European continent.[35] In particular, at the time of the dissolution of former socialist Yugoslavia, it was evident that the Western Balkans would represent an 'experimental playground for neoliberal capitalism',[36] subjected to external pressures aimed at integrating it in a precarious position within the core-European markets. As a result of the transition towards neoliberal capitalism, the post-Yugoslav region faced a progressive economic re-peripheralisation, entailing the '[re-]appropriation of previously socially-owned economic assets by new economic and political elites'.[37] Within this widespread and complex phenomenon, putting an end to welfare as a mode of re- and pre-distribution and production of the Common is of central significance.

The transition to neoliberal capitalism in Serbia

Upon the dissolution of the Socialist Federal Republic of Yugoslavia (SFRY), there was a temptation to re-peripheralise this area, adjacent to the central core of the EU and thus easily controllable. And this temptation was indeed given in to. During the transition, the previous socialist regime was converted not only into a liberal democracy but principally into free-market neoliberal capitalist country through externally-driven manoeuvres of economic liberalisation headed by the International Financial Institutions and the EU; the World Trade Organisation and the International Monetary Fund in particular pushed in this direction.[38] Economic liberalisation included privatisations, deregulation, labour flexibilisation policies, and de-unionisation, and the application of free-market principles and of minimum-state dogmas. Even if market socialism in Yugoslavia had already experimented with some market-oriented reforms[39] the impact of post-Yugoslav economic liberalisation has been clearly negative, especially affecting working-class conditions.[40]

The transition in Serbia was implemented through quite rapid shock-therapy at the end of the Yugoslav wars. During the unchallenged hegemony of the 'Washington Consensus' in the global political economy, shock therapy was considered more effective than a gradualist model. Nevertheless, by the turn of the millennium, doubts regarding its consequences in terms of rights deprivation, economic turnover (especially as it affected poverty and inequality), social security, and the long-term preservation of the newly established democracies were raised both at a policy level and in the critical literature, especially by authors of development and transition studies.[41] Serbia's transition was 'delayed', in comparison with the other former socialist countries, until after 2000. In fact, during the 1990s, due to the outbreak of the war and Milošević's regime, the NATO bombing, and UN sanctions, the transition proceeded slowly. Therefore, while some authors stress that the negative side-effects of the transition (the destruction of labour, social security, and equality) may be considered unintended and unexpected, we cannot accept this argument in the Serbian case even though it may well apply to cases of early transition. At any rate, Serbia faced this path almost a decade later, in a context of widespread criticisms of the neoliberal path of transition.[42] Hence, we argue that transition in Serbia has been systematically and deliberately exploited as a means of accumulating value in a few hands, to the progressive detriment of labour rights and redistributive welfare. In fact, as Will Bartlett has pointed out, even if the transition in Serbia was delayed, its neoliberal path was far more extractive of surplus value from the lower classes and workers than in other countries.[43]

As previously argued, the retreat of the state from its role of welfare provider plays a crucial role in enabling life-subsumption (in addition to labour-subsumption) in cognitive capitalism. The sandbox of transition-era Serbia was no exception. Former socialist Yugoslavia distributed large social cash transfers (almost equally per person), which contributed to the low level of income inequality.[44] In fact, Yugoslav welfare was generous and based on principles of solidarity and equality (with particular respect to the working class) and explicitly redistributive. Socialist welfare comprised: universal public education (at all levels), a universal health system and pension provisions, employment benefits distributed both in-cash and in-kind, indeed a comprehensive social assistance with a vast range of family benefits and income-support measures, in addition to low-cost or controlled rents.[45] This complex and comprehensive welfare was sustained by the mixed principle of contributions and solidarity: major benefits were organised on a contributory basis, while the minor benefits were not.[46]

More specifically, education was universal and free of direct or indirect fees, at all levels including higher education and university, even if some biases in access still existed (for example family connections).[47] Moreover, universal education was accompanied by strong pro-child policies directed both towards women, to guarantee high female participation in the labour market, and towards families, with generous family-allowances, much more so than in market economies, *de facto* introducing the principle of 'according to need' in welfare.[48] Aimed at mitigating inequality, social assistance was distributed almost equally per person. It was only at the moment of the transition that social transfers began to be focused exclusively on the poor, thus neglecting the broader problem of inequality.[49] The economist Branko Milanović, in one of the most comprehensive investigations of inequality in former Yugoslavia and during the transition,[50] explains how poverty-oriented social assistance became necessary to respond to GDP decline during the transition, but caused an expansion of both inequality and poverty, *de facto* widening the population base for targeted social assistance rather than increasing its efficiency. In addition, with the collapse of socialist Yugoslavia, both health and pension systems entered into crisis, particularly since such a generous socialist public welfare had to be maintained through (almost) full employment (because the contributory basis needed to be as broad as possible). This crisis owed to mass unemployment caused by privatisation, restructuring, and de-industrialisation policies.[51] On the other hand, social housing was a controversial policy in former Yugoslavia. In fact, housing was decentralised in the 1950s, leaving to the socially owned enterprises themselves the task of guaranteeing workers flats. However, decentralised housing policy jeopardised overall coverage and created a sort of income-in-kind inequality owing to housing inequality, while at the same time it was able to guarantee higher standards of houses at affordable prices, thanks to the self-management principle.[52]

Welfare's impact on income distribution in Serbia

To establish the impact of welfare inequality, any measurement of real income needs an estimate of the monetary value of public services provided through welfare. In other words, income should be considered not only as market income, but as disposable, consumable, and extended income (incorporating the welfare mechanism through direct and indirect taxes). In a short review like this, there is no space to develop such a comprehensive investigation of the demise of welfare as a means of redistribution in Serbia.[53] Nevertheless, some intriguing preliminary observations about welfare's impact on inequality can be made based on available data.

First of all, the comprehensiveness of welfare is an indirect indicator of its redistributive potential, through total spending on social services as a percentage of GDP. This indicator illustrates the declining trend of welfare. Generally speaking, post-socialist countries spend less on social protection than Western capitalist countries: since 2001, the proportion of GDP spent on welfare provisions in Serbia has been consistently lower than in the EU-28 average.[54] Moreover, the transition has been followed by various austerity measures aimed at debt reduction, which has required cuts in public spending, especially in social services. For this reason, the growing mass of unemployed and poor (whose numbers have further swelled, due to the severe consequences of the outbreak of the war and the reduction of productive output caused by both the conflict and the de-industrialisation process, which began with the privatisations) have been left with extremely weak social security. This has compelled them to turn towards self-employment and the informal economy in order to make ends meet, which also resulted in progressive exclusion from labour rights.[55] Serbia's social spending has been cut: from 2008 to 2016 expenditures fell by an average of 0.2% per year, reaching a minimum of 21.5% per GDP in 2016, while in the same year the EU-28 average was around 28.2% of total GDP.[56]

It is not possible here to discuss the problems of using synthetic indices of income inequality.[57] However, a Gini coefficient could be calculated in order to measure this inequality. All the data examined suggest that since the dissolution of socialist Yugoslavia, income inequality has dramatically grown in the region and in Serbia in particular. The most reliable estimate of the Gini in 1968 was around 24 points.[58] In 2015, it reached a peak of 40.5 points, according to World Bank estimates based on EU-SILC survey data – a figure significantly higher than the European average.[59] Other calculations estimate the Gini at even higher levels (depending on the definition of income used, on the Lorenz curve, but also on data sources and means of collection). For instance, the gigantic World Inequality Database (WID) calculates the after-tax Gini coefficient at 50 points in 2015. In any case, according to all the principal measurements, inequality has increased up to 2015; after that year the trend reversed, reaching a minimum in 2020 (33.3 according to the EU-SILC Survey and 42 points according to WID), as expected due to the equalising effect of the first wave of the Covid-19 pandemic; still, inequality in the region is among the highest in Europe.[60]

To avoid the potential ambiguity of synthetic indicators, income inequality may be measured through comparison of income shares between the richest 10% and the poorest 50% of the income distribution. Of particular interest is the comparison between the end of the 1990s, when the transition actually began in Serbia, and the most recent data (2020).[61] In 1999, the bottom 50% earned 20.8% of pre-tax national income and around 25.5% of post-tax national income, while the richest decile of the distribution possessed 30.8% of total pre-tax income, reduced to 25.9% when taking into consideration taxes. In 2020, the gap between the rich and the poor widened: the richest had 34% of pre-tax income and around 29% of post-tax income and the poorest only 17.8% of pre-tax income and 21% of post-tax income, due to the lower redistributive impact of tax-and-transfer mechanisms. Indeed, neoliberal manoeuvres to flexibilise labour and erode the pillars of welfare allowed value accumulation at the expense of the lowest deciles of the distribution, widening the gap between rich and poor. In fact, according to Bilhiana Mladenović,[62] income sources for the poorest income deciles deteriorated more in recent decades; the share of income from wages decreased between 2017 and 2018, while insufficient pensions and social transfers remain the primary source of income for the poor. On the other hand, the top 10% rarely stands on social welfare. This has further reduced the share of income enjoyed by the bottom 10% from 3.1% to 2.6% in 2018: the impressive 29% owned by top incomes appears more uneven.[63]

In the overarching context of the erasure of labour rights and the increasing power of capital over labour,[64] most of the relevant literature identifies the dismantling of welfare and its reduced capacity to carry out pre- and re-distribution as the main determinant of these extremely high levels of income inequality. While this is true, it leaves out a crucial new factor: within the current mode of value accumulation and dispossession in neoliberal and cognitive capitalism, the subordination of *social reproduction* to value accumulation plays a crucial role. In Serbia, welfare today has only a meagre distributive impact as compared to other European countries; differences in Gini coefficients calculated on market income and disposable income show significantly less redistribution derived from tax-and-transfer provisions in Serbia.[65] In fact, according to Arandarenko et al., it is 'interesting to note that the Gini coefficient for market income is within the EU average [...]: this indicates that the main reason for such a high inequality of disposable income in Serbia is the low redistributive role of social transfers and taxes'.[66] Consequently, Serbian welfare appears regressive instead of progressive: it provides limited support with scant coverage.

This regressivity is particularly evident in taxes on labour, which in 2001 were reformed with the introduction of a 10% flax tax on personal income and the abolition of vertical progressivity, since taxes depend more on the type of earning rather than on the overall amount.[67] Moreover, minimum contribution for social security is calculated at an excessively high level (40% of average gross wage), resulting in a heavy burden for minimum-wage or low-wage workers, informal workers, and part-time workers, disproportionately affecting the lowest strata of income distribution.[68] Progressivity would guarantee a vaster pool of resources to redistribute. Currently, the best-performing provision in positively affecting inequality is the pension system: nevertheless, the coverage is inadequate; the dependency ratio between pensioners and workers is increasingly unfavourable; early retirements, in combination with ageing of the population, is affecting pension checks; moreover, pension levels are insufficient to face the growing cost of living due to inadequate resources and the shrinking of the previously mentioned contributory base.[69] As a consequence of regressive taxes, social transfers – which are designed as poverty-reduction measures with little or no protection from social exclusion – are meagre and incomplete, with limited coverage.[70] Actually, biased eligibility criteria are common: for instance, the poverty line chosen to distribute cash-benefits is lower than the absolute poverty line in Serbia, and at the same time economies of scale are being implemented, thus penalising larger households.[71] Therefore, the impacts of social policy – mainly taking the form of cash benefits – on inequality mitigation are not uniform. For instance, the paltry unemployment protection is designed to exclude people working in the informal sector and the shadow economy, causing further marginalisation.[72] This is combined with almost non-existent active labour-market measures (expenditures were as little as 0.015% of GDP in 2014).[73] Overall, this brief overview of the quantitative impact of welfare on inequality shows that the economic degradation wrought by the transition to pure neoliberal capitalism has not been accompanied by adequately redistributive welfare.[74]

Conclusion

In this overview we have tried to disentangle the mechanisms characterising the valorisation process in neoliberal capitalism, with particular regard to those activities that may be called 'non-productive' labour, such as welfare services. In our view, these activities have been increasingly subordinated to the logic of capital accumulation. We argue that the more capitalism is moving towards bio-cognitive modes of accumulation, the more the labour theory of value intersects with a sort of *life* theory of value, meaning that the entire human being in his/her complexity, including his/her non-productive labour, is increasingly subjected to capital accumulation. In this sense, valorisation in neoliberal-cognitive capitalism results from the intersection of various mechanisms, among which are extraction, appropriation/ expropriation, dispossession, capture, neo- and post-colonisation, and (formal and informal) exploitation. In this sense, not only do welfare states act as means of pre- and re-distribution, but they are crucial to valorisation in modern neoliberal-cognitive capitalism. It is our view that strategies for the retrenchment, privatisation, and outsourcing of welfare are tantamount to capital-accumulation manoeuvres, as seen in increasing inequality, which is highly apparent in the case of Serbia. Serbia's transition from socialism to capitalism appears extremely extractive of surplus-value, resembling a modern 'enclosure' of the commons.

Overall, this development, which resembles a new round of 'primitive accumulation', occurred at the expense of the poorest in Serbia and led to a severe increase of income inequality – with all its consequences in terms of societal problems, economic instability, and democratic illegitimacy. It seems clear that this withering of welfare within the new round of primitive accumulation in Serbia represents a central process in neoliberal and cognitive capitalism, in which capitalism was able 'to redistribute rather than to generate wealth' (David Harvey), and that this produced a redistribution of wealth from the poor to the rich, from the working class to the capitalist class.

NOTES

1   'Bio-cognitive capitalism is a single body, inside of which the "real" sphere cannot be separated from the "financial," nor can the productive sphere be separated from the unproductive, or work-time from life-time, or production from reproduction and consumption. Rent is the main capturing tool of both surplus value and the desocialization/privatization of what is common' (Andrea Fumagalli, Alfonso Giuliani, Stefano Lucarelli, and Carlo Vercellone, *Cognitive Capitalism, Welfare and Labour: The Commonfare Hypothesis*, London: Routledge, 2019, p. 16.).

2   EU – SILC (European Union Statistics on Income and Living Conditions) Survey
     data are available through the Statistical Office of the Republic of Serbia (SORS)
     database. Calculations were done during a period of internship at the Institute for
     Economic Sciences in Belgrade (Serbia) in June and July 2021.

3   The results of the analysis are partially extracted from my master's thesis at the
     European Regional Master's Programme (ERMA) in Human Rights and Democracy
     in South-East Europe (Universities of Sarajevo and Bologna) and are to be expanded
     in my PhD research at the Scuola Normale Superiore. See Giulia Russo, *Rise of
     Capitalism and Demise of the Commons: a Case-Study on Inequality in Serbia*, <https://
     www.academia.edu/81385560/European_Regional_Masters_Programme_in_
     Democracy_and_Human_Rights_in_South_East_Europe_Selected_Master_
     Theses_2020_2021> (ERMA Selected Master's Thesis) <ERMA Selected Master
     Theses 2020-2021_academia.edu>, pp. 229-322; PhD research at the Scuola Normale
     Superiore on Inequality and Policies: The Impact of Labour, Tax and Welfare Policies
     on Income Inequality in Europe. The Cases of Denmark, Italy, Serbia and Slovenia.

4   On the welfare state: Asa Briggs, 'The Welfare State in Historical Perspective',
     European Journal of Sociology 2,2 (1961): 221-258, 228.

5   Gøsta Esping-Andersen, *The Three Worlds of Welfare Capitalism*, Cambridge: Polity,
     1990, p. 37.

6   Esping-Andersen, *The Three Worlds of Welfare Capitalism*.

7   Subsequent research has substantiated neither the Kuznets Curve nor Okun's
     efficiency-equality trade-off. On the contrary, the model of social welfare built into
     most of Western European countries after World War II moves in the direction
     of Engerman and Sokoloff's argument. The authors argue that factor endowments
     (conceived as the broad complexity of elements, assets and/or properties which shape
     homogeneity or heterogeneity within a group of people, such as income, wealth,
     property, access to public services, financial assets, or other kind of endowments in
     a material understanding) and thus the degree of (in)equality of a society, are related
     and causally related to the role of institutions. In this understanding, it is true that
     both factor endowments and the degree of inequality have influenced the direction
     assumed by institutions and policies; equally importantly, institutions – primarily
     through welfare – have affected the evolution of inequality, by shaping how factor
     endowments are distributed and the level of concentration of material and immaterial
     capitals, wealth, and thus political power.
     Stanley L. Engerman, Stanley L. and Kenneth L. Sokoloff, 'Factor Endowments,
     Inequality and Paths of Development Among New World Economies', NBER
     Working Paper 9259 (October 2002), <http://www.nber.org/papers/w9259>, p.
     17; Maurizio Franzini and Lucianao Marcello Milone, 'I Dilemmi del Welfare State
     nell'Epoca della Globalizzazione', in Nicola Acocella (ed.), *Globalizzazione e Stato
     Sociale*, Bologna: il Mulino, 1999, p. 17-76. Roberto Perotti , 'Growth, Income
     Distribution and Democracy: What the Data Say', *Journal of Economic Growth* 1 (1996):
     149-187.

8   The most relevant capitalist welfare regimes are the US-UK liberal model, the
     corporatist German welfare system, the social-democratic regime in Scandinavian
     countries, and Southern European familist welfare. See Giuliano Bonoli, 'Classifying
     Welfare States: A Two-Dimension Approach', *Journal of Social Policy* 26,3 (1997): 351-
     372; Chiara Saraceno *Il Welfare*, Bologna: il Mulino, 2013.

9   Joseph E. Stiglitz, *The Price of Inequality: How Today's Divided Society Endangers Our Future*, New York: W. W. Norton & Company, 2012 (reprint).

10   Esping-Andersen *Welfare Capitalism*.

11   Branko Milanovic, *Capitalism, Alone. The Future of the System That Rules the World*, Cambridge MA: Harvard University Press, 2019.

12   Thomas Piketty, *Capital and Ideology*, translated by Arthur Goldhammer, Cambridge MA: Harvard, 2020.

13   Anthony Barnes Atkinson, *Inequality: What Can Be Done?* Cambridge MA: Harvard University Press, 2015; Giuliano Bonoli and David Natali, *The Politics of the New Welfare State*, Oxford: Oxford University Press, 2012.

14   Bonoli and Natali, *The Politics of the New Welfare State*.

15   Felice Roberto Pizzuti, 'Considerazioni di sintesi': in Felice Roberto Pizzuti (ed.), *Rapporto sullo Stato Sociale 2019: Welfare Pubblico e Welfare Occupazionale*, Rome: Sapienza Università Editrice, 2019, pp. 11-53.

16   Mario Pianta, *Nove su dieci: Perché stiamo (quasi) tutti peggio di 10 anni fa*, Rome-Bari: Laterza, 2012; Maurizio Franzini and Mario Pianta, *Disuguaglianze. Quante sono, come combatterle,* Rome: Laterza, 2016.

17   Srećko Horvat, and Igor Štiks, 'Radical Politics in the Desert of Transition', in Srećko Horvat and Igor Štiks (eds), *Welcome to the Desert of Post-Socialism: Radical Politics after Yugoslavia*, London: Verso Press, 2015, pp. 1-17; Rachel Kurian and Ewa Cjharkiewicz, 'Violence in Transition: Reforms and Rights in the Western Balkans', *Global Campus Human Rights Journal* 1 (2017): 119-139; Milica Uvalić, *The Rise and Fall of Market Socialism in Yugoslavia*, Special Report (Berlin: Dialogue of Civilisations Research Institute, 2018).

18   Carlo Vercellone, 'From the Crisis to the "Welfare of the Common" as a New Mode of Production', *Theory, Culture and Society* 32,7-8 (1970): 85-99 (my brackets).

19   James Tobin, 'On Limiting the Domain of Inequality', *The Journal of Law & Economics* 13,2 (1970): 263-277, <http://www.jstor.org/stable/725025>; Fred Hirsch, *Social Limits to Growth*, New York: Routledge, 1978 (second edition); Debra Satz, *Why Some Things Should Not Be for Sale: The Moral Limits of Markets*, Oxford: Oxford University Press, 2012 (reprint); Michael Joseph Sandel, *What Money Can't Buy: The Moral Limits of Markets*, New York: Farrar, Straus & Giroux, 2013.

20   Cristina Morini and Andrea Fumagalli, 'Life Put to Work: Towards a Life Theory of Value', *Ephemera: Theory and Politics in Organisation* 10,3/4 (2010): 234-252.

21   Morini and Fumagalli, 'Life Put to Work', 235.

22   For a comprehensive explanation of life subsumption in bio-cognitive capitalism, see Morini and Fumagalli, 'Life Put to Work'; Vercellone, 'From the Crisis'; Andrea Fumagalli, Alfonso Giuliani, Stefano Lucarelli, and Carlo Vercellone, *Cognitive Capitalism, Welfare and Labour: The Commonfare Hypothesis*, New York: Routledge, 2019; Andrea Fumagalli, 'New Forms of Exploitation in Bio-Cognitive Capitalism: Towards Life Subsumption', in Fumagalli et al., *Cognitive Capitalism, Welfare and Labour;* Pierluigi Vattimo, *Governo e Potere dei Commons ai Tempi del Capitalismo Cognitivo: Alcune Esperienze di Autogoverno del Comune a Napoli e in Italia*, Napoli: La Scuola di Pitagora, 2022.

For the 'production of (wo)man for (wo)man', see Silvia Federici 'Social reproduction theory: History, issues and present challenges', *Radical Philosophy* 204 (Spring 2019):

55-57; Lucia Chistè, Alisa Del Re, and Edvige Forti (eds), *Oltre il Lavoro Domestico: il Lavoro delle Donne tra Produzione e Riproduzione*, second ed. Verona: ombrecorte, 2020.

23   Vercellone, 'From the Crisis', 87; Andrea Fumagalli and Stefano Lucarelli, 'Finance, Austerity and Commonfare', *Theory, Culture and Society* 32,7-8 (2015): 51-65.

24   Vercellone, 'From the Crisis', 90.

25   Enzo Mingione, David Benassi, and Andrea Ciarini, 'Inequalities and the City: Gender, Ethnicity and Class', in Anthony M. Orum, Javier Ruiz-Tagle, and Serena Vicari Haddock, *Companion to Urban and Regional Studies*, Hoboken NJ: John Wiley & Sons Ltd, 2021, pp. 373-397.

26   Vattimo, *Governo e Potere dei Commons*, pp. 59-66.

27   Vercellone, 'From the Crisis', 93.

28   Andrea Fumagalli, 'New Forms of Exploitation in Bio-Cognitive Capitalism: Towards Life Subsumption', in Fumagalli, Giuliani, Lucarelli, and Vercellone, *The Commonfare Hypothesis*, pp. 77-93.

29   David Harvey, *A Brief History of Neoliberalism*, Oxford: Oxford University Press, 2007.

30   Fumagalli, 'New Forms of Exploitation', 82.

31   Vercellone, 'From the Crisis', argues for a 'rentier model' of 'Accumulation through Expropriation' corresponding to the intensification of neoliberal policies of austerity and dismantling of the welfare state.

32   With the term 'imprinting', Chicchi et al. I am referring to a process in which 'labour and valorization do not coincide on the level of wages but they find different conditions of realization'. This process emphasises capital's capacity to derive surplus-value from subjectivity without necessarily passing through the wage convention. Federico Chicchi, Emanuele Leonardi, and Stefano Lucarelli, *Logiche dello Sfruttamento*, Verona: ombrecorte, 2016.

33   Antonio Negri, 'Postface': 174-177 in Fumagalli et al., *The Commonfare Hypothesis*, pp. 174-77.

34   Michael Hardt and Antonio Negri, *Commonwealth* Cambridge MA: Belknap/Harvard, 2011.

35   Milanovic, *Capitalism, Alone*; Piketty, *Capital and Ideology*.

36   Ivana Bajić-Hajduković, 'Introduction: Balkan Precariat', *Contemporary Southeastern Europe* 1,2 (2014): 1-6.

37   Chiara Bonfiglioli, *Gendering Social Citizenship: Textile Workers in Post-Yugoslav States* (CITSEE Working Paper Series 2013/30, University of Edinburgh), p. 25.

38   The transition to the capitalist mode of (re)production in post-socialist countries has been largely exogenous, especially in the case of the Western Balkans. In addition, the Copenhagen criteria, established in 1993 to define whether a country is eligible for accession to the European Union, specifically require free-market principles; Nigel Swain, 'A Post-Socialist Capitalism', *Europe-Asia Studies* 63,9 (2011): 1671-1695,1671; Ruth Mandel,'Transition to Where? Developing Post-Soviet Space', *Slavic Review* 71,2 (2012): 223- 233.

39   Albena Azmanova, '1989 and the European Social Model: Transition Without Emancipation?', *Philosophy and Social Criticism* 35 (2009).

40   It must be emphasised that these consequences were uneven. For instance, Slovenia performed and performs better than Bosnia- Herzegovina, Serbia, or Macedonia. In fact, Slovenia maintained certain continuities with the legacy of Yugoslavia, rather than breaking radically with the previous model, thus achieving better economic

performance. See Uvalić, *The Rise and Fall of Market Socialism in Yugoslavia*, pp. 58-59.

41   Arrigo Pallotti and Mario Zamponi, *Le Parole dello Sviluppo: Metodi e Politiche della Cooperazione Internazionale*, Bologna: Carocci, 2014.

42   Horvat and Štiks, 'Radical Politics in the "Desert of Transition"', p. 4.

43   Will Bartlett, Lecture: 'Inequality in the Western Balkans and Former Yugoslavia', London School of Economics and Political Science: International Inequalities Institute, 2017.

44   Branko Milanovic, Report: *Income, Inequality and Poverty during the Transition from Planned to Market Economy*, Washington, DC: The World Bank, 1998.

45   Will Bartlett et al. 'Income Inequality in Transition Economies: A Comparative Analysis of Croatia, Serbia and Slovenia', *Economic Annals* 64,223 (2019): 39-60.

46   Bartlett 'Inequality in the Western Balkans and Former Yugoslavia'.

47   Although it is far from my intention to romanticise the former Yugoslavia, the widespread criticisms highlighting its hidden inequalities in order to reject the legitimacy of calculations of inequality in socialist times (such as biases in access to various services, fringe benefits and privileges to *nomenklatura*) must be rejected. From the econometric perspective, fringe benefits and privileges (among which housing and education are particularly relevant) distributed to the upper strata were well-balanced by all forms of social incomes which, on the contrary, were distributed per capita with particular focus on the lowest deciles, *de facto* helping to reduce poverty while aimed at mitigating inequality. Therefore, the picture of income inequality is unlikely to radically change due to the combination of these benefits and privileges, even if difficulties in calculation hamper empirical testing. Moreover, I argue that hidden inequalities are not specifically socialist traits: clearly, liberal capitalist societies are not without various forms of hidden inequalities, well concealed behind the apparently neutral mask of meritocracy. In fact, the combination of hidden inequalities and power dynamics is even more evident in neoliberal capitalisms, as it allows for the increasing accumulation of political and economic power in order to maintain privileged positions and transmit them through new forms of feudalism.
For an econometric analysis of inequality, see: Milanovic, *Income, Inequality and Poverty during the Transition*, p. 15. On neoliberal capitalism, meritocracy, and inequality, see Stiglitz, *The Price of Inequality*. See also Michael J. Sandel, *The Tyranny of Merit: What's Become of the Common Good?*, London: Allen Lane, 2020; Mike Savage, *The Return of Inequality: Social Change and the Weight of the Past*, Cambridge MA: Harvard, 2021; Bartlett et al. 'Income Inequality in Transition Economies', 49-53.

48   Milanovic, *Income, Inequality and Poverty during the Transition*, p. 20.

49   Milanovic, *Income, Inequality and Poverty during the Transition*, p. 16.

50   Milanovic, *Income, Inequality and Poverty during the Transition*, p. 111.

51   Drenka Vuković and Natalija Perišić, 'Social Security in Serbia – Twenty Years Later', in Marija Stambolieva and Stefan Dehnert, Stefan (eds), *Welfare States in Transition: 20 Years After the Yugoslav Welfare Model*, Sofia: Grafimax, 2011, pp. 228-61; Will Bartlett, 'The Western Balkans', in David Lane and Martin Myant (eds), *Varieties of Capitalism in the post-Communist Countries*, London: Palgrave, 2007, pp. 201-20.

52   Mina Petrović, 'Post-Socialist Housing Policy Transformation in Yugoslavia and Belgrade', *European Journal of Housing Policy* 2 (2011): 211-231.

53   My current PhD dissertation at the Scuola Normale Superiore in Florence includes a comparative investigatioin of the distribution of market, disposable, consumable, and

extended incomes in Italy, Denmark, Serbia, and Slovenia since the end of the 1980s.

54   Liviu Chelcea and Oana Druță, 'Zombie Socialism and the Rise of Neoliberalism in Post- Socialist Central and Eastern Europe', *Eurasian Geography and Economics* 57,4-5 (2016): 521-544.
Lilijana Stokić Pejin and Jurij Bajec, *ESPN Thematic Report on Financing Social Protection: Serbia*, European Social Policy Network (ESPN): European Commission, 2019.

55   Will Bartlett, 'Economic Development in the European Super-Periphery: Evidence from the Western Balkans', *Economic Annals* 59,181 (2009): 21-44.

56   Stokić Pehin and Bajec, *Thematic Report*, pp. 4-5.

57   For instance, synthetic indicators such as Gini tend to flatten social conflicts among classes: the compression of the middle class at the lowest life-style levels is misunderstood in the Gini index, creating the appearance of stability. In fact, middle class 'disappearance' is the result of two opposite trends which counterbalance each other in synthetic indicators: on the one hand, there is the growth in inequality between the middle and the highest sections of the distribution; on the other hand, there is a decrease in inequality due to the flattening seen in the middle class in the lowest deciles of income distribution.

58   Bartlett et al., 'Income Inequality in Transition Economies', 40-41.

59   World Bank, *The Gini Index – Serbia*, <https://data.worldbank.org/indicator/SI.POV.GINI?locations=RS>.

60   European Union Statistics on Income and Living Conditions (EU-SILC Survey) 2020 <https://ec.europa.eu/eurostat/web/microdata/european-union-statistics-on-income-and-living-conditions >; World Inequality Database (WID), *Serbia*, <https://wid.world/country/serbia/>.

61   Shares of income per deciles of income distribution come from WID - *Serbia*.

62   Biljana Mladenović, *Income and Consumption Decile Analysis in the Republic of Serbia*, Belgrade: Social Inclusion and Poverty Reduction Unit of the Government of the Republic of Serbia, 2019.

63   Mladenović, *Income and Consumption in Serbia*, p. 3.

64   National income increasingly derives from rents rather than from labour in Serbia. In this connection, the ratio between capital income and labour income can be seen through data collected by WID, which clearly depicts the growing trend of capital income (from around 7% in early-2000, to 21.80% in the most recent year 2011 in contrast to labour income, which is slowly diminishing (from almost 90% to slightly more than 20% in 2011. See WID –*Serbia*.

65   On the other hand, social policy seems better-targeted to address poverty. In fact, according to my own calculation, based on data provided by the Institute for Economic Sciences in Belgrade and extracted by the Statistical Office of the Republic of Serbia (SORS) – SILC Survey, the percentage of people at risk of poverty before social transfers is around 28%, while after social transfers it falls to 23%. In addition, if we do not take into consideration the monetary value of social transfers in determining income sources for the bottom half of the distribution, the percentage of people at risk of poverty (or social exclusion) soars to 46.6%. EU-SILC Survey 2020.

66   Mihail Arandarenko, Gorana Krstić, and Jelena Žarković-Rakić, *Analysing Income Inequality in Serbia, Executive Summary: Analysing Income Inequality in Serbia. From Data to Policy*, Belgrade: Friedrich Ebert Stiftung, 2017, p. 5.

67   Saša Ranđelović et al., 'Labour Supply and Inequality Effects of In-Work Benefits: Evidence from Serbia', *Našegospodarstvo/Our Economy* 65,3 (2019): 1–22. Bartlett et al. 'Income Inequality in Transition Economies', 40-41.

68   Mihail Arandarenko and Vladimir Vukojević, 'Labor *Costs and Labor Taxes in the Western Balkans: Enhancing Efficiency and Equity: Challenges and Reform Opportunities Facing Health and Pension Systems in the Western Balkans*, pp. 119-160 (Washington: World Bank, 2008).

69   Vuković and Perišic 'Social Security in Serbia'; Lilijana Stokić Pejin and Jurji Bajec, *Thematic Report: Assessment of Pension Adequacy in Serbia 2017* (European Social Policy Network (ESPN), European Commission).

70   Friedrich Ebert Stiftung, *Inequality in South-East Europe,* (Dialogue Southeast Europe), 2018.

71   Olgica Ivančev, Milena Jovičić, and Tijana Milojević, *Income Inequality and Social Policy in* Serbia, v. 86, Wiiw Balkan Observatory 86 (2010), (Wiener Institut für international Wirtschaftsvergleiche).

72   Ivančev et al., *Income Inequality.*

73   Gordana Matković, *Position Paper: The Welfare State in Western Balkans Countries: Challenges and Options*, Belgrade: Center for Social Policy, 2017.

74   Branko Milanovic, 'The Two Faces of Globalisation: Against Globalisation as We Know It', *World Development* 31,4, (2003): 667-683; Will Bartlett, 'The Political Economy of Welfare Reform in the Western Balkans', in Caterina Ruggeri Laderchi and Sara Savastano (eds), *Poverty and Exclusion in the Western Balkans: New Directions in Measurement and Policy*, Springer: New York, 2013.

Marxist Christian Dialogue

TIME DIAGNOSES

Walter Baier, Cornelia Hildebrandt,
Franz Kronreif, Luisa Sello (Eds.)

Europe as a Common

Exploring Transversal Social Ethics

Contributions from: Baier, Bagnato, Bolesrecu, Brie, Callincos, Castellina, Coda,
Hildebrandt, Kronreif, La Prom, Livy, Mikonen, Pompen, Suchenas-Folaj, Toth, Zust, Pope Ferenc.

ZEITDIAGNOSEN

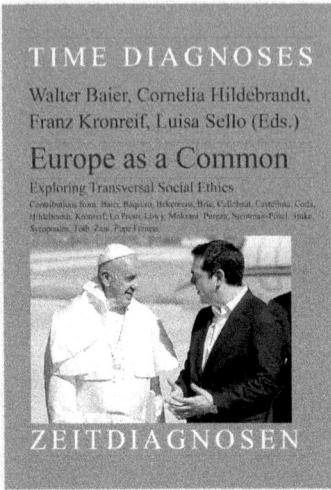

Europe as a Common. Exploring Transversal Social Ethics

Time Diagnoses, Vol. 46

edited by Walter Baier,
Cornelia Hildebrandt,
Franz Kronreif,
Luisa Sello

Publisher: LIT
Language: English
ISBN-13: 978-3643912985

To cope with the problems of today's world, we need to
enter into a dialogue regardless of political, religious and
philosophical beliefs – a transversal dialogue as Pope
Francis called for in the private audience, he gave to Alexis
Tsipras, Walter Baier and Franz Kronreif in September
2014. This conversation resulted in the DIALOP initiative –
a transversal dialogue between Socialists and Christians.
Since then, a network of universities and NGOs have been
exploring paths of what they call a transversal social ethics.
In this book authors from Austria, Belgium, Colombia,
France, Germany, Greece, Hungary, Italy, Portugal and
the Vatican air their views on topics like social equality,
European Unity, democracy, the commons and ecology.

The editors are the steering committee of the initiative
DIALOP – transversal dialogue project.

A Plea for a Left Religion Policy in Europe

Franz Segbers

In Europe fear is in the air – the fear of religion. As I write these lines, the writer Salman Rushdie is fighting for his life. In 1989 Iran's Ayatollah Khomeini issued a fatwa on his *Satanic Verses*; the book was said to be blasphemous and it was the duty of every Muslim to murder its author. On 12 August 2022 Rushdie was the victim of a life-threatening attack by an alleged fanatic of the Lebanese Hezbollah in the pay of Iran. A storm of outrage spread throughout the world. In almost kneejerk fashion *Neues Deutschland*, a German daily and representative of left journalism, commented on the attack: 'Religion is dangerous – worldwide.' As the attempt on Rushdie's life demonstrates, it said, a fallback into barbarism is always possible. 'This is a politically applied terror innate in all religions. The criminal history of Christianity may momentarily seem muted and that of Islam appear particularly aggressive – despite this the world religions are more or less similar because they do not want people to decide what is good for them.'

This commentary is representative of a broad left consensus: religions are violent and part of the repressive apparatus, which impedes free self-determination. Since all religions are considered per se irrational, prone to violence, and threatening to freedom, they have no place in an enlightened society. Pushing them into the private sphere is then a precondition for an open, tolerant society.

It is true that the history of religion's association with violence is a long one, reaching back to the Middle Ages, and in the recent past there have been religiously tinged wars in Yugoslavia, the radical Hindus against Muslims in India, the Islamist terror attacks, and, last but not least, the Islamist attack on the World Trade Center in New York. It seems right to conceptualise the history of religion as endangering tolerance and the internal peace of communities. According to a 1998 ISSP study, more than two-thirds of Western Europe's population are of the opinion that religion is 'intolerant'.[1]

One cannot, however, say that the carnage of the First World War, the atrocities of the Second World War, of the starvation in Ukraine, of the gulag or the Holocaust were caused by religion or religious intolerance. Rather they were the products of modern, secular ideologies, and state-organised brutality. 'The short century of extremes' from 1914 to 1989, as Eric Hobsbawm described it, was 'one of the most violent, bloodiest, and genocidal centuries in human history.'[2] In view of the different empirical experiences the sociologist of religion José Casanova has enquired into the origins of these widespread negative views of religion as intolerant and the catalyst of violence. Why does Europe prefer to ascribe outbreaks of violence to religions instead of analysing them as confrontations over state-building, geopolitical conflicts, or the consequences of European colonial expansion? For Casanova it is a secular construct that has the function of positively distancing the modern secular self-understanding from the 'people of other faiths' – whether the pre-modern Europeans or non-European religious people, especially Muslims. Secular Europe sees itself as an enlightened society and it confirms itself in this by discrediting religions in order to be able to make its own secularism into a condition for an enlightened and progressive politics. Here it appears, according to Casanova, that Europe has a problem – it has a 'fear of religion'.[3]

This assessment can explain the attitude of not a small sector of the left toward religion. Its understanding of religion is determined by the certainty that it is a pre-modern vestige which enlightened people, especially if they are politically engaged on behalf of emancipation from foreign rule, have grown out of. For them the decline of religion is a goal of historical development. Such a teleological theory of the development of religion has deep roots in the history of the Enlightenment in Europe and can also be found in Karl Marx. For him religion is a reflection of inverted social consciousness, which can only be overcome through a practical revolutionising of social conditions. Therefore he also calls the 'criticism of religion [...] the premise of all criticism', for 'struggle against religion is therefore indirectly a fight against the world of which religion is the spiritual aroma'.[4] We should add that a critique of religion that self-reflectively takes seriously basic historical materialist thinking must recognise that it cannot pronounce timelessly valid statements about religion in general; rather it is a specific historical constellations that must be analysed. If the economic base and the ideological superstructure change, then the relation of society and religion also changes, if the latter is its reflection.

The actually existing secularism in European countries

Today's European societies are pluralistic. Many religions and non-religious worldviews, as well as people with secular convictions, are represented in them. This variegated landscape is the result of two developments: the individualisation of convictions, which is also connected to the normalisation of the 'secular option',[5] as well as migration, especially the immigration of Islamic population groups. Not least through this, religion has again become an issue in public life, as the controversy over the hijab, for example, shows in many European countries. Questions such as those involving minarets, the construction of mosques, religious instruction, the training of Imams, shechita (Kosher butchering), and religiously motivated circumcision, etc. have become the objects of heated controversies in an increasingly secular public life for which religious convictions are alien and hardly still comprehensible.

The countries of Europe have shaped their relationship to the religious communities in the face of this religiously plural and secular constellation. The relationship, which has developed through a long process over centuries, is determined by the religious–legal arrangement with the Christian churches. It has not been clear up to now whether Europe's countries or the European Union will redefine their relation to religions so that other religions too and especially Islam can find their equal place free of discrimination. The countries are legally required – by their own constitutional traditions but also by international law (Article 18 of the UN's International Covenant on Civil and Political Rights), the European Charter of Fundamental Rights (Article 17), and the Treaty on the Functioning of the EU – to create non-discriminatory conditions that promote social integration.

The state/religion relation can be conceived in three basic forms, each of which typify a few important countries. First there are those countries that have a close relation between state and church in the form of a state church (for example, Denmark, England, and Greece); second there is the secular type of strict separation between state and church (for example, France), meaning a 'laicist' type of separation; and third the most widespread type, which is a relationship of cooperation between state and church (for example, in Finland, Italy, Austria, Germany).

Quite a few leftists see France, the motherland of the Enlightenment and of civil rights, as the model for the relation of states to religions. France is the only European state that is officially secular and that has declared the principles of *laïcité* to be one of the foundations of its republican democracy. This secularism according to the 1905 Law on the Separation of Church and State ensures the free exercise of religion and understands the churches as associations under private law without a special legal status. This means that the state is completely neutral toward religion. Since the 1990s a 'nouvelle laïcité' is gaining in importance. It no longer focuses on a too great influence of the church but is instead concerned with Islam. Through it the conservative and extreme-right camp has appropriated what was originally a left-republican principle in order to justify anti-Islamic requirements. A marker of national identity has been made out of a principle of arrangement between state and religion. In so doing the 'new secularism' has changed its subject – it is no longer a matter of the state's neutrality and the relation of state to religion but of an identity of its citizens. To be French means to be republican and secular, according to former president Sarkozy in 2008. While laïcité merely wanted to distance religion from the domain of the state, the new secularism is concerned to keep the social domain free of religious symbols, more precisely Muslim symbols. Its effect, as an expression of national identity, is therefore discriminatory, for it is only directed against Islam as a foreign religion. Laïcité becomes laicism, that is, no longer an arrangement between church and state but an ideology or conviction.

This reformulation of an original republican-left laïcité has split the left camp. The secular left is falling between the two fronts; it has problems with the return of religion in public life but has to distance itself from the taking over of laïcité by the right. Those on the left who defend Islam are disparaged as 'Islamo-gauchistes'. In view of this conflict the Marxist philosopher Étienne Balibar has advocated a 'complete philosophical and political reformulation'[6] of the principle of 'laïcité', in order to draw a new distinction between the religious and the political. Since there has been an identitarian turn in French secularism, Balibar argues that politics needs a clear secular standpoint and criticises the hardliners among French secularists for their xenophobic intolerance of French citizens of Arab and African descent.

By contrast to the French model, the counter-model, one that grounds religion in state constitutions, is found in European countries with long democratic traditions in which there are national and state churches, such as in England and Scotland in Great Britain, and the Lutheran-influenced states in Scandinavia (with the exception of Sweden). In these countries the state is identified with a confessional church not just ideally but also legally. As a whole, however, this state-church type is undergoing a process of gradual legal separation of church and state.

Between the two extremes of French laïcité and the state churches there is a broad palette of very different mixed forms with diverse kinds of cooperation on the basis of the institutional separation of state and religion in education, healthcare systems, social institutions, etc., as in Austria, Germany, and Italy.

All models in Europe are experiencing a certain legitimation pressure. Here we can distinguish two convergence tendencies of the different religious-constitutional systems: on the one side a reinforcement of the self-determination of religious communities vis-à-vis the state, and on the other side an increasing readiness on the part of the state to cooperate with religions on the basis of separation systems.

There are two understandings of secularity. The term 'secular' has always been subject to contradictory and even conflicting interpretations. On the one hand, the secularity of the state can represent a formal commitment to allow religious pluralism in a spirit of respect for everyone's religious freedom. On the other hand, the concept of secularity can also represent an attitude hostile to religion, which is detrimental to the exercise of religious freedom. It is therefore advisable to distinguish between an open 'political secularism' and various forms of republican 'doctrinal secularism'. Advocates of a doctrinaire conception of secularism generally hold that the practice of religion should be a private matter. By contrast, 'open secularism' emphasises the liberal goals of secularism – namely, freedom of religion, freedom of conscience, and equality.

The requirements of a left emancipatory religion policy

The concept 'religion policy' is in vogue. Within just a few years it has come onto the political agenda. For the right as well as the left, for church representatives as well as lay people, religion policy had long been a dangerous mixture where separation of state and church was seen as mandatory. However, not least due to migration, politics have become conscious of how strongly the religious landscape has been transformed and become plural. This is shown by the impressive career of the term 'religion policy'.

By now, all parties in Germany have nominated religion-policy spokespeople, and centres for research on the relation of religion to politics and study courses for religion and politics have been established. Christian Democratic foundations, such as the Konrad-Adenauer-Stiftung in Germany, are even asking for the establishment of religion policy as an independent field of politics. In the Rosa-Luxemburg-Stiftung, which is the political foundation corresponding to Die LINKE, there has for many years now been a dialogue over world outlooks, where questions of religion policy are also discussed. Just like the party Bündnis 90/Die GRÜNEN, Die LINKE has created a religion-policy commission.

The question then arises: What would a religion policy oriented to a left programme look like?

The separation of state and religion in a left programme

A point of departure is the separation of church and state, which is an old demand. Since the nineteenth century, with the declaration that religion is a private affair, this separation became a central demand of the socialist labour movement. When in 1875 in the Gotha Programme, the SPD defined 'religion as a 'private affair', the intention was not at all to limit the practice of religion to the private sphere; rather, the formula intended a right of defence against the then regressive Prussian state under Bismarck. This right of defence was formulated as follows by Marx: 'Everyone should be able to attend to his religious as well as his bodily needs without the police sticking their noses in.'[7] In 1904, at the Bremen Party Congress, Eduard Bernstein emphasised that religion is a cultural task: 'not a private affair but a public concern of great importance.' He demanded 'equal rights for the adherents of all religious and philosophical confessions, freedom of religious practice'. It is in this sense that religion is a private affair, not a state or party matter. In this spirit laïcité in France pursued, although in a different way, the goal of preventing the church and state from influencing each other.

The secular state is facing the challenge of giving diverse outlooks equal space without privileging any religion or world outlook. This is why the popular left demand of separation of church and state on the French model falls short. Laïcité in early twentieth-century France was politically necessary since the Roman Catholic Church held a monopoly position and fought against Enlightenment values. Laïcité was thus justified in order to secure democratic values or human rights, but it is not a timeless fundamental principle for a left emancipatory religion policy whose goal is freedom. It comes from a specific landscape of confessional politics, in which the state has to demarcate itself from a single, all-powerful church. But if laïcité, as an instrument of freedom, is maintained in a new – religiously plural – situation, its effect is obviously discriminatory against minorities, leading inevitably to tensions, above all with the new immigrants. Globalisation, immigration, and individualisation have so strongly altered Europe's religious landscape that the separation of religion and state is simply anachronistic.

The demand for separation of religious communities from the state addresses three fundamental requirements that a secular and pluralist society has to meet:

- freedom of conscience,
- the equality of citizens before the law,
- and the need to allow every voice to be heard.

The secular state's neutrality rests on two principles, namely equal respect and freedom of conscience, as well as on two regimes: the separation of church and state and the strict neutrality of the state toward all religions and secular tendencies. Respecting diversity is the goal of the secular neutrality of the state. The separation of state and religion is then the means of reaching this goal. Thus, a consistent separation of state and religious communities is not a goal in itself and is hostile neither to religion nor to the state. The goal is the complete pluralism of society in a context of strict equality. Left demands fall too short when in terms of religion policy they refer principally to the means, namely the separation of state and religion, and not to the goals to be achieved through this separation. In the context of freedom of religion or belief, non-discrimination requires a policy of deliberate 'non-identification' of the state with any particular religion or belief in order to be equally fair and inclusive vis-à-vis people of different faith orientations living under its jurisdiction.[8]

The established formula of the separation of church and state neither adequately conceptualises the complex interaction of religion and politics nor does it suffice as a maxim for religion policy. It is too indeterminate, for it says nothing about how this separation is to be shaped; this can, in fact, be liberal or illiberal, libertarian or dogmatic, cooperative or doctrinaire. But above all it cannot regulate the complex dealing with religious and moral diversity in modern societies. The separation of state and religious communities does not intend an unconnected separation but rather a 'respectful non-identification'[9] of the state with these communities. The prohibition of identification is the expression of the respect of the secular state for people's freedom of self-determination in matters of religion and world outlook.

Human rights are always rights aimed at the protection of minority rights vis-à-vis majorities. Precisely for this reason, the religious pluralisation of society requires a truly neutral state, for only then is it in a position to manage this diversity. A *laicist* state constitution, in which the state would identify itself with the non-religious, is only supposedly neutral. Actually, it represents a religion-free world outlook and conception of the Good. It follows that it does not treat citizens who accord a place for religion in their value system with the same respect and does not grant them the same free sphere for their development.

While from time immemorial questions of laws on religion played not an insignificant role in the founding of states in European space, this was not the case in the European Union. While, among the EU member states, *laïcité* is anchored in the French constitution, Ireland's constitution, and those of other EU member states, begin with an *invocatio Dei*. Yet this religion-constitutional diversity was not taken into consideration in the negotiations on the Treaty Establishing a Constitution for Europe. In the deliberations of the Constitutional Convention the formulation of a preamble in which Europe's cultural and religious heritage would be expressed played no role. By referring to its secular constitution, France pushed through a cliché-ridden minimal consensus that speaks only in general terms of the 'cultural, religious, and humanist inheritance of Europe'. The Preamble to the Charter of Fundamental Rights of the European Union only mentions being 'conscious of its spiritual and moral heritage'. But clearly there can be no provisions on the European ethos without a confirmation of its Judeo-Christian and humanist heritage.

This conflict situation confirms that there are exactly the two opposed versions of the state's worldview neutrality indicated above: a republican laicism or doctrinal secularism and a pluralist laicism or political secularism.[10] The secular republican version, as was finally implemented in the constitutional text, does not aim at a secular but at a secularist Europe that no longer affirms its origins but excludes the religious traditions of some member states. A laic understanding of the neutrality of the state tends to develop into a supposed religion-free public sphere that actually admits of no public sphere that is pluralist in terms of religion and world outlook in which freedom of religion and the pluralism rooted in it could function. The guarantee of equal freedoms requires a secular state that is neutral toward all citizens and their life plans; however, a generalisation of the secularised worldview in the sense of a republican secularism blocks precisely the guarantee of equal freedoms for all.

With Marx, from the 'critique of heaven' to the 'critique of earth', left religion politics needs the critique of religion. In so doing it stands in Marx's tradition, for whom the essential point was to transform the 'criticism of heaven' into the 'criticism of the earth'.[11] In this tradition it is the task of left policy on religion and world outlook to analyse and criticise the forces that hold up the existing order and veil its class antagonisms, in which communities of religion and world outlook also represent a sphere of the struggle for hegemony. For this reason religious and worldview communities are a contested locus in the endeavour 'to overthrow all relations in which man is a debased, enslaved, forsaken, despicable being, relations which cannot be better described than by the exclamation of a Frenchman when it was planned to introduce a tax on dogs: Poor dogs! They want to treat you like human beings!'[12]

A left approach to religion must always begin with a critical analysis of its functions. Religion has an ambivalent character: it can be liberating or oppressive, perpetuate injustices or set free forces of humanisation, promote visions of a solidary society or block them. Thus, for Marx religion is always both 'the opium of the people' and a 'protest against real distress'.[13] With Marx, therefore, the double task is to set free the energy that is dampened by religion as opium and to use the energy that lies in religious protest in order to find a way out of oppressive conditions.

Religion policy as a policy of diversity in a divided society

Since Europe has become more plural through the individualisation of lifestyles and the diminishing ties to religious communities, and through immigration, especially Islamic immigration, a left religion policy has to connect two problem areas: the relation of the state to religions and the problem of immigration and integration. The religion-policy debates in Europe are shaped by arguments from the right that deny equal participation to Islam, as a 'foreign' religion – but also by secularist voices, which want to entirely free public space of religion, critically oppose Islam, perceived as homophobic, misogynist, and anti-democratic.

From the doctrinaire secularist perspective, religion policy's focus is to keep public space free of religion. However, a religion policy that wants to navigate the present-day plurality of Europe's contemporary moral, religious, and cultural landscape has an entirely different point of departure. In dealing with diversity, it is not a question of a religious-secular multiculturalism; here what is at stake is nothing less than the core concern of the social left: equal rights of freedom for all and the solidary shaping of a society marked by social, cultural, and economic inequalities and discrimination and in which minorities are denied equal rights and recognition. For a secularist position that perceives religion as simply irrational and a barrier to freedom, it is largely not the religious concerns of minorities which appear to be worthy of protection but the secularity of the public sphere. This position therefore runs the risk of suppressing the integration-policy dimension of the human right to religious freedom. In so doing the disallowance of the religious from the public sphere doubly discriminates against a religious minority like the Muslims – as a population group with an immigration background and as members of an immigrant minority religion perceived as foreign.

In order for those in a society who are different to be equal it is time for a fundamental redefinition in the state-religion relationship that can create non-discriminatory and just legal conditions which promote integration. Pluralisation is not a mere adding up of different cultures, in which there is only the addition of something new to what already exists; rather, it changes everything. The task of a left religion policy consists in expanding existing regulations so that all citizens and their religious communities find a framework that recognises their religious or secular concerns but which in return also requires of them the equal recognition of other convictions. This above all involves the protection of people denied equal recognition and equal rights or who are exposed to massive disadvantages.

Only through the visibility of religious symbols, such as the yarmulke, cross, headscarf, or sheitel, the Jewish wig for women, can religious plurality become public. The question is: Do these symbols in public violate secular neutrality? Is there a tension between religious freedom and neutrality? Concretely: Should students be prohibited from wearing the headscarf in school? The principle of religious freedom aims to protect one's own way of life. The principle of state neutrality protects negative religious freedom and suggests a headscarf ban. This tension between religious freedom and neutrality can only be adequately resolved if an important boundary is drawn, that is, the boundary between the private and the public. The problem is not at all visibility (of religious symbols) in the public sphere but representation. The state must not issue prescriptions on clothing that impair the student's right to practice her religion; on the other hand, it can issue such prescriptions in the case of people whose role is to *represent* the secular state, for instance as judges.

The human right to freedom of religion as a contested right

Even if the human right to religious freedom has to be the point of departure and goal of left religion policy in Europe, human-rights demands cannot be won from state authorities simply through conflict-free derivation from the principle of human rights but are the result of a conflictual process of negotiation around the appropriation and configuration of rights.

For the left, Europe must be shaped as a pluralist space in which religions and secular convictions can be lived freely and with equal rights. Therefore, there must be an equitable way of dealing with all secular, religious, and other outlooks that concern ethical value systems and normative orientations, because in a pluralist society an answer to the question of what is good, just, and rational only exists in the plural. In a secular society of diversity, all points of view, whether religious or secular, have to be respected as equally important moral sources of a democratic culture. Since left religion policy aims at justly shaping the ethical-moral, cultural, religious, and spiritual diversity of society, it has an interest, from the point of view of civil society, in tapping into the diverse sources of humanity and solidarity, giving them space and promoting them. Left religion policy advocates religious and ideological autonomy and alliances with religious and ideological communities wherever and whenever these are concerned with a just, solidary, peaceful, and sustainable society. It therefore finds allies in the religions that are working for these social goals and bring to bear the emancipatory potential of religions. But they are also allies when it is necessary to combat attitudes and practices within the religious communities that violate human rights.

In religion policy the focus is predominantly not on the conflicts between 'the religious' and 'the secular'. The political task is rather the recognition of the foreign and the other. The European Union must become a place where citizens can practice the plurality of their religious and secular convictions without discrimination. Such a European Union would then be not only post-Christian and post-secularist, but also pluralist.

ADDITIONAL LITERATURE

Cornelia Hildebrandt, Jürgen Klute, Helge Meves, and Franz Segbers (eds), *Die Linke und die Religion: Geschichte, Konflikte und Konturen*, Hamburg: VSA, 2019.

Kommission Religionsgemeinschaften, Weltanschauungsgemeinschaften, Staat und Gesellschaft des Parteivorstandes der LINKEN (2021): *Linke Religionspolitik: Trennung von Staat und Kirche und der Vielfalt von Religionen und säkularen Weltanschauungen Raum geben*, Abschlussbericht <https://www.die-linke.de/partei/parteidemokratie/kommissionen/kommission-religionsgemeinschaften-weltanschauungsgemeinschaften-staat-und-gesellschaft/>, 2021.

Franz Segbers, *Religion nur Privatsache? Die LINKE, der Laizismus und das Menschenrecht auf Religionsfreiheit*, Rosa-Luxemburg-Standpunkte, 39/2016.

NOTES

1   ISSP Study, *International Social Survey Programme – Religion II – AZ* No. 3190 – 1998, <https://www.gesis.org/en/issp/modules/issp-modules-by-topic/religion/1998>.

2   José Casanova, *Europas Angst vor der Religion*, Berlin: Römerweg, 2015, p. 22.

3   Casanova.

4   Karl Marx, *A Contribution to the Critique of Hegel's Philosophy of Law*, Karl Marx and Frederick Engels, *Collected Works*, vol. 3, New York: International, 1975, p. 175.

5   Charles Taylor, *A Secular Age*, Cambridge MA: Harvard University Press, 2007.

6   Étienne Balibar, '*Laizität*', Wolfgang Fritz Haug (ed.), *Historisch-kritisches Wörterbuch des Marxismus*, vol. 4, Hamburg: Argument, 2012.

7   Karl Marx, *Critique of the Gotha Programme* [1875], Karl Marx and Frederick Engels, *Collected Works*, vol. 24, New York: International, 1989, p. 98.

8   See Heiner Bielefedt, Nazila Ghanea, and Michael Wiener (eds), *Freedom of Religion or Belief: An International Law Commentary*, Oxford: Oxford University Press, 2017 (reprint edition), p. 35.

9   Heiner Bielefeldt, *Streit um die Religionsfreiheit. Aktuelle Facetten der internationalen Debatte*, Erlangen, 2012, <https://islam.de/files/pdf/streit_um_religionsfreiheit_uni_rede.pdf>. p. 31.

10   Jocelyn Maclure and Charles Taylor, *Secularism and Freedom of Conscience*, Cambridge MA: Harvard University Press, 2011; *Laizität und Gewissensfreiheit*, Berlin: Suhrkamp, 2011, p. 39 ff.

11   Marx, *A Contribution to the Critique of Hegel's Philosophy of Law*, p. 175.

12   Marx, *A Contribution to the Critique of Hegel's Philosophy of Law*, p. 182.

13   Marx, *A Contribution to the Critique of Hegel's Philosophy of Law*, p. 175.

Anniversary

Fifty Years After the Coup d'État in Chile: Salvador Allende, a Revolutionary for the 21st Century

Mario Amorós

Salvador Allende made the ultimate sacrifice in defence of the democratic principles that had guided his country's life, in a La Moneda palace engulfed in flames after it had been bombarded from the sky. The events of 11 September 1973 made Allende one of the great political figures of the 20th century. However, his memory has been somehow caught up in the tragedy: his long and exciting political career before 1970, his defence of democratic and revolutionary socialism and his solidarity with the struggles of the Third World all fell into oblivion. Not even the great achievements of his thousand days in office are commonly recognised. And yet, together with 11 September, they trace the principles that guided his trajectory and shape his political legacy.

As historian Sergio Grez argues, from the mid-1930s onwards Allende embodied the 'historical continuity and the central line of development of the popular movement' in Chile.[1] He was born on 26 June 1908 in Santiago de Chile, seven months after the massacre at the Santa María school in Iquique (immortalised in the cantata composed by Luis Advis for Quilapayún in 1970), at a historical moment in which the working class was struggling to become a major actor in national life.

Allende became involved in social struggles during his time as a medical student at the Universidad de Chile, when he joined the demonstrations against the dictatorship of General Carlos Ibáñez (1927-1931), an activity for which he was imprisoned and temporarily expelled from the university. His interest in participation in the spheres of decision-making was apparent already in this period: at age 19, he was elected president of the Student Centre of the School of Medicine and, at 22, vice-president of the university's Student Federation. When he was around 15 or 16, an old anarchist carpenter of

Italian origin, Juan Demarchi, had provided Allende with his first books and conversations on libertarian–left ideals, and during his time at university he came into contact with the essential texts on Marxism.

One of the defining events in his political career was his participation in the founding in 1933 of the Socialist Party (PSCh), of which he soon became one of the main leaders, as regional secretary for Valparaíso in 1935, deputy secretary general in 1938 and secretary general between January 1943 and July 1944. Throughout his life, he was a proud socialist militant, as he explained in April 1973 to Marta Harnecker, then editor of the weekly *Chile Hoy*:[2] 'I have been everything in the party, from founder in Valparaíso, head of the cell, regional secretary, general secretary, general undersecretary, party deputy, party senator, party minister, party president. What has marked me most is the Socialist spirit, the generosity and fervour of thousands of militants I have met in my life, who never asked for anything personal and always had faith in the victory of the people to build socialism. Now, I can personally say that everything I am and have been I owe to the Socialist Party and to the people.'

In 1937, aged just 29, Allende was elected as a member of parliament. The following year he directed the campaign of Pedro Aguirre Cerda (leader of the Radical Party) in Valparaíso, who won the historic presidential elections of 25 October 1938 as the Popular Front candidate, breaking a long century of oligarchic hegemony. As a member of parliament and as Health Minister between 1939 and 1942, Allende pursued several important projects to improve the precarious living conditions of the country's vast majority.

In the years that followed, Allende made some decisive moves. In 1945, he won a seat in the Senate for the southern provinces, until then a conservative fiefdom, and confirmed his growing prestige in national politics. In 1948, he criticised the persecution of the Communist Party by the government of President Gabriel González Videla and argued that socialist principles were imbued with a profound humanism and inseparably intertwined with human rights and civil liberties. Thus, upon voicing his opposition to the proscription of the Communist Party, he stated in the Senate: 'We Chilean Socialists, who widely recognise many of the achievements of Soviet Russia, reject its type of political organisation, which has led to the existence of a single party, the Communist Party. Nor do we accept several of the laws that have been introduced in that country and that restrict individual freedom and proscribe rights that we consider inalienable to the human person.'[3]

In 1951, when most of the Chilean Socialists decided to back the presidential candidacy of the ex-dictator Ibáñez, with a populist project reminiscent of Peronism, he opted to leave the Popular Socialist Party[4] and launched his candidacy for the 1952 presidential elections with the support of a minority sector of the Socialists and the underground Communist Party, in a coalition that was called Frente del Pueblo (People's Front).

Although he barely won 51,975 votes, the first of his four presidential candidacies gave concrete expression to an aspiration he had expressed early on. Already back in 1944, as secretary general of the PSCh, he had stated: 'We socialists call on the Left to unite around a programme; a programme that we will agitate from the streets and from Parliament; a programme of national interest, which will unite the maximum of wills around it.'[5] From 1951 onwards, Allende became the great champion of left-wing unity, which came to fruition with the creation of the Frente de Acción Popular (Popular Action Front) in 1956 and the reunification of the Socialist Party in 1957. In the 1958 elections, he fell just 33,000 votes short of reaching the presidential palace known as La Moneda: 'Allendismo' was born, a popular movement that was formed around a political proposal to transform the country and which went beyond the boundaries of the Socialist and Communist parties, though their unity of action provided its foundation.

Before the triumph of the Cuban Revolution in January 1959, the united Chilean left (a fact as exceptional in the context of the Cold War as the unique revolutionary identity of Chilean socialism) was already an alternative power in the land. This led the successive tenants of the White House to order a massive intervention in its politics to prevent Allende's triumph at all costs. In 1964, with a gigantic 'terror campaign' and the support of the right wing, the Christian Democrat Eduardo Frei defeated him, but on 4 September 1970, Unidad Popular achieved the longed-for triumph. It had won narrowly at the polls, but after an agreement with the Christian Democratic Party (PDC), it managed to defeat the manoeuvres that Washington and the Chilean right organised to thwart Allende's election as president by the National Congress. For the first time, a Marxist had taken over the national government in a democratic election, and Allende did so at the head of a coalition that brought together 'Marxists, secularists, and Christians', as he proudly characterised it.[6]

President Allende immediately ordered the application of the programme of Unidad Popular, and his government proceeded to build the so-called Social Area, 'the embryo of the future socialist economy', i.e. through the nationalisation of the industries most crucial to national development, of the big copper, coal, and iron ore mines, and of banking. This decision hurt the interests of the bourgeoisie and, in reaction, the Christian Democrats pushed through a constitutional reform aimed at paralysing the process of building socialism. The conflict over defining the separate areas of the economy, and in particular over the importance of the nationalised sector, in which the working class participated in company direction and management, was a constant through those thousand days. It proved irresolvable because of the conflicting interests and the stalemate in the state institutions, despite Allende's repeated attempts, right up to the last day, to reach an agreement with the Christian Democrats.

The Unidad Popular government also eradicated *latifundia* landed estates and freed the peasants from an almost feudal prostration, to instead recognise them as fellow citizens. The most significant achievement came on 11 July 1971 with the historic nationalisation of the big copper mines, the most important sector of the national economy, 'the salary of Chile' in the words of the President of the Republic. Allende's decision to subtract large amounts of 'excess profits' from the compensation to be paid to the US multinationals intensified Washington's economic blockade; but its dislike of the Unidad Popular government went beyond monetary interests and was justified mainly by political and ideological reasons. Hence Nixon's well-known orders to Kissinger, as early as September-November 1970, to unleash a covert campaign of aggression against Chile.

After the left's victory in the municipal elections of 1971, taking 50.86% of the votes, on 21 May of that year, in his historic first Message to the Plenary Congress, President Allende set out the foundations of the 'Chilean road to socialism', which captivated the attention of millions of people on all continents. This meant the construction of a socialist society with absolute respect for political pluralism, democratic principles, and human rights: 'We are treading a new path; we are marching without a guide through unknown terrain; our compass is our fidelity to the humanism of all times – particularly Marxist humanism – as we set as our true North the project of the society we desire, inspired by the most deeply rooted yearnings of the Chilean people.'[7]

Allende always deeply valued the possibility of building socialism under such conditions. So, at the May Day rally in 1971 organised by the Central Workers' Union, he told the hundreds of thousands of people gathered: 'Think, comrades, that in other places the peoples rose up to make their revolution and were crushed by the counter-revolution. Torrents of blood, prisons, and death mark the struggle of many peoples, on many continents, and, even in those countries where the revolution triumphed, the social cost has been high, a social cost in lives that are priceless, comrades. A social cost in the human existences of children, men, and women that we cannot measure monetarily. Even in those countries where the revolution triumphed, it was necessary to overcome the economic chaos created by the struggle and the drama of combat or civil war.'[8] The assassination of prominent Christian-Democratic leader Edmundo Pérez Zujovic by an ultra-left group on 8 June 1971, opened up a gulf between Unidad Popular, in a minority in the National Congress, and Christian Democracy. It tipped this latter toward an alliance with the right-wing National Party, which was concretised throughout 1971 and 1972 in various by-elections and in the 'March of the Empty Pots' on 1 December 1971, toward the end of Fidel Castro's visit to Chile. Throughout those three years, Allende tried to reach an agreement with the Christian Democrats to form a large national majority for the transformation of the country, in line with many aspects of the programme of the Social-Christian candidate from 1970, Radomiro Tomic. But little by little this party moved closer to the right – and with the election of Senator Patricio Aylwin as its party president in May 1973, it definitively opted to instigate the coup d'état.[9]

From the beginning of 1972, a political crisis became apparent in the Unidad Popular as a result of disagreements over strategy, faced with the contradictions, challenges, and opposition generated by the construction of socialism. If at first this dispute set the Communist Party in opposition to the Revolutionary Left Movement (MIR, a party which was integrated into Unidad Popular), the Unidad Popular meeting in Lo Curro in June 1972 would give vent to the two visions of economic policy, and of the revolutionary process in general, as articulated around Salvador Allende and the Communist Party,[10] on the one hand, and the Socialist Party, on the other.

However, the strikes and lockouts orchestrated by the employers' unions and the middle and professional sectors in October 1972 diluted all those differences for several weeks. This could be seen in the gigantic popular mobilisation in support of the government, which prevented the country from outright collapse. As a last resort, President Allende brought three high-ranking officers of the Armed Forces into his cabinet, among them the Commander-in-Chief of the Army, the constitutionalist General Carlos Prats. Such major military participation in the Executive – unheard of since the turbulent period of 1925-1932 – was evidence of Allende's interest in incorporating the armed forces into a project of national sovereignty, but also of the degree of divisions in a country polarised between capitalism and socialism.

In December 1972, Salvador Allende embarked on a historic tour of Mexico, New York, the Soviet Union, and Cuba, demonstrating his enormous international prestige. Surely, already much earlier in his political life, Allende had taken a keen interest in struggles around the rest of the world. In the 1930s he had supported the struggle of the Second Spanish Republic against fascism, in the 1940s that of the Allies against Nazi-fascism, in the 1950s he condemned the overthrow of Arbenz in Guatemala, and in the 1960s he supported the Cuban Revolution and the struggle of the Vietnamese people while repudiating the Marines' 1965 invasion of the Dominican Republic. In his speech to the United Nations General Assembly, he spoke out on behalf of the peoples of the Third World who were fighting for their economic independence and aspired to use their natural wealth for their own development:

> The future action of the collectivity of nations must emphasise a policy that has all peoples as its protagonists. The Charter of the United Nations ws conceived and presented in the name of 'We the Peoples of the United Nations'. International action must be directed to serve the man who does not enjoy privileges, but who suffers and labours: the miner in Cardiff like the *fellah* in Egypt; the cocoa worker in Ghana or Ivory Coast as well as the peasant in the highlands of South America; the fisherman in Java as well as the coffee farmer in Kenya or Colombia. It should reach the two billion neglected beings whom the collectivity is obliged to incorporate into the present level of historical evolution and to recognise as having "the value and dignity of a human person", as the preamble of the Charter sets out.

From the most important tribune on the planet, and with the solemnity and dignity with which he dressed his most important speeches, President Allende also denounced imperialism's attempts to overthrow the constitutional government over which he presided:

> The refusal of [US manufacturing firm] ITT to accept a direct agreement and our knowledge of its cunning manoeuvres have forced us to send a nationalisation bill to Congress. The decision of the Chilean people to defend the democratic system and the progress of the revolution, the loyalty of the Armed Forces to their country and its laws, have thwarted these sinister initiatives. I accuse ITT before the conscience of the world of trying to provoke a civil war in my country. This is what we call imperialist action [...] The aggression of the big capitalist companies aims to prevent the emancipation of the popular classes.[11]

In March 1973, after two and a half years in office, and even amidst a serious economic crisis largely caused by the opposition's strategy, Allende had higher popular support than any president over the previous two decades.

The 43.4% vote won by Unidad Popular prevented the opposition from removing him through constitutional channels, but also already showed the latter that their last resort, before the presidential elections scheduled for September 1976, would be a coup d'état. On 21 May, Allende spoke before the joint Congress in defence of the 'Chilean road to socialism' and democratic freedoms and warned the country of the danger of civil war. Pablo Neruda would do the same one week later in a dramatic speech broadcast on the public television channel and in the last interview he gave, published by the Argentine magazine *Crisis* in August that year.

Hours after the failed military coup of 29 June, Allende gave a speech before thousands of people from the balcony of La Moneda. When he heard slogans calling for the closure of the National Congress, in the hands of a seditious opposition that was blocking government action, and the arming of the people, the president said that, if necessary, he would call a plebiscite to settle the political conflict, but added:

Comrades, the people already knows what I have repeatedly told it. The Chilean process has to go through the proper channels of our history, our institutions, our characteristics and, therefore, the people must understand that I have to remain loyal to what I have said; we will make the revolutionary changes in pluralism, democracy, and freedom [...].[12]

After that failed uprising, a dramatic appeal by the archbishop of Santiago, Cardinal Raúl Silva Henríquez, opened the way for the final stage of negotiations between Allende and the Christian Democrats. But that party's leadership, headed by Aylwin, under the heavy influence of former president Eduardo Frei and fuelled by CIA dollars, rejected the minimum agreement which the president had proposed. On 23 August, following the resignation of General Prats, the president appointed as the new commander-in-chief the army's number two, General Augusto Pinochet, who had Prats's confidence and until then had exhibited impeccable loyalty to his constitutional duties as head of the Santiago garrison in 1971 and chief of the army's General Staff since 1972.

On Sunday 9 September, hours after Allende explained to Pinochet his intention to call a plebiscite on the morning of 11 September as a solution to the serious political conflict dividing the country, the General decided to join the coup plot. Two days later, each man chose his place in history: Pinochet led a coup d'état that annihilated a democracy which was then unparalleled in Latin America. He now became the head of a dictatorship that for seventeen years exhibited a total disregard for human dignity. From April 1975 it would pursue the neoliberal agenda in the most brutal fashion. Allende, for his part, was loyal to the promise he repeatedly made to the

Chilean people: he would not hand over to any coup leader the popular mandate he had democratically received.

In 1970 Salvador Allende had earned the nickname of 'comrade president'. It reflected his efforts dating from the student mobilisations against the Ibañez dictatorship, the short-lived Socialist Republic of 1932, the foundation of the Socialist Party, the construction of the Popular Front, and his role, over a quarter-century, as an MP, health minister, senator, and four-time presidential candidate. 'I have no other weapon than persuasion and the moral authority that I may enjoy, for having been a man loyal to the people', he said on 27 October 1971 before the workers at the Chuquicamata mining complex.[13]

As President of the Republic, he on many occasions addressed the workers, peasants, youth, women, students, the humble people of Chile, with deep respect and warmth. He always frankly explained to them his vision of the situation in the country and the revolutionary process. He insisted endlessly on the need to strengthen the commitment to the construction of socialism. His words were also full of affection. For example, after the hours of uncertainty and disturbance on 29 June 1973, on that cold winter night, he said goodbye from the balconies of La Moneda with these words:

> Comrades, there are still some fascist groups out there, be careful, don't fall into provocations. You must have confidence in the government, which has shown its strength this morning and we will continue to show it. Comrades, stay in your homes, join your wives and children in the name of Chile. Carry my love, my respect, my admiration and my faith to each of your homes.

All these feelings came together in his words of 11 September 1973:

> Workers of my homeland: I want to thank you for the loyalty you always had, for the trust you placed in a man who was only the interpreter of great yearnings for justice, who pledged his word that he would respect the Constitution and the law and did so [...]. Radio Magallanes will surely be silenced and the quiet metal of my voice will no longer reach you. No matter, you will still hear it, I will always be with you. At least my memory will be that of a worthy man who was loyal to the loyalty of the workers.[14]

That same day, Salvador Allende became a legend of the 20th century. The shocking images of the bombing of La Moneda; the drama and almost poetic beauty of his last speech on Radio Magallanes; his death in defence of one and a half centuries of democratic development in Chile and of the revolutionary project to which he devoted his whole life; and the grim military dictatorship that took hold of the country – all this gave his name a universal dimension, synonymous with values like democracy, social justice, pluralism, human rights, freedom, and socialism.

In 2023 Salvador Allende is back. The young man who committed so early in life to the values of democracy and socialism, who devoted his whole life to making them a reality. The MP and senator who promoted so many initiatives to improve the living conditions of the working classes. The socialist militant who devoted his energies to uniting the left around a political programme to transform Chilean reality. The doctor with a deep social vocation. The President of the Republic who nationalised copper and eradicated the latifundia, promoted worker participation in the management of the national economy, turned peasants into citizens, drove the distribution of half a litre of milk a day to each child, and created the Quimantú National Publishing House. The comrade of Víctor Jara, Inti-Illimani, Isabel Parra and Quilapayún. The man who defended a new world economic order at the UN and who, faced with the most powerful nation on the planet, stood head held high for his people's determination to build socialism. That boy who talked and played chess with old Demarchi in his modest workshop in Valparaíso, the mason proud of his ancestors (especially his grandfather, Dr. Ramón Allende Padín) and, with him, that immense and beautiful popular movement that opened wide the doors of history one starry night in September 1970. He is back.

Salvador Allende and the left lost the first battle; they could only be defeated by the violence of the Armed Forces who trampled on their constitutional obligations. However, the political project of Unidad Popular, its struggles and its ideals, are still valid in the 21st century: the profound and radical democratisation of society, in all spheres, including the economy. The commemoration of the 50th anniversary of the coup d'état in 2023 will be an international event that should motivate reflection not only on Allende's political trajectory, his government, and the evolution of Chile in the 20th century, but also on the challenges of the transformative left in the 21st century.

Along this road, we will be accompanied by the 'quiet metal' of Allende's voice, the unforgettable example of the Comrade President, who called us to hope even on that black 11 September of 1973:

Workers of my country: I have faith in Chile and its destiny. Other men will overcome this grey and bitter moment in which betrayal is trying to impose itself. Keep on knowing that sooner rather than later, the great avenues will open again, down which free men will pass to build a better society.

NOTES

1   Sergio Grez Toso, 'Salvador Allende en la perspectiva histórica del movimiento popular chileno', <http://www.scielo.cl/scielo.php?pid=S0718-23762004000200014&script=sci_arttext>.

2   This weekly, created in April 1972, was one of the best and most pluralistic publications of the Chilean left during the Unidad Popular period. See the complete collection online: <http://www.socialismo-chileno.org/PS/ChileHoy/chile_hoy/chile_hoy.html>.

3   Gonzalo Martner (ed.), *Salvador Allende 1908-1973. Obras Escogidas (1939-1973)*, Santiago de Chile: Antártica, 1992, pp. 143-145.

4   In the 1940s, Chilean Socialism went through a deep crisis. The debate over the party's position in the face of the outlawing of the Communist Party triggered a fresh split and, while the anti-communist wing of the party kept the name Partido Socialista de Chile, prominent leaders such as Allende, Raúl Ampuero, Clodomiro Almeyda, and Aniceto Rodríguez founded the Partido Socialista Popular (Popular Socialist Party).

5   *Rambo de Liberación*, Archivo Salvador Allende, no. 5. Mexico City, 1990. pp. 193-204.

6   On Christians' participation in the Chilean revolution, see Mario Amorós, 'La Iglesia que nace del pueblo. Relevancia histórica del movimiento Cristianos por el Socialismo', <https://rebelion.org/docs/75701.pdf>.

7   Martner, pp. 323-352.

8   *El pensamiento político de Salvador Allende*, Santiago de Chile: Quimantú, 1971. pp. 197-211.

9   On Christian Democracy and the coup d'état, see Mario Amorós. 'Una responsabilidad jamás asumida', Interferencia.cl, Santiago de Chile, 4 August 2020, <https://interferencia.cl/articulos/una-responsabilidad-historica-jamas-asumida>.

10   On the political relationship between Salvador Allende and the Communist Party of Chile, see Mario Amorós, 'Por un rojo amanecer', *Mundo Obrero*, Madrid, September 2003, <https://www.rebelion.org/docs/35207.pdf>.

11   Patricio Quiroga (ed.), *Salvador Allende: Obras escogidas (1970-1973)*, Barcelona: Crítica, 1989, pp. 333-357.

12   Víctor Farías, *La izquierda chilena (1969-1973). Documentos para el estudio de su línea estratégica*, Vol. 6, Santiago de Chile: Centro de Estudios Públicos, 2000, pp. 4771-4776.

13   'Los trabajadores y el Gobierno Popular', Archivo Salvador Allende, no.8. Morelia, 1990, pp. 73-81.

14   Martner, pp. 669-671.

Authors and Editors

Mario Amorós is a member of the editorial board of *Mundo Obrero* in Spain. He is the author of fourteen books on the history of Chile over the last half-century, including reference biographies of Pablo Neruda, Augusto Pinochet, and Miguel Enríquez (secretary general of the Revolutionary Left Movement, MIR). In March 2023, he published a biography of Víctor Jara, and an updated version of his biography of Salvador Allende will appear in September this year.

Athena Athanasiou is Professor of Social Anthropology and Gender Theory at Panteion University of Social and Political Sciences (Athens), Director of the Laboratory of Anthropological Research and Dean of the Faculty of Social Sciences, and a member of the editorial advisory boards of *Critical Times*, *Feminist Formations*, *Philosophy and Society*, *feministiqá*, and the *Journal of Greek Media and Culture*. She is the co-author, with Judith Butler, of *Dispossession: The Performative in the Political* (Polity, 2013) and most recently of *Agonistic Mourning: Political Dissidence and the Women in Black* (Edinburgh University Press, 2017).

Walter Baier is an economist in Vienna, was National Chairman of the Communist Party of Austria (KPÖ) from 1994 to 2006, an editor of the Austrian weekly *Volksstimme*, Political Coordinator of the transform! Europe network from 2007 to 2020, and currently President of the Party of the European Left. His books include *Linker Aufbruch in Europa?* (Steinbauer, 2015) and most recently *Marxismus: Geschichte und Themen einer praktischen Theorie* (Mandelbaum, 2022).

Étienne Balibar has held positions at Paris–Nanterre, Kingston University London, UC Irvine, and Columbia University. He is author of *Reading Capital* (Verso, 2016 [1965], with Louis Althusser et al.), *Race, Nation, Class. Ambiguous Identities* (Verso 2011 [1991], with Immanuel Wallerstein), *The Philosophy of Marx* (Verso, 2017), and numerous other works, of which the latest is *On Universals. Constructing and Deconstructing Community* (Oxford, 2020).

Aristides Baltas is a philosopher of science and physicist who has served as Greece's Minister of Culture and Sports and Minister of Culture, Education, and Religious Affairs in the cabinet of Alexis Tsipras from 27 January 2015 to 4 November 2016. He is currently Emeritus Professor of Philosophy of Science at the National Technical University of Athens and President of the Nicos Poulantzas Institute. His *Peeling Potatoes or Grinding Lenses: Spinoza and Young Wittgenstein Converse on Immanence and Its Logic* was published by the University of Pittsburgh Press (2012).

Ulrich Brand is Professor of International Politics at the University of Vienna. Together with Markus Wissen he coined the term 'imperial mode of living' – their *The Imperial Mode of Living: Everyday Life and the Ecological Crisis of Capitalism* (Verso, 2919) has been translated into eleven languages. Brand is director of the Latin America Research Network at the University of Vienna, a member of the recently established Environment and Climate Hub. He is editor of the monthly *Blätter für deutsche und international Politik* and a co-founder and member of Diskurs – Der Wissenschaftsnetz <https://www.diskurs-wissenschaftsnetz.at/>.

David Broder is a translator and historian of Italy. He is co-editor of the *transform! europe yearbook* and Europe editor at *Jacobin magazine*. His books include *Mussolini's Grandchildren: Fascism in Contemporary Italy* (Pluto, 2023), *First They Took Rome: How the Populist Right Conquered Italy* (Verso, 2020), and *The Rebirth of Italian Communism, 1943-44: Dissidents in German-Occupied Rome* (Palgrave Macmillan, 2021). He teaches twentieth-century European history at Syracuse University.

Ankica Čakardić is Associate Professor and Chair of Social Philosophy and Philosophy of Gender at the Faculty of Humanities and Social Sciences in Zagreb and a member of the editorial board of *The Complete Works of Rosa Luxemburg* (Verso). She is the author of *The Spectres of Transition. Social History of Capitalism* (in Serbian, 2019), *Like a Clap of Thunder. Three Essays on Rosa Luxemburg* (Rosa Luxemburg Stiftung, 2019) and *Rebellious Mind. Essays in Radical Social Philosophy* (in Serbian, 2021).

Eric Canepa is a music historian and co-editor of the *transform! europe yearbook*. From 2001 to 2006 he was the Coordinator of the Socialist Scholars Conference/Left Forum in New York and from 2008 to 2012 Co-coordinator of the Rosa Luxemburg Foundation's project North-Atlantic Left Dialogue.

Steven Forti is a lecturer at the Department of Modern and Contemporary History at the Universitat Autónoma de Barcelona. His research focuses on fascism, populism, nationalism, and the extreme right with a special focus on comparative and transnational history. His most recent book is *Extrema derecha 2.0. Qué es y cómo combatirla* (Siglo XXI de España, 2021). He is currently local coordinator of the European research project 'Analysis of and Response to Extremist Narratives' (ARENAS).

Alberto Garzón Espinosa is an economist, member of the Spanish Communist Party, General Coordinator of Izquierda Unida, and Spain's Minister for Consumer Affairs. He is a researcher at the Pablo de Olavide University in Seville. As a student he co-founded Students for a Critical Economy; he earned his Master's in International Economy and Development at the School of Business and Economic Sciences at the Complutense University of Madrid.

Haris Golemis is a Greek economist who worked at the Research Department of the Bank of Greece, was scientific advisor to the Federation of Greek Bank Employees, and consultant to the United Nations Centre on Transnational Corporations. From 1999 to 2017 director of the Nicos Poulantzas Institute, he is now a member of the Editorial Committee of the Greek newspaper *Epohi*, Scientific and Strategic Advisor to the Board of transform! europe, and co-editor of the *transform! europe yearbook*.

Boris Kagarlitsky began his political activity in Moscow co-producing samizdat journals for which he was arrested in 1982. As a deputy to the Moscow City Soviet he was arrested again in 1993 under Boris Yeltsin In 2008 he founded the internet journal *Rabkor*, a leading intellectual voice of the Russian left. In 2022 he was declared a 'foreign agent' for protesting against the Russian invasion of Ukraine but refused to leave the country. His latest book is *Between Class and Discourse: Left Intellectuals in Defence of Capitalism* (Routledge, 2020).

Dunja Larise has held senior post-doctoral positions at the European University Institute in Florence, Sciences Po in Paris, and Yale University, among others. She coordinates the 'Austro-Marxism' project supported by Transform Europe, Rosa Luxemburg Stiftung, and the City of Vienna. Her *Helene Bauer: Political Economy and Social Sciences Between Two World Wars* (Sage) will appear in late Autumn. With Walter Baier she is the editor of the forthcoming *Max Adler, Hans Kelsen, and Käthe Leicher on the Theory of State and Democracy* (Historical Materialism).

Mariana Mortágua is the National Coordinator of Portugal's Left Bloc (Bloco de Esquerda). She earned her PhD in economics at the School of Oriental and African Studies at the University of London. At the age of 27 she was elected deputy to the Assembly of the Republic in 2013 and re-elected in 2015, 2019, and 2022. In parliament she has been a member of the Economy and Public Works Commission, the Budget, Finance and Public Administration Commission and the Eventual Commission for Monitoring the Measures of the Financial Assistance Programme for Portugal. She is active in women's rights and LGBT movements.

Jukka Pietiläinen is Director of Left Forum, Finland and a member of the board of transform!. He holds a PhD in social sciences from the University of Tampere and was senior researcher on Russian media and society at University of Helsinki.

Gavin Rae is a sociologist and activist living in Warsaw. He has written extensively on political and economic events in Poland and Central and Eastern Europe. He is a co-founder of the Polish Transform group: Forward (Naprzód).

Panos Ramantanis works in the field of political communication and political analysis. He is a regular columnist for the newspaper *Epohi* and the website Left.gr, and his scholarly work in social and political theory has appeared in *Theseis*. His analyses centre on the state, multi-level class conflicts, and power relations.

Giulia Russo is a PhD candidate in Political Science and Sociology at the Scuola Normale Superiore in Florence. Her research interests include the role of the state in the dynamics of accumulation, centralisation, and concentration of capital, and income and wealth distribution. Her current research focuses on the taxation of wealthy elites and corporations, focusing on the tax-dodging industry and its role in capitalist accumulation.

Franz Segbers studied theology and social sciences and worked in Germany in the Industrial Mission, after which he did his doctoral work in social ethics on strikes and lockouts. While working at the Social Academy of the Protestant Church, he graduated with a thesis on business ethics. Until his retirement, he was a professor of social ethics at the University of Marburg. He is a member of the working group on ideological dialogue in the Rosa Luxemburg Foundation and of the religious policy commission of the party Die LINKE.

Michalis Spourdalakis is Professor Emeritus at the National and Kapodistrian University of Athens. Outside Greece he has taught and lectured in Canada, the US, Spain, Italy, China, Turkey, and Korea. Some of his many publications in the field of political sociology have appeared in

Spanish, Chinese and Korean. From 2016 to 2018 he was chair of Greece's Committee for the Dialogue for Constitutional Reform. He is member of the Executive Board of the Nicos Poulantzas Institute.

Göran Therborn is professor emeritus of sociology at the University of Cambridge and affiliated professor of sociology at Linnaeus University, Sweden. His latest books are *Inequality and the Labyrinths of Democracy* (Verso, 2020), and *Cities of Power* (Verso, 2017). His current work involves comparisons of the second and the twenty-first centuries.

Antonios Tzanakopoulos is Professor of Public International Law at the Faculty of Law of the University of Oxford and Fellow in Law at St Anne's College, has taught at numerous universities throughout Europe and Asia. He has acted as counsel or advisor, providing expert opinions in a number of cases before international and domestic courts and tribunals, including the International Court of Justice and arbitral tribunals. His latest book is *Research Handbook on the Law of Treaties* (Elgar, 2014).

Hilary Wainwright is an Associate of the Transnational Institute and a founder and co-editor of *Red Pepper*. From 1978 to 1982 she worked with the Lucas Aerospace Shop Stewards Combine Committee and from 1982 to 1986 as Deputy Chief Economic Advisor to the Greater London Council. Her latest book is *A New Politics from the Left* (Polity, 2018).

transform! european network for alternative thinking and political dialogue

office@transform-network.net
Gusshausstraße 14/3
1040 Vienna, Austria

Austria

Institute of Intercultural Research and Cooperation – IIRC★
www.latautonomy.com

transform!at
www.transform.or.at

Cyprus

Research Institute PROMITHEAS★
www.inep.org.cy

Czechia

The Institute of the Czech Left (Institut české levice)★
www.institutcl.cz

Society for European Dialogue – SPED
e-mail: malek_j@cbox.cz

Denmark

transform!danmark
www.transformdanmark.dk

Finland

Left Forum
www.vasemmistofoorumi.fi

Democratic Civic Association – DSL
www.desili.fi

France

Espaces Marx
www.espaces-marx.fr

Foundation Copernic★
www.fondation-copernic.org

Foundation Gabriel Péri★
www.gabrielperi.fr

Institut la Boétie
institutlaboetie.fr

Germany

Journal Sozialismus
www.sozialismus.de

Rosa Luxemburg Stiftung RLS
www.rosalux.de

Institute for Social, Ecological and Economic Studies – isw
www.isw-muenchen.de

Greece

Nicos Poulantzas Institute - NPI
www.poulantzas.gr

Hungary

transform!hungary★
www.balmix.hu

Italy

transform! italia
www.transform-italia.it

Cultural Association Punto Rosso (Associazione Culturale Punto Rosso)
www.puntorosso.it

Fondazione Claudio Sabattini★
www.fondazionesabattini.it

Lithuania

DEMOS. Institute of Critical Thought★
www.demos.lt

Luxembourg

Transform! Luxembourg★

Moldova

Transform! Moldova★
e-mail: transformoldova@gmail.com

Norway

Manifesto Foundation★
www.manifestanalyse.no

Poland

Foundation Forward / Fundacja Naprzód
www.fundacja-naprzod.pl

Portugal

Cultures of Labour and Socialism - CUL:TRA
e-mail: info@cultra.pt

Serbia

Center for Politics of Emancipation - CPE★
www.pe.org.rs

Slovenia

Institute for Labour Studies - IDS★
www.delavske-studije.si

Spain

Europe of Citizens Foundation - FEC
www.lafec.org

Foundation for Marxist Studies - FIM
www.fim.org.es

Instituto República y Democracia★
www.institutorepublica.info

Iratzar Foundation (Basque Country)★
www.iratzar.eus

Neus Catalá Foundation (Catalonia)
neuscatala.cat

Sweden

Center for Marxist Social Studies
www.cmsmarx.org

Turkey

Left Blog – Sol Siyaset★
http://solsiyaset.org/

UK

The World Transformed – TWT★
www.theworldtransformed.org

Transform! UK – A Journal of the Radical Left
www.prruk.org

★ *Observers*

www.ingramcontent.com/pod-product-compliance
Lightning Source LLC
Chambersburg PA
CBHW072059040426
42334CB00041B/1464